C.P. (Bud) Lathrop
P.O. Box 3754
Fullerton, Ca 92634

# Medieval, Renaissance and Folklore Studies in Honor of John Esten Keller

## Juan de la Cuesta
## Hispanic Monographs

Series: *Homenajes*, Nº 1

# Studies in Honor of
# John Esten Keller

JOHN KELLER IN HIS STUDY AT HOME IN LEXINGTON (APRIL, 1980)

# Medieval, Renaissance and Folklore Studies In Honor of JOHN ESTEN KELLER

*Edited by*

JOSEPH R. JONES
*University of Kentucky*

Juan de la Cuesta
Newark, Delaware

The Publisher wishes to thank Professor R. M. Flores of the
University of British Columbia for providing the original
Juan de la Cuesta decorated capital letters which begin each article.
Hal Barnell of New York City has prepared the decorated J
in the style of the old Cuesta letters.

ISBN: 0-936388-04-8

PRINTED IN THE UNITED STATES OF AMERICA

# Contents

# JOHN ESTEN KELLER III

EW FACULTY and graduate students have occasionally admitted to me, after meeting John Keller for the first time, that they were surprised by his youthful appearance and by his affability—as if medievalists were all old and grumpy, by definition. The reason, of course, is that John's scholarly production is so large that Hispanists who have never met him assume that he must have lived a long time to have written so much; and it is hard to believe that the forty-ish, athletic man seen in the photo could have been born in 1917. The backhanded compliment to John's affability is a tribute to his reputation for taking vigorous action when his social or pedagogical ideals are challenged.

John's strong character is hereditary. Dr. John Esten Cook, the ancestor whose name he bears, is remembered principally not for his innovations in the field of medical education in Kentucky but for his writings against Presbyterian heresies. John's parents, Owen Bullit and Mary Louise Welch Keller, were both militant partisans of the Confederacy and its traditions, steadfastly refusing to the last to alter their views or genteel life-style in the face of drastic changes in contemporary Southern society. An example of this family conservatism—what John's critics call his intransigence—is the letter he wrote to Professor Kampf, who was elected president of the MLA at the chaotic meeting in 1969. John, who had been a member of the MLA for twenty-five years, president of the South Atlantic MLA, member of the Executive Council, etc., resigned from the Association in protest and sent the new president a letter excoriating him for his political pronouncements and calling him Mein Kampf. Obviously such sarcasm, however traditional in Humanist circles, is not calculated to win over the opposition. But it brings him the grudging admiration even of his opponents.

John came to the professorship of Spanish at his alma mater, in his native city, by a roundabout way. When he started his university career, he planned to become a botanist, and he undertook the study of Spanish in preparation for a botanical expedition to South America. But the language quickly replaced botany as his passion. (He still retains a fondness for the natural sciences. He has a splendid garden and a large greenhouse, where he cultivates tropical plants as a concession to his interest in equatorial America. Once in a while, this inclination for nature is reflected even in his publications, such as an essay on Quiroga in *Repertorio americano*, or a study of the skink's habits published in the *Audubon Society Bulletin*. After taking bachelor's and master's degrees at the University of Kentucky in 1940 and 1942, John accepted the post of Spanish instructor at Staunton Military Academy. In the middle of his first year, he was drafted, only to return six months later, discharged for bad eyesight. The unchanging routine of secondary education quickly bored him, and he was anxious to get back to the stimulation of university life. In the fall of 1943, therefore, he entered the University of North Carolina as a teaching assistant, to begin work on a doctorate. UNC, the oldest state university in America, already had a distinguished tradition in both Spanish and medieval studies. Sturgiss Leavitt, "el alcalde de Zalamea," the spiritual father of several generations of young Hispanists, and Urban T. Holmes, the American dean of Old French and Romance studies, were among the faculty. It was Holmes who interested John in early Spanish literature. John spent the next three years in the picture-postcard surroundings of Chapel Hill taking courses and completing his dissertation on *The Exemplum in Spain* (1946).

In the meanwhile, he had married Dinsmore Davis, whom he had met during his undergraduate years. With his wife and firstborn—John Esten Keller IV, who came into this world three months after his father became a *philosophiae doctor*—the new Dr. Keller returned to the University of Kentucky as Assistant Professor. The University in Lexington was at that time a small state institution specializing in agricultural sciences, engineering, and law; but it was in the process of becoming the state's research center, not only for the sciences applicable to local economy but also for medicine, the arts, and subjects that would have amazed Daniel Boone, such as Japanese. It did not have the prestige of UNC or the intellectual atmosphere to foster the kind of scholarship John hoped to pursue, and he missed Chapel Hill. After brief stays at Kentucky (1946-47) and Tennessee (1947-50), he received what he wanted, an offer from North Carolina; and he and his growing family, which now included Laura Dinsmore, born in 1950, moved to Chapel Hill.

In its congenial atmosphere, John began to fulfill the promise seen by Leavitt and Holmes; he published dozens of articles on medieval literature, folklore, and medieval culture, as well as an edition of *El libro de los engaños*. In 1957, he was promoted to professor and began teaching Old Spanish and medieval literature, while directing graduate students' work (twenty-three dissertations and numerous master's theses during his sojourn in Chapel Hill). In addition to his scholarly work, John published translations and adaptations of medieval tales; he even wrote a novel about Isabel la Católica and Columbus which lies unpublished in a desk-drawer. He lectured far and wide: Oxford, Toronto, London, Coimbra, Seville, and—eventually—more than forty American, Canadian, and foreign universities. His patience and meticulous attention to detail made him ideal as an editor, and the UNC press and journals (*Romance Notes*, the UNC series in romance languages and comparative literature) sought his help. He has been, or is now, on the editorial board of the *Bulletin of the Comediantes, Southern Folklore Quarterly, Crítica hispánica, Hispania, Kentucky Folklore*, and the *Kentucky Romance Quarterly*, among others.

During the years at UNC, (1950-67) the University of Kentucky was losing its provincial aspect, broadening its faculty, establishing a cosmopolitan community of native and foreign scholars. North Carolina on the other hand, was becoming more rigidly conservative in its curriculum, and the stubborn resistance to change in the

Romance Languages faculty in particular annoyed John sufficiently to make him consider some of the offers which poured in
every year. Finally, the Dean of the College of the University of
Kentucky (Paul C. Nagel, a distinguished historian who currently
heads the American Historical Society), came to him with a prop-
osal which no one with an interest in furthering Hispanic studies
could refuse: a combination of professorship, chairmanship, and
deanship, authorization for six new faculty members and for
library acquisitions, and a special arrangement for doctoral candidates who wished to transfer from UNC to Kentucky. Keller
agreed, provided he could find a group of congenial colleagues
interested in revitalizing the program of Hispanic studies at an
institution which was just beginning to gain a reputation for the
quality of the faculty. After several months of negotiation, John
announced that he and three colleagues from UNC, as well as
three other young scholars and twenty-five graduate students,
would go to Lexington. The announcement fell on UNC like a
bomb. The American scholarly community, which thrives on professional gossip, watched with malicious curiosity not only the
embarrassment of UNC at losing its most distinguished Hispanist
and virtually all of its doctoral candidates in Spanish, but also the
supposedly impractical efforts of John and his associates to form
another Spanish department when there were already numerous
excellent, prestigious ones in this country. (At the time, John
attributed their scepticism to envy, saying, *¿Quién es tu enemigo? El de
tu oficio.*) Even today, thirteen years later, academicians still talk
about the "Chapel Hill Exodus." An impartial observer can see,
however, that the Romance Languages Department at UNC was
not permanently damaged and that John's hopes for making Kentucky a center of Hispanic studies was not fanciful either. Perhaps
the most convincing evidence are the fifty-two Kentucky Ph.D.'s
(thirteen under John's direction) and numerous MA's, the reorgan-
ization of the *Kentucky Romance Quarterly* (Keller, editor in chief), the
establishment of the *Kentucky Studies in Romance Languages and Literatures* (Keller, editor in chief), and the increasing activities of the
department in national and international Hispanic circles.

As for his private life, John lives like a Southern gentleman, in
an elegant Colonial house, with his wife, who is a collector of
eighteenth-century furniture, a dog of uncertain pedigree, and an

enormous tabby cat. His daughter Laura, now a lawyer working for the state's department of ecology, and her husband live nearby. Dr. John Esten Keller IV, alias Jack, an archaeologist for the federal government, and his wife visit regularly from their home in Louisiana.

       🌿      🌿      🌿

One wonders what there is left for John to accomplish. Since coming to Kentucky, he has been through the administrative *cursus honorum*, has received special leaves of absence for research, two sabbaticals, the Sang Award (a prize for contributions to graduate education), and a grant from the department of Health, Education, and Welfare to further his study of medieval literature and the arts; his colleagues have elected him Distinguished Professor for 1979, and he continues to be deluged with requests for lecture appearances and visiting professorships. John himself refuses to speculate about his own future or the future of the American university system. Not long ago at a SAMLA meeting, a group of scholars asked him his views on this subject, and on such related matters as public indifference, undergraduate hostility to languages, and dangerously shrunken budgets. How can so obviously "irrelevant" a department as that of Spanish and Italian survive, they wanted to know, at a medium-sized state university? John answered with two famous quotations and his customary Stoic line: "St. Teresa tells us how to face these problems: '...todo se pasa; Dios no se muda; la paciencia todo lo alcanza.' America's current isolationist mood and resistence to expansion are a passing phase. Common sense will eventually prevail. Nobody can ignore the importance of language study; and for Americans, the most practical language is Spanish, the speech not only of our neighbors but of twenty million fellow-Americans. *'Paciencia y barajar.'*" And following his own advice, John continues patiently to cultivate his garden.

John's students like to tell new arrivals a joke (which used to be applied to U. T. Holmes), a compliment to his medieval enthusiasms: "When Dr. Keller dies, his tombstone will read, 'HERE LIES

JOHN ESTEN KELLER III. BORN 1917. DIED 1285.'" But anyone who knows John, knows that he is not hankering to revive the days of Alphonse the Learned: he is the very type of the modern American academician, a combination of scholar and businessman. It is this mixture of erudition and practical intelligence that has made him one of the most eminent Hispanists in the American academic community.

JOSEPH R. JONES
University of Kentucky
Lexington, Kentucky
December 1980

# PUBLICATIONS

## BOOKS

*Motif-Index of Mediaeval Spanish Exempla*. Knoxville: University of Tennessee Press, 1949, xvii+67 pp.

*El libro de los engaños*. (Critical Edition) Studies in the Romance Languages and Literatures, no. 20. Chapel Hill: University of North Carolina Press, 1953, xiii+56 pp.

*El libro de los engaños*. (Revised Spanish Edition). Textos Antiguos Españoles, no. I. Valencia: Artes Gráficas Soler, 1959. Studies in the Romance Languages and Literatures, no. 20., 2nd ed., Chapel Hill: University of North Carolina Press 1959, xvii+60 pp.

*El libro de los gatos* (Critical Edition). Madrid-Valencia: CSIC, 1958, 150 pp.

*The Book of the Wiles of Women*, a translation of the *Libro de los engaños*. Studies in the Romance Languages and Literatures, no. 27. Chapel Hill: University of North Carolina Press, and Translation Series of the MLA, no. 2, 1956, 60 pp.

*A Brief History of Spanish Literature* (With N. B. Adams) 3rd ed. College Outline Series. Paterson: Littlefield and Adams, 1974, 185 pp.

*El libro de los exenplos por a. b. c.* (Critical Edition). Madrid-Valencia: CSIC, 1961, 449 pp.

*España en su Literatura* (with N. B. Adams). New York: W. W. Norton and Co., 1962, 2nd ed. 1972, xii+490 pp.

*Hispanoamérica en su Literatura* (with N. B. Adams, Elizabeth Daniel, and John Fein). New York: W. W. Norton and Co., 1965, 477 pp.

*Breve Panorama de la Literatura Española* (with N. B. Adams). Madrid: Editorial Castalia, 1964, 259 pp.

*The Abencerraje and the Beautiful Jarifa* (Bilingual Edition). Spanish text by Francisco López Estrada, trans. John E. Keller. Studies in Comparative Literature, no. 33. Chapel Hill: University of North Carolina Press, 1964, 86 pp.

*El libro de Calila e Digna* (Critical Edition with Robert W. Linker). Madrid-Valencia: CSIC, 1965, xxxix + 374 pp.

*Alfonso X, el Sabio.* World Author Series. New York: Twayne, 1968, 198 pp.

*El Libro de Buen Amor,* translated by Elisha Kent Kane. Introductory study by John E. Keller. Chapel Hill: University of North Carolina Press, 1968.

*The Scholar's Guide,* a translation of the *Disciplina Clericalis* of Pedro Alfonso (with Joseph R. Jones). Toronto: Pontifical Institute of Mediaeval Studies, 1969, 117 pp.

*Gonzalo de Berceo.* World Author Series. New York: Twayne, 1972, 198 pp.

*The Book of Count Lucanor and Patronio,* a translation of the *Conde Lucanor of Don Juan Manuel* (with Clark Keating). Lexington, Ky.: University Press of Kentucky, 1977, 201 pp.

*Pious Brief Narrative in Medieval Castilian and Galician Verse.* Lexington, Ky.: University Press of Kentucky, 1978, 142 pp.

*Barlaam e Josafat* (Critical Edition). Madrid-Valencia: CSIC, 1980, xiv + 456 pp.

*Así Somos: Lecturas del Mundo Hispánico* (with Gregorio Martín and M. Laurentino Suárez). Lexington, Mass.: D. C. Heath, 1980.

*Don Quixote de La Mancha (Part II),* a translation of Alonso Fernández de Avellaneda's *Segundo tomo del ingenioso hidalgo don Quixote de la Mancha* (with Alberta Wilson Server). Newark, Del.: Juan de la Cuesta—Hispanic Monographs, 1980, xiv + 350 pp.

## BOOKS IN PRESS, FINISHED OR UNDERWAY

*Iconography and Narrative Art in Medieval Spanish Fiction* (with Richard P. Kinkade). Lexington, Ky.: University Press of Kentucky. Accepted, April, 1980. Written under a grant from the National Endowment for the Humanities. In press.

*Old Spanish Literature—A Selected Bibliography* (with James F. Burke). Toronto: University of Toronto Press. Accepted, June, 1978. In press.

*The Book of Tales by A. B. C. of Clemente Sanchez de Vercial,* translated from the fifteenth-century Spanish (with L. Clark Keating). Under consideration by the Pontifical Institute of Mediaeval Studies in Toronto.

*Etymologies of St. Isidore of Seville,* a translation from the Latin (with Joseph R. Jones). In progress.

*Iconography and Narrative Art in Medieval Spanish Fine Art—Tapestries Sculpture, Frescoes, Paintings, Carvings, etc.* (with Richard P. Kinkade). In progress. Under a grant from the National Endowment for the Humanities.

## INTRODUCTIONS AND FOREWORDS

Foreword to *Mediæval Studies in Honor of Urban Tigner Holmes, Jr.* Chapel Hill: University of North Carolina Press, 1965, pp. 10-15.

Foreword to *Hispanic Studies in Honor of Nicholson B. Adams.* Chapel Hill: University of North Carolina Press, 1966, pp. 9-12.

Preface to *The Literary Mind of Medieval and Renaissance Spain: Essays by Otis H. Green.* Lexington, Ky.: University of Kentucky Press, 1970, pp. vii-xi; Introduction, pp. xiii-xxvi.

Foreword to *Studies in Honor of Everett W. Hesse.* Madrid-Mexico City: Porrúa (Studia Humanitatis), 1980.

Foreword to *Formulaic Diction in the* Poema de Fernán González *and the* Mocedades de Rodrigo, by John S. Geary. To appear in Studia Humanitatis, 1981.

## ARTICLES

"Horacio Quiroga," *Cartas y Comentarios. Reportorio Americano* XLIV, no. 10, p. 156.

"Elements of White Magic in Medieval Spanish *Exempla.*" In *Romance Studies Presented to William Morton Dey.* Studies in the Romance Languages and Literatures. Chapel Hill: University of North Carolina Press, 1950, pp. 85-90.

"Estudios recientes sobre la clasificación folklórica de obras españoles." *Filología* II, no. 1 (1950), pp. 85-90.

"The Motif-Index." *South Atlantic Bulletin* XVII, no. 2 (1951), pp. 1, 6, 7.

"A Tentative Classification of Themes in the *Comedia.*" *Bulletin of the Comediantes* V, no. 2 (1953), pp. 17-23.

"*Gatos* not *Quentos.*" *Studies in Philology* L, no. 3 (1953), pp. 437-45.

"Old Spanish *Garpios.*" *Hispanic Review* XXII, no. 3 (1954), pp. 227-32.

"El cuento folklórico en España y en Hispanoamérica." *Folklore Americas* XIV, no. 1 (1954), pp. 1-14.

"The Present Status of Motif Classification of the *Comedia.*" *Bulletin of the Comediantes* VI, no. 1 (1954), pp. 12-14.

"Motif-Index of *Ysopete Ystoriado*" (with James H. Johnson). *The Southern Folklore Quarterly* XXVIII, no. 2 (1954), pp. 85-117.

"A Note on King Alfonso's Use of Popular Themes in his *Cantigas*." *Kentucky Foreign Language Quarterly* I, no. 1 (1954), pp. 26-31.

"Source of the 'Hard Luck Stories.'" *North Carolina Folklore* III, no. 1 (1955), pp. 11-12.

"The Lapidary of the Learned King." *Gems and Gemology* IX, no. 4 (1957-58), pp. 105-10 and 118-21.

"The *Libro de los exenplos por a. b. c.*" *Hispania* XL, no. 2 (1957), pp. 179-86.

"Daily Living as Presented in the *Canticles* of King Alfonso the Learned." *Speculum* XXXIII, no. 4 (1958), pp. 484-89.

"The Virgin Mary as Rival of Saint James in the *Canticles* of King Alfonso the Wise." In *Middle Ages-Reformation-Volkskunde (Festschrift for John G. Kunstmann)*. Chapel Hill: University Press of North Carolina, 1958, pp. 75-82.

"The Motif of the Statue Bride in the *Canticles* of King Alfonso the Learned." *Studies in Philology* LVI, no. 3 (1959), pp. 453-58.

"Folklore in the *Canticles* of Alfonso X." *The Southern Folklore Quarterly* XXIII, no. 3 (1959), pp. 175-83.

"The Source of 'The Wolf, the Fox and the Well.'" *North Carolina Folklore* VII, no. 2 (1959), pp. 23-25.

"Some Translations of the *Cantigas de Santa Maria*." *Romance Notes* II, no. 1 (1960), pp. 63-67.

"Daily Living as Revealed in King Alfonso's *Cantigas*." *Kentucky Foreign Language Quarterly* VII, no. 4 (1960), pp. 207-10.

"The Depiction of Exotic Animals in *Cantiga* XXIX of the *Canticles of Holy Mary*." In *Festschrift in Honor of Tatiana Fotitch*. Washington, D.C.: The Catholic University of America, 1962, pp. 247-53.

"The Question of Primary Sources." In *Medieval and Renaissance Studies in Honor of B. L. Ullman*. Rome, 1964, pp. 118-23.

"A Medieval Folklorist." In *Folklore Studies in Honor of Arthur Palmer Hudson*. Chapel Hill: University of North Carolina Press, 1965, pp. 19-25.

"The Spanish Chaucer." In *Lectures in the Humanities*, Fourteenth and Fifteenth Series. University of North Carolina (1969), pp. 95-115.

"New Lights on *Calila e Digna*." In *Hispanic Studies in Honor of Federico Sánchez Escribano*. Madrid, 1969, pp. 25-34.

"Traducciones del *Libro de buen amor* al inglés." In *Actas del I Congreso Internacional sobre el Arcipreste de Hita*. Barcelona: EDITA S.E.R.E.S.A., 1973, pp. 318-22.

"The *Libro de buen amor* in English Translations." In *Medieval Studies in Honor of Robert White Linker*. Madrid: Editorial Castalia, 1973, pp. 112-40.

"Las traducciones castellanas de las *Cantigas de Santa Maria*." *Boletín de la Real Academia Española*, LIV, Cuaderno CCII (mayo-agosto, 1974), pp. 221-93.

"Some Stylistic and Conceptual Differences in Texts *A* and *B* of *El libro de los engaños*." *Estudios Hispánicos* (1975), pp. 100-15.

"An Unknown Castilian Lyric Poem: the Alfonsine Translation of *Cantiga* X of the *Cantigas de Santa Maria*." *Hispanic Review* 43, no. 1 (1975), pp. 43-47.

"A Re-examination of Don Juan Manuel's Narrative Technique: 'La mujer brava.'" *Hispania* 58, no. 1 (1975), pp. 45-51.

"From Masterpiece to Résumé: Don Juan Manuel's Misuse of a Source." In *Estudios literarios de Hispanistas norteamericanos dedicados a Helmut Hatzfeld con motivo de su 80 aniversario*. Madrid: Ediciones HISPAM, 1975, pp. 41-50.

"Some Stylistic and Conceptual Differences in Texts *A* and *B* of the *Libro de los engaños*." In *Studia Hispanica in Honorem Rafael Lapesa*, vol. III. Madrid: Editorial Gredos, 1975, pp. 275-82.

"The Enigma of Berceo's Milagro XXV." *Symposium* XXIX (1975), 361-70.

"A Feasible source of the Dénouements of the *Exemplos* in *El conde Lucanor*." *American Notes and Queries* XIV, no. 3 (1975), pp. 34-37.

"Verbalization and Visualization in the *Cantigas de Santa Maria*." In *Oelschläger Festschrift*. Chapel Hill: Estudios Hispanófila 36, 1976, pp. 221-26.

"More on the Rivalry between Santa María and Santiago de Compostela." *Crítica Hispanica* I, no. 1 (1979), pp. 37-43.

"On the Morality of Berceo, Alfonso X, Don Juan Manuel and Juan Ruiz." In *Homenaje a Don Agapito Rey, trabajos publicados en su honor a cargo de Josep Roca-Pons*. Bloomington, 1980, pp. 117-30.

"The *Canticles of Holy Mary* of King Alfonso the Wise." *Kentucky Review* I (autumn 1980).

## CONTRIBUTOR TO

Stith Thompson's *Motif-Index of Folk Literature. New Revised and Enlarged Edition*. Bloomington and Helsinki: 1957-59. Over 1000 items.

Medieval Spanish Dictionary to be published by the MLA. Over 1000 items.

*An Anthology of Medieval Lyrics*. New York: The Modern Library, 1962, pp. 303 and 305. Translations for Medieval Spanish and Portuguese Verse.

*An Anthology of Medieval Spanish Literature.* Washington, D.C.: the Catholic University of America, 1962, pp. 135, 173, 175. Edited Selections of Medieval Spanish fiction.

*Laurel Masterpieces of World Literature. Medieval Age.* New York: Dell, 1960. Translations from Medieval Spanish and Portuguese.

## BOOK REVIEWS

Since 1959 some fifty or so book reviews distributed through *Speculum, Romanic Review, Hispanic Review, Hispania, Filologia, Modern Language Journal, South Atlantic Bulletin, Southern Folklore Quarterly, Books Abroad, Renaissance Review* and others.

## EDITORSHIPS AND EDITORIAL BOARDS

Managing Editor of *University of North Carolina Studies in the Romance Languages and Literatures,* 1960-67.

Associate Editor of *Bulletin of the Comediantes,* 1962-66.

Book Review Editor of *Southern Folklore Quarterly,* 1960-73.

Assistant Editor of *Romance Notes,* 1960-67.

Editor-in-Chief of *Kentucky Romance Quarterly,* 1967-.

President of *Romance Monographs,* 1970-.

Associate Editor of *Kentucky Folklore,* 1975-.

Editor-in-Chief of *Studies in Romance Languages* of the University of Kentucky.

Member of the Editorial Board of *University of North Carolina Studies in Comparative Literature,* 1963-67.

Member of the Editorial Board of *Studia Humanitatis,* 1979-.

Member of the Editorial Board of *Crítica Hispánica,* 1979-.

Member of the Editorial Board of *Hispania,* 1972-1980.

Member of the Editorial board of Juan de la Cuesta—Hispanic Monographs, 1979-.

# Studies in Honor of
# John Esten Keller

# Folktale Types
# from North Carolina

RALPH S. BOGGS

URING THE YEARS of my professorship in the University of North Carolina at Chapel Hill (1930's and 40's), where I taught courses in the history of the Spanish language and phonetics, and medieval literature, I always remained faithful to my first love: folklore in general and folk narrative in particular. In the course I gave on medieval Spanish literature, naturally nothing was dearer to my heart than the exempla, and a kindred spirit appeared in that course in the form of John Esten Keller. I first knew him as a graduate student there, although he had first appeared in this world, unbeknown to me, on the 27th day of September 1917, when I was a junior in high school not too far away, in Indianapolis. Needless to say, we became fast friends, and have kept in contact, even to this day. I began to build a folklore curriculum by introducing a general course on the science of folklore in January 1930, and in my memo to the dean of the graduate school of October 3, 1939, I laid out the plan, including several departments, for an M. A. major or Ph. D. minor in folklore. When I left Chapel Hill for Miami in 1950, I recommended that my courses, both in Spanish and in folklore, be turned over to John. They were. And in his letter of August 21,

I

1951, John says, "I have a great deal to thank you for . . . If you feel in the mood to offer comment or advice, please do so." These two things I found quite unusual—that the administration followed my advice and that John asked for it,—both after I was gone, for the proverb says: The dead and the absent have few friends. It is quite satisfying, for historical perspective, to be able to turn to my seventy-odd bound volumes of "Biographic documentation". John went on to distinguish himself in the field of the exempla.

In Chapel Hill I quickly perceived that there was a rich well-rooted, and still thriving traditional culture, and I soon began to collect folktales from all parts of the state, from the coast to the mountains, mostly from whites in rural areas. As a sampling, I published 57 of them in the *Journal of American folklore* in 1934 (vol. 47, no. 186). I have several hundred tales in my manuscript collection, and the intention to prepare them for publication someday. However, being skeptical of good intentions, even my own, I offer here a brief survey of this collection.

Many of the North Carolina folktales are known internationally. They vary in details, but in basic plot patterns there is a surprising uniformity in a rather large stock of tales known in many nations. Let us see what character North Carolina's folktale stock manifests in the light of international tradition. Since many of my readers will be familiar with the Aarne-Thompson international tale classification, let us follow its general ordering of materials.

My *Comparative survey of the folktales of ten peoples* (Folklore Fellows Communications, no. 93, Helsinki 1930) indicates that the popularity of animal tales varies considerably from one country to another: Lapland 30 percent, Spain 15 percent, Hungary 7 percent. Only about a dozen appear in my North Carolina collection. Here are four examples, excluding such well-known classics as Tarbaby and the Wolf and three little pigs.

In Cherokee County I was told that Br'er Bear went fishing, and on the way met Br'er Rabbit, who wanted to go along. Br'er Bear said he might, but when they got there, Rabbit wouldn't fish. He just rolled in ther sand and ate grass. Bear caught a whole string of fish and started home. Rabbit ran through the woods and played dead in the middle of the road. Bear came along and said, "Look, a dead rabbit!" and he went right on. Rabbit ran through the woods again and laid himself in the road. Bear came along and said, "Another dead rabbit! If I had this one and the one I saw back yonder, I'd have enough to make myself a meal." So he laid down his fish and went back to get the other rabbit. As soon as he was gone, Rabbit jumped up and ran off with the fish. This well-known European folktale is known also in India, Egypt and Africa, among North American Indians, in the Bahamas and Brazil.

I have variants from seven counties of the Crop Division tale. The one from Mitchell county says that the Devil and Bobtail took a notion to make a crop together. So they planted corn. When the crop was made, they went to decide how to divide it. The Devil left it up to Bobtail to say how they should divide it. Bobtail, seeing the fine ears of corn, said he'd take what grew on top of the ground, and the Devil could have what was in the ground. The next year the Devil said now it was his turn to choose, and he'd take what grew on top of the ground and Bobtail could take what grew in the ground. The Devil thought he'd get the best of Bobtail, but this time they'd planted potatoes, so that's how Bobtail beat the Devil. This tale seems to be best known in northern Europe, though it is also known in India, medieval Spain, Switzerland, the West Indies, and among the American Indians and Negroes, as well as among the Missouri French.

In Edgecombe County I heard a version of Partgone, Halfgone, Allgone. Bear, Fox, and Rabbit cooked a pot of peas for dinner. Then they went out to the field to work. Rabbit got hungry thinking about those nice peas. Finally he couldn't stand it any longer, so he put his paw up to his ear and made out like he heard his wife calling him, and went up to the house and ate some peas. When he got back to work, he told Bear and Fox his wife had given birth to a child. They asked him if he had named the child yet, and he said yes, they'd decided to call it PARTGONE. Rabbit went on working, but he couldn't get his mind off of those peas, so finally he made out like his wife was calling him again. "She must be having twins," he said, and up to the house he went again, and ate some more peas. When he came back to work, he told Bear and Fox she'd given birth to another child. They asked what he was going to name it, and he said HALFGONE. They worked on a spell, but old Rabbit still kept thinking about those peas, so he put his paw up to his ear again, and said, "She must be having another one." Off he went up to the house and licked the pot of peas clean. When he came back, he said they'd decided to call the third child ALLGONE. When they went to wash up for dinner, and came out, Rabbit was all gone, and so were the peas. This is part of a tale family listed by Thompson in his *Motif-index* as K372, found in northern Europe, Russia, France, Louisiana Creole, Missouri French, Canadian French, Scotland, Portugal, Africa, Japan, among the American Indians, New Mexican Spanish, along the U. S. South Atlantic seaboard, and in the West Indies.

The fourth and last animal tale I shall cite is from Edgecombe County, the classic Cheese in the Well, with a fine local touch of philosophy. One night Rabbit was out walking and came to a well. He looked in and saw a big yellow ball. It was the reflection of the moon, but he thought it was a big cheese. Two buckets on the ends of a rope hung from a pulley over the well. Rabbit got in one and went down, faster than he liked, till he hit the water. He found no cheese. He couldn't get out, so he began to cry. Fox came by and heard him, looked in the well and said, "What's the matter, Rabbit?" "I was crying for joy, Mr. Fox. Look at the big cheese I found down here. Come down and eat some." Fox jumped in the other bucket. He was heavier than Rabbit, so he went down fast, and Rabbit came up. As they passed on the way, Rabbit, said, "That's the way it goes, Mr. Fox: some coming up, others going down." Two themes combine here: diving for the cheese, and bucket rescue from the well, which, between them, have variants too numerous to mention here.

The ordinary tales about people instead of animals, told in a serious rather than a humorous vein like the joke, including tales we typically associate with our fairytale books, appear to be almost unknown in the genuinely oral tradition of North Carolina, in strong contrast with European countries, where this category is the largest, running from thirty to sixty percent in those included in my *Comparative survey*. Although I looked for this category insistently, I usually got in its stead local anecdotes, often "scary", and legends—about graveyards and haunted houses, witches and ghosts. Perhaps the most popular tale in this whole category is "Big 'fraid and little 'fraid". It is told in a humorous vein. I have variants of it from fourteen counties. A short composite form follows.

A boy brought in the cows from pasture every evening, but he played around and wouldn't get home until after dark. On his way home he had to pass a graveyard, so his father decided to scare him so he'd be afraid to come home after dark and would come home earlier. His father put on a sheet and hid behind a tombstone. His pet monkey put on a sheet from the cradle and hid behind another tombstone, but the father didn't see the monkey. When the boy came along, the first thing he saw was the monkey wrapped in the baby's sheet, and he said, "Oh, look at that little 'fraid! I never saw such a little one!" The old man knew he wasn't little, so he decided there must be a real 'fraid around there, so he ran for the house. The monkey set out after him, and the boy cried, "Run, big 'fraid, or little 'fraid'll catch you!" Evidently *'fraid*, for *afraid*, is a local word for *ghost*, and is often taken by outsiders for *Fred*. Indeed, the local pronunciation does tend to reduce the diphthong *ai* to *e*. This tale has been reported from Ontario, Philadelphia, and through the South from Virginia to Miami and Louisiana, but it is not listed in Aarne-Thompson, and it is certainly a far cry from the European favorites: Dragon-slayer, Magic Flight, Fearless Boy, Hansel and Gretel, Red Riding Hood, Cinderella, Snow-White, etc., which evidently live in North Carolina only in children's books.

Jokes and anecdotes constitute the third and last of the major categories in Aarne-Thompson, and in my *Comparative survey* (FFC 93) they generally comprise 20 to 30 percent of the European tale stocks listed. In my North Carolina collection two-thirds fall in this category, double the number of the first two categories combined. This situation appears to be typical of the United States in general. The favorite group in this humorous category consists of tales of exaggeration, huge lies, popularly called "tall tales". In them what is most obviously impossible appears to be the most hilariously funny, according to our folk taste. This leads to competition and liars' clubs, resulting in an endless effort to improve the old and fabricate something new and better. Thus in this group we are faced constantly with a mixture of truly folkloric old traditional themes plus continually appearing new themes which may or may not survive until they gradually acquire the traditional traits of true folklore.

The tale of the Irishman and the reflection of the moon illustrates rather fully the combined characteristics of this group: an old traditional theme, known in India and Europe, as well as in the United States and Canada, with exaggeration based on incredible stupidity, applied to newly arrived immigrants. It says that four Irishmen saw the reflection of the moon in a river, thought it was a silver plate, and determined to get it. One Irishman grasped a tree branch extending over the river, the second hung on to the feet of the first, the third, to the feet of the second, and the fourth, to the feet of the third. The fourth could reach the water, but just as this human chain was completed, the first man, gripping the branch, said, "Wait till I spit on my hands and get a firmer grip." With that, they all fell into the river. When they got out on the bank, the first one counted them, to see if they were all there. He forgot to count himself, so they thought one was missing. The second one counted, with the same result. So they all stuck their noses in the mud and then counted the impressions. In this way they discovered they were all there. Or were they?

The supreme ability of the mosquito to make a pest of himself attracts much attention to him, and he is featured in many jokes. The mosquito in combination with the "green" Irishmen produced the following. Two Irishmen recently arrived went to a hotel where mosquitoes were particularly bothersome. They got under the bed and pulled the bedclothes down all around the bed. Now safe from the mosquitoes, one stuck out his head to see if they had all gone. He saw fireflies, and he said to his companion, "They've got out their lanterns to look for us." I collected this tale in Beaufort County, on the coast, where I can personally testify to the aggressiveness of mosquitoes, in 1932, and in that same year this tale was published in Blum's *Farmers and Planters Almanac* at Winston-Salem.

Perhaps not so well-known is the mosquito tale I collected the next year in both Henderson and Mitchell Counties. In substance, it says that a man traveling on foot stopped at a house along the road when night fell and asked for a place to stay, but he was told they had a full house. He saw a big iron washpot in the yard, turned it upside down, and curled up under it. Mosquitoes there had stingers so long that they came right through the iron pot and stung him. He went up to the house and borrowed a hammer. During the night, the folks in the house heard a terrible banging outside, but they weren't about to investigate. Next morning, though, they went out and saw the man curled up on the ground. Their washpot was gone. When he awoke, they asked him where the pot was, and he explained that when the mosquitoes stuck their stingers through the pot, he'd hit them with the hammer and brad them to the pot. Finally there got to be so many of them that they just flew away with the pot.

The most popular numbskull tale, often told of an Irishman, is "The ass's (or mare's) egg." I found it in ten different counties. It has been reported from India, China, Turkey, various European countries, and in America, from Ontario to Oklahoma, among Whites, Negroes, and Indians alike. In his introduction to *Uncle Remus, his songs and his sayings*, Joel Chandler Harris says, "There is an anecdote about the Irishman and the rabbit which a number of Negroes have told me with great unction, and which is both funny and characteristic, though I will not undertake to say that it has its origin with the blacks." In Hyde County I was told a common saying there was "Well, he's hatched a mare's egg!" meaning he has told something exaggerated or impossible. Users of this expression often are unfamiliar with the story, of which I offer here a version from Edgecombe County. A man who had never seen a donkey saw some pumpkins growing in a field, and asked the farmer what they were. The farmer thought such a silly question deserved a silly answer, so he said they were donkey eggs. The man said he'd just bought a farm and would need a donkeky, so the farmer gave him a pumpkin and told him to take it home and sit on it for a week to keep it warm and it would hatch out a fine young donkey. But after the man sat on it all day and all night, his joints got so stiff he couldn't stand it any longer. He felt a soft spot in the pumpkin, and decided it was getting rotten rather than ready to hatch, so he got up and kicked it down a hill. It struck a rock and broke all to pieces. That scared a rabbit that was behind the rock, and it jumped up and ran away. The man thought it had jumped out of his pumpkin and was his young donkey, so he ran after it calling, "Come back here! Don't you know your daddy?" But the rabbit was long gone.

The dictionary says our slang word *bunk* comes from *buncombe*, and some champion liars around Asheville reminded me that this is the name of their county, which has given this word to the Eng-

lish language, thanks to them and their colleagues who have cultivated the gentle art of prevarication for generations. They told me
that after the Civil War Yankees flooded the South, and they
recalled one who stayed at a local hotel. The hotel keeper, aware of
the tricky Yankee reputation, asked this one to show him a trick.
The Yankee agreed, and when he was ready to leave the hotel, he
bored a hole in one side of a barrel of wine, and asked the hotel
keeper to plug it with his thumb. Then he bored a hole in the
other side of the barrel, and asked the hotel keeper to plug it with
his other thumb. Then the Yankee left without paying his bill,
knowing the hotel keeper would not lose his wine to come after
him.

Southerners could be tricky too. In Clay County I was told that
Sam Hooks went into Joe Merritt's store in Hayesville and told Joe
he had no money but would give him a mortgage on some hogs he
had up on the mountain, if Joe would give him rations till his crop
was ready. Joe accepted the mortgage and gave him rations all
summer. In the fall when Joe tried to collect, Sam told him to take
the hogs, but to slip up on them easy, because they were
groundhogs.

Anecdotes about a preacher and related religious activities
enjoy limited popularity, especially in northern Europe and predominantly non-Catholic Christian countries, which are noted also
for their lack of folk legends about miracles and edifying experiences of saints and the Virgin Mary, so abundant in countries dominated by the Greek and Roman Catholics. Some of these tales are
of rather limited circulation, but many others are more widespread
internationally than one might expect. Let us consider both types,
beginning with the international.

An old woman was quite impressed when her preacher said
that all that was given for a good cause would come back to the
giver tenfold. She decided to try out this principle and gave the
preacher her best cow. Next morning she heard unusual stomping
and snorting outside. She looked out and saw her cow had wan-
dered back home followed by nine of the preacher's cows. She told
the preacher he surely spoke the truth. My version from Wake
County ends here, but in a Norwegian version, after some argument, the preacher and the peasant who got his cows agreed that
the one who could say "Good morning" to the other first would

keep the cows. The peasant was up first and witnessed a scene between the preacher and his housekeeper, after which the preacher let the peasant keep the cows. This tale appeared in medieval Latin, in Bédier's *Fabliaux*, and in various European languages.

Apparently of only limited circulation is another church jest I found in Wake County. A parrot on a ship heard the captain say to his men "All hands below!" so often that it learned to repeat these words quite clearly. The ship was wrecked. The parrot reached shore on a piece of driftwood, and took refuge in the rafters of a church. Sunday morning, in the midst of the preacher's sermon, the parrot cried out from above, "All hands below!" Everyone listened, but heard nothing more, so the preacher continued to preach. But soon the parrot shrieked again, "All hands below!" This time everyone was scared and ran out of the church. The parrot decided it was time for him to leave too, so he flew down and perched on the shoulder of a crippled old lady, the last one out, just as she reached the door. When she felt claws on her shoulder, she cried, "Please, Mr. Devil, I'm not a member of this church!" I have found no parallels from other nations.

However, an inappropriate answer to a rhetorical question asked by a preacher in his sermon is a well-known European pattern which I found in Buncombe County in the following form. One Sunday morning the preacher sent a fellow to Paul, the local bootlegger, to get him a bottle of moonshine. Later that morning the fellow came back to the church just as the preacher, in the midst of his sermon, asked a rhetorical question: "And then what did Paul say?" The fellow thought the preacher was talking to him about Paul the bootlegger and not Paul the Apostle, so he said, "Paul said you couldn't have any more till you pay him for the last bottle you bought."

Another for which I lack parallels from abroad, also from Buncombe County, is about a man famed as being the biggest eater in the county. He was invited to a home for Sunday dinner. The host's favorite word was *reasonable*. When all were seated at the table, the host bowed his head to ask the blessing and said, "Lord we thank thee for these victuals thou hast set before us. Bless a REASONABLE portion of them for the sustenance of our bodies. We ask it in Christ's name. Amen." When the host pronounced loud and long his favorite word, *reasonable*, the big eater felt someone kick his leg under the table.

But in Buncombe County, far more popular than such subtleties of language are tales that magnify the truth without limit, told in a spirit plainly seen in the next two examples.

Once there was a boy who had such tough feet that he could dance on chestnut burrs, and he cut his initials in a rock with his big toe nail. The second has more elaboration: Once a farmer noticed the corn in his crib was disappearing fast, so he kept watch and early one morning he saw many squirrels across the creek that came by his barn. Beside the squirrels was a pile of shingles. Each squirrel took one, set it on the water, sat on the shingle, stuck his tail up for a sail, sailed across, got an ear of corn, sailed back, and went away to a big hollow treetrunk. The farmer got some friends, and they chopped on this treetrunk all day long. At night they went around the trunk to see how far they had cut through it, and found another bunch of men chopping on the other side.

The theme of "Who's holding whom?" is popular in a variety of forms, especially in western North Carolina. I offer a version from Onslow County because of its local slavery setting. When the master gave out food to the slaves, Jim would always refuse to take any meat, saying he had some left over from the last time. Every now and then the master would miss a hog. He suspected Jim, so he borrowed a tame bear from a neighbor and put it in his hogpen one night. Jim came in the dark, thought the bear was a hog, and got a helper, because it was so big. "Go in and pull him out, Joe," Jim said to his helper. But Joe replied, "You go in, Jim; you know more about this business than I do." So Jim went in, but instead of getting hold on the bear, the bear got a hold on Jim. When Jim didn't come out, Joe said, "Do you want me to come in and help you hold him, Jim?" Jim replied, "Help me hold him, hell! Come help me turn him loose!"

Of restricted north European currency is the story of the escape by the bear's tail, which appears to be quite popular in North Carolina, for I found it in five counties. In Burke County it was told to me as an actual experience. A man came to a hollow treetrunk about twelve feet high. He thought there might be some bear cubs in it, so he climbed to the top of it, broke off some pieces of bark, and threw them inside, thinking he'd find out that way if the mother bear was inside. The treetrunk was rotting, and the part he was sitting on broke off. He fell down inside, right among the bear cubs, and could not get out. The mother bear came back and climbed down inside, hind end first. He grabbed her tail, poked her rear end with his hunting knife, and she climbed back up and pulled him out.

In Surry County Bill Kitchen was picking blackberries when he met a big black bear. He ran, and the bear came after him. Finally he came to a stream frozen over, and skidded out on the ice. But the bear was afraid to go out on the ice, so Bill got away. When people reminded him he met the bear while he was picking black-berries, so it must have been summer, and the stream could not have been frozen over, he said, "Why that bear ran after me all through the fall and into the winter."

And so we could continue, with the tale of the man who replaced the hollow log into which the rabbits jumped with a solid log painted black on the end to look hollow, so the rabbits knocked themselves out butting their heads against that solid log; of the man who could not find his pigs because they had eaten their way inside a pumpkin and were lost from view; of a camp under the shade of a cabbage; and of a potato so long only one end of it could be gotten into the fireplace, while the other end stuck out of the cabin door and had to be sawed off.

But let us end this sojourn with Tarheel folktales by recalling that beautiful valley in Mitchell County, in which there were no graves because no one ever died there. Traveling through that valley one day, I heard a man crying. Then I saw him, sitting in his cabin door. He was wrinkled and gray, with long whiskers,—the oldest man I had ever seen. Hoping I might help, I asked the reason for his grief. He said his father would not approve of the marriage he had planned. I asked to meet his father. He took me inside the cabin, and there sat an even older man, cracking hickory nuts with his teeth. I told him he should use a hammer, for he would break his teeth, but he told me his father was using the hammer in the other room, to mend his grandfather's shoes.

# The Popularization of Legal Formulæ in Medieval Spanish Literature

BRIAN DUTTON

OR SEVERAL YEARS now there has been a lively interest, reflected in the ever growing bibliography on the subject, in binary expressions, legal formulæ, Classical phrases etc. in vernacular literature of the Middle Ages, epic, *clerecía*, chronicles, *caballería*, scientific prose etc. For a wide ranging discussion of these aspects, and the bibliography, I would refer to Colin Smith's *Estudios cidianos* (Madrid, 1977), in particular the chapter on "Realidad y retórica: El binomio en el estilo épico," pp. 161-217.[1] Here Smith surveys not only the epic, but also Berceo, the *Libro de Alexandre*, various *Crónicas* and numerous other works in Romance and in Latin, including Old French. He shows how

---

[1] Since the bibliography given by Colin Smith is quite extensive, I will not repeat it here. I would like to express my thanks to Alan Deyermond, who with his usual generosity read a first draft of this article and made many useful references. He informed me of two forthcoming articles germane to this topic, by David Hook in *Iberoromania* and Jack Walsh in *Romance Philology*.

many of the binomial phrases are in fact common formulæ found in legal documents in both Latin and the vernacular. The simplest illustration would be the term *sanus et salvus, sano y salvo, sain et sauf, safe and sound,* which has become a set phrase in frequent use in many languages (p. 168). Others dealt with by Smith include *señores e amigos* (p. 165), *de buena voluntad, de buen corazón,* (pp. 165-66), *grandes e chicos* (178-79), *mayores e menores* (179-81), *moros e christianos* (181-87), *mugeres e varones* (187-89), *legos e coronados* (191), *casadas e por casar* etc. (192-93), *yermo e poblado* (194-96), *exidas e entradas* (197-98—for the last two see also p. 216), *della e della part* (198-99), *noche e día* (199-200), *ivierno e verano* (200) etc. In his conclusions, Smith states (pp. 209-210):

> Es muy notable el uso tan constante de las parejas en el lenguaje jurídico de todos los tiempos, con el mismo empleo a dos niveles, "real" y formulaico, con la misma evolución y adaptación lentas. Creo que a pesar de existir muchos estudios de este lenguaje para la historia del léxico y de la diplomática, en algunos aspectos todavía está por investigar: orígenes, desarrollo, contenido estético, estructuras... Es un lenguaje influido desde luego por las hablas corrientes y las tradiciones literarias y religiosas, pero también es una ingente masa lingüística que se mueve *motu proprio.* Su influencia en el latín literario fue grande... y en las nacientes literaturas vernáculas incalculable, como hemos visto ya, y como volveremos a ver, en el *PMC* entre otros muchos textos. Este lenguaje jurídico tenía como una retórica propia tanto latina como vernácula, de mucha autoridad, culta por definición pero accesible a muchos; y no había que ir a las escuelas para aprenderla.

The last words of this paragraph are clear enough: the basic implication is that a large number of people would be familiar with legal phraseology without having to attend Law School. In this article I hope to demonstrate that this was indeed the case, and also to show some of the mechanisms that made this general intelligibility of legal formulæ possible. This also has considerable implications for the whole question of epic phraseology and vernacular literature in general.

Smith demonstrates rather convincingly (*Estudios* pp. 63-85) that the author of the *Poema de mío Cid* must have been quite familiar with the law, and almost certainly a legal professional. Since this is also true of Gonzalo de Berceo in an even more demonstrable way,[2] I will deal mainly with Berceo, but also refer to other texts. Previously I indicated the clear presence of epic formulæ and reminiscences, at times *a lo divino*, in Berceo's works.[3] Bermejo Cabrero's study (see note 2) amply demonstrates his knowledge of legal language and procedures, so that Berceo could use legal formulæ in his works and expect them to be as readily understood as epic ones.

First, however, we should document two facts: (a) that the gen-

---

[2] See my "The Profession of Gonzalo de Berceo and the Paris MS of the *Libro de Alexandre,*" BHS, 37 (1960), pp. 137-45. In reference to legal elements in Berceo's *Milagros*, see José Luis Bermejo Cabrero, "El mundo jurídico en Berceo," *Revista de la Universidad de Madrid, Nos. 70-71 (1969: Homenaje a Menéndez Pidal, II)*, pp. 33-52.

[3] See my "Gonzalo de Berceo and the *Cantares de Gesta,*" BHS, 38 (1961), pp. 197-205, and also my "El reflejo de las literaturas romances en las obras de Gonzalo de Beceo," in *Studia Hispanica in Honorem R. Lapesa*, II (Madrid, 1975), pp. 213-24 and "French Influence in the Spanish *mester de clerecía,*" in *Medieval Studies in Honor of Robert White Linker*, ed. B. Dutton, J. W. Hassell and J. E. Keller (Madrid, 1973), pp. 73-93. More general data on this and other aspects may be found in Joaquín Artiles, *Los recursos literarios de Berceo* (Madrid, 1968[2]). Pages 175-84 of my edition of Berceo's *Vida de San Millán*, Obras Completas, I (London: Tamesis, 1967), are also quite relevant, as far as epic elements are concerned. The other volumes are as follows. II, *Milagros de Nuestra Señora* (1971), III, *Duelo de la Virgen, Himnos, Loores de Nuestra Señora, Signos del Juicio Final,* (1975); IV, *Vida de Santo Domingo de Silos* (1978) and V, *Sacrificio de la Misa, Vida de Santa Oria, Martirio de San Lorenzo* (in Press).
I have used the following sources for legal documents:
AU: Antonio Ubieto Arteta, *Cartulario de San Millán de la Cogolla (759-1076)* (Valencia, 1976)

CH: Antonio Durán Gudiol, *Colección diplomática de la Catedral de Huesca*, 2 vols. (Zaragoza, 1969)

CSM: Dom Luciano Serrano, *Cartulario de San Millán de la Cogolla* (Madrid, 1930)—only for documents after 1076.

CDR: Ildefonso Rodríguez de Lama, *Colección diplomática de la Rioja (923-1168)*, tomo II (Logroño, 1976).

DL: Ramón Menéndez Pidal, *Documentos lingüísticos de España*, I, *El reino de Castilla (Madrid 1919, reprint 1966)*

Oña: Juan del Alamo, *Colección diplomática de San Salvador de Oña*, two vols. (Madrid, 1950).

eral public would be familiar with legal documents at least aurally and (b) that as witnesses they were of almost all social stations, except for the serfs, who did not count and are often mentioned only as part of the property belonging to the land being sold or leased.[4] Despite the fact that all documents were composed in Latin in the earlier period, we find constant references to them being read aloud to the witnesses and parties. This point is frequent in all cartularies, but does not seem to have entered into the discussion on legal formulæ in vernacular texts. Obviously, if all parties were to understand what was read out to them, the documents must have been recited in some form of Romance, even though they were written in Latin. Most of the examples given here are from the general region of La Rioja, from the ninth to the thirteenth centuries, in order to show that Berceo's immediate public would have had a long and direct experience of such texts, aurally at least. Later I will show the demonstrable effects of this "oral vernacularization" of Latin legal phrases on the language of the documents themselves.[5]

---

[4] Three quotes to illustrate the point: *Oña* 259 (1177) "Hanc ergo hereditatem...cum solaribus et collaciis et aliis possessionibus"; 313 (1196) "...hereditates, collacios nostros et ganados..." The *collazo* was a serf, who belonged to the land just as the trees and rivers did, and who could be bought and sold with it. The lot of the serfs is clear in *AU* 223 (1045) in which bishop Sancho of Nájera ruled that a certain "...mulier rustica...idens se sublimiorem suis vicinis, nolebat ire cum illis in officio operis agrorum..." was in fact "ex tribu servili...genitam", and ordered "ut semper operaretur cum vicinis suis...cum omni genere suo...per secula cuncta." The common justification for this state of affairs was that the serfs descended from Cain, and they had to expiate the murder of Abel.

[5] Of interest in this connection is the important study by Derek Lomax, "The Lateran Reforms and Spanish Literature", *Iberoromania*, I (1969), pp. 299-313. The policy of making available hagiographic, liturgical and paraliturgical texts in the vernacular also has obvious effects, through need, in secular matters too. Innocent III called the IVth council in 1215.

*AU*

2 (800)     Ego Vitulus cum fratre meo Erbigio legente audivi-
            mus, manus nostras signo fecimus...

3 (807)     Ego Eugenius et mei socii hec scriptura legente
            audivimus...

16 (873)    ...qui hanc cartam fieri iussimus relegentem audi-
            vimus...Cf. 30 (930), 37 (945), 38 (945) relegendo
            cognovi; 43 (947), 91 (972), 95 (975), 129 (1006),
            130 (1007) etc.

112 (997?)  Et ego Elvira et filio meo Alvaro qui hunc pactum
            fieri audivimus facere, relegentem cognovimus...

141 (1010?) ...et omnes Matutensi concilio audientes et testi-
            ficantes...

207 (1036)  Ego igitur Garsea rex hunc testamentum audivi,
            assensum prebui et confirmavi.

310 (1060)  Ego Garcia Fortuniones, qui hanc paginam fieri
            iussi, legentem audivi et confirmavi.

313 (1061)  Ego Fredinandus rex hanc cartam legentem audivi,
            assensum prebui et confirmavi.

*CDR*

102 (1132)  ...in conspectu totius populi uirorum et mulierum
            attendentium fuit lecta, recitata et predicta...
            scriptura...

117 (1138)  Ego quidem Maria Lopiz istam cartam fieri precepi
            et coram parentibus meis legere feci et lectam
            laudavi et roboravi.

131 (1142)  ...detulit hanc cartam Iohannes prior...ad
            Chell, in medio concilio lecta et affirmata fuit,
            coram subscriptis testibus...

In *CDR* 11 (1052?) there is even a "physical formula": "Toto
Concilio de Sancti Salbatore quod de aures audivimus de occulos
vidimus hic testes sumus." *Cf.* 86 (1126)

An early document from Huesca, *CH* 1 (551) is interesting in
the different formula: "Vincentius, in Christi nomine diaconus,
hanc cartulam donacionis quam feci propria manu signavi, relegi et
subscripsi..."

Vernacular documents are often just as specific, as these
examples show, even though the actual formula is in Latin at
times.

*DL*

5 (1220)     *La Montaña.* Huius rei sunt testes qui hoc uiderunt et audierunt...

12 (1156)     *Campó.* Testes qui ibi fuerunt et audierunt....

44 (1214)     *Castilla del Norte.* Estos son ueedores et oidores...

57 (1244)     *Miranda de Ebro.* Hujus rey sunt testes qui lo uieron e que lo oyeron...

93 (1241)     *San Millán.* Sabida cosa sea a quantos esta carta udieren e uidieren que...*Cf.* 98 (1249), 100 (1254) 101 (1259) etc. for this very common *incipit.*

113 (1212)     *Cervera.* Testimonias por mano postas qui esto uidieron et odieron...

165 (1220)     *Burgos.* E desto son testigos que lo uieron e odieron...

270 (1212)     *Toledo.* E son testimonias deste pleito oydores e ueedores...

Finally, on this particular topic, I quote *DL* 266 (1206) *Toledo:*

> ...e escribieron sos nomres, proprias manos, e los que non sopieron escrebir, escrebieron por ellos...

This quote makes it clear that literacy was not required of a witness, or even expected, but simply the ability to hear and understand the document as it was read out aloud.[6] It should be remembered that the idea persisted for some time that "written" language was Latin, and *sermo rusticus* was spoken, a decadent form of the language once common to all:

---

[6] *DL* 189 (1237) *Burgos,* specifically states "Et estos fueron testigos ante qui fue esta uendida fecha & estas cartas robradas & que fueron clamados pora oyrlo". Compare 278 (1236) *Toledo,* "Et los que este priuilegio ondrado leyeren, o gelo leyeren..." This document is of special interest, since it was "traslatada del priuilegio arauigo" granted by Alfonso VI in 1102, but it contains the formula "tierras labradas & por labrar"—see Smith, pp. 192-193. For other examples see "solares poblados & por poblar" 52 (1230) *Castilla de Norte;* 168 (1220) *Burgos;* 172 (1224) *Burgos,* 175 (1226) *Burgos* etc. "Labrado e por labrar" occurs in 113 (1212) *Rioja Baja* and "solares uassallos, poblados & por poblar, & con todas sus heredades labradas & por labrar" in 224 (1223) *Valladolid.*

La antigua e primera lengua latina era a todos comun e
una, asy a ninnos commo a honbres e mugeres, e asy a aldea-
nos commo a çibdadanos.[7]

As these documents were read out to the witnesses and parties,
the reader probably did not think he was "translating", but merely
reexpressing learned language in vernacular, popular speech.[8]

Our next point is to identify the classes of people who acted as
witnesses in these documents. Naturally, the social standing of the
main parties is often reflected in that of the witnesses to the document. For this reason I think it would be otiose to quote examples
of noblemen, court officials or ecclesiastics in general as witnesses.
We do occasionally find groups of witnesses without such titles as
*senior* or *dominus*, as in AU 238 (1078) and 242 (1079), and may
assume that they were commoners at least. Often the town council appears *en bloc*, as in *concilio de Sancti Romane testes*, AU 434 (1076)—
compare 244 (1046) in which a *ferrero* appears with *totum concilium de
Azofra*. There is an *aurifice* in 321 (1062). It is much to be regretted
that we do not have a complete cartulary from San Millan from
1077 onwards, such as we have for Oña. However *DL* will fill the
gap and give us a general picture for Castile, with the added advantage of mixing urban and rural settings in wider variety. In *DL* 19
(1201) *Campó*, the witnesses are divided into three groups, *fijosdal-
go ... clérigos ... labradores*, corresponding to the *defensores, oradores, labradores* of the three estates. Such divisions occur with frequency, and
since any person who was neither noble nor cleric was automatically assigned to the *tiers état*, it is in their ranks that we will find
the economically productive members of society who could contribute most in cash and kind to the prosperity of the monasteries. If
my hypothesis concerning the economic motives that lie in part
behind the composition of Berceo's works is valid, then the effec-
tiveness of his use of legal formulæ in them is at once apparent.[9]
Here are some specific examples from *DL*:

---

[7] E. J. Webber, "A Spanish Linguistic Treatise of the 15th Century",
*RPh*, 16 (1962-1963), quote from p. 35.

[8] This concept remained fairly constant from the time of St. Jerome's
*Vulgata*, and its final breakdown was one of the reasons for the Lateran
Reforms discussed by Lomax—see note 5.

[9] See my edition of the *Vida de San Millán*, pp. 163-175, chapter VII. 1.

*Campó:* 32 (1259) yuguero, texedor; 33 (1259) pellegeru.
*Castilla del Norte:* 52 (1230) çapatero; 54 (1231) ferrero.
*Rioja Alta:* 94 (1242) carpentero; 105 (1279) cozinero, carpentero, azemilero.
*Rioja Baja:* 113 (1212) zapatero; 120 (1250) fferrero.
*Burgos:* 157 (1206) atuarero, portero; 158 (1207) moninero (*sic*), el bufon; 164 (1214) luuero; 165 (1215) iuguero; 178 (1227) carpentero; 192 (1241) carpentero, tornero, corronero, calzador, feuillero, frenero.
*Osma:* 214 (1225) pescador; 216 (1227) pastor; 217 (1233) molinero.

The documents from Huesca in *CH,* since they reflect a more concentrated urban society, often specify witnesses by name and profession or trade in greater variety: 196 (1151) zapatero, carnicero; 220 (1155) pellizero; 227 (1158) feltrero; 239 (1164) lanero: 293 (1173) mercero; 351 (1180) macelero; 394 (1184) cocinero; 489 (1195) carcelero; 492 (1195) mege (médico); 504 (1195) "Testes visores et auditores Arnal tayllador, Domenge ortolan, Fortanus serraler, Bernat de Modiran bayart..." 508 (1195) harinero; 559 (1199) trapero; 652 (1205) adobador; 706 (1209) cazador; 749 (1212) molinero etc. I have used these documents from Huesca since those available from San Millán usually have monks and ecclesiastics as witnesses, though professions are not lacking in *DL* Rioja Alta—see above. The general class of the third estate that could serve as witnesses was made up of precisely those members of society with enough of an economic stake in life to be contributors to the needs of a monastery such as San Millán de la Cogolla, namely, at the lowest but most practical level, artisans and craftsmen, blacksmiths, butchers, carpenters, cobblers, fishermen, haberdashers, glovers, leatherers, millers, tanners, weavers etc. Their products correspond to some degree to the contributions demanded under the *Votos de San Millán.*[10]

---

[10] The forged *Privilegio de los Votos,* dated 934 but in fact composed in the early years of the XIIIth century (text in *Obras* I, pp. 1-8 and *AU* 22, pp. 33-40), lists the following products as required annual payments to San Millán de la Cogolla: carneros, sayales, lienzos, pozales de vino, cera, cirios, quesos, rejas de hierro, acero, odres de aceite, pescados, plomo, corderos, panes, gallinas, anguilas, bueyes, arienzos y dineros. Other professions mentioned among witnesses in *DL* include odrero, hornero,

There is yet another dimension: legal documents were much more a part of daily life and aural experience in the Middle Ages than today. Publication implied not gazettes and classified sections in newspapers, but public proclamation and recital. Moreover, even for simple sales of property, the formal witnessing of the document could be quite a memorable ceremony with its own reward, since often the buyer provided a meal for the seller and the witnesses. This was known as the *alboroque, robra* or *raisce* in Castile, and as the *aliala* in Aragon:

60 (1094)    Aliala II panes, III galletas bino medio kantaro, una spatula de porcho, II conellos.

131 (1130)   ...et in aliala expensimus in pane et vino et pisce VIII solidos.

196 (1151)   Aliala inter pane et vino et pisce que vocatur salmon et alias cosas quod ibi fuerunt opus, XV solidos.

342 (1178)   Aliala X solidos costa inter pane et vino et caro.

406 (1186)   Et dedit...ad comer ad illas fidanças et ad illas testimonias...de pane et de vino et de pisce et de alias cosas quod fuit opus, quod costavit X solidos.

*AU*

197 (1032)   ...in roboratione XXV panes et argenzata et media de vino et uno ariete et tozino...

212 (1037)   ...in alboroc...V camelas de vino in XII argenzos et quinque argenzos in carne...

238 (1045)   ..et raisce...II camelas et media de vino, VI panes et II caseos.

*CDR*

44 (1098)    ...precium...XXXIII solidos argenti cum suorum aluoroz sicut nobis usum est.

46 (1100)    ...precium...XIII solidos cum sua iantare.

97 (1129)    ...precio...CCCXX solidos...cum consueto prandio.

207 (1159)   ...per CC morabetinos bonos melequinos cum suo albaroc...

---

aceñero, albardero, ballestero, herrador, pregonero, alcabalero, cirujano, aceitero, conejero, escobero, porquerizo, montero, plomero, cristalero, mercader etc.

*DL*

112 (1169)   ...sum bene paccato de isto precio cum sua iantar ...

114 (1235)   ...dados e pagados cum sua jantar...

120 (1250)   ...de los quales morauedis somos bien pagados e dela jantar...

123 (1258)   ...& son bien pagados con so iantar conplida...[11]

In view of this evidence, I think we can see clearly how the Romance versions of Latin legal formulæ (and from about 1200, the Romance formulæ used in vernacular documents) passed into commonly understood phrases, and often commonly used expressions. These could be exploited for effect (and as ready-made formulaic hemistichs) in vernacular literature, not only as a phraseology familiar to those experienced in law and diplomatic, but also as a stock of expressions that would be understood by the lay public.

There is one further point to be noted, and one that is of great importance. This concerns the changes that took place in Latin formulæ in the eleventh century, as part of a process to make the documents more intelligible. A simple example of this development is the gradual change from *spontanea voluntate*, which is extremely common in the eleventh century, as in *AU* 150 (1013), 168 (1017), 176 (1022), 184 (1028) *et passim*, through such forms as *spontanea bona voluntate CH* 442 (1189) *CDR* 118 (1138), to the form *bona voluntate CH* 442 (1187), etc., most abundant. This then becomes the *de buena voluntad* of *DL* 25 (1220), 48 (1225), 51 (1230) etc. There is in *DL* 157 (1206) *Burgos*, the expression "ex mea bona voluntate uendo e robro..." This formula often occurs with *corde*, as in *placuit mihi toto corde, spontanea voluntate AU* 234 (1045), 298 (1058) etc., or *placuit mihi obtimo corde et bona voluntate CH* 422 (1187)—see also 434, 438, 439, 444, 473 etc., and 480 (1194) *de bono corde et optima voluntate*, also 568. Compare this with *DL* 214 (1225) *Osma: de buen coraçón e de buena uoluntad*, and *cf.* 225, 273, 314, 322 etc. In *AU* we find 242 (1046) *toto cordeque voluntate* and in 279 (1051) *omni voluntate*—see also 286 etc. These phrases provide Berceo with formulaic hemistichs

---

[11] The amounts spent on these meals range from 5-10% of the sale price, which gives some idea of the nature of some of these feasts— whole salmon, rams etc. imply quite a celebration!

that also occur as set expressions in the *PMC* and many other texts:

> de buena voluntad *SMill.* 200c; *SDom.* 87c; *Milag.* 98a, 856b etc.
>
> de toda voluntad *SMill.* 129d, 148b; *SDom.* 10a, 75a, 496d, 632d, etc.
>
> Compare also *de todo coraçón* Sacr. 223c, 264d. See C. Smith, p. 165.

It could easily be objected that these phrases are so commonplace that the parallels with legal documents are purely coincidental. However, if we examine another one, I think the objection becomes invalid.

Berceo uses the adjectives *sano e alegre* constantly to refer to people who have been cured of serious ailments, as in:

| *SDom.* | 291a | Alegre e bien sana | metióse en carrera. |
|---|---|---|---|
| | 314c | bien sana e alegre | fue la duenna su vía. |
| | 548d | sano e bien alegre | tornó a su posada. |
| | 635a | Sano e bien alegre | tornó a Celleruelo. |
| *SLor.* | 83b | cobró toda la lumne, | fue alegre e sano. |

If we look at Latin documents of the eleventh century, we find the formula, much used in the first clause of wills, that is clearly the origin of *sano y alegre*:

> *AU*
> 299 (1058) ...ego...sana et integra mente...
> 406 (1073) ...ego...mea sana et integra voluntate...

This is confirmed absolutely by the equivalent Romance formula:

> *DL*
> 102 (1262) *Rioja Alta:*...yo...seyendo sano e alegre e en mi buena memoria...
> 115 (1237) *Rioja Baja:*...jo...sana e alegre e en mi bona memoria...
> 210 (1217) *Osma:*...hyo...sano e alegre...
> 225 (1225) *Valladolid:*...ego...sana hi alegre he de buena uoluntad...

Another phrase that Colin Smith deals with briefly is *ivierno e verano*. This again is of legal origin, being used in reference to grazing rights. Smith himself quotes a document of 1044 from

Silos *in hieme quomodo in estate* (p. 200). This is explained by a document from La Rioja, dated 1122:

> ...concedo quoque vobis quod in illa nostra defesa cavalli vestri pascant cum ganato nostro ab introito mensis martii usque ad festum Sancti Michaelis; postea pastus defese sit comunis nobis et vobis... *CSM* 303.

Given the hot, dry Castilian summer, grazing was more abundant from September to March—hence only the horses were allowed grazing on the *dehesa* from March to Michaelmas. The phrase also exists in Romance:

> DL 115 (1237) *Rioja Baja*:...ganados de los frayres de Casanueua proprios e de sus pastores...que pascan hiuierno e verano...

The phrase also occurs in *SMill.* 172d; *SDom.* 47a, 191d, 356d; *Milag.* 306d, 503c. It is an inclusive phrase to mean "all year long", just as *noche e día* was used to cover the whole twenty-four-hour period, not just the hours of daylight possible when *día* alone was used.

Another phrase much used is the pair *vestir e calzar*:

*Milag.*
| | | |
|---|---|---|
| 233c | si algo li menguasse | en vestir o calzar. |
| 363c | assín como estava | calzado e vestido. |
| 760a | Avía qé vistir, | avía qé calzar. |

*Soria*
| | | |
|---|---|---|
| 142c | todas bien aguisadas | de calçar e vestir. |

*SLor.*
| | | |
|---|---|---|
| 82d | en tus manos me meto, | vestido e calçado. |

In documents we find the origin of this formula, as part of the inclusive expression to indicate complete support, as in *bed and board* in English:

*Oña*
| | | |
|---|---|---|
| 293 (1191) | ...concedo tibi... uictum et uestitum et calciamentum et pallium... |
| 296 (1192) | ...monachorum indumentis et calciamento... |

*DL*
86 (1227)    *Rioja Baja*:...uostros obos de a uostro cuerpo, en
             comer e beber, e uestir e calzar...

Next, there is one phrase that I have so far found only in
thirteenth-century Latin documents, but I suspect that, from the
context, it too is a much older formula, *menudo e granado*. It occurs in
Berceo in *SMill*. 464a, 477a; *SDom*. 452b; *Sacr*. 254a; *Signos* 9a, 20b,
70a; *Milag*. 478b, 836c, 890bc. In documents I have found the following examples:

*Oña*
438/439 (1225)    ...primitiis et decimis tam minutis quam gra-
                  natis...
566 (1264)        ...quantas calonnas hy uinieren, menudas et
                  granadas...
649 (1276)        ... el tercio del diezmo granado e menudo-
                  ...todel diezmo menudo e granado...
*DL*
135 (1266)        *Alava*:...de todo lo al que christianos deuen
                  dezmar entergadament, de menudo e de gra-
                  nado...

The context seems to indicate that the phrase was originally associated with tithing—*minutum* probably connected with the widow's
mite of *Mark* 12:42, and *granatum* originally representing kind, particularly grain crops, whence it came to be associated via *menudo*
with large and small. Daniel Devoto also associates this expression
and *tardío e temprano* with tithing—which is also the origin of such
expressions as *non valer una fava/ arveja/ chirivia/ nuez* etc.[12]

Finally, there is the phrase *della e della part*, which Colin Smith
relates to the literary phrase *huc atque illuc*, (p. 198). However, the
phrase does occur in a document from San Millán:

---

12 See Daniel Devoto, "Tardío e temprano", in his *Textos y contextos:
estudios sobre la tradición* (Madrid, 1974), pp. 52-61. The phrase *tardío e temprano* has a biblical base—see *James* 5:7 "El labrador atiende buen fruto de
su tierra paziblemente, fasta que reciba ende fruto temprano e tardío" in
*Nuevo Testamento, versión castellana de hacia 1260*, ed. Spurgeon W. Baldwin
and Thomas Montgomery (Madrid, 1970), *Anejos de la BRAE*, XII, p. 398.
The Vulgate gives *temporaneum et serotinum*. Devoto does not give this
reference.

DL
91 (1237) ...el concejo de Madriz aia los morauedis, saluos los casamientos que anden ad della e della part con so fuero...

This seems to be a clear derivation from the common formula *ex utraque parte*, as in *CDR* 202 (1158) *testes ex utraque parte*. Compare this with 196 (1157) *fidiator de saluamento ex parte abbatis... Ex parte don Paschal...* [13]

*This brief and limited excursion into legal formulæ, principally as present in the works of Berceo, has been, I think,* sufficiently rewarding, in the light of the evidence concerning the mode of transmission of such expressions from Latin documents to common parlance, to permit some general observations in conclusion. It does seem that the practice of reading out aloud documents to witnesses in a form that they could understand (clearly not the Latin in which they were actually drafted), made this vernacularized legal phraseology generally available and usually quite intelligible, though predictably with some confusion, as can be seen in the change from *sana et integra mente* to *sano e alegre*. The above material seems to show that there was a constant flow of such terminology and expressions into the daily speech of the people.

Berceo's use of epic phrases and terminology simply indicates that the genre was thriving during his lifetime. In the same way, his use of legal terms and phrases only demonstrates his and his public's familiarity with the contents and language of agreements, leases, sales, exchanges, wills etc. in legal dress. This is an element that I believe this study has shown to be a perfectly valid assumption. It has for some time been clear that the author of the *PMC* and Berceo were professionals or paraprofessionals in law and court procedures,[14] but now it seems understandable that they should use "shop" terms and concepts in their vernacular works,

---

[13] Compare the following from *DL*: 34 (1284) *Campó*, "Desto son testigos rogados de ambas las partes por testimonio..." and 62 (1270) *Castilla del Norte*; 116 (1237) *Rioja Baja*, "son testimonias por mano puestas, dambas las partidas". The San Millán document that actually uses *della e della part* (*DL* 91) describes the dispute as being "entre el concejo de Madriz de la una part, e delos barrios de Santurdi e de Barrio nouo de la otra".

[14] See Smith, *op. cit.* pp. 15-34, 65-85, esp. 77-78.

since the evidence adduced shows that their public would be, aurally at least, experienced and familiar with the formulæ, expressions and turns of phrase they use, derived from their professional experience. It is also important to realize that these expressions would have a particular resonance, and carry associations and connotations that would be clear and quite unmistakeable. The prospect is however a little daunting, as A. C. Spearing points out in discussing the phrase "governour of this gyng", which suggesyts "Boss of this gang", whereas other contexts indicate that it meant more like "lord of this company". Spearing remarks " ... but we can only guess at the number of similarly mistaken responses that we do not notice and cannot correct".[15]

Add to this the further question of the problems faced by early vernacular writers. When the various forms of Romance began to give expression to literary creation, one must assume that there was rather a limited battery of terms and phrases to express the finer intellectual and aesthetic points that distinguish "literature", if the writer was restricted to the day-to-day speech of the general mass of the people. This language provided the basic morphology and syntax, the general grammar and lexis, as both grammatical particles and the nomino-verbal semantic elements with which the language operated—concrete objects, basic emotions and human inner activities, covering the social structure under which they lived and the general area of human needs, relationships and experiences. Such early vernacular writers must have been perforce educated to read and write, which implies education in Latin. When they began to write in the vernacular—presumably for a listening audience—they were obliged to force, as it were, the old wine of Latin intellectuality into the inadequate new bottles of popular speech. At any stage, the presence of Latinisms and *semicultismos* is clear evidence of this process.[16] Hence, for quite a long period, there would be an element of novelty in the use of, say,

---

[15] *Criticism and Medieval Poetry* (London, 1964), Chapter I, "Problems for the Critic", quote from p. 7.

[16] See José Jesús de Bustos Tóvar, *Contribución al estudio del cultismo léxico medieval* (Madrid, 1974), *Anejos de la BRAE*, and my "Some Latinisms in the Spanish *mester de clerecía*", KRQ, 4 (1967), pp. 45-60.

legal terms in vernacular works that quite escapes us now, for
most of them smack of hoary antiquity, of precisely the quality
these time-honored expressions had for Cervantes, who parodied
them in *Don Quijote*, as Smith illustrates (pp. 193 and 206).[17]

UNIVERSITY OF ILLINOIS

---

[17] There are two fundamental studies that should be kept in mind as
trailblazers in this whole question, namely P. E. Russell, "Some Problems of Diplomatic in the *Cantar de Mio Cid* and their Implications", *MLR*,
47 (1952), pp. 340-349 and Alan Deyermond, *Epic Poetry and the Clergy*,
(Támesis, London, 1968) esp. pp. 63-80 and the excursus on *merinos*, pp.
217-220. Antonio Ubieto Arteta, "Observaciones al Poema de Mio Cid",
*Arbor*, 37 (1957), pp. 154-170 also merits special mention.

# The Ideal of Perfection: the Image of the Garden-Monastery in Gonzalo de Berceo's *Milagros de Nuestra* Señora

JAMES BURKE

HE FIRST MIRACLE OR EXEMPLUM in Gonzalo de Berceo's *Milagros de Nuestra Señora* tells of the marvelous chasuble which the Virgin gave to St. Ildelfonsus of Toledo because he had been instrumental in establishing a new feast of the Incarnation in a time more propitious for the proper observation of such a feast. The miracle exists in the Latin source which is either the one used by the poet or one very similar to it. Berceo adds, however, as Brian Dutton, the latest and perhaps best editor of the *Miracles* notes, a curious statement concerning the chasuble: "...diole una casulla sin aguja cosida; / obra era angélica, non de omne texida." (60c)[1] Of course if the chasuble comes from the Vir-

---

[1] Gonzalo de Berceo, *Obras completas* II: *Los Milagros de Nuestra Señora*, ed. Brian Dutton (Colección Támesis, Serie A—Monografías, XV, London, 1971), p. 52. All quotations from the *Milagros* and from its Latin sources will be taken from this edition.

gin, one might expect that no man or woman wove it. But does Berceo have any particular reason for adding these lines? The next archbishop of Toledo, one Siagrius, demands to vest the chasuble although he obviously is by no means worthy to do so. The chasuble promptly deals with this usurpation of the rights of his predecessor by strangling him.

The miracle which is number 25 in manuscript I, that of Santo Domingo de Silos, is the story of a church which was robbed, "La iglesia robada." Traditionally most editors have followed the order of manuscript I. Dutton, however, chooses the order of manuscript F, that of the Real Academia de la Lengua, which switches "La iglesia robada" to place number 24 while making 24 in manuscript I, the story of Theophilus, the final one. Dutton likes the order of F better he tells us, because the last three quatrains of the Theophilus story, all of which end with the word *Amen* and which exhort the Virgin to remember the poet, seem more appropriate as an ending.[2]

If we look at the theme of "La iglesia robada" it is possible to see that the miracle parallels the first in the collection in two very significant ways and that, therefore, from a structural point of view it is more appropriate as an ending for the work. The two thieves who proceed to loot a church and the cell of the nun who maintains the church are only stopped when they attempt to pull from an image of the Virgin in the church a beautiful white veil which covers the head of the statue. The veil sticks so tightly to the hand of one of the thieves that he cannot detach it. Further the Virgin causes both thieves to lose their memory and to become totally disoriented so that they cannot escape from the church before help arrives.

In the first miracle the Virgin has granted a particular wondrous fabric product to a faithful servant. In the last her image is covered (protected) by another piece of material. Further Berceo tells us that the nun-guardian has only one thing of value: " . . . avié magra sustancia, assaz poca ropiella, / pero avié un panno era cosa boniella, / pora mugier de orden cubierta apostiella." (874*bcd*) Although the poet does not make the connection explicitly, one infers that the nun's veil parallels the one on the statue of the

---

2 *Ibid.*, p. 17.

Virgin. As she cares for the marian shrine, so the Virgin cares for her and the token of her esteem is the veil. In the first miracle the chasuble deals with the usurper; in the last the veil does likewise with the thieves.

The protective power of the covering veils reappears and is clarified in Miracle 14 which is the story of the image of the Virgin miraculously respected by a fire. In this *exemplum* a fire breaks out and all is burned save the statue, the veil which covers it, and a *flabellum* hanging near the image. In the Latin source which the poet probably used, a parallel is drawn between the way in which the image is saved from the fire and the perpetual virginity of Mary. As the fire did not touch the image, so she was unbothered by the concupiscence of the flesh. "Digna prorsus ostense sunt miracula quia illius ymaginem ignis tangere non valuit, que corpore et mente semper virgo permanens carnis concupiscenciam nullatenus scivit." (p. 117) Berceo at the beginning of the miracle takes great pains to describe the rich quality and appearance of the veil: "... de suso rica impla en logar de cortina, / era bien entallada e de lavor muy fina, / valié más assi pueblo qe la avié vezina." (320*bcd*) At the end of the *exemplum* the poet departs from the Latin by not making a direct comparison between the viriginty of Mary and the pristine state of the image. Instead he broadens the scope of his analogy to a more general conclusion:

> La Virgo benedicta, reína general
> como libró su toca de esti fuego tal,
> asín libra sus siervos del fuego perennal,
> liévalos a la Gloria do nunqua vean mal.   (329)

In effect Berceo establishes the sheltering powers of the veil. He will reinforce this idea in Miracle 19 where he dramatically demonstrates the protective powers of the Virgin's clothing:

> Yo en esto estando, vino sancta María,
> cubrióme con la manga de la su almexía;
> non sentí nul periglo más que quando dormía,
> so yoguiesse en vanno más leida non sería.   (448)

The eminent anthropologist Victor Turner in his study of the phenomenon of pilgrimage in Christian culture has noted that in patrilineal, partimonial societies the maternal bond and image is used to express the unity of the community as a whole. This pro-

tective, maternal communitas is often portrayed as "white," "pure,"
"primary," and "seamless."[3]

It is thus not surprising to find that the imagery of the Christian dispensation has adopted a symbol which conforms to such a
pattern. According to an ancient legend repeated many times
among the Church Fathers the Virgin could be compared to a
weaver who had woven the robe of flesh which was to be torn
upon the cross.[4] The image of unity then moves metonymically
from the body of Christ to the seamless tunic which he was wearing and for which the soldiers cast lots so that one of them could
have it whole. (John 19:23-24) The Fathers of the Church came to
view this tunicle as representing the unity of the Church and
hence of all creation.[5]

In addition there existed an ancient tradition particularly prevalent and extended in the Eastern Church which was related very
much to the theme of the return to paradise. In this scheme Mary
has the role of Eve in reverse. The physical mother of humanity
gave to her progeny a garment of skins as a result of her sin and
that of Adam in the Garden of Eden. The New Eve, Mary, given to
her spiritual children a new garment, the flesh of Christ, which
will reverse the effects of the primordial fall.[6]

The frame within which Berceo places his 25 miracles, the
Introduction, is, of course, a return to paradise:

> Yo maestro Gonçalvo de Verceo nomnado,
> yendo en romería caecí en un prado,
> verde e bien sençido de flores poblado . . .    (2abc)

---

[3] Victor and Edith Turner, *Image and Pilgrimage in Christian Culture*
(New York, 1978), pp. 199, 254-55.

[4] See Hilda Graef, *Mary: A History of Doctrine and Devotion*, I (London
and New York, 1963), p. 71 and also P. Saintyves, *Essais de folklore biblique:
magie, mythe, et miracles dans l'ancien et le nouveau testaments* (Paris, 1922), pp.
420-21. M. Morreale discusses the knowledge of this tradition in Spain
in relation to the renderings of the Passion of Christ which Juan Ruiz
presents. "Una lectura de las 'passiones' de Juan Ruiz (*LBA* 1043-1066)",
*BRAE*, 55 (1975), pp. 331-81 at 372.

[5] Saintyves, p. 419.

[6] Graef, pp. 60 and 71.

This is a place, as Leo Spitzer has noted in his study of world harmony, of complete perfection, concord, and order.[7] The very word *sençido* applied to the *locus amoenus* means 'whole'. In stanzas 8 and 9 the birds which inhabit the garden sing sweetly in carefully modulated tones. The three groups who respectively produce the base note of the octave, its fifth, and the octave of the fifth bring forth the kind of parallel polyphony which was allegorically utilized in the Middle Ages to suggest the totality of the world soul.[8] In stanza 11 we are told that this garden "siempre estava verde en su entegredat." (c) In stanza 14 it is specifically compared to paradise: "...semeja esti prado egual de Paraíso." Stanza 15 says that the fruit of the trees of this garden would never have produced the lamentable effect which Adam and Eve suffered. Stanza 19 explains that this meadow is the Virgin while stanza 20 goes on to make an explicit analogy between the completeness and perfection of this *locus amoenus* and that of the Mother of Christ:

> Esti prado fue siempre verde en onestat
> ca nunca ovo mácula la su virginidat;
> post partum et in partu fue virgin de verdat,
> illesa, incorrupta en su entegredat.

We learn in stanza 25 that the trees in the garden are the miracles which Mary produces. Then finally after a long series of traditional, topical references and descriptions of the Virgin the poet tells us that he intends to ascend into these miracle-trees in order, one would infer, to entertain and impress his reader-listener with the powers of Mary. The first miracle, that of the chasuble of St. Ildelfonsus, follows immediately.

It would seem that Berceo has reversed the traditional struc-

---

[7] *Classical and Christian Ideas of World Harmony: Prolegomena to an Interpretation of the Word "Stimmung"*, ed. Anna Granville Hatcher (Baltimore, 1963), pp. 54-57.

[8] *Ibid.*, p. 36. See also John Hollander, *The Untuning of the skies: Ideas of Music in English Poetry 1500-1700* (Princeton, 1961), p. 56. Melissa C. Wanamaker, *Discordia Concors: The Wit of Metaphysical Poetry* (Port Washington, N.Y. and London, 1975), p. 8 points out that the metaphysical poets in England accepted the medieval idea that the tempering of discords in the musical universe should be paralleled by similar tempering in a writer's poetry.

ture which the Christian puts on the new garments of Christ before proceeding to effect his return to paradise. The pilgrim Gonzalo enters the marian *locus amoenus* and then removes his clothing: "...descargué mi ropiella por yazer más vicioso..." (6c) He puts on as it were the protective ambiance of the garden itself which, of course, metaphorically stands for the Virgin.

The idea that the Christian imagination should seek in Paradise a more perfect garment than the one of flesh and fabric bequeathed to him by Eve is an old one as Terry Comito has pointed out.[9] Comito has traced and discussed the image of the "proud earth's new garment" as it develops from its Classical base in the poetry of the Carolingian singers and those in the *Carmina Burana*. (126) This idea of the earth's donning a raiment of greenery and flowers in the spring is fused with motifs of spiritual renewal and restoration at Easter so that all Creation could be contemplated *"sub specie renovationis."* (128)

This is, of course, a lyrical, metaphorical conceptualization perfectly adapted for poetry. A more practical mode, one combining the themes of garden and renovation, which would have allowed the Christian to perfect himself if he so desired would have obviously existed.

The principal manner by means of which such perfection was thought to be achievable in this life in the Middle Ages was through the monastic vocation. The individual who professed as soon as he pronounced his vows was seen to be dead to the world.[10] His old garments were removed and he received a tunic which was understood as a symbol for his renewal in Christ. This tunic was known as the *vestis angelica* or the *angelica* and eventually even the adjective came to be synonymous with the idea of "monastic habit." Once the neophyte wore this habit he could begin to mold his life toward the greatest degree of completion possible in this world. In the later Middle Ages it became customary for seculars who wished to obtain for themselves before dying the merit of monastic life, which they of course had never lived, to

---

[9] *The Idea of the Garden in the Renaissance* (New Brunswick, NJ., 1978), p. 129.

[10] See Dom Jean Leclercq, *The Life of Perfection*, trans. Leonard J. Doyle (Collegeville, Minn., 1961), especially pp. 97, 119-25.

don the *angelica*.[11] The chasuble which the Virgin gives to St. Ildelfonsus is described as *angelica* and one wonders if the poet had in mind the well-known monastic garb.[12]

It became common in the later Middle Ages to view the monastery as a kind of earthly paradise.[13] For example St. Peter Damian represented the great monastery of Cluny as an eden watered by the four rivers which had poured out of the primeval garden: "Vere claustrum est paradisus."[14] Those who have seen examples of cloisters built during this period and afterwards will have recognized the kind of archetypal plan which evolved and which managed to imply the paradisical ideal.

Now the cloister-paradise provided excellent opportunity for the perfection of that individual who could afford to abandon the vagaries of everyday life. But as Juan Manuel was well aware everyone could not assume the monastic role if the life of the world

---

11 *Ibid.*, p. 17. See also Comito, p. 128 and the remarks of John Bugge on the *vita angelica* in *Virginitas: An Essay in the History of a Medieval Ideal* (The Hague, 1975), p. 34. Bugge also demonstrates how the ideas of the virginity of Mary served as the ideal for integrity and wholeness in the medieval period.

12 It is interesting to note the reasons for the establishment of the new feast of the Virgin on December 18 by the Tenth Council of Toledo. First the same event should be recalled or commemorated on the same day throughout the Church if schism is to be avoided. "Quum nicil fidei sinceritas por diversitatem adversum incurrat et unitatem catholicae regulae varietas nulla decerpat, est tamen quod nisi temporum unitate servetur et discidium indiscissae unitati parturiat et sacramentorum unitate constare non valeat". (*Concilios visigóticos e hispano-romanos*, ed. José Vives, Barcelona, Madrid, 1963, p. 308). A feast in honor of the Virgin outside of Lent (where the Annunciation almost always falls) was being celebrated on many different dates throughout Spain. "...quoniam transducti homines diversitate temporum dum varietatem sequuntur, unitatem celebritatis non habere probantur". (p. 309) It was necessary to fix one date as the valid moment for the celebration of the feast. Thus even the very setting of the date of the feast has to do with a concern for unity, an integrity of worship.

13 See García M. Colombás, *Paradis et vie angélique: le sens eschatologique de la vocation chrétienne*, trans. Dom Suitbert Carron (Paris, 1961), pp. 248-49, 234-35 , and 164-65. Leclercq, *op.cit.*, also discusses the same idea at numerous points.

14 Quoted in Colombás, footnote 3, p. 243.

were to continue.[15] The monastic ideal could only apply to a certain proportion of the population. Was the life of perfection embodied in the garden monastery to be denied to all others?

Gonzalo de Berceo provides the solution. An old, established tradition to which constant reference was made in the liturgy and in sermons compared the Virgin to a garden, the restored earthly paradise. Other traditions declared the perfection of her physical as well as her spiritual presence. By poetically combining the two themes he could give to everyman, as he lived his daily life, a means by which to restore and perfect himself. Thus the *Milagros* open with the well-known idea, drawn out and elucidated in many ways, of the Virgin as the perfect antitype to the lost Eden. The poet makes clear that this *locus amœnus* is far superior to that of any earthly monastic setting: "...que avié de noblezas tantas diversidades / que no las contarién priores nin abbades." (10cd)

This introduction serves as a frame for the 25 miracles, but, of course, the overall meaning or significance suggested in the introduction would have to be translated into terms which would be more directly intelligible. Thus, I believe that Berceo set up a subframe in the first and last miracles which effected this transmutation. The metaphorical value of the Virgin as garden-paradise is transposed and carried to the reader-listener by metonymical links with her in the first and last *exempla*, links given in terms of clothing. Again ancient tradition associated the Virgin with clothing—Christ's tunic which he wore to the cross and the new garments which the renewed Christian would put on as a sign of his orientation toward perfection.

Further as Comito has noted the idea of clothing is fused with the concept of perfect garden as paradise in the widely used image of the "earth's proud new garment". Thus not only was the Virgin associated in the Middle Ages with garden and with clothing; these two latter concepts were also closely related to one another independently. Berceo then had available to him well established tradi-

---

[15] "Et si todas las gentes pudiessen mantener esta carrera, sin dubda ésta sería la más segura et la más aprovechosa para aquellos que los guardassen; mas, porque si todos lo fiziessen sería desfazimiento del mundo..." *El Conde Lucanor*, ed. José Manuel Blecua (Madrid, 1969), p. 303.

tions which interrelated the three major elements of his *Miracles*—Virgin, perfect garden, and clothing.

Ernst Cassirer in volume II of the *Philosophy of Symbolic Forms* has studied the manner in which primitive societies understood the metonymical relationship.[16] The part is not a subordinated division or fraction of the whole. It is the whole. It shares all of the important qualities, attributes, and properties of the greater portion. Cassirer's discussion of alchemy, astrology, plant and mineral lore in the Middle Ages proves that this mythological mode of thought still pertained to a great degree during that period. The idea is still prevalent in the Renaissance and Golden Age in Spain as is seen in Juan de Pineda's *Diálogos familiares de la agricultura cristiana*. "La orden natural y de perfeción pide ser primero el todo que su parte, pues el bien de la parte se ordena para el todo, y del todo viene la perfeción a la parte ...y esta prioridad se reduce a la conque el fin es primero en la intención, pues para él se ordenan las demás cosas... "[17]

Thus the pilgrim—everyman enters the *locus amœnus* which metaphorically stands for the Virgin and also for the idea of shelter and protection. Once there, in the midst of its delights, he removes his clothes in order to better enjoy the atmosphere of the place. Metaphorically he has assimilated himself to the Virgin and by putting on this "proud garment" has monastery-garden and perfection-completion metaphorically attributed to him. But there remain the practicalities of the situation. Metaphor is always theoretical; two things are like one another, but other than this likeness there may be no firm connection between them. Metonymy is on the other hand always real. That which establishes or declares a metonymical link between two things is the fact that they are physically related one to the other. In addition in the ancient, mythological worldview that which was physically connected to something else shared in a very real sense the qualities of that to which it was joined.

Now the *Milagros* as a work is basically about a very, very good

---

[16] *The Philosophy of Symbolic Forms: Mythical Thought*, II, trans. Ralph Manheim (New Haven and London, 1964), pp. 38, 49-50, and 62-65.

[17] Ed. Juan Meseguer Fernández (BAE 163, Madrid, 1963), pp. 225-26.

connection—that of the sinner to the Virgin. This is not a metaphorical link but a real one. Therefore after the introduction comes the first *exemplum* in which a real bond is established between Mary and her servant, Ildefonsus; she gives him the wondrous chasuble. The next *exemplum* is the story of the sacristan who committed fornication but is nevertheless saved from a troop of demons by the Virgin: "... mientre fue en el cuerpo fue mi acomendada..." (89c) There follows the story of the sinning cleric buried at his death in unconsecrated ground because of his sins. He too was a follower of Mary: "... por cancellario mío yo a éssi tenía . . . " (109d) She causes his body to be disinterred. The onlookers find a beautiful flower growing out of his mouth and the body completely sound and untouched. The theme of wholeness established in the introduction and translated into new terms by the chasuble has returned.

The rest of the *Miracles* ensue in similar fashion. The lesson is given again and again. He who is a follower of Mary enjoys a unique protection in this life and also afterwards. That protection is because the perfection of being which characterized the whole (the Virgin) will also touch him as something intimately attached to her.

University of Toronto

# "La Huella del León" in Spain and in the Early Sindibad Tales: Structure and Meaning

T. A. PERRY

LTHOUGH IT HAS RECEIVED little attention from literary critics, the parable of the lion or, as it has come to be known in Spanish criticism, the "Huella del león" must surely count as among the finest in world literature. The tale is preserved in ten extant versions of the so-called oriental strain of the Sindibad collections[1] and in a number of partial and derivative versions as well.[2] Leaving aside the per-

---

[1] For a concise summary of the main versions and their early editions, see Alfons Hilka, ed., *Historia Septem Sapientum*, Sammlung Mittellateinischer Texte, IV (Heidelberg: Carl Winter, 1912), pp. vii-xxv. The study of Sindibad has been updated by Morris Epstein, *Tales of Sendebar. An Edition and Translation of the Hebrew Version of the "Seven Sages"* (Philadelphia: Jewish Publication Society, 1967). See especially Epstein's bibliography and, on the question of the extant versions, pp. 3-5, 19-21 and Appendix A. In their probable chronological order, the extant versions are as follows: 1. The Syriac *Sindiban* (ca. 10th century); 2. the Greek *Syntipas* (second half of the 11th century), based on the Syriac version; 3. the Hebrew *Mishle Sendebar* (12th or 13th century); 4. the Old Spanish *Libro de los engaños*, claiming to be a translation of a now lost Arabic version (1253); 5-7. three Persion texts, the latter two being derived from the first (late 12th century to 1375); 8-10. the Arabic *Seven Vizirs* (14th Centuryt), included in the three manuscript versions of the *Thousand and One Nights*.

[2] The so-called "forme primitive" (Victor Chauvin, *Bibliographie des*

plexing and unsolved question of origins that has occupied scholars almost exclusively, I propose to examine some variant and structural aspects of the "Huella del león," principally in the oldest known versions,[3] with a view to describing their possible meanings for their copyists/translators and readers. Since detail is of the essence, may I be permitted to quote the tale in its entirety:[4]

> El privado dixo: —Oý dezir que un rrey que amava mucho a las mugeres e non avia otra mala manera sinon esta; e seýe el rrey un dia ençima de un soberado muy alto; e miró ayuso e vido una muger muy fermosa, e pagóse mucho della, e enbió a demandar su amor; e ella díxo que non lo podria fazer, seyendo su marido en la villa; e quando el rrel oyó esto, enbió a su marido a una hueste; e la muger era muy casta e muy buena e muy entendida.
>
> E dixo: —Señor, tu eres mi señor e yo so tu sierva, e lo que tu quesieres, quiérolo yo; mas irme he a los vaños afeytar. —E quando tornó, diól un libro de su marido en que avia leyes e juyzios de los rreyes de commo escarmentavan a las mugeres que fazian adulterio, e dixo: —Señor, ley por ese libro fasta que me afeynte.
>
> E el rrey abrió el libro e falló en el primer capitulo commo devia el adulterio ser defendido, e ovo gran verguença, e pesól mucho de lo quel quisiera fazer; e puso el libro en tierra e

---

ouvrages arabes, 12 vols. [Liège, 1892-1922], 7:121) of our tale, by al-Jahiz (d. 868 or 869), includes the theme of the trace of the lion but not the wife's chastity; it is translated by A. González Palencia, "La Huella del León," RFE 13 (1926): 46-47. For some later versions of the "Huella" see ibid.; also Stanislao Prato, "L'Orma del Leone," Romania 12 (1883): 535-65 and 14: 132-35 (not listed in Epstein). For Juan Manuel's version (Lucanor 50), see below.

3 For the focus of our study, the Libro de los engaños, I use John Keller's excellent edition, published in the University of North Carolina Studies in the Romance Languages and Literatures, no. 20 (Chapel Hill: University of North Carolina Press, 1953). For the Syriac version see Frédéric Macler, trans., Contes syriaques. Histoire de Sindban (Paris, 1903), pp. 20-22. Epstein's edition of the Hebrew Mishle Sendebar is the best (see note 1). Although the Latin text published by Hilka (see note 1) has been called a translation of the Mishle Sendebar, for our purposes its variants are of sufficient interest to list it as a separate version.

4 Ed. Keller, pp. 7-8. I have added some accent marks for the sake of clarity.

sallóse por la puerta de la camara, e dexó los arcorcoles so el lecho en que estava asentado; e en esto llegó su marido de la hueste, e quando se asentó el en su casa, sospechó que y durmiera el rrey con su muger. E ovo miedo e non osó dezir nada por miedo del rrey e non osó entrar do ella estava; e duró esto gran sazon, e la muger dixolo a sus parientes que su marido que la avia dexado e non sabia por qual rrazon.

E ellos dixieronlo a su marido: —¿Por que non llegas a tu muger?

E el dixo: —Yo fallé los arcolcoles del rrey en mi casa e he miedo, e por eso non me oso llegar a ella.

E ellos dixieron: —Vayamos al rrey, e agora démosle enxenplo de aqueste fecho de la muger, e non lo declaremos el fecho de la muger; e si el entendido fuere, luego lo entenderá. —Estonçes entraron al rrey e dixieronle: —Señor, nos aviemos una tierra e diémosla a este omne bueno a labrar que la labrase e desfrutase del fruto della; e el fizolo asi una gran sazon e dexóla una gran pieça por labrar.

E el rrey dixo: —¿Que dizes tu a esto?

E el omne bueno rrespondió e dixo: —Verdat dizen que me dieron una tierra asi commo ellos dizen; e quando fuy un dia por la tierra, fallé rastro del leon e ove miedo que me conbrie; por ende dexé la tierra por labrar.

E dixo el rrey: —Verdat es que entró el leon en ella, mas non te fizo cosa que non te oviese de fazer, nin te tornó mal dello; por ende toma tu tierra e labrala.

E el omne bueno tornó a su muger e preguntóle por que fecho fuera aquello, e ella contógelo todo e dixole la verdat commo le conteçiera con él; e él creyóla por las señales quel dixiera el rrey, e despues se fiava en ella mas que non dante.

It is most interesting that the earliest extant versions of the "Huella" story all agree in their thematic structures, as we shall see, and disagree only on details. One significance of this observation was not lost on generations of students, who have tried to uncover or reconstruct the original version from which all others have derived. In such an endeavor even variants serve, by comparison and elimination, to focus on what the historical source may have been. Although the goal may never be reached, the by-products of this research—the extant versions themselves—are perhaps of as great interest as the so-called original, since each presents its own interpretation, mainly through its variants. Such versions have special interest, it seems to me, in cultures where transmission is oral or through manuscript rather than printed form, since each successive version may represent a rethinking rather than a mere copying of the *materia*, the received thematic materials. The matter is analogous to the interest generated by the successive versions of Montaigne's *Essais* or Robert Lowell's poems, where each stage *can* be understood by reference to the earlier versions and yet each is also interesting in its own right.[5] In the context of the "Huella" story, the "authors" of the extant versions re-read their *materia* in terms of traditional motifs—motifs that, let it be said once and for all, may or may not have been intended in the Ur-version of the tale. Variants thus become signposts alerting the reader to literary analogues too well-known to require more explicit reference. Such details usually have no inherent importance; rather, they suggest comparisons that can be tested as possibly valid readings of a particular episode. By such hints or allusions we are invited to compare the tale of the Lion with possible paradigms, in an exercise that promises delight less from the surface texture of the parable than in the intellectual and moral insight resulting from the comparisons. Let the reader seek the level that best befits him!

## A. THE SETTING: A KING'S LUST

How does the king fall in love? The Syriac version is paradigmatic in its simplicity: "il y avait dans le temps un roi à qui rien ne plaisait tant que l'amour des femmes. Un jour qu'en regardant, il en aperçut une fort belle, la passion entra dans son coeur et il s'enflamma d'amour pour elle."[6] The king loves beautiful women, he sees a beautiful one.... Details and circumstances are irrelevant, and the reader is free to imagine whatever situation he wishes. But not so in the other versions. The Latin text is perhaps the most naïve: "Tunc quedam puella pulcra ad videndum floreque eleganti coniuncta erat marito, *cuius domus iuxta domum regiam sita erat.*

---

[5] On this point see the interesting discussion of Gerald L. Bruns, "The Originality of Texts in a Manuscript Culture," *CL* 32 (1980): 113-29.

[6] Trans. Macler, p. 20

Quam Rex adamauit."[7] What exactly did the translator/adaptor wish to convey by this extra detail? Perhaps he was responding to a need for realism, for giving *some* concreteness to the psychological generality of the Syriac version. Or, in terms of the social situation of the story, we are thus informed that either women in general or this particular woman would otherwise not have been available to view. Whatever the reason, the author seems to be responding to the same motivation that produced a similar gloss in the *General Estoria*. In the famous story of David and Bathsheba (2 Samuel 11), the biblical account is similarly vague as to Bathsheba's location with respect to the King: "E en la ora de la tarde leuantose Dauid de su lecho e andudo por el acotea del alçaçar e vio una muger que se lauaua, e la muger era de buena vista mucho."[8] In the *General Estoria* we have the following explanation: "acaesçio un dia que se leuanto el de dormir despues de la siesta; e andauase por una almoxaua de su palaçio. E auie y estonçes un judio que dezien Vrias, e era casado; e llamauan a su muger Bersabe. *E auie sus casas de faz de las del rey.*"[9]

What may seem mere realistic detail takes on more literary and allusive dimensions when we examine the other versions. In the *Libro de los engaños*, as we have seen, the king is pictured as on a very high *soberado*,[10] and this gives him a wide-ranging view and perhaps also the ability to see into surrounding houses. The true sense of the passage, however, seems to be most clearly presented in the Hebrew *Mishle Sendebar*: "While standing on his roof, he beheld a

---

[7] Ed. Hilka, p. 5; italics are in text to indicate that this explanation occurs only in the Latin version. Yet *Mishle Sendebar* also explains (Epstein, p. 90) that the husband was a "neighbor of the king." A similar gloss has strongly ironic tones in Marie de France's "Lai du laüstic", where it is advanced as one of the causes of the undying love between lady and lover: "Tant pur ceo qu'il ert pres de li" v. 28.

[8] I quote from the 14th century *Biblia medieval romanceada Judio-cristiana*, ed. José Llamas, 2 vols. (Madrid, 1950), 1:447).

[9] Alfonso el Sabio, *General Estoria, Segunda Parte*, eds. A. Solalinde, L. Kasten and V. Oelschläger, 2 vols. (Madrid: CSIC, 1961), p. 365; italics added.

[10] Joan Corominas lists "piso alto de una casa" and "techo" as two of the meanings of *sobrado*, in his *Diccionario crítico etimológico de la lengua castellana*, 4 vols. (Madrid: Gredos, 1954).

most lovely maiden." In three of the Hebrew manuscripts[11] the use of *gag*, roof, is a clear allusion to 2 Samuel 11:2: "It happened, late one afternoon, when David arose from his couch and was walking upon the roof [*gag*] of the king's house, that he saw from the roof a woman bathing; and the woman was very beautiful" (Revised Standard Version). The detail is an invitation, for those who wish, to compare the two tales that follow, and still other signs point in the same direction. The Hebrew version shows a general interest in 2 Samuel by including two tales that appear in no other extant versions: the flight of Absolom and his death.[12] Another curiosity, this time in the Spanish text, is the designation of the location of the entire story as Judea: "Avia un rrey en Judea que avia nonbre Alcos" (ed. Keller, p. 1). The name Alcos is still a puzzle, but Judea of course belonged to the Tribe of Judah, ancestor of King David, and the lion of the parable could find no more appropriate reference than to the lion of Judah (Gen. 49:9). Finally and most explicitly, among the edifying remarks contained in the book presented by the faithful wife to the king, the Vatican manuscript of the Hebrew version adds: "also written there was the story of David and Bathsheba, the wife of Uriah, and the words of Nathan the Prophet."[13]

It seems, then, that the David/Bathsheba episode was very much on the mind of some medieval transmitters of the *Sindibad* stories, for reasons which we shall see. Curiously, the comparison has been bypassed by modern critics, who have been content with vague and passing allusions. Chauvin noted the possible relationship in a footnote, and A. González Palencia observed that the "huella del León" theme "puede referirse al episodio de David con Betsabe."[14] In our study of the "Huella" we shall be most attentive

---

[11] Cited in Epstein, p. 92.

[12] Ibid., pp. 228-39

[13] Ibid., p. 95, n. 1

[14] Chauvin, *Bibliographie*, 7:122; A González Palencia, "La Huella del León," *RFE* 13 (1926): 46; the same author's allusion in *Versiones castellanas del "Sendebar"* (Madrid-Granada, 1946), p. xxix, is less satisfactory in that it refers to the unsolvable problem of the tale's "remoto origen." Stanislao Prato attempts to delineate the moral superiority of the "Huella" lady over Bathsheba in "L'Orma del Leone," *Romania* 12 (1883): 563-64. In his translation of "The King and the Wazir's Wife" of the *Thousand and a Night* Richard F. Burton denies the possible relation (Benares, 1886), 6:129.

to its structural similarities with the story of King David and Bathsheba.

### B. THE STRUCTURE OF "LA HUELLA DEL LEÓN" AND FURTHER BIBLICAL PARALLELS

The givens are a man and a woman. The man is an essentially virtuous king with a weakness for beautiful women; the woman is beautiful but also virtuous and clever. The action starts when the two come into contact, by the accident of the king seeing the woman. The story has three distinct episodes or acts: 1) the woman's escape from the king; 2) the husband's return and separation from his wife; 3) the trial (in form of a parable) and judgment. The restitution implied in Act 3 is not acted out. It is stated by the teller and can differ from version to version.

ACT ONE is inherently undramatic because the man is a king and therefore, by definition, can have whatever he wishes. The woman's reception is no mere hyperbole but rather descriptive of the real situation, as countless tales of harems will attest: "Señor, tu eres mi senor e yo so tu sierva, e lo que tu quesieres, quierolo yo." The husband's presence is a mere cosmetic difficulty and he can therefore be promptly dispatched or simply imagined absent. The focus of interest is the lady's trick and the king's ensuing change of heart. Depending on our point of view, therefore, this episode could be entitled either "The Lady's Escape" or "Le Roi converti" (Chauvin)[15] or, as we shall propose later, "La Vergüenza del Rey." Whichever way one views it, it is an uplifting one-acter with lots of local color and sublimated eroticism (the king's polite but forceful entry, the bath and, in some versions, the dinner) and a happy ending. It is entirely self-contained and could end with the king's departure, except for the *huella*: the king "forgets" something under the bed.[16]

Beyond the points of contact already mentioned between the "Huella" and 2 Samuel 11, one is tempted to compare the person

---

[15] Chauvin, *Bibliographie*, 7:120-21.

[16] The same is of course true in 2 Samuel 11:2-6. The incident would be over save for the tell-tale "huella" of the King, i.e. Bathsheba's discovery that she is pregnant.

of the two kings, similar not only in their being virtuous but also in their one weakness. Is this not the sense of Nathan's scathing reference to David's "wealth," that is to say, his harem (2 Samuel 12:2)? There are biblical grounds for suspecting King David of a fondness for women, a tendency transmitted to his favored son Solomon. At least, there can be little doubt that such impressions have been conveyed to many readers. Referring to David's wives, the *Arcipreste de Talavera* exclaims how the King, "aun non farto su voluntarioso apetito de quantas a su mandado tenia, e fermosas e tales como un rey por poderio tener podia...."[17] Moreover, one may see Uriah's convenient military absence echoed in the choice of the Spanish text to send the husband off to the army. The significant difference is in the reaction of the two wives. Of Bathsheba we are told simply: "erat autem mulier pulchra valde" (Vulgate). In his edition John Keller noticed the apparently conscious imitation of the biblical phrase and stressed its contrastive meaning by placing it at the end of the paragraph: "e la muger era muy casta e muy buena e muy entendida." In view of what develops in the two stories between the wives and the kings, one would be tempted to view the "Huella" as a deliberate rewriting of the 2 Samuel episode, giving the lady more moral character and the king more scrupules.[18]

ACT TWO belongs entirely to the husband, who returns and discovers that the king has been there. At this juncture several courses of action are open to him. He could kill his wife for adultery,[19] or he could plot against the king (e.g. Count Julian against Rodrigo), if the thing can be confirmed. This is an important point,

---

[17] Alfonso Martínez de Toledo, *Arcipreste de Talavera o Corbacho*, ed. Michael Gerli (Madrid: Cátedra, 1979), p. 101.

[18] I discuss the exegesis of the 2 Samuel text and also the moral status of Bathsheba in medieval Spain in a forthcoming article. See also below, n. 31.

[19] An interesting testimony on this possible course of action comes from Nahmanides (Rabbi Moses ben Nahman), who lived in Catalonia in the 13th century: "It is a custom today in some parts of Spain that a wife who commits adultery is handed over to her husband, who may condemn her to death or let her live, as he wishes"; Commentary on Gen. 38:24, in *Perushei ha-Torah*, 2 vols. (Jerusalem: Mossad harav Kook, 1969), 1:218 (in Hebrew).

since the moral of the story *as part of the collection*[20] (and not in itself, which may be a different matter) seems to advise prudence: King, don't kill your son on appearances; husband, don't commit an act of folly on suspicions or *huellas*! But within the tale itself this uncertainty remains in the background, and the husband's decision to separate himself from his wife is explained in all versions as due to fear of the king: "e ovo miedo e non osó dezir nada por miedo del rrey e non osó entrar do ella estava." The action of this Act is thus inaction: the husband discontinues all relations with his spouse.

The action of ACT THREE involves removal of the suspicion hanging over the wife so that reconciliation can occur. Suspicion is removed through the king's a) admission that he indeed was present (suspicion justified), b) assertion that there was no wrongdoing on the part of the wife, and c) promise for the future. Since confrontation is dangerous—the king may regret his failure or resent the reproach—a particular form of mediation is devised, a parable.

One of the hidden gems of world literature, the parable of the lion invites comparison with the famous parable of Nathan the Prophet (2 Samuel 12:1-4) which follows upon the David/Bathsheba story. The tactic in both instances is to present, within a judicial setting, an instance of criminal behavior that forces the king, acting as judge, to deliver a guilty verdict, whereupon the invented crime is related (by accepted symbolic properties: wife/lamb, wife/field) to the person of the judge himself: the condemnation applies to him! Yet, at least one difference exists between the two stories. David's repentance is a private affair with no public consequences—indeed, Uriah is dead and Bathsheba already his

---

[20] If the "único objeto" of the collection is "mostrar los engaños, astucias y perversidades de la mujer" (Menéndez y Pelayo)), then the placement of this *exemplum* of womanly virtue at the beginning of the collection (it occurs as the first *exemplum* in all extant versions) makes no sense whatsoever, unless by "astucias" we include *virtuous* cleverness, in which case the book's supposed anti-feminism must now be seen as the argument that women are superior creatures for good as well as for ill. Feminine wiles would therefore be "exemplary" in the original sense of being simply outstanding, without the more modern and optimistic nuance of "deserving to be imitated." On this latter point see Daniel Devoto, *Introducción al estudio de Don Juan Manuel y en particular de "El Conde de Lucanor"* (Madrid: Castalia, 1972), p. 170.

wife. In the "Huella" story, however, the king's acknowledgement has social value, since otherwise no reconciliation can take place between the husband and his estranged wife.

A detail in some Hebrew manuscripts suggests a more fruitful comparison. When the king departs, he leaves behind not a ring or a slipper, as some versions would have it, but his *mateh*, his royal staff. The *mateh* that jumps to mind is Judah's staff that he leaves with Tamar disguised as a harlot and that reappears during the trial precisely as a *huella del león*, evidence that the Lion of Judah has indeed left his trace (Gen. 38:18). What makes this comparison so attractive is the utterly *respectful* attitude of the plaintiffs. Whereas Nathan's parable was pure effrontery and trickery (noble, to be sure, since it effected David's sincere repentance), revealed as such in the startling second of declaration: "You are that man!", there is a connivence in both the Genesis and "Huella" stories between the king, who is fully aware of his guilt *before* giving the judgment of self-condemnation, and the plaintiffs, who fully submit to the king's mercy and make clear that no threat of a more public disclosure is being used to pressure the king into compliance.[21] Connivence is perhaps the wrong word, since the tacit understanding between king and plaintiff is that the motives of mutual self interest are as rigorously excluded as blackmail: the king is being asked to act because that is the right thing to do, he is invited to be "royal in his confession."[22] The appeal is thus to the king's own ideal self image, done in a manner that is respectful and, indeed, self-sacrificial. If it is improper to embarrass the king, it is proper to give him occasion to be embarrassed by inviting him to respond to his own sense of *vergüenza*.

---

[21] In the relatively modern version of Firuz (mid-eighteenth century but reflecting a much earlier story), we are assured that "volvió el marido [Firuz] con su mujer, y ni el cadi, ni nadie de los que estaban en la sala, sospechó siquiera del pleito, sino el rey, Firuz y el hermano de la mujer"; in González Palencia, "La Huella del León," p. 51.

[22] For interesting materials on the trial of Tamar see Louis Ginzberg, *The Legends of the Jews*, 6 vols., 5th ed. (Philadelphia: Jewish Publication Society, 1956), 2:35, 5:335. According to St. Augustine, "Judah means confession"; "Reply to Faustus the Manichaean, in *Nicene and Post-Nicene Fathers of the Christian Church*, ed. P. Schaff (Buffalo, 1887), 4:307.

C. *Conde de Lucanor* 50
AND THE MEANING OF THE "HUELLA DEL LEÓN"

The question may now be raised as to the possible relation between the "Huella" and *Lucanor* 50, "De lo que contesçió a Saladín con una dueña, muger de un su vasallo." Against an impressive gathering of critics Daniel Devoto has denied the connection by observing that what is essential in our story is precisely "la huella del león," "es decir, el hecho de que el marido advierta que su señor corteja a su mujer, y este elemento falta por completo en nuestro ejemplo [i.e., *Lucanor* 50], donde la mujer se desempeña por sus proprios medios y donde su marido no desempeña papel alguno."[23] To recast Devoto's criticisms in terms of our analysis, *Lucanor* 50 would be comparable only to Act One of the "Huella," and Devoto feels that Act 1 does not contain the essence of the story.[24]

It is certainly possible to agree that *Lucanor* 50 and Act One of the "Huella" are similar, with the single and unimportant difference of the interspersed search for the knowledge of "la mejor cosa del mundo." The absurd length of the quest reminds us of Dacier's version of the "Huella," which presents a king more intent on touching the heart of the lady than forcing her[25]—how else can we understand his agreeing to an adventure that, in its difficulty, takes on the dimensions of a love-trial: he could have forced the lady outright! Structurally, however, the quest is simply another delaying tactic, comparable in function to the bath and ointment ploy in other versions.

The similarities between *Lucanor* 50 and the "Huella"—the entire story, not merely Act One—are perhaps more pervasive,

---

[23] Devoto, *Introducción al estudio de Don Juan Manuel*, p. 462. For *Lucanor* 50 I use Don Juan Manuel, *El Conde Lucanor*, ed. José Manuel Blecua (Madrid: Castalia, 1969), pp. 243-53.

[24] Devoto is thus in agreement with G. Palencia, "La Huella del León," p. 53: "Con la primera parte de esta redacción, es decir, con la astucia de la mujer para librarse de las solicitaciones del rey, y faltando la segunda parte, o sea el símil de la tierra o de la finca, como símbolo para tranquilizar al esposo, se relaciona el cuento que trae el conde Lucanor..., el ejemplo 50."

[25] "Ce n'est pas un Souverain qui parle & qui veut être écouté; c'est un amant qui prie & que voudroit toucher"; M. Dacier, "Notice d'un ms. grec de la Bibliothèque du Roi," *Histoire de l'Académie de Inscriptions* (Paris, 1780), 41:549.

however. Juan Manuel's central theme of *vergüenza*, which Devoto seems to take as separate from the "Huella" comparison,[26] is of the substance of the latter story as well. This is clearly the case for the ending of "Huella," for only *vergüenza* or conscience[27] could have motivated the king's "confession." But *vergüenza* is operative in the first episode as well as in the final one:

> E el rrey abrió el libro e falló en el primer capitulo commo devia el adulterio ser defendido, *e ovo gran vergüença, e pesól mucho de lo quel quisiera fazer*; e puso el libro en tierra e sallóse por la puerta de la camara. (p. 8, italics added)

It thus seems possible to apply the title "La Vergüenza del rey" both to Act One and also, with a slightly different emphasis,[28] to the entire tale. In the first instance the king's *vergüenza* is his blushing shame; he is caught off guard and is forced to do the right thing in spite of himself, as it were. As with David before Nathan, he is reminded of something that he never should have forgotten. The *vergüenza* displayed by the king in the final act is of a more public and enduring nature, however, since it initiates a process *for the future* that is the reverse of the one ascribed to the King Vitiza in the *Primera Crónica*:

> Vitiza que fasta estonces fiziera su mal et su luxuria a ascuso, començó dalli adelant a fazer lo en descubierto ante todos, et afloxo las riendas, esto es *el costrenimiento de la uerguença*, et non se retouo de fazer toda nemiga et todo peccado [referring especially to sexual sins].[29]

The king's *vergüenza* and repentance thus lead to not only a restoration of the status quo but also an implied promise to mend his one

---

[26] Devoto, *Introducción*, p. 462: "Por lo que respecta a la vergüenza como fuente de virtud...."

[27] For the synonymy of *conçiençia* and *vergüeña* see, for example, Fernán Pérez de Guzmán, *Generaciones y semblanzas*, ed. R. B. Tate (London: Támesis, 1965), p. 14.

[28] The pun on *vergüenza*—meaning both blushing shame and conscience—explains the success of Gracián's "Et si vergüenza hobiere, nunca fará cosa por que la haya"; quoted in Devoto, *Introducción*, p. 462.

[29] *Primera Crónica General de España*, ed. Ramón Menéndez Pidal (Madrid: Gredos, 1955), p. 304.

vice. The Hebrew version is especially emphatic on this point, as the king declares during the trial:

> It is true that the lion did come there and found *her*[30] cluster of grapes lovely and good. But he did not eat of *her* fruit nor did he break down the fence [of *her* modesty], nor will he return there again.[31]

Juan Manuel's version, while omitting the theme of the *husband's* discovery, thus captures the perhaps deeper theme of the king's repentance, and precisely in the *two* stages of rethinking the matter that characterize the "Huella": a) the initial withdrawal from the act and b) the later confirmation that this withdrawal is related to a change in character. What *Lucanor* 50 adds—without, however, changing the nature of the argument—is greater emphasis, indeed a meditation, on the *nature* of repentance.

The connection between Juan Manuel and "Huella" may be further clarified by considering the real function of the *huella* itself. As observed earlier, Act One is self-contained and is related with what follows only by the *huella*, which is dropped or forgotten. However, in the Spanish text the *huella* is psychologically moti-

---

[30] Ed. Morris Epstein, p. 101. The use of possessives in the Hebrew text, not rendered in Epstein's translation, makes the king's confession much more explicit.

[31] It is perhaps as a lesson in royal *vergüenza* that the "Huella" takes its place as an *exemplum* both in the copious literature of *castigos*, of advice to reigning monarchs, and in the *Sindibad* collection itself. A "mirror of Princes " contemporary with the *Libro de los engaños* gives expression to a real danger of royal power by explaining to the Prince the advantages of being *casto*: "las gentes...non han duda que les tomará las mugeres nin las fijas nin les fará ende desonrra nin mal" John K. Walsh, ed., *El libro de los doze sabios* (Madrid, 1975), pp. 79-80. *Luxuria*, he continues, leads only to defeat and destruction, witness the examples "en el rey David e el destruymiento que Dios fizo por su pecado..., e en el rey Rodrigo que perdió la tierra de mar a mar" (pp. 80-81). The answers given by the "Huella," therefore, are both that the king should set the right example of *vergüenza* and also, that failing, that ladies also play an active role in teaching morals. It thus teaches a more positive role of women than that proposed by the *Primera Crónica General*, where La Caba finally succumbs to King Rodrigo "por ser mujer," and especially the story of David and Bathsheba, where the lady seems neither to have resisted nor to have cared to resist.

vated rather than accidental, since the king's absentmindedness and hurried departure are seen to result from his *vergüenza*. The result of this virtuous and felicitous carelessness, the *huella*, not only generates those tensions associated with the husband's discovery, it also leads to restitution and even a higher state than before. This is the case, as we have seen, for the king's confession, which completes the process of repentance. But it is even more true for the wife, since from now on her husband "despues se fiava en ella *mas* que non dante." Rather than Devoto's view of the *Huella* as concerning primarily the *husband's*[32] awareness and role in the story, therefore, we propose to consider the *huella* as but the visible link between the king's two *vergüenzas* and also, as regards the lady, both as the occasion of her escape and as initiating a process whereby her virtue is vindicated and rewarded. If this view is correct, then Juan Manuel's *Lucanor* 50 is indeed a "version" of the "Huella del león" since it preserves the essential functional aspects of that tale.

THE UNIVERSITY OF CONNECTICUT

---

[32] This view can find support in the al-Jahiz version (see above, n. 2), where the husband has a leading role because his *bon mot* about the lion earns him a generous subsidy from the monarch. In this early version, however, the lady is without virtue and the king unrepentant.

# Self-Conscious References and the Organic Narrative Pattern of the *Cantigas de Santa Maria* of Alfonso X

JOSEPH T. SNOW

N THE PAST, various attempts have been made to determine the personal role of Alfonso X in the works which so proudly bear his name. Most all critics are agreed that the most personal of these is his anthology of miracles and hymns to the Virgin, the *Cantigas de Santa Maria*, but the same critics allow as Alfonso did not write all 420 of them while they differ on the extent of his participation. There are, I think, more fruitful ways to go about detecting the role(s) Alfonso played in the *Cantigas*, a truly monumental work for scholars of language, literature, art and music, aptly called by Menéndez y Pelayo "la Biblia estética del siglo XIII."[1] One such way is to explore the image patterns that persist throughout and which,

---

[1] The statement was made in a thoughtful review of the Academy edition of the *Cantigas* (2 vols. 1889) which appeared in *La Ilustración Española y Americana* of 1895. It is more accessible reprinted in the Edición Nacional of his *Obras completas*, I (Madrid: CSIC, 1941), pp. 161-189.

taken as a whole, may shed light on the overall design Alfonso had in mind.² Another is to study closely related groups of poems—for example, those centering on a particular city or Marian shrine—for the kind of information a segment may tell us about the larger whole.³ A third, which I intend to pursue in this study, concerns internal references of a self-conscious nature.

By self-conscious references is meant the following: the text of an individual poem which a) acknowledges, or refers to, another text in the *Cantigas*, b) demonstrates an awareness of its own role as part of a collection, or c)wrestles with literary problems they themselves pose as they are being written and added to the expanding anthology.⁴ While a full catalogue of all such internal references—and I cannot be yet certain that I have not missed several that must be included—cannot be presented here, the examples I have chosen will trace for us the hand of a master architect-designer at work. More patient and detailed study may

---

² See, for example, the image patterns of the troubadours discussed in J. Snow, "The Central Rôle of the Troubadour *Persona* of Alfonso X in the *Cantigas de Santa Maria*, *BHS*, 56 (1979), 305-316.

³ There are several interesting studies on shrine-related miracles: J. Leite de Vasconcellos, "Santa Maria de Terena no século XIII," *O Archeólogo Portuguès*, 10 (1905), 340-343; P. Aguado Bleye, *Santa María de Salas en el siglo XIII: Estudio sobre algunas cantigas de Alfonso el Sabio* (Bilbao, 1916); J. Filgueira Valverde, "Poesia de santuarios," in his *Sobre lírica medieval gallega y sus perduraciones* (Valencia, 1977), 117-39 [the original article was printed in 1958]; John Esten Keller, "King Alfonso's Virgin of Villa-Sirga, Rival of St. James of Compostela," in *Middle Ages-Reformation-Volkskunde: Festschrift for John G. Kunstmann* (Chapel Hill, 1959); ibid, "More on the Rivalry Between Santa María and Santiago de Compostela," *Crítica hispánica*, 1 (1979), 37-43; J. Snow, "A Chapter in Alfonso X's Personal Narrative: The Puerto de Santa María Poems in the *Cantigas de Santa Maria*," *La corónica*, 8 (1979), 10-21. for a more complete survey, see items (p. 132) listed under "CSM, Classification of" in J. T. Snow, *The Poetry of Alfonso X, el Sabio: A Critical Bibliography* (London, 1977).

⁴ For a full treatment of one such poem, see J. Snow, "Poetic Self-Awareness in Alfonso X's Cantiga 110," *KRQ*, 26 (1979), 421-432. The concept is fascinating and may be explored to advantage in Martin Stevens' "The Performing Self in Twelfth-Century Culture," *Viator*, 9 (1978), 193-213 and, to a more general degree, in Richard Poirier, *The Performing Self* (London: Chatto & Windus, 1971). Another treatment of the idea is Leo Spitzer's "Note on the Poetic and Empirical 'I' in Medieval Authors," *Traditio*, 4 (1946), 414-422.

yet reveal that this designer was also the principal mason of the edifice. For the moment, let us search for clues in the carefully-worked stones.

The references I have compiled are grouped into four divisions: references which anticipate poems to follow; references to previous poems; references to the *Cantigas*; references, finally, to the poem itself.

I. References which anticipate later compositions.

These are often fairly general in nature; that is, they may not signal a particular text at all but rather contain an allusion to all the poems to follow, or to a particular type of poem. Here is the earliest example, from Prologue B:[5]

1.      Onde lle rogo, se ela quiser,
        que lle praza do que dela disser
        *en meus cantares* ( . . . )
        que me dé gualardon ( . . . )
        e queno souber,
        por ela mais de grado trobará. (39-44)

There are anticipated here several *cantares* with their words and music. They are offered as the service of the troubadour who here addresses his leige lady (Mary) as a supplicant. Already a reward for them is anticipated, such a one as will make others take up the singing of her praises. The service is clearly defined: *dizer loor* (l. 15). He is thus, while he sings about his service, actually performing it. This conceit becomes a continuing thread in the ongoing narrative of the *Cantigas* and is to reappear with some frequency, as in our next example from CSM 131:

2.      deron aa Virgen loores assaz
        por este miragr'e por outros que faz
        *grandes e fremosos pera retraer.* (92-94)

Here the joy of the artist at work is expressed in the work which brings him that special joy. In other compositions we have the same vein of internal self-reference but we are clearly now in the middle of the process, for its continuance is roundly affirmed.

---

[5] All quotations and numbering are from the 3-volume edition of the *Cantigas* prepared by Walter Mettmann (Coimbra, 1959-64). A fourth volume, a glossary, was published in 1972.

3.      De mi vos digo que a loarei
        mentre for vivo, e *sempre direi*
        ben dos seus bẽes... (CSM 170, 24-26)

4.      Santa Maria *loei*
        e *loo* e *loarei*. (CSM 200, refrain)

5.      por que a *loo* sempr'e *loarei* (CSM 339, 72)

Another kind of reference falling into this same category appears
in the third person, but describes the activities of the troubadour
king in terms which our reading of the earlier poems helps us fully
to understand.

6.      E des ali adeante *serviu mais*... (CSM 295, 62)

We remember that the Prologue B poem defined this service with
precision: *dizer loor,* "dizer" of course taken in a more narrow, com-
positional sense. This increased service to the heavenly *domna* is
reflected yet once more in the awe of Alfonso's unknown collabor-
ator in CSM 345: "demais trobando / andava dos seus miragres"
(13-14) in which the adverb serves not as a measure of degree of
excess but as a sign of admiration for the intensity of the involvement of the troubadour in the work-service of his Lady.

II. REFERENCES TO PREVIOUS POEMS.

These include both direct and indirect allusions to or citations
of compositions the poet assumes have already been circulated
among his public. These are of two natures. One kind will refer to
a poem quite close in sequence; the second will cite from poems
from earlier compilations of the *Cantigas,* of which there seem to
have been three.[6] In either case, it is expected that the matter

---

[6] A first redaction was probably completed after 1257, the year in
which Alfonso took up his 18-year quest of the crown of the Holy
Roman Empire (the title is used in the Prologue A poem): this codex is
called the Toledo manuscript, although it now reposes in Madrid's Biblioteca Nacional. The second redaction is in two parts now; the first is
Escurial T.I.1 and the second belongs to the Biblioteca Nazionale in Flor-
ence. The third and last redaction, with 420 separate texts, is Escurial
B.I.2. Internal events that can be dated seem to indicate a terminus of
1279-81 for compilation: it may, of course, have been completed a bit
later.

being discussed in the present poem will be enriched by a full knowledge of the larger context. Here are some rather specific examples. In the far right hand column are listed the earlier *cantigas* to which reference has been made.

1.  En Monsarraz, de que *ja vos contei*
    (CSM 52, 10)  CSM 48

2.  A que en *nossos cantares* nos chamamos Fror das flores
    (CSM 366, refrain)

    ...é Sennor das sennores
    (CSM 366, 73)  CSM 10

3.  A que por gran fremosura é chamada
    Fror das frores  (CSM 384, refrain)  CSM 10
    and 366

4.  A que avondou do vinno aa dona de Bretanna
    ar avondou... (CSM 386, refrain)  CSM 23
    (epigraph)

5.  ...aquel miragre, que foi dos maravillosos
    Que a Virgen groriosa fezess'en aquel logar
    (CSM 159, 33, 35)  CSM 8

6.  *quand'en Bitoira* morou un an'e un mes,
    jazendo mui mal doente...
    (CSM 235, 65-66)  CSM 209

7.  que o guareçera ja d'outras grandes doores
    (CSM 366, 18) CSM 209, 235,
    and 279

8.  Aquel Rei *fora enferm'en Sevilla*
    de grand'enfermidade a maravilla,
    de que guariu... (CSM 367, 26-28)  CSM 366

Example 1 shows us a poem harking back to another just four places earlier and still in the mind of the poet-designer: but the implication is that the public will also have this recent composition in its memory and understand the allusion. The second and third examples may well be part of a longer series of such references. Recalled is the text of the most famous of all the *Cantigas*, number 10. It happens also to be a crucial poem in the narrative imbedded in the

collection of miracles and hymns to the Virgin.[7] In it the troubadour promises to renounce all other women if Mary will have him
as a suitor. This particular internal reference has been cited often
but almost no one has noticed that our example 2 carries a double
citation from the refrain of cantiga 10, as the quoted last line
reveals.[8]

Such citations as these are formulaic, of course, but their use
here to recall specific poems heightens their non-poetic importance
for us. Note the certainly deliberate recall of the same image just
two poems later (example 3). The literally dozens of *sennor das sen-
nores* conceits help further to establish and define—through frequent repetition (which also depends on the audience's familiarity
with the larger context)—Alfonso's submissive role before Mary
who in her roles as Mother of God, Mediatrix between heaven and
earth, and Queen of Paradise, rules over Kings. In our number 4
Mary performs a wondrous deed in the third reworking of the
growing collection similar to one referred to already in the first
"edition" (see note 6). Compare the citation given with the text of
the epigraph to CSM 23: "Esta é como Santa Maria acrecentou o
vỹo no tonel, por amor da bõa dona de Bretanna." The final three
examples also require fairly specific knowledge of accounts already
anthologized and, as shown, form a chain of linking references
from within.

There are, of the same type, less specific references than the
ones just recounted which reflect implied awareness of other
poems in the *Cantigas*.

---

[7] The significant fourth stanza is worth quoting as it brilliantly, if
succinctly, frames the moment in which the spiritual odyssey is begun in
earnest:

> Esta dona que tenno por Sennor
> e de que quero seer trobador,
> se eu per ren poss'aver seu amor,
> dou ao demo os outros amores.

[8] Cantiga 10 surely is the most anthologized of the *Cantigas* in modern collections; it seems to be also the most frequently recorded. With
the charm and simplicity of its text and the strong allusive nature of its
refrain, it surely must have been beloved even in its own time. Its
important role in the setting of the theme in the opening poems and its
later echoes hint strongly that it was intended by Alfonso as a keystone
in the larger edifice of the structure.

9.        ...e ja *vos en dix outros* [miracles of Chartres] *ben oistes*
          de quaes                                    (CSM 148, 8)

The earlier compositions are 24 and 117 and the assumption is
that the reader/listener will know them. Perhaps a more important
assumption that each example points up is that the order of compositions is not casual. The poems are intended to be taken up in
the order of their arrangement. In the following examples, the
audience's appreciation of other miracles associated with
the shrines of, respectively, Santa María de Terena (Portugal) and
Santa María de Vila Sirga, is noted by the poet.[9]

10.       E dos miragres enton da virgen ali contaron
          que faz grandes en Terena... (CSM 224, 41-42)

11.       que fez a Madre do Rey
          en Terena, e mui ben sey
          que outros y, com'apres'ey,
          fez muitos e faz cada dia
          aos que os van buscar y.        (CSM 283, 15-19)[10]

12.       [a miracle] *que fezo en Vila-Sirga, ond'outros muitos sabemos*
                                                    (CSM 268, 8)

13.       Esto foi en aquel tenpo que a virgen começou
          a fazer en Vila-Sirga miragres...
                                          (CSM 278, 13-24/14)[11]

The following refrain from CSM 202, the contents of which
treat of some troubadour other than Alfonso, has a general tone
which gives it a subtle linkage with the already cited Prologue B
poem (see I.1 and commentary).

14.       Muito á Santa Maria, Madre de Deus, gran sabor
          d'ajudar quen lle cantares ou prosas faz de loor.

And not only that, but it also is a harbinger of the goodwill
Alfonso expects Mary to show toward such service in his poem of
"pitiçon", CSM 401. Ever since this theme was announced in Pro-

---

[9] See again note 3.

[10] Other CSM which deal with the shrine at Terena are 197-199,
223, 224, 228, 275, 283, 319, 333 and 334.

[11] The other miracles at Vila-Sirga are related in CSM 31, 217, 218,
227, 229, 232, 234, 243, 253, 268, 278, 301, 313, and 355.

logue B, there is a continuing hope expressed for the great *galardon* desired : salvation. Here is one of many examples.

15.          ...de que gran'merce'espero          (CSM 336, 13)

Alfonso is not alone in this enterprise, as we see when he speaks of another troubadour who receives Mary's divine aid (italics mine):

16.          ...que mentre vivesse
             polo seu amor trobasse, *de que nos trobamos*
                                                  (CSM 363, 27-28)

The last examples from this group are all in poems which come at the end of the *Cantigas*. The internal reference to previous compositions is clarion clear.

17.          Pero cantigas de loor
             fiz de muitas maneiras          (CSM 400, 2-3)

18.          Macar poucos cantares acabei e con son,
             Virgen, dos teus miragres...          (CSM 401, 2-3)

19.          Non catedes a como pecador
             sõo, mais catad'a vossa valor
             e por un muy pouco que de loor
             dixe de vos, en que ren non menti.
                                                  (CSM 402, 3-6)

It should be evident that a single intelligence has been crafting the shape, content, and sequencing of the poems in the *Cantigas*. Also taking shape is the notion that the whole is intended to form a narrative in which the larger narrative—Alfonso's quest for salvation—is carefully inset with smaller ones—Mary's favor to all his family and court, the shrine miracles cycles, and so forth—in an interlocking, if somewhat freeform structure.

III. References to the *Cantigas de Santa Maria.*

The rich referencing of the following examples is logically to the very compilation for which each of the cited poems' text and music is intended.

1. E daquest'un gran miragre oyd'ora, de que fix
   un cantar da Virgen santa [que] eu dum bon om'aprix,
   e *ontr'os outros miragres porende mete-lo quix*
   (CSM 84, 6-8)

2. Dest'un miragre quero contar ora,
   que *dos outros non deve seer fora*     (CSM 69, 5-6)

3. Desto direi ũu miragre que en Tudia avẽo
   e *porrey-o con os outros, ond'un gran livro é chẽo,*
   de que fiz cantiga nova con son meu, ca non allẽo
   (CSM 347, 5-7)

4. [This miracle] metudo dev'a seer *ontr'os preçados*
   (CSM 198, 9)

5. E eu aqueste miragre *farei põer entr'os teus miragres...*
   (CSM 219, 53-54)

6. *Ontr'os outros* que oystes...       (CSM 225, 11)

7. E porend'*ontr'estes outros miragres* será contado
   (CSM 254, 7)

8. ...e *d'ontr'outros* traladar-o mandei     (CSM 284, 7)

Here the self-conscious reference is only too evident. A more coy type of reference—and one in line with statements about the magnitude of the project made in the opening and closing poems—is this one in which Mary's deeds are described:

9. cujos miragres / *non caben en volume.*

(CSM 116, 66-67)

While this is true, since miraculous events are an infinite series for the Mother of God, we are constantly being made aware that *some miracles*—as in examples 1-8 above—are being fitted into *this volume.*

One place where the volume is actually named is in *cantiga* 209. It recounts an illness which befell Alfonso and which brought him to the brink of death and beyond the aid of the very best physicians. He is cured when he has *o livro dela* placed on his stomach: the epigraph to this narrative tells us that the volume was "o livro das Cantigas de Santa Maria." Since *Cantiga* 209 belongs to an expanded compilation of Alfonso's *repertorio marial*, the reference is likely to the first redaction of 100 poems (the Toledo codex, now in the Biblioteca Nacional de Madrid). Although Alfonso did possess other collections of miracles—and none of them must be excluded from consideration—Alfonso's recovery here makes the obvious candidate his own *Cantigas de Santa Maria*. It would not only be fitting, since Alfonso and his family have a long and strong Marian tradition and of favor associated with them, but it would also imply a degree of gratitude on Mary's part for the service thus far performed (e.g., the *CANTIGAS*) in her name and to her greater glory. Furthermore, it would be hard to imagine Alfonso not resorting in his great hour of need to this most personal of collections, in which his own search for the reward of eternal salvation is the central story.

In the following example, the unidentified reference also seems to have been to the alfonsine *Cantigas*. Mary performs a miracle for Pedro Lourenço, an illuminator working at Alfonso's court. One of the casual descriptions of this figure is that:

> 10.  *os seus livros* [Mary's] pintava ben e aginna.(CSM 377, 8)

He may either have been involved in many *mariales*, which would explain the plural, or he may have participated in the several "editions" of the *Cantigas*. While I think the context justifies both, I favor the latter meaning as it would draw support from the many other internal references imbedded in the work. That the whole seems to conform to an imposed design or pattern now seems a safe conjecture. Whether or not Alfonso had a few or many collaborators, there were surely established standards for most of the poems. In addition to artistic worth, and perhaps musical value, we should perhaps also be thinking in terms of relevance. Alfonso has already created for himself a place in the *Cantigas de Santa Maria* as a second protagonist and his story evolves: it has a beginning, a middle, and an end, as I have shown (see note 2). Other poets aware of the norms of the early version (Toledo) would submit poems which could fit into the overall story or, failing that, compose new versions of standard or local Marian wonders which would contain just such internal references as we have been discussing. These would enhance their being selected, if in fact they had not already been commissioned by Alfonso. In this sense, too, the king and patron could still honestly call all the poems his as he does in our final example (but see also I,2 and II, 2, above):

> 11.  e nos roguemos *en nossos cantares*          (CSM 406, 69)

IV. REFERENCE TO THE POEM ITSELF.

Many of these deal with technical problems inherent in the undertaking of a repertory or catalogue of Marian praise. Others deal with such opening statements as those heralding what is to follow in the text, or establish a close relationship between text and poet. In each we are made aware of the poet at his work.

1. Desta razon vos direi
   un miragre que achei
   escrito, e mui ben sei
   *que farei*
   *del cantiga saborosa*                    (CSM 106, 5-9)

2. de que *fiz cantiga nova*, con *son meu ca non allẽo*(CSM 347, 7)

3. E daquest'un miragre mostrarei en tal guisa
   *que dos outros da Virgen, será muy grand'enquisa*
                                             (CSM 148, 5-6)

4. ...e creed'a mi
   que *mayor deste non vos posso contar*    (CSM 226, 8-9)

5. ...ben sõo fis e sei
   que non oistes *d'outro nunca tal retraer*   (CSM 251, 7-8)

6. avẽo mui gran miragre, onde *fiz cobras e son*
                                             (CSM 293, 8)

In most of the above examples, we are not dealing so much with the presence of an "I" as we are with his own critical judgment of the poem (or song), because it is a "new" form or style, because it is "delightful," or because none better can be found. We are reminded that the words and the music are not borrowed but newly *trobadas*. There is pride, innovation, and a desire to please in the individual poems of the *Cantigas*, even as the poet is forced to wrestle with some of the aesthetic problems of sufficiently praising a *domna* whose praises are, by definition, infinite.

There are a few further references to the poem itself which are of a different kind: they tell us, in both instances for which I have examples, more about King Alfonso's relationship to this great compilation. In the first instance, the King is featured in the account, although in the third person. He is so moved by the events which fill him with awe that

7. chorou muit'ant'a omagen e *fez tod'est'escrevir*

                                             (CSM 295, 60)

Alfonso, seeing a good opportunity, commissions the poem which he will then fit into its place in his personal story of involvement with Mary. In the second instance, the author (I incline towards Alfonso himself) speaks in the royal plural form.

> 8. E desto *cantar fezemos* que cantassen os jograres
> (CSM 172, 33)

The meaning is ambiguous for the italicized words do not automatically imply authorship (cf. "fiz cobras e son" in example 6 above) and certainly do not exclude it. Since Alfonso did, however, adopt for most of his appearances in the *Cantigas* the persona of the troubadour, who often merely wrote songs which would be then sung or performed by the *jotglar*, it seems that the "voice" in 172 belongs to that of the persona adopted by Alfonso. This is not very far from what Alfonso intended for these songs after his death: "que sean todos en aquella iglesia do nuestro curpo se enterrare, e que los faga cantar en las fiestas de Santa Maria."[12]

What can we surmise from this brief survey of a system of co-ordinated internal references in the *Cantigas de Santa Maria*? It must be said that traditional *Cantigas* critical study has commented some of these same examples although not always in the light of the full collection, and certainly not with a view to perceiving a special order or rationale for the disposition of the poems. I do not believe that sufficient attention has ever been paid to the possibility that Alfonso (and his anonymous collaborators) revitalized the medieval Marian collection by making it over into a work of art, as text, as music, as illumination. In none of those collections I have seen, or seen described, in Latin or vernacular (prose or verse), had there been any attempt to graft onto the trunk of the traditional material (the wonders performed by Mary) the vital limb of another organic tradition: the spiritual biography. In the examples brought to bear on the central thesis of this study, we have also been able to see *internal* evidence of other structures or processes familiar to students of Alfonso's poetry. One is the succession of versions of the *Cantigas* which culminates in the lavish Escorial

---

12 From Alfonso's final will, reproduced in *Antología de Alfonso X, el Sabio*, ed. A. G. Solalinde, Austral 169, 5th ed. (Madrid: Espasa-Calpe, 1965), p. 236.

T.I.1. manuscript, recently reproduced in full color with meticulous precision.[13] Another would be the details which accumulate and tell us snippets about what Alfonso was like, how he reacted, and so forth. He is frequently depicted throughout the *Cantigas*, most especially in attitudes of praising, in illustrations of the miracles in which he is featured and in those accompanying the lyric *loores* (nos. 10, 20, 30, etc.) This latter feature is also part of the unique structural design of the *Cantigas* and has been the subject of much attention.[14]

One positive result of this survey is the clearer outline of an overall and intentional internal pattern. Out of a tradition in which the arrangements of the Marian narratives had little impact on the whole—in which the free substitution of the individual tales would not affect the end result—Alfonso fashioned a more formal arrangement. It must be noted, so that we do not overstate the case for deliberate architectural arrangement, that many of the narratives of the *Cantigas* can also be freely interchanged with no visible effect on the end result. However, given the very surprising number of individual accounts that have internal references which justify their coming *before* or *after* other narrations, or groups of narrations, we are left to conclude that there is a purpose and design which distinguish the *Cantigas* from all others of its kind.

Alfonso's assumption of overall control of the unfolding of the ever-growing Marian anthology makes it unique in its genre. In its texts he asks that all contributors—himself included—strive for the new, aim for the best, reflect the aesthetic test that the praise of the Heavens' Queen presents. He creates for the purpose of this collection the image of the troubadour (himself) in search of his lady Mary's guerdon. His own role is subordinate to Mary's in the same way that the troubadour is subject to his *domna*. The success of the *Cantigas* as a work of art was to be achieved through the

---

[13] *El "Códice Rico" de las Cantigas de Santa Maria* [= Escurial T.I.1], 2 vols., Madrid: Edilán, 1979. The first volume contains the full-size, six-color facsimile on 516 pages of parchment paper. Volume 2 contains studies of the manuscripts, philological and literary studies, treatments of the illuminations and the music, etc. It is an incredible achievement in modern bookmaking.

[14] See the items in the bibliography (note 3) gathered under the rubric, "Loores", (p. 133).

search for the best artistic talents available, for each new, expanded version of the work was more elaborate and beautiful than its predecessor. Alfonso spent almost three decades in this vast project. To him, we may be sure, its value lay not only in its beauty, its unparalleled depiction of daily life, and the vast spectrum of Marian exploits set forth. To him it must also have been a record of his spiritual journey through trying times: in it would live after him a poetic record of his own faith and service to a higher cause. The care and concern for assuring that the record would not be obliterated or obscured is seen, I am convinced, in the placement of the poems in a discerning pattern consistent with the natural evolution of a narrative.

Seen in this light, with the help of the internal references which—once revealed—provide greater definition to the conscious pattern of the whole, the *Cantigas* of Alfonso may be said to predate the more perfect "autobiographies" of Dante's *Vita nuova* and the *Canzoniere* of Petrarca. Far from being a rehashing of traditional materials in a new idiom, the *Cantigas de Santa Maria* turns out to be one of the truly important poetic documents we possess, more important even than Menéndez y Pelayo's bold claim, with which this study began (see page 53), was able to envision when first made almost a hundred years ago.[15]

UNIVERSITY OF GEORGIA

---

[15] A much abbreviated version of this study was initially read as a paper at the 1979 meetings of the Mountain Interstate Foreign Language Conference held at Institute, West Virginia. Professor Keller presided over a stimulating Medieval Spanish meeting organized by himself and Professor Roger Tinnell (who was absent on this occasion). I had fully intended to dedicate this *esbozo* to him then, although in the 90 degree temperatures in which all were forced, willy-nilly, to read their papers it completely went out of my mind at the appropriate time. I am very happy to be now able to contribute to his *Festschrift* this piece on one aspect of the *Cantigas*, a work he has loved and helped to make more widely-known for several decades. All modern *Cantigas* scholars are deep in his debt.

# El "ome mui feo": ¿Primera aparición de la figura del salvaje en la iconografía española?

José Antonio Madrigal

I

## Introducción

M. Azcárate, en el único estudio dedicado exclusivamente a la iconografía del hombre salvaje en España, indica que la temática del mismo hace su aparición hacia "la primera mitad del siglo XIV, en la decoración de cajitas de marfil, piezas de orfebrería, orlas de manuscritos y, posiblemente, en los tapices que en los palacios sustituían a las pinturas en la decoración de los muros."[1] Dicha aseveración, repetida en un estudio mío,[2] es incorrecta debido a que, por lo menos, existe un

---

[1] J. M. Azcárate, "El tema iconográfico del salvaje," en *Archivo Español del Arte*, 82 (1948), 81. En adelante, Azcárate.

[2] José A. Madrigal, *El salvaje y la mitología, el arte y la religión* (Miami: Ediciones Universal, 1975), pág. 33. En adelante, Madrigal.

caso previo donde aparece la figura de este ser hetereogéneo. La referencia es a la Cantiga Nº 47, de Alfonso X, titulada "Esta é como Santa Maria guardou o monge, que o demo quis espantar por lo fazer perder."[3] Antes de proseguir al estudio de ella, que irá precedido por algunas observaciones generales sobre el tema, quiero expresarle al profesor John Keller, quien me indicó la existencia de un salvaje u "ome mui feo," como se describe en el poema, mi agradecimiento profesional por haberse dado cuenta de algo que hasta hoy día había pasado desapercibido a los investigadores.

Concomitantemente, debe aclararse que si la temática del salvaje en el arte iconográfico español puede adelantarse alrededor de medio siglo—se cree que *Las cantigas* se terminaron uno o dos años antes de la muerte de Alfonso en 1284—, no puede afirmarse categóricamente que ésta es su primera aparición, ya que lo mismo que se descubrió (descubrir en el sentido de reconocer su importancia) la figura del salvaje en *Las cantigas*, puede salir a relucir otro caso similar que remonte sus orígenes a una fecha anterior. Sin embargo, lo que sí puede afirmarse sin duda alguna es que no es hasta la primera mitad del siglo XIV que el tema adquiere verdadera popularidad. Consecuentemente, con el pasar de los años dicha difusión va aumentando paulatinamente hasta llegar a penetrar y enriquecer no sólo la iconografía y la literatura ibérica, sino también la del resto de Europa. De ejemplo, puede destacarse el teatro español de los siglos XVI y XVII donde se capta ricamente su difusión, variedad e importancia socio-filosófico-religiosa.[4]

---

[3] Alfonso el Sabio, *Cantigas de Santa Maria*, ed. Walter Mettmann (Coimbra: Acta Universitatis Conimbrigensis, 1959-72), págs. 137-38.

[4] Véanse los siguientes estudios: José A. Madrigal, *La función del hombre salvaje en el teatro de Lope, Tirso y Calderón*, University of Kentucky, 1973 (disertación) y Oleh Mazur, *The Wild Man in the Spanish Renaissance and Golden Age Theatre*, University of Pennsylvania, 1970 (disertación).

## II

### La figura del salvaje

Hasta ahora se ha hablado brevemente del hombre salvaje, de su popularidad y, sobre todo, de su posible primera representación iconográfica. No obstante, todavía está por definir. A continuación se trazará, de forma muy sucinta e introductoria, un bosquejo de su imagen visual y de su importancia simbólica; primordialmente para beneficio de los que no conocen el tema y también para poder facilitar el estudio de la función que desempeña en la cantiga.

Su definición no es tarea fácil. Al contrario, presenta toda clase de dificultades debido a que no puede hablarse de una creación concebida por un individuo en una época específica. Su trayectoria cronológica, según la han reportado y descrito historiadores, filósofos, literatos, periodistas, etc., incluye innumerables períodos históricos que abarcan desde las descripciones de pueblos salvajes, los escitas por ejemplo, por escritores griegos como Herodoto (¿484-420? a. de J. C.) hasta la noticia, divulgada por la prensa, que en este año (1980) varios campesinos en la China comunista han visto criaturas peludas que han calificado de "hombres salvajes."

Frente a este panorama histórico e idiosincrásico tan diverso, no es de extrañar que el salvaje haya sido objeto de múltiples interpretaciones. Si para Herodoto y otros escritores de la Antigüedad podía representar un ser primitivo, ya fuera noble o innoble, durante la Edad Media iba a adquirir una fisonomía más mítica, teniendo de ancestros a panes, sátiros, faunos, centauros, etc. Es interesante que, con los descubrimientos, el aspecto primitivista y antropológico vuelve a dominar la filosofía de la época y, como consecuencia, se le pone más atención al indio, a los pueblos salvajes y a los seres abandonados o refugiados en la selva que a la concepción del salvaje que hereda muchas de sus características de los semidioses míticos. En otras palabras, cuando se trata de definir a esta criatura tan heterodoxa hay que tener en cuenta que el vocablo "salvaje" ha llegado a abarcar una galería de seres que se proyectan en forma de semidioses rurales mitológicos y sus reminiscencias artísticas; hombres primitivos como los escitas en la Antigüedad y los indios durante el Renacimiento; individuos forzados a vivir en bosques, incluyendo a los que allí eran abandonados por sus mismos padres como resultado de haber alcanzado un físico desproporcionado debido a los excesos en el comer y en el beber; locos obstinados a vivir entre los animales; niños que, por diferentes razones, eran abandonados en la selva casi siempre por su madre; y el hombre de las selvas que tiende a predominar en la iconografía, festivales y representaciones teatrales medievales.

A esta última clasificación pertenece el "ome mui feo." En cuanto a su físico, las características más comunes que tienden a estar presentes en su concepción medieval son: cuerpo con muy poca vestimenta, casi siempre hecha de piel de animales; cuerpo velludo, o por lo menos cierta presencia de pelo en el cuerpo y en la cabeza, pero sin llegar a descender a la figura de un animal; decoración vegetal que algunas veces lleva una sobre su tronco; y un palo o sachiporra que usa y tiende a connotar su asociación con la fuerza bruta que se encuentra en *natura*. Como resultado de esta apariencia, su significado fue variado y su popularidad extensa. Ahora bien, si en algunas ocasiones aparece en función decorativa, o sea como un ser de índole positiva e inofensiva, la mayoría de las veces simboliza lo contrario. Richard Bernheimer, mejor que nadie, ha definido su significado, al igual que su causalidad:

> Individual and social factors thus contribute toward the genesis of the wild man: individual insofar as the awareness of disturbing, untried, elementary forces in each of us is the prime factor in his formation; social, since the restraints which prohibit direct and destructive utterance are always exerted by the human group, for the sake of goals and concerns.... The wild man's existence is therefore a life of bestial self-fulfillment, directed by instinct rather than volition, and devoid of all those acquired tastes and patterns of behavior which are part of our adjustments to civilization. He embodies a negative ideal in all of its harshness and one-sidedness.[5]

Dado lo dicho, debe hacerse patente su herencia mítica. Sin embargo, tomando en consideración que representa el lado inferior de la persona al igual que el inconsciente en su aspecto atrevido y

---

[5] Richard Bernheimer, *Wild Men in the Middle Ages* (Cambridge: Harvard University Press, 1956), pág. 4. En adelante, Bernheimer.

regresivo,[6] es más significativa su irónica popularidad, ya que, si por un lado estos rasgos lo hacían un ser favorito y muy imitado en festivales y bailes que exhibían características exóticas y eróticas, por otro lado su figura es empleada en lugares religiosos a pesar de la Iglesia haber tratado por todos sus medios de erradicar su aceptación.[7] Como resultado, su popularidad se extiende hasta los sitios más vedados de las iglesias, catedrales, capillas o conventos. En estas edificaciones, los dos lugares más populares eran las fachadas y las tumbas, construidas con elaboradas decoraciones para personas de elevado rango social o religioso.

Dichas manifestaciones representan, como se ha mencionado, un cambio sorprendente en la idiosincrasia religiosa de la época, sobre todo, si se tiene en consideración que antes del siglo XV, época en que empiezan a aparecer, sólo ocupan tales decoraciones figuras de santos, profetas, apóstoles, ángeles, arcángeles, etc. Las iglesias del mundo hispánico constituyen la sorprendente mayoría donde se le da entrada al salvaje en sus decoraciones heráldico-religiosas.[8] La iglesia de San Gregorio en Valladolid ofrece un ejemplo excelente de lo acabado de mencionar. Construida a fines del siglo XV, parece haber sido el primer templo en utilizar en su fachada a estos seres peludos,[9] los cuales ocupan, dentro de la complicada configuración escultórica, un lugar prominente. Los salvajes

---

[6] Juan Eduardo Cirlot, *Diccionario de símbolos* (Barcelona: Ediciones Labor, 1969), págs. 410-11. En adelante, Cirlot.

[7] Véase Madrigal, caps. II y III.

[8] Es de notarse que en otros países de Europa no se ve la cantidad de ejemplos que existen en España. Las excepciones son más bien en Francia e Inglaterra. En el primero, en la iglesia de Semur-en-Auxois, Provenza, construida a mediados del siglo XIII hay una escultura de un hombre que está contando dinero. Se deduce claramente que el motivo de esta asociación es didáctica ya que la ganancia, aparentemente excesiva o deshonesta, tiende a ser calificada como algo que no se deriva de la facultad superior de la persona. Otro ejemplo es el de un tapiz que se conserva en Notre Dame, Nantilly, donde se representa una danza de salvajes. En Inglaterra existen algunas pilas bautismales que participan del tema al tener esculpido al salvaje apoyando el escudo heráldico de algunas familias nobles. Hasta cierto punto, susituyendo a otros animales, como el león, en función de protector.

[9] Marqués de Lozoya, *Historia del arte hispánico* (Barcelona: Salvat Editores, 1931), pág. 39.

que aparecen en ella están situados en las jambas, mientras el centro consiste de una fuente que baña toda la fachada, aún los lugares más remotos, y de donde sale el árbol de la vida—en una de sus tantas bifurcaciones se encuentra el escudo de armas de Fernando e Isabel. En cuanto a la función de los salvajes, también bañados por el agua de la fuente, Richard Bernheimer opina, al contrario de J. A. Azcárate quien cree que sólo poseen función decorativa, que ellos tienen que ser considerados como parte intrínseca y pertinente la brote de agua de la fuente, al cual es un símbolo de energía vital en la oración de fertilidad que representa la magnífica decoración de la fachada (Bernheimer, pág. 183). Ahora bien, el concepto de fertilidad aquí expuesto no debe entenderse en un sentido inmoral o pagano, como normalmente se interpreta, sino dentro de un marco religioso y de acuerdo con la idea ortodoxa de la procreación. Sin duda alguna, es una manera ingeniosa de usar una criatura que simboliza lo erótico y lo instintivo y modificarla para servir unos fines diferentes.

Otros ejemplos de su ubuicidad pueden observarse en el claustro de la Catedral de Toledo y en la capilla del Convento de Medina del Pomar. En la primera hay una incrustación donde aparece un salvaje luchando contra un centauro (Azcárate, lámina I, figura 4), y en la otra se ve un salvaje sosteniendo una espada (Azcárate, lámina I, figura 3). En los dos iconos, la función más probable e indicada parece ser la de proteger y guardar. Esta vez, en vez de utilizar el motivo de la fertilidad, representan la idea de la fuerza hercúlea y animalezca que se creía ellos poseían.

Sin embargo, no siempre aparece en un ministerio positivo. Sólo baste mirar su función en la decoración exterior del sepulcro de Don Juan de Luna (Azcárate, lámina IV, figura 3) y el del Arzobispo Juan de Cerezuela (Azcárate, pág. 91). En ellos su función parece basarse en sus cualidades negativas, quizás para ilustrar que, si el salvaje se encuentra permanentemente en la parte de afuera del sarcófago, el difunto puede ahora disfrutar de una duradera y definitiva paz espiritual, en la cual no pueden entrar las pasiones y los deseos e instintos irracionales que simboliza. O sea, su posición en la parte exterior parece indicar que el difunto goza de una paz espiritual donde no existen los azotes de las tentaciones pecaminosas de la carne.[10] Otra ilustración donde el salvaje tiene

---

[10] Para una discusión más detallada, véase Madrigal, págs. 46-48.

un papel antagónico bien delineado, es la cantiga de que es objeto este estudio y que se analizará en la próxima división.

## III

### EL "OME MUI FEO"

La Cantiga Nº 47, que se reproduce a continuación, consiste, como es costumbre en las *Cantigas de Santa María*, de seis paneles o divisiones que visualmente ilustran lo que se relata en el poema.

En él, se cuenta el milagro de cómo Santa María protege a un monje que había caído en un estado de gran embriaguez, por el engaño del diablo. El monje, a pesar de ello, quería ir a la iglesia a arrepentirse de su pecado pero el diablo, que quería apoderarse de su alma, le puso en su camino tres obstáculos—un toro, un salvaje y un león—para infundirle miedo y así alejarlo de la iglesia y del perdón que quería obtener.

Si la tradición del diablo de asumir formas animalescas, además de estar bien documentada, ha adquirido dimensiones populares, su asociación con el salvaje no ha sido extensamente explorada y sólo existen unos pocos estudios que le han dedicado cierta atención.[11]

Tal asociación parece haberse basado en dos factores: en la tendencia de la Iglesia de calificar de diabólico y asociar con el diablo todo lo que ella consideraba heterodoxo; y, sobre todo, en la semejanza entre la figura heterogénea y peluda del salvaje y las formas animalescas que se creía el diablo adoptaba o encarnaba para entrar en contacto con sus seguidores. Igualmente, no debe olvidarse que los seres peludos, como menciona la Biblia,[12] constituían un recinto excelente para encarnar el espíritu demoníaco. También debe traerse a colación el caso de Nabucodonosor, el más antiguo de

---

[11] Véanse Bernhemier, págs. 36, 60-66, 96-100 y Madrigal, págs. 41-48.

[12] San Jerónimo, al traducir la Biblia del hebreo al latín, en la sección donde Isaías profetiza la desolación que reinará en Palestina dice: "et pilosi saltabunt ibi." Esta traducción que en español significa "y los peludos bailarán o saltarán allí" indica no sólo que la asociación con el diablo, sino también con figuras míticas (sátiros, faunos, sileno, etc.) que habían sobrevivido en la mentalidad medieval. De acuerdo con R. Bernheimer, San Jerónimo usa la palabra *pilosi* para traducir del hebreo *se' irim*, vocablo que

## Cantiga Nº 47

### Descripción de los seis paneles

1. Como o demo fez o monje bever tanto vȳo que sse enbriagou.

2. Como Santa Maria livrou o monge do demo que lli pareceu en figura de touro.

3. Como Santa Maria livrou o mongedo demo que lli pareceu en figurad'ome mui feo.

4. Como Santa Maria livrou o monge do demo que lli pareceu en figura de muy bravo león.

5. Como Santa Maria castigou o monge des que o livrou do demo e do vȳo.

6. Como o contou aos monges e loaron muito a Sancta Maria.

transformación a un estado inferior. La historia, que trata sobre el castigo que Dios le impone por su extremada soberbia y desobediencia, describe cómo cambia su apariencia al crecerle el pelo y vivir ínfimamente entre las bestias. En otras palabras, se convierte en un salvaje, quizás estableciendo un precedente que va a servir de modelo a la leyenda de San Juan Crisóstomo, la cual recoge su metamorfosis de ermitaño a salvaje al caer preso de sus instintos lascivos. Antes de proseguir debe indicarse que en festivales de la Edad Media, como el celebrado en Dresden en la corte de Federico Augusto de Sajonia, el salvaje también se encuentra asociado con la figura del diablo.

Desde un punto de vista teológico, merece mención el escritor alemán J. Gailer von Kayserberg, quien dedica parte de su libro, titulado *Di Emeis*, a estudiar teológicamente la relación que él cree existe entre el salvaje y el diablo. Entre las cinco categorías de salvajes que enumera se encuentra una titulada *diaboli*[13] dando a entender que una de las diferentes maneras en que el diablo opera es bajo la forma del salvaje y la irracionalidad y lascivia que representa.

Retornando a la cantiga, si el lector se fija puede observar que el león y el toro, a pesar del simbolismo positivo que poseen casi siempre en la simbología cristiana,[14] aparecen como animales fieros que tratan de prevenir físicamente que el monje pueda entrar en la iglesia a arrepentirse. El autor parece haber optado por incluir estos animales basándose en que ellos también simbolizan cualidades negativas, específicamente los deseos instintivos del ser humano

---

parece haberse empleado en el folklore judío para denotar demonios que residen en lugares desiertos (Bernheimer, pág. 96).

Para añadir más a la confusión entre las reminiscencias míticas rurales y el demonio, la versión King James cambia la palabra *pilosi* por la de 'sátiro': "and satyrs shall dance there," Isa. 13:21

[13] Las otras categorías son: *solitari* (ermitaños como Aegidus, Onuphrius, María Magdalena y María Egipciaca); *sacchani* (el salvaje tradicional que lo identifica con el sátiro); *hyspani* (las criaturas salvajes de tierras extranjeras que se enumeran en *Merveilles du Monde*); y *piginini* (pigmeos). J. Gailer von Kayserberg, *Die Emeis* (Strassburg, 1509-1519). Información tomada de Bernheimer, pág. 199.

[14] J. A. Pérez-Roja, *Diccionario de símbolos y mitos* (Madrid: Editorial Tecnos, 1962), págs. 227 y 339.

(Cirlot, págs. 283 y 457). El salvaje, el segundo obstáculo, además de estar representado como una criatura que por su aspecto horrible y significativo color negro[15] induce al miedo y, como resultado, debe prevenir que el monje prosiga al interior de la iglesia, también simboliza el estado de embriaguez[16] en que se encuentra dicho cura. Debe recordarse que uno de los atributos más sobresalientes en su simbología, principalmente por su relación con las divinidades paganas rurales mencionadas anteriormente y lo que éstas representan, es el de encarnar las fuerzas inferiores de la naturaleza. En otras palabras, los tres obstáculos sirven para recordarle e incitar al monje a continuar una vida desordenada y regida por los sentidos, que ya había empezado al embriagarse. No obstante, a pesar de la posibilidad de que el autor hubiera querido traer esta dimensión a la historia, lo más probable es que el toro, el salvaje y el león hayan tenido una función que básicamente los limitaba a imponer el miedo, al igual que prevenir corporalmente que el monje entrara a arrepentirse de su transgresión.

Para concluir, baste recalcar que ya sea en heráldica, en asuntos religiosos, en representaciones teatrales, en festivales, en literatura, en arte, etc., el salvaje hace acto de presencia; hecho que atestigua la gran popularidad y difusión que llegó a alcanzar su temática en la Edad Media. Sin embargo, lo más significativo de este trabajo es el indicar que, cualesquiera que hayan sido los motivos del autor al incluir el "ome mui feo" en la Cantiga Nº 47, representa una de las primeras muestras de la figura del hombre salvaje en la iconografía española, alrededor de medio siglo antes de lo conocido hasta ahora. Análogamente, su concepción, aunque bastante similar a las posteriores, ofrece un rasgo no observado en las otras: el color negro. Si es simbólico del pecado o si solamente se usa su cromatismo para crear el miedo, es algo que no puede determinarse con certeza pero, indudablemente, hace que esta miniatura adquiera aún más originalidad e importancia.

Auburn University

---

[15] Que yo recuerde ésta es la única ocasión en que se describe al salvaje de color negro.

[16] En el *Roman de Fauvel* (siglo XIV) las miniaturas que lo ilustran contienen personas embriagadas y disfrazadas de salvajes, toros y leones participando en un *charivari*, una serenata bulliciosa que tenía el propósito de ofender a unos recién casados.

# Possible Comic Elements
## in the *Cantigas de Amigo*

### ROGER M. WALKER

OR A LONG TIME it has been conventional to divide the non-religious Galician-Portuguese lyrics of the thirteenth and fourteenth centuries into three virtually watertight compartments. In doing so, of course, literary critics and historians have simply been following the divisions of genre set out in the *Arte de trovar* which prefaces the *Cancioneiro da Biblioteca Nacional*.[1] The *cantiga de amor* has generally been regarded as the least successful of the three types of poem, being considered as little more than a rather pale copy of the Provençal *canso*, simpler in form, less brilliant in concept, less dazzling in style, and more anemic in attitude. The *cantigas de escarnho e mal dizer* have been recognized as witty satires and lampoons which often show considerable intellectual and poetic skill; but because of their frequently scabrous nature and their foreign (Provençal) inspiration, they have tended to be rather quickly skipped over by conservative-minded and nationalistic critics. It has always been universally

---

[1] *Cancioneiro da Biblioteca Nacional (Colocci-Brancuti)*, ed. Elza Paxeco Machado and José Pedro Machado, 7 vols. (Lisbon: Revista de Portugal, n.d.), I, 15-30, at pp. 15-17.

claimed (and, in fact, still is) that the great glory of the *cancioneiros* is the *cantiga de amigo*, the haunting, gentle, timeless manifestation of a young girl's love, a type of poem that corresponds to nothing in the Provençal lyric. Even now, most critical attention devoted to medieval Galician-Portuguese poetry is concentrated on the *cantiga de amigo*.[2]

A few critics, however, have attempted to show that there may be some evidence of cross-fertilization between the three genres, that they are not quite so totally independent of one another as is usually assumed. In what I regard as a very important article, C. P. Bagley has demonstrated that the Provençal-inspired sophistication of the *cantiga de amor* influenced the pseudo-popularism of the *cantiga de amigo*, and, conversely, that the simplicity and gentle melancholy of the *cantiga de amigo* affected the tone and content of the *cantiga de amor*.[3] Although Bagley at times tends to overstate her case, there is little doubt that her basic point is totally valid. From a different angle Frank R. Holliday has shown that there is little doubt that there was some influence of the satirical tradition of the *cantiga de escarnho* on the *cantiga de amor*.[4]

These two critics have done something to restore a balanced view of the *cancioneiros* as a whole. After all, it should not surprise us that there should be some interaction between the three types of poem, since they were obviously written for the same audience

---

[2] Of the fifty Galician-Portuguese lyrics anthologized by Francisco Luis Bernárdez, *Florilegio del Cancionero Vaticano* (Buenos Aires: Losada, 1952), only eight are *cantigas de amor*, whereas thirty-nine are *cantigas de amigo*. In even recent histories of literature much more space is devoted to the *cantiga de amigo* than to other genres: see, for example, A. D. Deyermond, *A Literary History of Spain: The Middle Ages* (London-New York: Benn-Barnes and Noble, 1971), pp. 10-21. It is significant that the most stimulating study on Galician-Portuguese poetry of recent years is devoted to the *cantiga de amigo*: Stephen Reckert, Roman Jakobson, and Helder Macedo, *Do Cancioneiro de Amigo*, Documenta Poética 3 (Lisbon: Assírio and Alvim, 1976).

[3] "*Cantigas de amigo* and *Cantigas de amor*," *BHS* 43 (1966), 241-52.

[4] "The Frontiers of Love and Satire in the Galician-Portuguese Medieval Lyric," *BHS* 39, (1962), 34-42. Cf. also Peter Dronke, *The Medieval Lyric* (London: Hutchinson, 1968), p. 151. Actual parodies of the *cantiga de amor* are mentioned in Kenneth R. Scholberg's *Sátira e invectiva en la España medieval* (Madrid: Gredos, 1971), pp. 125-29.

and, more importantly, by the same poets.[5] In this article I wish to push this line of enquiry a little further and suggest that there may be some influence of the bawdy, satirical *cantiga de escarnho* on the delicate, *saudosa cantiga de amigo*. Holliday looked for such influence and (rather regretfully, it seems) concluded that "we are faced with a fact, the almost complete absence of comic, satirical or sacrilegious elements in the *cantiga de amigo*."[6] A. D. Deyermond arrives at a similar conclusion: "satirical elements have been found in some *cantigas de amor*, though there are few or none in the *cantigas de amigo*."[7] The only scholar, to my knowledge, who has actually claimed to find satirical intent in a *cantiga de amigo* is Brian Dutton. He suggests that Pedro Annes Solaz's poem "Eu velida non dormia" is "an ironic comment on a liaison between a Muslim minstrel and a *soldadera*, in the highly original and subtle form of a delicate lyrical poem."[8] The general view of critics is still, however, that the *cantigas de amigo* are to be taken totally seriously. In the face of this well-nigh universal opinion, it is perhaps necessary to justify my persistence in searching for comic elements in the *cantiga de amigo*, to suggest reasons why I believe that such elements may exist.

In the first place, one must again stress the fact that the *cantigas de amigo* are *not* popular or traditional poems, despite what many Iberian and particularly Portuguese, critics may think.[9] On the con-

---

[5] All three types of poem were written by the following poets: Afonso Meendez de Beesteiros, Afonso Sanchez, Airas Nunes, Bernal de Bonaval, D. Denis, Estevam da Guarda, Joam Airas, Joam Baveca, Joam Servando, Juião Bolseiro, Lopo, Lourenço, Paio Gomez Charinho, Pedro Amigo de Sevilha, Pero Viviaez, Vasco Perez. In this connection it is also worth remembering that Alfonso el Sabio wrote scurrilous *cantigas de escarnho* as well as the *Cantigas de Santa Maria*.

[6] "Extraneous Elements in the *Cantiga de amigo*," *Revista da Faculdade de Letras*, 3rd series, 8 (1964), 151-60, at. p. 160.

[7] *A Literary History*, p. 15; cf. "broad humour—absent from the *cantigas de amigo* and rare in the *kharjas*—is more frequent in *villancicos*." (ibid., p. 23)

[8] "*Lelia doura, edoy lelia doura*, an Arabic Refrain in a Thirteenth-Century Galician Poem?" *BHS* 41 (1964), 1-9, at p. 8.

[9] See, for example, Hernâni Cidade, *Poesia Medieval: I. Cantigas de Amigo*, 3rd ed. (Lisbon: no publisher given, 1959), p. vi: "frescas e fragantes flores naturais circuladas de viva seiva do húmus nacional, entre multidão de flores de papel, de convencional recorte."

trary, they are all the work of highly sophisticated poets, many of whom also contribute to both the courtly *cantiga de amor* and the witty *cantiga de escarnho* genres (see note 5 above). The comparisons that are so often made between the *cantiga de amigo* and the *kharja* and the *villancico* are not, therefore, totally valid. Both the *kharja* and the *villancico* are, for the most part, genuinely popular poems which were collected by, but not composed by, cultured poets. If it can be shown, as it undoubtedly has been by Holliday, that there are irreverent elements in some *cantigas de amor*, why should we exclude the possibility of similar elements in the *cantigas de amigo?*

Secondly, we must remember that medieval poets were above all entertainers: they wrote for a specific public to a much greater degree than most later poets. The public of the Galician-Portuguese poets was aristocratic, cultured, leisured, and perhaps a little jaded. By the time the concepts and themes of courtly love reached the western Iberian Peninsula, they had already been in existence for well over a hundred years. Furthermore, courtly-love poetry, even in Provençal, exploits an extremely narrow range of feelings and emotional situations; the possible variations are, therefore, somewhat limited. The range is narrower still in the *cantigas de amor*, as Bagley has shown.[10] The fact that satirical elements creep into the *cantiga de amor* can, I think, easily be explained as a reaction against an overworked convention or, in Holliday's words, "the desire for originality in dealing with a somewhat hackneyed type of poem."[11]

It is also legitimate to see the *cantiga de amigo* as, at first, another aspect of this reaction against a tired convention, as a search for new inspiration, just as the vogue in Spain for ballads and *villancicos* in the sixteenth and seventeenth centuries was, at least in part, a reaction against overworked Petrarchism. In both cases, cultured poets were looking to popular poetry for something new and fresh. However, we know that there exist cynical and obscene ballads and *villancicos*; why, then, must we deny any possibility of similar elements turning up in the *cantigas de amigo?*[12] The range of

---

[10] "Courtly Love-Songs in Galicia and Provence," *Forum for Modern Language Studies* 2 (1966), 74-88.

[11] "The Frontiers," p. 42.

[12] It is interesting that a recent article on the *kharjas*, another type of

situations and sentims in the *cantiga de amigo* is also rather limited, so that, although the first poets to try composing in the new genre may well have been charmed by the freshness of something new, we are entitled to ask how long that charm lasted. Is it not possible that familiarity with this new type of poem produced a certain amount of cynicism and parody, just as familiarity with the courtliness of the *cantiga de amor* also produced a certain amount of irreverence?

Thirdly, so far as I can discover, the Middle Ages did not have the same awesome respect for the popular and the primitive that we have today. They did not exhibit paintings by children and chimpanzees; they did not make a cult of improvised music; they had little concept of "the noble savage." Art was regarded as a skilled craft with rules and conventions that had to be learned and adhered to, not as an outpouring of feeling. In view of this, we cannot assume that the imitation of popular poetry by the *cantiga de amigo* poets or the inclusion of snatches of popular song in their compositions by the *muwashshah* poets necessarily implies any great respect for the people who produced their sources of inspiration (see note 12 above). So far as one can gather, the attitude of the average medieval aristocrat towards the peasant was far from being one of respect, understanding, sympathy, or affection.[13] Most of them would certainly not have shrunk from making fun of their simplicity and lack of sophistication.

Fourthly, medieval society is not, in general, noteworthy for its respect for women, unless of course they happened to be one's social superior and could be of some use in gaining preferment.

poem which, like the *cantiga de amigo*, has perhaps been treated too solemnly, suggests that they are in fact "farce" (*hazl*); see Jareer Abu-Haidar, "The *Kharja* of the *Muwashshah* in a New Light," *Journal of Arabic Literature* 9 (1978), 1-13.

[13] A good example of this attitude is to be found in the very textbook of courtly love, Andreas Capellanus's *De Arte Honeste Amandi*: "We say that it rarely happens that we find farmers serving in Love's court, but naturally, like a horse or a mule, they give themselves up to the work of Venus, as nature's urging teaches them to do. For a farmer hard labor and the uninterrupted solaces of plough and mattock are sufficient. And even if it should happen at times, though rarely, that contrary to their nature they are stirred up by Cupid's arrows, it is not expedient that they should be instructed in the theory of love, lest while they are devoting

Despite the apparent idealization of women in conventional courtly poetry, she is still an object. This poetry, with very few excep-
tions, is written by men and is concerned with the man's suffering,
the man's reactions, the man's claims; the woman remains a shad-
owy being at whom the poet's protestations and moans are
directed. The lady in a courtly poem may be an object of adoration,
rather than an object of derision and possession (as she largely was
in reality), but she is an object nevertheless. It is not until we reach
the sentimental romance in the fifteenth century that we find any
real attempt to understand and sympathize with the woman's
point of view.[14] I would argue, then, that it is rather hazardous to
believe that in the *cantiga de amigo* the Galician-Portuguese poets
should *all* suddenly start taking seriously the sexual feelings and
emotional longings of women.

Finally, we must not forget that there is a long tradition of
bawdiness in medieval literature and art, some of it extremely
obvious, some of it extremely subtle. In view of this, it is again
very difficult to believe that every one of the 512 surviving *cantigas
de amigo* is totally serious, that there is not a hint of parody, humour, or cynicism in any one of them.

I hope enough resaons have been put forward to enable us to
recognize that the possibility (if nothing more) of the presence of
"extraneous elements" in the *cantiga de amigo* is not such an outrage-
ous proposition as it may seem. Before going on to outline what I
think these elements are, however, I must make it clear that I too
believe that many, probably most, of the surviving *cantigas de amigo*
are intended to be taken seriously. Some of them are magnificent
and very moving poems, capturing with great skill a young girl's
yearning for her lover; the best of them survive any comparison

---

themselves to conduct which is not natural to them the kindly farms
which are usually made fruitful by their efforts may through lack of culti-
vation prove useless to us. And if you should, by some chance, fall in love
with some of their women, be careful to puff them up with lots of praise
and then, when you find a convenient place, do not hesitate to take what
you seek and to embrace them by force." (Andreas Capellanus, *The Art of
Courtly Love*, trans. John Jay Parry [New York: Ungar, 1959], pp. 149-50.

[14] A possible exception may be the romances of Chrétien de Troyes;
but he was, after all, writing under the patronage of Marie de
Champagne.

with similar songs in other languages. Peter Dronke endorses this view by entitling his chapter in *The Medieval Lyric* on European female love-poetry simply "Cantigas de Amigo." Nonetheless, I believe that in at least four main areas humorous elements can be found in the *cantigas de amigo.*

First, in some poems the poet descibes an intrinsically humorous situation. In a work by Juião Bolseiro, for example, we have a mother complaining to her daughter that the latter has stolen her lover:

> Per vós perdi meu amigo,
> por que gram coita padesco,
> e, pois que mi-o vós tolhestes
> e melhor ca vós paresco,
>     non ajade-la mia graça
>     e dê-vos Deus, ai mia filha
>     filha que vos assi faça,
>     filha que vos assi faça.
>         (Nunes, Nº CCCC)[15]

This seems to me to be an essentially farcical situation, since the middle-aged woman in pursuit of sex has always been, albeit unfairly, a figure of fun. It would be reasonable to suppose that a sophisticated court audience, predominantly male, would also find this poem amusing. A less broadly humorous situation is found in a poem by Martin de Padrozelos:

> Por Deus que vos non pês,
> mia madr'e mia senhor,
> d'ir a Sam Salvador,
> ca, se oj'i van tres
>     fremosas, eu serei
>     a ũa, ben o sei.
>
> Por fazer oraçon
> quer'oj'eu alá ir,
> e, por vos non mentir,
> se oj'i duas son
>     fremosas, eu serei
>     a ũa, ben o sei.

---

[15] All quotations are from *Cantigas d'Amigo dos Trovadores Galego-Portugueses*, ed. José Joaquim Nunes, 3 vols. (Coimbra: Imprensa da Universidade, 1926-28).

I é meu amig', ai
madr', e i-lo-ei veer,
por lhi fazer prazer;
si oj'i ũaa vai
    fremosa, eu serei
    a ũa, ben o sei.
                (Nunes, Nº CCCLVI)

Here the poet openly equates the pilgrimage with an opportunity
to meet a lover. He is not, of course, the only Galician-Portuguese
poet to do so,[16] but the wit of this poem arises from the progres-
sion of the girl's argument, from asking her mother's permission
to go to San Salvador, through lying about her real intentions, to
finally confessing why she intends to go, whatever her mother
says.[17]

Secondly, a number of poems seem to poke fun at the naiveté
of the peasant characters for the amusement of the sophisticated
audience. Surely we are meant to smile at Joam Airas's ambitious
mother urging her daughter to make the most of herself in order
to get her man:

Ai mia filha, por Deus guisade vós
que vos veja [e]sse fustan trager
voss'amigu, e tod'a vosso poder
veja-vos ben con el estar en cos,
    ca, se vos vir, sei eu ca morrerá
    por vós, filha, ca mui ben vos está
                (Nunes, Nº CCLXXXVI)

The same theme runs throughout the poem's three stanzas and,
although the girl does not speak, we sense that she has some
doubts about the seductive powers of *fustan*, doubts that would
surely be shared by a richly-clothed courtly audience. Other poems
make the girl, rather than her mother, the butt of some gentle
humor. In a poem by Pero de Ponte we find an illustration of the
gullibility of a peasant-girl, in what could be described as a post-

---

[16] See, for example, the *cantigas de romaria* of Joam Servando (Nunes,
Nos. CCCLXIV-CCCLXXIX), and those of D. Afonso Lopez de Baian
(Nunes, Nos. CLXXII-CLXXV).

[17] This poem is seriously misread by Dronke (*The Medieval Lyric*, p.
105): he takes the *senhor* of the second line to refer to the girl's father.

*pastorela* situation: she has obviously believed the cynical flattery of a passing *escudeiro* and blames herself for his failure to return:

—Vistes, madr', o escudeiro
que m'ouver' a levar sigo?
menti-lhe, vai-mi sanhudo;
mia madre, ben vo'lo digo:
 madre, namorada me leixou,
 madre, namorada mi á leixada,
 madre, namorada me leixou.
   (Nunes, Nº CCXXXVIII)

A similar situation exists in a poem of Fernan Rodriguez de Calheiros:

Madre, passou per aqui un cavaleiro
e leixou-me namorad' e com marteiro:
 ai, madre, os seus amores ei;
  se me los ei,
  ca mi-os busquei,
  outros me lhe dei;
 ai, madre, os seus amores ei.
   (Nunes, Nº LXVI)

I shall return to this poem in another context later.

Thirdly, I believe that there may be some humorous intention behind the repeated use of folkloric symbols in the *cantigas de amigo*. This is, of course, a very controversial point, since it involves some of the most famous and highly regarded *cantigas*. Many of the recurrent symbols are undeniably phallic: stags, pine trees, fountains, to name but the most obvious. This is universally recognized; but what has not been considered is the effect such patent symbols might have had on a court audience all too familiar with obscene double-meanings and innuendoes in the *cantiga de escarnho*. The justly famous poems of Pero Meogo all feature stags (in one case, hinds), one of the oldest and most widely used masculine symbols.[18] Fine as these poems are, I feel sure that at least some

---

[18] These poems are the subject of a recent study by Alan Deyermond, "Pero Meogo's Stags and Fountains: Symbol and Anecdote in the Traditional Lyric," *RPh* 33 (1979-80), 265-83. Deyermond treats the poems as totally serious; but it is interesting that he quotes an example of a comic use of stags in a Spanish traditional song (p. 272).

members of a medieval audience would not be able to conceal a sly
grin at such a passage as:

> Vai lavar cabelos
> na fria fontana,
> passa seu amigo
> que a muit'ama,
> > leda dos amores,
> > dos amores leda.
>
> Passa seu amigo,
> que lhi ben queria;
> o cervo do monte
> a augua volvia,
> > leda dos amores,
> > dos amores leda.
> > > (Nunes, Nº CCCCXV)

The poem of Meogo just quoted also involves the obvious symbolism of the girl's hair, which has a long history of association
with sex, from nuns shaving their heads to signify their vow of
chastity down to the song in *South Pacific* "I'm gonna wash that man
right out of my hair." Many other *cantigas* feature the girl's hair as
a symbol of her sensuality. One of the most blatant, to my mind, is
by Joam Zorro:

> —Cabelos, los meus cabelos,
> el-rei m'enviou por elos;
> > madre, que lhis farei?
> > —Filha, dade-os a el-rei.
>
> Garcetas, las mias garcetas,
> el-rei m'enviou por elas;
> > madre, que lhis farei?
> > —Filha, dade-as a el-rei.
> > > Nunes, Nº CCCLXXXV)

In this little poem, incidentally, we once again see the mother as a
semi-comic figure, urging her daughter to please the king. It does
not need too much imagination to visualize the assembled court at
this point ironically cheering their king, who would presumably
blush gracefully!

Finally, I am convinced that certain recurrent words and expressions in the *cantigas de amigo* have double meanings. Other critics have already shown quite conclusively that such double meanings exist in the *cantigas de amor*[19] and in the late fifteenth-century Castilian *canciones*.[20] If we accept that the *cantigas de amigo*, despite their surface popularism, are as highly stylized and conventional as either of these types of poem, then it is surely possible to accept that such key words as *falar* and *ver* may express on occasion more than their literal meaning. If such is the case, the following stanzas from poems by Joam Airas de Santiago and Dom Denis take on a whole new significance:

> Meu amigo, vós morredes,
> por que vos non leixam migo
> falar e moir'eu, amigo,
> por vós e, fé que devedes,
>     algun conselh'i ajamos,
>     ante que assi moiramos.
>         (Nunes, Nº CCLXXXVIII)

> —Non poss'eu, meu amigo,
> con vossa soidade
> viver, ben vo-lo digo,
> e por esto morade,
>     amigo, u mi possades
>     falar e me vejades.
>         (Nunes, Nº XXIX)

In the poem of Fernan Rodriquez de Calheiros mentioned earlier ("Madre, passou per aqui un cavaleiro..."), the second stanza begins:

> madre, passou per aqui un filho d'algo
> e leixou-m'assi penada, com'eu ando:
>     ai, madre, os seus amores ai.
>         (Nunes, Nº LXVI)

---

[19] See, for example, A. J. Saraiva, *História da Cultura em Portugal*, I (Lisbon: Alta Cultura, 1950), pp. 279-356; Segismundo Spina, *Do formalismo estético trovadoresco*, Cadeira de Literatura Portuguesa 16 (São Paulo: Faculdade de Filosofia, Ciências e Letras da Universidade, 1966), pp. 176-85.

[20] Keith Whinnom, "Hacia una interpretación y apreciación de las canciones del *Cancionero General* de 1511," *Filología* 13 (1968-69), 361-81.

Surely *penada* is deliberately chosen because of its closeness to *pre-nada*, which of course adds extra zest to the idea of the girl abandoned by her knightly lover.[21]

My purpose in this short article has not been to undermine the respect and affection which the *cantigas de amigo* deservedly enjoy. I am sure that most of these poems were delivered to and received by their audiences with serious appreciation and enjoyed for their freshness and apparent spontaneity as a relief from the hackneyed conventions of courtly love expressed in the *cantigas de amor*. But I am equally sure that courts with a highly developed taste for innuendo must have smiled from time to time at the naiveté of the peasant as shown in many songs and at some of the more obvious double meanings and phallic symbols. I am also convinced that these sources of humor were not unintentional, but deliberately presented as such by the poets.

BIRKBECK COLLEGE, UNIVERSITY OF LONDON

---

[21] It is possible that, to minds accustomed to double-meanings, *coita* (which occurs in so many *cantigas*) may have associated itself with *coito*. I have, however, been unable to ascertain when the latter word entered the peninsular languages; it could well have been later than the fourteenth century. The earliest use of *coito* in Spanish recorded by Corominas is in Juan de Mena's *Coronación* of 1438; see *DCELC*, 4 vols (Berne: Francke, 1954), *s.v.* coito.

# Un fragmento inédito
## de *Dichos de sabios*

AGAPITO REY

N LA BIBLIOTECA MENÉNDEZ PELAYO de Santander se conserva un manuscrito que contiene el texto del *Libro de los cien capítulos* que hemos utilizado en la edición de esa obra. Trátase del manuscrito 128: 129 folios, letras del siglo XV o XVI. Descríbelo Miguel Artigas, *Boletín de la Biblioteca Menéndez Pelayo*, VI (1924), pág. 108. Es un manuscrito defectuoso, falto de varios folios. El texto empieza en el fol. 53a: "Este es el libro de los cien capitulos en que fabla de los dichos de los sabios." Sigue la tabla del contenido de los cien capítulos y el texto de los sólo cincuenta de que consta la obra.

El manuscrito tenía una extensa laguna que comprendía los capítulos 27-32, fols. 41-44, págs. 35-39 del texto impreso. Alguien trató de completar ese deficiente manuscrito insertando folios arrancados de otro manuscrito con texto diferente pero de la misma naturaleza que el del *Libro de los cien capítulos*. Los folios fueron incorporados al manuscrito sin siquiera tratar de que ambos textos empalmaran ni al principio ni al final del injerto. Tampoco hay división de capítulos ni epígrafes que correspondan a los cinco sustituidos, que son los siguientes: 27. Que fabla de la sufrencia; 28. De las maneras de los omnes que son de buen talante; 29. Que fabla de las buenas maneras. 30. Que fabla de la nobleza que ha de auer en todos los omes buenos. 31. De la cortesia. 32. De la humildad que han de auer los omes. La laguna comienza en el fol. 41r, pág. 35 de nuestro texto: "non te tienen pro en ningua guisa." En el manuscrito M esa línea es la última del folio, con la variante " . . . ninguna cosa." Sigue la sustitución, fol. 49 de nuestra numeración: "dixo mas, la lengua del sesudo . . . ," sin terminar la frase. En el texto impreso termina en el capítulo xxxii, pág. 39, línea 30: "non se mueue el monte por el viento . . . "

La única división en capítulo con epígrafe hállase en el fol. 58a: "Capitulo de unos sabios que non supieron sus nonbres." Corresponde a un epígrafe parecido en *Buenos proverbios*, Knust, pág. 374.

Conócense del *Libro de los cien capítulos* cuatro manuscritos: A. 9216, Biblioteca Nacional, Madrid, fols. 22-61; B. 6608, Biblioteca Nacional, fols. 31-73; C. 8405 Biblioteca Nacional, fols. 116-147; M. 128, Biblioteca Menéndez Pelayo, Santander, fols. 53-100. Este es el defectuoso con la interpolación arriba descrita; sustituye a los fols. 75-83 que faltaban.

En los manuscritos A y B aparece nuestro texto junto con el *Libro del consejo e de los consejeros* de Maestre Pedro y *Castigos e documentos* atribuido a Sancho IV de Castilla. En un manuscrito dice don Sancho haber terminado la obra en 1292 cuando la toma de Tarifa; en otro se pone la fecha de 1293. Son obras contemparáneas y Billy R. Weaver trata de explicar esas dos fechas. Weaver acepta la identificación de Maestre Pedro con un Pedro Gómez Barroso que andaba en la corte de don Sancho como el autor del *Libro del consejo e de los consejeros* y sugiere la hipótesis, respecto a *Castigos e documentos*, "that the work was completed in 1292, that after the work was finished Maestre Pedro copied it and appended his own *Libro del consejo* to it, adjusting the colophon date to the correct date of 1293 . . . as a reward for services rendered Sancho interceded with the archbishop of Toledo on behalf of Maestre Pedro," *Studies in honor of Lloyd Kasten*, Madison, 1975, p. 296.

El agustino Arturo García de la Fuente publicó un extenso estudio: *Los "Castigos e documentos" del Rey Don Sancho IV el Bravo*. El Escorial, 1935. Había de servir de introducción a una edición crítica. Se publicó primero en *Religión y Cultura*, XXVI, 236-248, 341-365; XXVII, 316-322; XXVIII, 71-90, 380-399 (1934); XXIX, 27-41 (1935). Lo cito en mi edición, pero la ficha bibliográfica se extravió en la impresión.

Dice José Pérez Carmona que la edición que García de la Fuente tenía preparada para la imprenta fue destruida con otros muchos papeles y el Padre Arturo asesinado en El Escorial en 1936 durante la guerra civil: "Fragmentos de otro códice de los "Castigos e documentos" atribuidos a Sancho IV," *Boletín de la Academia Española*, 39 (1959), 73-84. Son fragmentos más breves que los perdidos en Sigüenza; abarcan unas ocho páginas incompletas. Habían sido empleados como forro de otra obra, como los de Sigüenza.

El *Libro de los cien capítulos* lleva por subtítulo "Dichos de sabios en palabras breves" (fol. 22v). Es en efecto uno de los muchos manuales de consejos y lecciones morales comunes en la Edad Media, dirigidos a la educación de príncipes y gobernantes. Mostrábase la lección por medio de *exempla*, apólogos, fábulas y dichos de sabios y filósofos, sacados de la tradición literaria o de las sagradas escrituras. Es fondo cumún a todas esas colecciones, y algunos de los ejemplos aparecen, más o menos modificados, en varios textos. Además de las arriba mencionadas, las más intimamente relacionadas son *Poridad de poridades*, *Bonium o Bocados de oro*, *Buenos proverbios* y *Flores de filosofía*. Algunas colecciones llevan el título general de "Dichos de sabios" o "Dichos de filósofos." El manuscrito escurialense E. III. 10, que es el que utilizó Knust, lleva por título: "Este libro es llamado *Bocados de Oro*." Luego, en el texto, pág. 80: "Dichos de filósofos;" más adelante, págs. 402-415: "ejemplos de los sabios antiguos." La versión contenida en el Ms. 8405 de la Biblioteca Nacional comienza: "Estos son los dichos del propheta Sed y Sus castigos" (fol. 40). El Ms. 6545 de la misma biblioteca va rotulado en el tejuelo: "Estos son dichos de Aristotiles e sus castigos;"; contiene *Bocados de Oro*, con un fragmento al principio de *Poridad de poridades* (Kasten, p. 24). Existen otras versiones más o menos completas: Ms. H. III. 24, Escorial: "Dichos e castigos de profetas que toda verdad fablaron" (fols. 84-91). Véase Zarco, *Catálogo* I, 233.

Otro texto todavía inédito hállase en el Ms. L. I. 12, Escorial, fols. 208-218: "proverbios y sentencias breves espirituales y morales." Comienza: "Dios no siempre te pide todo lo que tu puedes [dar]." Los manuscritos escurialenses B, II, 19, B. LV. 10, K. III. 12 contienen "Dichos de sabios y filosofos." Trátase de una traducción del catalán al castellano hecha por Jacobo Zadique de Uclés en 1402: lo "mando trasladar don Lorenzo Xuares de Figueroa, maes-

tre de Santiago . . . e fue trasladado por un judio su fisico" (B. II.
19, fols. 127-156).

El manuscrito 8405 de la Biblioteca Nacional, fols. 40-116, contiene unos "dichos de filósofos," comenzando por los de Sed como
en *Bocados de Oro*; termina como el texto en la edición de Knust.
Sigue en el mismo manuscrito, sin separación alguna, fols. 117-
147, un texto del *Libro de los cien capítulos*, que contiene sólo cin-
cuenta, aunque hay epígrafes para todos los cien, idénticos a los del
manuscrito 128 de la Biblioteca Menéndez Pelayo. Para más
amplias descripciones de los manuscritos de El Escorial véase
Zarco, *Catálago*.

*Buenos proverbios* nos da el título en el prólogo: "Este es el libro de
los buenos proverbios que dixeron los philosophos y los sabios antiguos . . . " Consérvase el texto en dos manuscritos escurialenses:
H-III-1 y L-III-2, que utilizaron Knust y Sturm en sus respectivas
ediciones.

Estos dichos de sabios son anónimos, traducciones del árabe.
*Buenos proverbios* procede de una obra de Husiain ibn Ishaq, como lo
indica Sturm en la introducción a su edición crítica.

Como ya dejamos apuntado, el texto de los folios sustituidos
por los cinco capítulos en el texto del *Libro de los cien capítulos* en el
manuscrito 128 de la Biblioteca Menéndez Pelayo no corresponden
ni empalman con el original. El contenido de esos folios es similar
al de las varias colecciones de dichos de sabios que hemos mencionado. Pone énfasis en el saber hablar y saber callar, porque por el
habla se conoce al hombre. Se condena la codicia y la soberbia, y se
recomienda no revelar secretos a nadie y no acompañarse de mala
gente, de mentirosos. Guarda cierta relación con *Bocados de Oro*
(Knust, 336 ss).

Al transcribir el texto resolvemos las abreviaturas y añadimos
puntuación y división en párrafos.

## Bibliografía

*Bonium* o *Bocados de Oro*, seguida de "Dichos de sabios," ed. Hermann
Knust, "Mittheilungen aus dem Eskurial," *Bibliothek das Literarischen
Vereins in Stuttgart*, t. 141, Tubingen, 1879.

*Libro de los buenos proverbios*, ed. H. Knust en *Dos obras didácticas y dos leyendas*,
Bibliófilos españoles, Madrid, 1878; ed. crít. Harlan G. Sturm,
Lexington: U. of Ky. Press, 1969.

*Castigos e documentos*, ed. A. Rey, Bloomington: Ind. U Press, 1952; P. García de la Fuente, Arturo, *Los "Castigos e documentos" del Rey Don Sancho el Bravo*, El Escorial, 1935.

*Libro del consejo e de los consejeros*, ed. A. Rey, Zaragoza, 1962.

*Libro del Caballero Cifar*, ed. Charles P. Wagner, Ann Arbor, 1929.

*Flores de filosofía*, ed. H. Knust en *Dos obras didácticas*, Madrid, 1879; A. Rey, ed. *Libro de los cien capítulos*.

*Poridad de las poridades*, ed. Lloyd Kasten, Madrid, 1957.

*Proverbios morales* de Sem Tob, ed. I. González Llubera, Cambridge, 1947.

Sánchez Vercial, Clemente, *El libro de los enxemplos por A. B. C.*, ed. John E. Keller, Madrid, 1969.

*Libro infinido* (Libro de los castigos o consejos) por Don Juan Manuel, ed. José M. Blecua, Madrid, 1952.

Weaver, Billy R., "The Date of Castigos e documents para bien vivir," *Studies in Honor of Lloyd Kasten*, Madison, 1975, 289-300.

Zarco Cuevas, Julián, *Catálogo de los manuscritos castellanos de la Real Biblioteca de El Escorial*, 3 vols., Madrid, 1924-1929.

# Dichos de sabios

[49] Dixo mas: la lengua del sesudo es en su coraçon, e el coraçon del loco es en cabo de la su lengua, ca quequier que pase por su coraçon dizelo luego. E puna luego todavia en acostunbrar las buenas maneras, e ayuda la buena natura con la buena costunbre e ayudarte ha contra las mas [malas] costunbres, e tollera de ty el destoruo de la nescesidat. E vemos muchos onmes que andan en malas carreras e conosciendo la buena carrera, mas non pueden yr a ella, tanto se apodero dellos la antigua mala costunbre, mas apremiando sus almas en usar poco la buena yra perdiendo la mala. Dixo otrosi: conviene al omne que muestre cada dia ansi mesmo todas sus obras, e que pune de saber que dizen del sus vezinos e los que han con el de dar e de tomar, e que cosa es con que lo alaban e con que lo denuestan. Quando andoviere por esta carrera non se asconderan, non se asconderan del ninguna de sus tachas. Dixo mas: pon a tus desengañadores e a tus amigos por espejo a las tus obras asi como pones el fierro açecalado por espejo a tu rostro; e a ti mas menester te es que enderesces la tu natura e las tus obras

que afeytar la tu forma. Dixo otro: el que mucho se paga de si son muchos los que se despagan del, e el que escatima non a otro que escatimar, e el que non pedrica a si non se pedrica por nengunt pedricador. E dixo: [50] si quisieres que el tu seso vença a la tu voluntat non te guies por las tus cobdicias; e para mientes a la fin, e sepas que mas dura el repentir en el coraçon que la cobdicia, ca la verguença es aber con temor, si ha fecho lo que non deuia fazer ante quien es mejor que el. E esta natura non es sinon el que ha alma verdadera de las cosas fermosas. El mejor de todos los omnes es el que se amansa siendo el alto, e el que aborresçe el mundo siendo el valloso [sic], e el que se mesura seyendo poderoso.

Mandaron a un sabio que afirmase el fecho deste mundo e del otro e dixo: este mundo es sueño e el otro es departimiento, e el mediano entre ellos es la muerte, e nos somos las vanidades de los sueños. Pregunto un omne a un sabio: ¿que ganaste por el tu saber en la tu fe? Dixo: afirmo el saber la razon e tolliola escasa, e soluio la dubda, e que en que me trabajar en toda mi vida. E dixo mas: marauillado me fago del coraçon que ama este mundo e del alma que quiere y fincar, e los dias lievan nuestras vidas; pues ¿como amamos en lo que non ha firmidunbre, e como puede dormir el ojo que non sabe si se abrira mas despues de aquel dormimiento si non se lo abriere ante Dios para resçibir el galardon? E dixo: el de grant coraçon es el que ha mas sabor de la aspera palabra del desengaña-dor quel falago del engañador, ca non es seruiçio de Dios en [51] penar la natura nin en dexar cresçer mucho sus cabellos, mas en tener el alma de non yr a las viles cobdiçias. Dixo mas: si quisieres que las tus bondades sean grandes en los ojos de los omnes, e sean pequeñas en los tuyos. Dixo otro: si tu sabes que eres non te nuzira lo que los otros dizen de ti; e non punes de ganar lo que otro te podria toller, e si dubdares en alguna cosa, dexala.

Dixo otrosi: mas vale buen fablar que buen callar, ca el callar non tiene pro sinon al que calla, e el fablar tiene pro a los que oye. E el callar es dormiente del seso e el fablar es despertamiento. E dixo: aconpañeme con los ricos e fue grande el mi duelo, porque veia mejores paños que los mios, mas fermoso afeytamiento que el mio; e aconpañeme con los pobres e folgue. Dixo mas: como el fierro quando no lo usan cubrelo orin fasta que lo desgasta, otrosi el seso quando esta de balde vencelo la nesçedat e matalo. E asi como el viento açiende el fuego e lo faze cresçer, otrosi las cuytas fazen cresçer las bondades del bueno. E dixo: asi como fierue la olla e se sale por fuerça quando ençienden el fuego, otrosi la mançebia quando ençiende la cobdiçia sale de su derecho. Ansi como queda la olla de feruir quando ponen agua fria sobre ella, otrosi se amata la mançebia por las sotiles pedricaciones, e ansi como la saeta quando fiere en alguna piedra se torna atras contra el ballestero, otrosi la mala [52] palabra quando la dixeren del omne bueno non se apega en el, mas tornase al que la dize. E Dixo: asi como el viso quando enferma vee unas ymaginaçiones non verdaderas, otrosi el alma quando non es bien clara vee mentirosas opiniones que no pueden ser.

Dixo mas: asi como la criatura mientra es en el vientre, e despues que sale, gusta el sabor del dormir e la sotileza del leer, fallase mejor que con lo que antes era. Otrosi los omnes mientra son en este mundo non quieren ende salir, e despues que del salen e van al otro mundo conosçen la su mejoria, asi como el enfermo quando ha en el fiuza que non morra de aquel mal, piensa de él el fisico e mandal fazer lo quel tiene pro, e viedale lo que le tiene daño; e quando pierde del la fiuza quitase de él el fisico e dexal comer de todo lo quel cobdiçia. Otrosi el omne quando ha buena voluntad guiale Dios por fazer bien, e quando non la ha dexalo seguir sus cobdiçias de manera que se conplira la su mala fin.

E asi como se aprueban los vasos del barro si son sanos o quebrantados por sus suenos por ferir en ellos, otrosi el omne porque es fecho de lodo se prueba por su fabla si anda derecho o errado. E asi como el sabio creçe cada dia el su saber e puja la su bondat porque la su vida es provechosa, e cunplese la pro quando se le sale el alma del cuerpo, otrosi la vida del nesçio es en su daño porque cada dia creçe la su vileza e [53] la su malicia e la su muerte e cunplese la su tenpestat. E dixo: si amostrares al sesudo, agradesçet gelo, e si endre[sç]ares al nesçio, denostar te ha. Dixo: el amor de tu amigo es tuyo en la tu tenpestat. E dixo: el cabdal del sesudo es sufrençia, e el cabdal del loco es soberuia. El que mostrare la tu nesçedat, galardonagelo tu en sofrirgelo. Dixo mas: el que es perezoso en su obra cobdiçia lo que otro gana. E dixo mas: el que puede escusar los omnes onrranle e precianle. El que cata las cosas dos vezes non se repiente. El primero ardor es con voluntat e el segundo es con seso. Dixo: el saber es lunbre del seso, pues puna en alunbrar el tu seso, E honrra al grande de dias porque conosçio a Dios antes que tu, e enpiada al pequeño porque se engana por el mundo mas que tu, ca non se levanta la onrra de la yra con el quebranto de la escusa. Dixo: otra que tengas que tarda la respuesta del tu clamor, porque tu erraste la carrera con los pecados. E grand ocasion es la verguença de los enemigos, e la mayor es auerlos menester. La mas fuerte lid es lidiar omne con la su yra. Dixo: la verdat es el mandadero de los mandaderos que envia Dios a los sus sieruos, pues nol deue nenguno tornar sin recabdo, e el que lo faze non lo faze sinon a Dios. Dixo: sofrid la tenpestat, tenpestat del vagador, ca el venturado es el que conosçe a Dios e faze su mandamiento.

El que amochigua la su ganancia [54] fincable mengua la su ganancia fincable. Los que mucho aman a Dios e lloran quando fazen sus oraciones fallan ende tan grand alegria como si fuesen cercados de la pro e de la su fin; e non la fallan tanto los mentirosos que rien, mintrosos neçios. Dixo mas: Asi como conviene a los buenos asi de amar a los buenos, asi les conviene de desamar a los malos. El buen seso cubre todas las manchas del omne e afeyta todas las sus maldades e faze auer la graçia de Dios.

Fijo, ruega a Dios que non hayas mala muger e guardate de la buena, ca las mugeres van tarde al bien e ayna al mal. Fijo, mercat con Dios e venir te han las ganançias sin cabdal. Fijo, muestra al que non sabe de lo que tu sabes del saber de los sabios; e non te aconpañes a los malos por que non seas tenido por atal como ellos; e non fies en cosa en que eres oy vivo e cras muerto. Fijo, sey todavia con los sabios, ca Dios aviva los coraçones e las palabras de la sabençia como aviva la tierra con el agua de la lluvia.

E dizen que la fuesa de Logines es entre la mesquita del arenal e el logar do fazen el su mercado, e alli ha fuesas de setenta profetas que murieron despues de Logine, e açertaron los fijos de Ysrrahel fasta que murieron todos de fanbre.

Fijo, teme a Dios; non fagas muestra a los omnes que le temas por que te honrre. Fijo, quando vieres logar de fabla de Dios posa con ellos, ca si fueres [55] sabio cresçera el tu saber; sinon fueres sabio mostrar te han, e si Dios les fiziere bien seras parcionero con ellos en el bien. E non poses en el logar do fablan de Dios, ca si fueres sabio non te aprovecharas en el tu saber, e si fueres nesçio, en la tu nesçedat, ca si Dios se ayra sobre ellos abras tu pro con ellos. Fijo, abe verguença de Dios en quanto es mas açerca de ty, e teme a Dios en quanto ha mas poder que tu.

La pregunta es la meytad del saber; mesurar la vida es la meytad del gouernamiento. Como el enemigo con el dar se torna
amigo, otrosi el amigo con la seberuia tornase enemigo. E el dicho
muestra qual es el seso, pues cata lo que dizes; e en acomendarse
omne a Dios fuelga, e el galardon del que miente es de nunca ser
creydo. Nunca cuentes nuevas al que vees que nunca te creera, nin
pidas al que te non dara, nin prometas lo que non podras conplir,
nin fies lo que non eres seguro de lo poder pechar, nin te atrevas a
lo que non podras auer.

Quitate de conpaña de mentroso, e si non lo podieres escusar,
non lo creas. Fijo, non veas seer del mas alto logar de la casa del
palaçio; e mas vale que te suban alla que non te deçendan dende.
Los envidiosos son mas que los buenos, ca ellos cuydan quel enbi-
dioso ha mas de lo que ha. Fijo, castigate [56] que temas a Dios, ca
es bien para ti e derecho. E non se vazie el tu coraçon de pensar en
Dios. E asi como es el fablar en Dios mejor que las otras fablas, asi
es Dios mejor que las sus criaturas. Fijo, non quieras en el serviçio
de Dios rrepto de nengunt rreptador. Fijo, faz la oraçion que te es
mandada, ca asi es la oraçion como la naue en la mar, sy estuerçe
estuerçen quantos en ella son, e si se pierde la naue pierdense
quantos en ella son.

Fijo, cosa que cada dia e cada noche cuydas que la dexaras non
vale nada, e cata todavia como lieues vianda della. Quanto el rey
adelantare tanto le faz tu mayor honrra commo puede auer omne
obedeçimiento de otro e el non puede auer obedesçimiento de su
alma. La buena voluntat es una manera para servir a Dios e el
omne. El buen oyr es buena manera de seso, e ser de buen talante
es una franqueza, e buena respuesta es manera de saber. Si ouieres
de enbiar en algunt mandado a algunt mandadero enbia omne
sabio, e si non lo podieres auer vete por ti. Non te sigas en el que
te dize mentira por otro, ca el la dira de ty a otro. Mas ligero es de
mouer las peñas de sus lugares que fazer entender al que non
puede entender. No rrenuçies a la tu alma cosa que es vergueña a
los omnes por la dezir por tu luenga [sic] ca mayor [57] vergueña
deues auer de Dios que de los omnes. E non porfies, ca la porfia
faze verter las sangres. Ama sienpre cyr mas que dezir. Quitadvos
de malos omnes e saluar se han vuestros coraçones. De dos sufri-
mientos son, el uno es sofrir omne lo que aborresçe que es derecho
de lo fazer, el otro es sofrir de non fazer lo que demanda su volun-

tat porque non es derecho de lo fazer. Tres omnes non son conosçidos sinon en tres cosas: non es conosçido el sufrido sinon en la su yra, nin el buen barragan sinon en la lid, nin el amigo sinon quando lo ha menester su amigo. Las malas son sospechar en el amigo e descobrir la poridat, e fiar en todo omne, e fablar mucho en lo que non aprovecha, e demandar buenos fechos a los malos. En dos cosas non presta el consejo: en fazer omne malandante siendo el bienaventurado, o fazerlo bienandante siendo el malaventurado. En dar la cosa por fecha ante que sea fecha es franqueza; el pensar es espejo del omne en que vee la su fermosura e la su tacha. Non seas sospecha [sic], ca la sospecha non dexa amor nin dexara entre ti e nengunt tu amigo.

El seso sin enseñamiento es como el arbol que non lieua fruto; e mostrar buena cara e salut a los omnes, e ser bueno en dar e tomar, e en dexar vaberia faze al omne ser amado de los omnes. Quando Longine llego a muerte lloro, e dixole el [58]: padre, ¿por que lloras? ¿es por desmayamiento de la muerte o es porque dexas el mundo? E dixole: non lloro yo por ningunas cosas desas, mas lloro porque he de andar grand camino e tengo de pasar fuerte puerto e lieuo poco conducho e grand carga e non se si se me aliuiara de aquella carga ante de llegar al cabo del camino o si non. E quando acabo de dezir pasose deste mundo.

## Capitulo de unos sabios que non supieron sus nonbres

Dixo un sabio: non dexes de fazer bien por que veas mucho que te lo non conosçen, ca el bien fazer es mejor que non el galardonamiento por el. Dixo otro: conviene al sesudo que non se trabaje sinon en lo que puede fazer, nin fable sinon en lo que le aproveche, nin despienda quanto gana, nin demande galardon si non quanto ha fecho pro, nin prometa si non lo que pudiere conplir. Dixo otro: non tornes a tu yerro porque estorçiste del. Dixo otro: el omne non se puede bien escusar de se allegar a los omnes, ca alguna pro le viene por ellos, mas convienele que se guarde mucho dellos, ca las grandes tenpestades dellos se levantan. Dixo otro: el que se trabaja de lo quel nuze non puede entender que es lo que le aprovecha. Dixo otro: el omne non puede estorçer en este mundo de la vida trabajosa; si non comiere morra, e si comiere algunt poco

demas de lo que le cunple enbargarse ha, e si comiere mucho enfer-
mara, e si comiere menos [59] de lo que ha menester habra fanbre.
En pos desto es lo que omne ha de seguir por ser mas sano. Dixo
otro: asconbra la tu lengua en dezir verdat e guardate mucho de
jurar, e si esto fizieres endresçar se ha todo tu fecho e presçiar te
han mas lo omnes e sera creyda la tu palabra e el tu renunçia-
miento escuchado, e valera esto en el otro mundo. Dixo otro: non
presçia este mundo mas que el otro sinon el codiçioso; e es como el
que quiere mas la miel con la benganbre; vuelta non es vianda provechosa. Dixo otro: maravillado me fago de los que se preçian por
ser linpios siendo suçios, e por sabios siendo nesçios, e por verdade-
ros siendo mintrosos. Dixo otro: non te pagues de la forma que es
fermosa de fuera e fea de dentro, nin de lengua escorrecha e dulce
siendo mintroso, nin del que ha mucho auer e non lo despiende asi
como deue, nin del que se preçia por los que son pasados, nin del
rey poderoso siendo torticero e robador. Dixo otro: si gostares el
sabor de las çiençias, propiamente de la thologia, non abras ningunt cuydado de ningu[n]a sabor sentible, e aborresçeras el mundo
e fallaras tu alma mas poderosa. Dixo otro: la riqueza verdadera es
la de los sabios que fazen las buenas obras e se quitan de pecados;
los que saben la poridat de la obra de Dios en este mundo mientra
viven e en el otro despues que mueren; e esta es la mayor ventura
que puede ser. Dixo otro: el que ha en este mundo fiuza mintrosa
abra en el otro desfiuzia verdadera, porque la carrera de la [60]
verdat es esperar. Dexaronla los cobdiçiosos e siguieron sus saberes en este mundo por mengua de alcanzar la verdat. Dixo otro:
non te ayudes por el que corronpio su fę por este mundo, mager
ayas grand poder por te defender, ca non sabes qual sera la fin del
fecho con el, ca el que faze mal a si non somos seguros que non
faga mal a otros. Dixo otrosi: si tu punares en fazer buenas obras e
foyr de las malas por el temor de Dios e por el su amor abras por
ello provecho en este mundo e en el otro la vida perdurable. Dixo
otro: mostrar al omne las poridades es grand pecado, ca es como
quien echa agua clara en el çieno fediondo que corronpiese el agua
e finca el çieno como se era en antes. Dixo otro: los estados de los
omnes mudanse todavia, pues en el que fias en la tu vida, requie-
rele toda ora e catalo bien si esta firme o non. Dixo otro: estar otro
debalde aduze la nesçedat, e la neçedat faze al omne ser deson-
rrado. Dixo otro: porque demandaron los omnes la folgura en este

mundo cayeron en grand lazerio; e como se guia el omne a la folgura que non sabe nin sabe qual es carrera para ella. Dixo otro: el
trabajo que tiene aventura maguer sea lazerio es mejor que la folgura que tiene desaventura.

Dixo otro: non puedes escusar en este mundo muchas cosas, e
puedes escusar otras, e pues sigue las que has menester e dexa las
otras. Dixo otro: la vianda e el agua e lo que se guarda el cuerpo de
calentura e de frio e el logar para [61] morada, esto todo podras
fallar en cada tierra, mas si non te cunpliere lo que te es menester
seras sieruo de las tus cobdiçias. Dixo otro: poca pro tiene al que
dize por su lengua «yo so siervo de Dios» e sus obras obedesçen al
diablo; antes les es este derecho enpeçedor e mortal. E dixo: la vida
del omne en este mundo non puede escusar las cosas deste mundo;
e los sabios toman dellas aquellas que non pueden excusar. Dixo
otro: despues que el mundo te ha de matar, mata tu la tu alma en
este mundo e abras la vida fincable en este mundo e en el otro.
Dixo otro: non desfinojes de allegar despues que eres mejor en el
tienpo que te conviene que en el tienpo pasado. E dixo: non a pro
en mucho dormir, mas daño es, pues acostunbra la tu alma tan
bien fazer de dia como de noche, bien por tal que non haya la mey-
tat de la tu vida de balde. Dixo otro: pon tu vida en trasmudar de
una çiençia a otra e non trastuelgas la tu alma despues que acaba-
res de orar a Dios sinon en esto. Dixo otro: la buena alma non
puede folgar en este mundo, pues non ayas fiuza de auer folgura si
non fueres bueno. Dixo: puna en fazer bien en qualquier estado,
quier que sea de sanidat o de enfermedat, ca mas vale fazer bien en
la tu enfermedat que en la tu sanidat; e si non la pudieres fazer por
ti mesmo por tu enfermedat que ayas mandalo fazer por ty; e
como quier, la tu alma non dexe de orar e de onrrar a Dios. E dixo
otro: convienete que [62] resçibas de la vianda aquello que te cunple, e guardate de cobdiçiar las cosas sabrosas, ca son tenpestades
cargadas. Dixo otro: non te ayudes de omne mintroso en grand
cosa nin en pequeña, ca el mintroso es atal como el omne muerto,
que do quier que le pongan faze daño. Dixo otro: si tu ouieres
piadat faze lazrar el tu cuerpo en seruiçio de Dios. E dixo otro:
quantos cuydan que fazen bien a sus almas e a ellos que se esfue-
rçen en las perder. Dixo otro: el que ama a Dios con verdadero
amor non aborrexce la muerte, nin teme a Dios con verdadero
amor el que faze algund pecado. Dixo otro: non cuydes que te apro-

veche el saber que es obedencia si non obrares las cosas de la obe-
dençia. Dixo otrosi: el que ouiere amor contigo por los saberes del
mundo abra desamor contigo por los desaberes del mundo; el otro
que ouiere amor contigo por el bien ningunt mal non vos puede
partir. E dixo otro: conosçer a Dios el que lo ama con verdadero
amor non se enbarga el su seruiçio, seruiçio de otro omne ninguno.
Dixo otro: pon buen estado a tu alma por todos los pecados grandes e pequeños, e puna en estorçer de todos; e quequier que fagas
de bien te abonda. E dixo otro: todos los omnes del mundo son
seruidores a los sabores, pues sey tu de los seruidores a Dios e non
de los seruidores de los sabores. Puna de non semejar a las bestias,
mas de samejar a los angeles que nunca cansan de seruir a Dios.
Dixo otrosi: el que quiere saber . . .

Indiana University

# Juan Ruiz:
# Sacerdotal Celibacy and
# the Archpriest's Vision

DOROTHY CLOTELLE CLARKE

NE OF THE STRONGEST UNDERCURRENTS in the *Libro de buen amor*[1] is Juan Ruiz's oblique argument against the Church's rule of sacerdotal celibacy. If the *presión* of the opening prayer (1, 2, 3) is figurative, and the bonds are of human flesh, the argument begins there; if not, it opens with the presentation of the poet's major premise, thrice stated in the prose prologue, where the point is made clear that, along with insufficiency of good understanding and will and memory, sin derives from fallible human *nature*: "... ante viene de la flaqueza de la natura humana que es en el omne que se non puede escapar de pecado" (p. 7). "E viene otrossí por razón que la natura umana (que) más aparejada e inclinada es al mal que al bien e a pecado que a bien" (p. 9), and "... porque es umanal cosa el pecar" (p. 9), he insists. Needless to say, the sin he has uppermost in mind is *loco amor*.

The essence of Juan Ruiz's ideas on nature's role in love as carnal desire, especially as they are developed in his work, had been expressed well before Juan Ruiz's time, notably in the very widely

---

[1] Juan Ruiz, *Libro de Buen Amor*, ed. Raymond S. Willis (Princeton University Press, 1972). Numbers in parentheses refer to stanzas as numbered in this edition. All quotations, though with punctuation removed in order to allow freedom of interpretation, are also from the Willis edition.

known twelfth-century love treatise written by another cleric,
Andreas Capellanus, who, in discussing specifically "The Love of
the Clergy," a chapter that may well have been the germ cell of
our poet's work, states: "Now the clerk is considered to be of the
most noble class by virtue of his sacred calling, a nobility which we
agree comes from God's bosom and is granted to him by the
Divine Will [...] But so far as this nobility goes, a clerk cannot
look for love, for on the strength of it he ought not to devote
himself to the works of love but is bound to renounce absolutely
all the delights of the flesh [...] So it is very clear that a clerk, so
far as concerns the distinction of this clerical nobility, cannot love,
and thus it would be improper for me to treat of his love according
to the dignity of this rank and the nobility of the order. A clerk
ought therefore to be a stranger to every act of love [...] But
since hardly anyone ever lives without carnal sin, and since the life
of the clergy is, because of the continual idleness and the great
abundance of food, naturally more liable to temptations of the
body than that of any other men, if any clerk should wish to enter
the lists of Love let him speak and apply himself to Love's service
in accordance with the rank or standing of his parents [...]"[2]

In any case, before the end of st. 76, the poet has acknowledged
himself as God's archpriest (6), has stated the theme of his work
by repeating Aristotle's observation that all [male] creatures in the
world strive for two things, the two being *mantenencia* and *juntamiento con fembra plazentera* (71),[3] has declared that he a sinner like
anyone else has loved women (76),[4] and has contended that, in
respect to this love, nature itself exerts a driving force far more
powerfully on humans than on other creatures: "Digo muy mas el

---

[2] Andreas Capellanus, *The Art of Courtly Love*, trans. John Jay Parry
(New York: Frederick Ungar Publishing Co., 1959 ¿1964¡), Book I, ch. VII,
p. 142. Note, then, the humor in st. 583*a*, 598, 600*ab*.

[3] Although the two are constants in the work, and sometimes rivals
(e.g., 982, 1399), and at one point join in triumph as Don Carnal and Don
Amor, the latter is the more conspicuous in the *Libro*.

[4] Of verse 76*a* ("e yo porque so omne como otro pecador"), as is frequently the case in the *Libro*, multiple interpretations are possible, depending on the reader's punctuation: "and I, because I am a man(,) like any
other (,) (a) sinner." Here, any one of the three possible connotations is
acceptable.

omne que toda criatura / todas a tiempo cierto se juntan con natura / el omne de mal seso todo tiempo sin mesura / cada que
puede quier' fazer esta locura" (74).[5] To his argument concerning
human nature, he adds the platitude concerning God's intention,
that is, that God would neither have made woman of man, nor
have given her to man for a companion, had He considered her an
evil thing (109); and, significantly, he makes it clear also that God
was the creator of nature: "Yo creo los astrólogos verdad natural-
mente / pero Dios que crió natura e acidente / puédelos demudar e
fazer otramente / segund la fe católica yo d'esto só creyente" (140).
He explains that the power exerted by general human nature on
the human individual, in regard to *juntamiento*, can be augmented by
the influence of Venus (152); and he argues, further, that since it
was under her sign that he was born, or so he believes, he is dou-
bly obliged to love the ladies—alas! however unrequited (153, 154).

Thus established, via both authority—Cato, Job, David, the
Decretal (Prologue, pp. 7-8), Aristotle (71)[6]—and logic, the fact of
virtual unalterability of the helplessness of man in regard to his
attraction to woman,[7] the Archpriest sets about demonstrating via
a series of love episodes the devastating hold that unfulfillable
desire has on the mind of the cleric, who is forced to spend his
waking and his sleeping hours in vicarious experiences and com-
pensatory imaginings. Of such insubstantiality, if it has no more
basis in fact than do the other tales of its kind that follow it in the
book, is the account of the futile courtship in which a virtuous lady
outwits him (77-104), and so gives the poet an excuse to retell and
to sermonize on two fables—that of the sick lion (82-88) and that
of the mountain (here the earth) and the mole (98-100). Refurbish-
ing another well known tale,[8] he poses as the motivating charac-

---

[5] Again, punctuation changes meaning: "el omne de mal seso" can
mean 'the man of poor sense' or 'man, of poor sense'.

[6] One wonders, however, whether it is through slyness on the poet's
part that the most frequently quoted authority in this prologue is Biblical
David, whose sinful love story is the first to come to the Archpriest's mind
in his bombast against Don Amor in regard to *luxuria*. (258-259)

[7] Unless the Archpriest is insinuating that Don Amor breaks down *all*
resistance, only the truly saintly may be excepted: "nunca te pagas de
omnes castos e dinos e santos" (388), says the Archpriest to Don Amor.

[8] Andreas Capellanus, *op. cit.*, Book II, ch. VII, sec. xvi (p. 174).

ter, and pretends to have been a victim of his own stupidity in entrusting his case to a male go-between (115-121, Cruz). Again assuming the guise of the would-be seducer, he fabricates another wooing scene, this time founded on the old dog-and-thief fable, and in it, like the thief, he is thwarted in his quest. The Archpriest's inclination to fantasize is now apparent, as is the fact that Juan Ruiz has indirectly declared his *acipreste* a purely fictional character, apart from the author.

Concurrent with the theme of *juntamiento* as a phenomenon of nature, God's creation, and reinforcing the argument against man's violation of that nature, is the theme of frustration, often the source of ironic-to-bitter humor, and sometimes the source of pathos, as in the passage on the canonical hours. From the implication of frustration in the references to captivity and prison, in the book's opening quatrains, and man's struggle against his own propensity for evil, specifically *loco amor*, as noted in the prose prologue, through repetition of the prison motif—Amor's *presos* (110), the imprisoned astrologers (132, 139)—and the crucifixion metaphor (112), and the confession that "a muchas serví mucho que nada acabecí" (153) because "el Amor siempre fabla mintroso"(161) and "lo que semeja non es" (162), to the climactic outright statement on unfulfilled desire, "nunca puedo acabar lo medio que deseo / por esto a las vegadas con el Amor peleo" (180), the ill effects of repressed instinct are apparent, for Amor, as we are about to learn first-hand, is not *el buen amor de Dios e sus mandamientos* explained in the prose prologue (p. 7). As the open conflict begins, we can see frustration pressuring to the point that the Archpriest's equilibrium is destroyed, and in anger he personifies, and derangedly conjures up the apparition of, his old tormentor, upon whom he proceeds to vent his wrath—to no avail, he comments, if Juan Ruiz was punning on the words *con vino*: "Dirévos una pelea que una noche me vino / pensando en mi ventura sañudo e non con vino [*non convino* ?] un omne grande fermoso mesurado a mí vino" (181). Hereupon begins the Archpriest's vision,[9] in which a

---

[9] In this study I "distinguish between ordinary dream and the vision vouchsafed by heaven. The events of the latter were doubtless conceived as existing on a plane of greater reality." (Chandler Rathfon Post, *Mediaeval Spanish Allegory* (Cambridge: Harvard University Press, 1915), p. 291.

parody of the medieval debate (here *desmesura* vs. *mesura*, Archpriest vs. Don Amor) is merged with a sermon-within-a-sermon (parodying the epic-within-an-epic?). The Archpriest plays a dual role in the vision, one that of Don Amor's antagonist, and the other that of editorial commentator (e.g., 891, 892).

One implicit lesson contained in the vision is that frustration leads to defeat, and therefrom to the commission of the very act that has been forbidden. "Con saña que tenía fuilo a denostar" (182), says the Archpriest, launching into his obloquy, in which he alternates abstraction and exemplum in his discussion, one by one, of the deadly sins, in his attempt to rid himself of an importunate *vecino* (181) who pesters day and night—"sin piedad me matas de noche e de día" (214)—and who comes invariably dragging in his wake every one of those sins, the last one of which, significantly, is *acidia*. The Archpriest is so overwrought that he monopolizes the floor until he exhausts his fund of uncensurable arguments (421-422), whereupon Don Amor, with *mesura*, serenely triumphs, and the aggressor meekly follows his lead, even going so far, at a later encounter, as to kneel before him, obsequiously begging him to be his guest (1260-1261), and opening his house to him (1262).

The Archpriest berates Don Amor for adding hypocrisy to sloth: "Otrossí con acidia traes ipocresía" (319), and so prepares a fitting nexus (and inserts a sly insinuation concerning clerics' easy life and leisure time?[10]) between the enumeration of the sins and the equivocal passage on the canonical hours (374-387), crux of his anti-celibacy argument and emotional apex in the first half of the vision (and the *Libro*), to be counterpoised structurally, near the end of the vision, by the lengthy diatribe against Death (1520-1568), point of consummation of the inevitable love-death union.

In the "Canonical Hours," while he is exposing and criticizing the degradation of the pornographic parodies of religious rites, parodies that cause the mind to wander during worship time, and evoke lustful longing instead of reflection on the intended meaning of the religious observation, Juan Ruiz depicts the pathetic state of mind resulting from denial of nature. Frustration leads to obsession, as the poet obliquely had forewarned in st. 214 ("sin piedad me matas noche e día"), and the obsession becomes so intense that

---

[10] See quotation above, by Andreas Capellanus.

all exterior circumstances are converted to one object, on which the celibate rivets his attention. Otis H. Green has supplied the major clue to the underlying obscene meaning of this passage. By beginning with the references, in his *Spain and the Western Tradition*,[11] to *coplas* 375*a* and *cd*, 384*b* (p. 56), and 381*d*, but substituting a specific strictly anatomical for the personal reference in the not entirely euphemistic word *amiga* (375 and consistently thereafter), and remembering that the *tú* throughout the passage is still Don Amor who is being angrily addressed by the frustrated Archpriest, the reader will find that the remainder of the scabrous meaning will fall into place, and he can easily decipher the hardly sotto voce message contained in the passage.[12] There are only two characters involved in this episode: Don Amor and the Archpriest. All other references that seem to be to persons or apparent personifications are figures of speech (euphemisms) connoting parts, products, or actions of the body, and the Archpriest, continuing his vituperation, and now speaking in *garçón-golhín* (374, low-life lingo—hence the *amiga, vieja, dueña,* etc.) is berating Don Amor for tantalizing said *amiga* to a point beyond endurance. The force at work here is the cleric's mind, and the scene is an amplification and exemplification of a section of a statement made in the prologue's *Breve*: "comoquier que a las vegadas se acuerde [omne] pecado e lo quiera e lo obre, este desacuerdo [...] viene otrossí de la mengua del buen entendimiento, que lo non ha estonce, porque omne piensa vanidades de pecado" (pp. 7-9). At every call to worship, night and day reminding the cleric of his vows and his erstwhile idealism and the pleasures foregone, the victim's mind is driven mercilessly and tormented, at Don Amor's behest, by a lower region of his being— when his thoughts should be focused on the highest point of human aspiration—and his resultant condition and attempted relief must be veiled by an act of hypocrisy.

---

[11] Vol I. (Madison, The University of Wisconsin Press, 1963), pp. 53-60.

[12] For the probable base meaning of line 377*d*, which apparently was taken from Genesis 38:9 (on Onan), read *verter* for *verte*. The term *esquima*, generally understood to mean 'harvest', makes perfect sense since, via synecdoche, it would also mean 'seed'. Could it also contain a hint of *quimo* 'chyme', to suggest consistancy?

This depiction of the interminably repeated process of nature's tyrannic urging and of a cleric's predicament in a vain struggle to still his passion, demonstrates by way of example the futility of the self-defeating man-made rule of total abstinence, and the harm that comes of a good carried to such an extreme that, paradoxically, *mesura* disregarded, the good becomes an evil. The irony of the conflicting exterior/interior—i.e., the surface *buen amor* in the Church's call to worship, and the obscene subsurface *loco amor* concealed by the goaded cleric's hypocritically assuming the attitude of prayer—could hardly be more impressive, or the sarcasm more biting, as the symbols of sacred love evoke *luxuria*.[13] The joking hardly hides the hurt.

As the vision continues, Don Amor, with the greatest of aplomb, and well supported by his underling Hypocrisy, downs his helpless opponent in less than two-thirds the time and space (424-575) needed by the Archpriest to wear himself down in argumentation (188-422), and hustles off to work, leaving his wife and his servant Pamphilus with the mop-up. "Partióse Amor de mí e dexóme dormir / desque vino el alva pensé de comedir / en lo que me castigó e por verdad dezir / fallé que en sus castigos usé siempre vevir" (576), muses the Archpriest. Don Amor's departure suggests a comment and a question. The lines just quoted indicate that the episode is a vision, since the Archpriest fell asleep—or believed he did—only *after* the recounted action had taken place; and probably that, since daybreak came even later, the whole epi-

---

[13] The wandering mind at worship time is a *clerecía* "confession" topos, of which our passage is an elaboration in which the errant thoughts are specified. Stanza 180 of Gonzalo de Berceo's confession in the *Loores de Nuestra Señora*, clearly foreshadows Juan Ruiz's passage on the Hours: "Quand era en la glesia las oras m'enojavan, / los pensamientos vanos de seso me sacavan; todas las vanidades allí me remembravan, / mezquino peccador, ¡tan mal me engannavan¡" ed. Brian Dutton, *Obras completas*, vol. III (London: Tamesis Books Limited, 1975). Pero López de Ayala, like the others, stressing deceit, confesses to having broken the Third Commandment in the same way: "De oír dezir las oras non tomé devoçión, / en la tu casa santa nin la pedricaçión: / en vanos pensamientos puse mi coraçón, / mentir, e escarnir era mi entinçión." "*Libro de poemas*" o "*Rimado de Palaçio*", vol. I, ed. Michel García (Madrid: Gredos, 1978), st. 30. The *Libro rimado de Palaçio*, vol. I, ed. Jacques Joset (Madrid: Alhambra, 1978) varies slightly in textual details, but not in meaning.

sode to this point does not contain much, if any, truth (in medieval lore it was the dreams occurring at daybreak that contained revelation of truth).[14] Ironically enough, too, the vision was useless for the Archpriest's purposes, for he is no further advanced in the situation than he was when he started, with an Amor who is *mintroso* (161).

Why the artifice of a vision? is the suggested question. Perhaps for the borrower of tales to be able to utilize literary sources (e.g., the *Pamphilus*) more freely and humorously than he might otherwise have been able to do? Perhaps to justify the use of allegorical figures such as Don Amor, Don Carnal, and Trotaconventos in an otherwise realistic-seeming work? Perhaps merely to poke a little fun at vision-allegory literature itself, so popular at the time? Perhaps to illustrate in a grandiose way one of the great themes of his work, illusion versus reality? Or perhaps because he could be more daring than he might otherwise be in striking his blows at the rule of celibacy—a disclaimer, as it were—since patent fiction bears less onus than does apparent truth, and the visionary cannot be held responsible for the content of vision or dream? Some of each, but mainly the daring, one may suspect. Or is the whole thing but one grand parody on the epic vision or dream, in which a supernatural figure appears to the hero and advises or inspires him?[15]

Possibly as further insurance against censure, or to enhance the truth of the message, the Archpriest casts himself, still within the vision, into a second and therefore deeper vision (vision-within-a-vision), which, he believes, comes at dawn, apparently during his sleep (576), though no direct mention of his state of consciousness is made after line 576a, unless it is contained in a lost passage. Venus and Pamphilus appear in the order designated by Don Amor. Venus appears in person, and Pamphilus transforms himself and the Archpriest together into a single character, whose name, according to Trotaconventos, is Sir Melon of the Garden (727, 738), or simply Sir Melon (873, 891), or, once his

---

14 "Post mediam noctem, cum somnia vera" (Horace, *Satires*, I, 10, 33); "Ma se presso al mattin del ver si sogna" (Dante, *Inferno*, XXVI, 7); "Nell'ora che [...] presso alla mattina, [...] e che la mente nostra peregrina [...] alle sue vision quasi è divina" (Dante, *Purgatorio*, IX, 13-18).

15 See M. H. Abrams, *A Glossary of Literary Terms* (New York: Holt, Rinehart and Winston, 1957 [1966]) p. 29.

goal is accomplished, since all men do likewise, Sir Melon Garden-son (via false etymology,[16] 881), but whom Doña Endrina, not entirely obfuscated by the insidious procuress, calls Fita (845).[17] This hybrid character fades away at the end of a single episode, however, and the Archpriest is only himself thereafter. In this second vision state the Archpriest not only talks but acts, albeit cowardly, for the most part, in contrast to his boldness of speech in the outer vision.

Repeatedly, during the vision, the Archpriest demonstrates the tenacity of obsession. He figures himself—in wishful thinking—first,with the help of Venus, as the neo-Pamphilus just mentioned (580-591), borrowed from *Pamphilus* ("que lo feo de la estoria dize Pánfilo e Nasón", 891); eventually as the unwilling object of desire, in varying degrees, on the part of four *serranas* (950-1042), when he learns that *mantenencia* is sufficiently powerful to distract the mind from *juntamiento*, and that a *serrana*, only a syllable removed from the nymphomaniac *rana* of st. 407-414, woman and sturdy though she be, can fall prey to the snares of Don Amor (975-992); and even as the suitor of a virtuous nun, in a fanciful tale (1332-1507), which gives him the opportunity to protest the Church's wasting of womanhood (1500), but then, in a fleeting moment of respite from the tyranny of the flesh, to admit that pleasure can be had in platonic love: "mucho de bien me fizo con Dios en limpio amor / en quanto ella fue biva Dios fue mi guiador" (1503). Lesser exploits round out his saga, though he never, in the *Libro*, except, if even then, under duress (first two *serranas*, 971, 983 and 992) succeeds in breaking his celibacy vow.

Although Juan Ruiz does not indicate specifically the end of the vision, we may assume that it coincides with the end of the epitaph for Urraca (1576-1578), since the sermonet that follows, on the Christian's defensive weapons against the Devil, though a natural reflection on the phenomenon of death and sin just experienced, is not fictionwise connected with anything in the vision, but appears, rather, as an afterthought in which the poet summar-

---

[16] See Dayle Seidenspinner de Núñez, "The Poet as Badger: Notes on Juan Ruiz's Adaptation of the *Pamphilus*," *Romance Philology*, XXX (1976), 123-34 (p. 126).

[17] Don Melón de la Huerta, Don Melón, Don Melón Ortiz. *Melón* may also mean 'badger' or 'mongoose' (see n. 16, above).

izes soberly and in abstract terms the lively vision-sermon on sins, and offers for each a specific catechistic counteractive, also presented in abstract terms. The poet, reassuming his initial posture of sermonizer, opens his sermonet by addressing his audience *juglar* fashion: "Señores, acordadvos del bien, sí vos lo digo" (1579), and speaks, minus some of the humor, with the same voice he had at the beginning of the great sermon (i.e., that of the poet himself, *not* through a character, but addressing his audience directly), which also had been introduced with a *juglar* formula, "Si queredes, señores, oír un buen solaz" (14), and continued intermittently through the book. The whole book-sermon, in which, Juan Ruiz claims, "Fablévos en juglaría" (1633), is brought to a close formally with the Archpriest's vision-influenced (1608) observations on the attractions of brevity and smallness, beginning, again *juglar* fashion, with "Quiero abreviaros, señores, la mi predicación" (1606). What follows in the way of love episode (Don Furón, 1618-1625), seems anti-climactic but for the fact that it serves as one more lesson in which by his own inconstant behavior the Archpriest gives proof of Don Amor's falseness, and as a final reminder that obsession, though possibly attenuated, has not been eradicated from the Archpriest's mind. In its post-vision position it also parallels the three pre-vision love tales and, though it lacks the intrigue interest of the earlier pieces, harmonizes with them in relative brevity and choice of character, and serves as the final panel of the vision's frame.

Lest he be held responsible for having overstepped the bounds of daring, the poet offers the seemingly discrete "Cántica de los Clérigos de Talavera" episode (1690-1709) as the requisite palinode (or parody of one?), in which, to offset the impression gained by anyone who failed to "bien juzgar la mi entención por que lo fiz' e la sentencia de lo que y dize" (prologue, p. 11), he scores and ridicules his fellow clerics for not keeping the vow that his Archpriest so eagerly sought to break—or is the "Cántica" a parting shot at that very vow?[18]

UNIVERSITY OF CALIFORNIA, BERKELEY

---

[18] For important background, see A. N. Zahareas, "Celibacy in History and Fiction: The Case of *El LBA*," *I & L*, I (1977), pp. 77-82; "Structure and Ideology in the *LBA*," *La Corónica*, 7 (1979), 92-104; "On the Sources of the *LBA* and the Interpretation of Medieval Texts," *La Corónica*, 8 (1979).

# Juan Ruiz's Attitude
# to Literature

ALAN DEYERMOND

HE *Libro de Buen Amor* PRESENTS what may be a unique difficulty in medieval literature. Some texts, such as the *Cantar de Mio Cid*, have a clear meaning, and critical argument is confined to the reasons which lie behind that meaning and to the ways in which the author's intention is artistically realized. Other texts—for example, *La Celestina, Sir Gawain and the Green Knight*, Villon's *Testament*—are more controversial, but at least we all know what questions we should ask, and any one critic knows his or her view of the answers that emerge. Most critics of the *Libro de Buen Amor*, however, confess themselves baffled for at least part of the time, and it is hard even to reach agreement on what questions one should ask of the work. The only other medieval Spanish text I know that approaches this level of difficulty is the *Razón de amor*, and even there we are spared one of the *Libro de Buen Amor*'s most perplexing features: its protean vocabulary. In the *Razón*, each word seems to retain throughout the poem its initial meaning (whatever that may be), whereas in the *Libro* many words, starting with those of the title, treat the reader like Alice's flamingo-croquet mallet, that turns round and looks her in the eye whenever she tries to hit the ball, or Thurber's bed, that converts itself into a card-table in the middle of the night.

I propose to deal in this paper with one of the less intractable problems (in the sense that the questions are fairly clearly defined): the problem of the Archpriest's attitude to literature. First, I should like to direct attention to the proliferation of genre terminology, especially at the beginning of the *Libro*. We all know that Juan Ruiz enjoys enumerations: musical instruments, nuns' electuaries, the skills of a mountain-dweller, the names of the go-between, the faults of Don Hurón, and, in a more diffuse form, the soldiers of Doña Cuaresma and Don Carnal. But this is different. This is not an enumeration, but a plentiful and varied use of genre terminology, again and again. Let me exemplify, starting where the first (1330) version of the *Libro* seems to have begun:

11 prosa    canto
12 cantares    librete    rimar
13 libro
14 romançe
15 trobas    cuento rimado    dezir    saber sin pecado
       razón    fablar
16 libro
19 cantar de sus gozos[1]

This use of terminology continues, though not as intensively. It may be objected that the terms are, on the whole, vague either because of their generality (*libro*) or because they have no fixed meaning (*trobas*).[2] That is true, just as it is true of almost all genre terminology used by medieval Spanish writers outside the restricted spheres of rhetoric and versification.[3] Juan Ruiz's usage is distinguished from that of his Spanish contemporaries not by its

---

[1] My quotations are taken from the Clásicos Castellanos edition by Jacques Joset (Madrid: Espasa-Calpe, 1974).

[2] This point has been noted before, e.g. by Olga Tudorica Impey, "Los *topoi* y los comentarios en el *Libro de buen amor*," *NRFH*, 25 (1976), 278-302, at p. 285.

[3] Middle English terminology seems to have been rather more consistent: see Paul Strohm, "Some Generic Distinctions in the *Canterbury Tales*," *Modern Philology*, 68 (1970-71), 321-28; "*Storie, Spelle, Geste, Romaunce, Tragedie*: Generic Distinctions in the Middle English Troy Narratives," *Speculum*, 46 (1971), 348-59; and "The Origin and Meaning of Middle English *Romaunce*," *Genre*, 10 (1977), 1-28.

generality or its imprecision, but by its frequency. The number of genre terms used in his *cuaderna vía* stanzas is surprising (they are rare in the lyrics). In the first hundred stanzas of *cuaderna vía*, I have counted thirty-five genre or related terms, used on fifty-three occasions. In the same hundred stanzas, there are nine references to sources or authorities, sometimes vague ("los antiguos astrólogos," "el sabio"), more often precise (Aristotle, Cato, *Ysopet*, Plato, Ptolemy, Solomon).

This impression of an intense preoccupation with literature— its creation, its types, its effects—is reinforced as we go through the *Libro*. As I have said, genre terminology is not usually as frequent or as varied in later parts of the *Libro*, but one seldom goes for very long without encountering it. I have made a preliminary index, which contains nearly one hundred and thirty terms, used on nearly three hundred and fifty occasions; and this does not include the numerous occasions on which generic terminology is applied to the speech of the characters. I know of no other work that approaches this level of frequency or of variety.

Juan Ruiz's terminology does not provide a satisfactory generic classifcation, for two main reasons. First, the same word is used for two or even three generic meanings:

| | |
|---|---|
| çiençia | art of poetry (Prose prologue, p. 14) scientific treatise (123a) |
| ditado | content of letter (1077a) doctrinal observations? (1129d) poem (p. 14, 91c, 1044d) |
| escarnio | joke (100c) satire (908b) |
| estoria | picture (1571c)[4] story (297c, 909a, 1048e, 1571d, etc.) |
| fabla | doctrine? (429b) proverb (80c, 111a, 919a, etc.) story (96d, 407d, 892b, etc.) |

---

[4] *Estoria* is the reading in the manuscripts. Joset accepts Chiarini's emendation to *escoria* (Corominas emends to *esordia*). *Estoria* is shown to be correct, and interpreted as "picture," by Steven D. Kirby, "'Escripto con estoria' (*Libro de buen amor*, st. 1571c)," *Romance Notes*, 14 (1972-73), 631-35. I dissent, however, from Kirby's view that *estoria* in the following line has the same meaning; here, the required sense seems to be "story."

| fablilla | proverb (179c, 870a) |
| | story (1400d) |
| fazaña | proverb, *sententia* (580a) |
| | story (188d, 457a, 474a, etc.) |
| nota | contents (1068c, 1074d, 1193a) |
| | poem (p. 14) |
| razón | message (1198d) |
| | story (460a, 1631d) |
| | work (15d, 68c, 425c, etc.) |
| romançe | story (904a) |
| | work (14b, 1148c, 1634b) |

Secondly, the same genre or related concept may be represented by many words:

| story | estoria, fabla, fablilla, fazaña, juguete, razón, romançe |
| proverb | fabla, fablilla, fazaña, parlilla, pastija, pastraña, proverbio, retraher, and the periphrastic "como dize la vieja" |
| poem | canción, cantar, cántica, cantiga, canto, chançón, chançoneta, ditado, nota, rima, troba (and if these mean different kinds of poem, I do not see how we can learn to distinguish them)[5] |

It will be clear that I am not trying to make a case for Juan Ruiz as literary theorist, but merely recording his interest in literature. So far I have dealt only with generic or quasi-generic terms. There are also, though on a smaller scale, stylistic comments, categories of poet or performer, and explicit references to sources, authorities, and other literary works.

This last category reveals an apparent paradox: there are eight vague terms for sources (e.g. "el sabio") and some thirty names of authors or works. Of these, however, ten are Biblical or patristic,

5 Anthony N. Zahareas, *The Art of Juan Ruiz, Archpriest of Hita* (Madrid: Estudios de Literatura Española, 1965), says that the Archpriest "shows awareness of the diversity of his poetic production by constantly labeling his compositions correctly" (p. 65), but the terms quoted by Zahareas mostly refer to content, and he does not attempt to distinguish between, e.g., *rima* and *troba*.

eleven are legal (usually from canon law), and of the nine more literary ones four are primarily philosophical (Aristotle, Cato, Plato, Ptolemy). The only references to more imaginative literature are to *Ysopet*, Ovid, *Pamphilus*, *Flores y Blancaflor*, and *Tristán*. We know that the Archpriest read more widely than that, so why are there not more references to creative writers? It is true that such references are comparatively uncommon in poetry of that time, so their scarcitry in the *Libro de Buen Amor* may not be significant. It is, however, possible that, in the context of Juan Ruiz's other references to literature, it indicates a much stronger interest in his own creative process than in that of other writers.

Be that as it may, a clear impression of intense concern with his own poetic creativity is given by stanzas 1631-34, in which Juan Ruiz sums up the purpose of his work:

> Fizvos pequeño libro de testo, mas la glosa
> non creo que es chica, ante es bien grand prosa;
> que sobre cada fabla se entiende otra cosa,
> sin lo que se alega en la razón fermosa.
>
> De la santidat mucha es bien grand liçionario,
> mas de juego e de burla es chico breviario;
> por ende fago punto e çierro mi armario:
> séavos chica fabla, solaz e letuario.
>
> Señores, hevos servido con poca sabidoría;
> por vos dar solaz a todos, fablévos en juglaría;
> yo un gualardón vos pido: que por Dios, en romería,
> digades un paternóster por mí e avemaría.
>
> Era de mill e trezientos e ochenta e un años
> fue conpuesto el romançe por muchos males e daños
> que fazen muchos e muchas a otros con sus engaños,
> e por mostrar a los sinples fablas e versos estraños.

This is a protestation of didactic aim, certainly, but what are we to make of "mostrar a los sinples fablas e versos estraños"? The ambiguity of that line, which was in the original version of the *Libro*, is almost entirely removed by the words of the prose prologue, probably added in 1343:

> E conpóselo otrosí a dar algunos leçión e muestra de
> metrificar e rimar e de trobar; ca trobas e notas e rimas
> e ditados e versos fiz conplidamente, segund que esta
> çiençia requiere. (p. 14)

His verse is highly skilled, Juan Ruiz tells us—a claim made also by the poet of the *Libro de Alexandre*. Ruiz, however, goes further: he stresses the variety of his work, and claims that it is his mission to show people how to write poetry.[6]

In one sense, this fits what may be a mid-fourteenth-century pattern. Juan Manuel, as we all know, wrote a general prologue to his works, explaining his aims, and Ian Macpherson has commented perceptively on his view of the writer's task.[7] Guillaume de Machaut, a contemporary of Juan Manuel and of Juan Ruiz, did much the same.[8] These two writers, however, differ strikingly from Juan Ruiz in one way. Neither Machaut nor Juan Manuel is notably modest, and both can at times be arrogant, but as far as I know neither of them says at any point that it is his function to show his compatriots how to write. Juan Ruiz's sense of mission goes even further than Garcilaso's well-known dismissal of his poetic predecessors in Spain, because Garcilaso at least acknowledges his debt to the Italians. The Archpriest of Hita acknowledges a debt to no poet. The extent of his claim is uncertain, because we do not know who "los sinples" of 1634d or "algunos" of the prologue are. They can hardly, I suppose, be the uneducated in any literal sense. It is likely that they are poets whose work the Archpriest considers inadquate in some way, but whether they are a defined group or contemporary Spanish poets in general remains doubtful.

---

6 His statements are discussed by Zahareas, *The Art of Juan Ruiz*, pp. 62-69, 172-74. Zahareas concludes that he is serious in what he says about his art, even if in nothing else. Irma Césped B., "Las composiciones líricas en el *Libro de Buen Amor*," *Boletín de Filología* (Chile), 23-24 (1972-73), 29-60, is more hesitant, but does not deny that one aim of the lyrics may be to set a poetic example (p. 30).

7 Macpherson, "Don Juan Manuel: The Literary Process," *Studies in Philology*, 70 (1973), 1-18. Two versions of the general prologue to Juan Manuel's works are extant, one of them being what has hitherto been described as the first prologue to *El conde Lucanor*; see Germán Orduna, "Notas para una edición crítica del *Libro del conde Lucanor et de Patronio*," *BRAE*, 51 (1971), 493-511.

8 See Kevin Brownlee, "Guillaume de Machaut's Concept of Poetic Identity: The Example of the *Dits amoureux*," unpubl. diss., Princeton University, 1979. Kevin and Marina Brownlee are now preparing an article comparing Machaut and Juan Manuel in this respect.

With a poet as fond of parody and ambiguity as Juan Ruiz, one is bound to wonder whether such a sweeping claim is seriously meant. There are statements of modesty to be set against it ("Señores, hevos servido con poca sabidoría"), but these are, of course, topoi.[9] Now, a topos may be sincerely used—that is how it came to be a topos in the first place. On the other hand, it may be mere formality or protective coloring. A statement which is not a topos—and the Archpriest's literary claims are not—is much less likely to be a formality.[10]

There is ample evidence to support a serious reading of Juan Ruiz's literary manifesto. He does indeed use a wide variety of verse forms and of poetic genres, and he extends his range by parody: of the *alborada* (in the Canonical Hours passage and perhaps in stanza 1022), of the spring song (two lazy men; Clérigos de Talavera), and of the *pastorela* (*serrana* episodes).[11] His interest in the writing of lyrics, already strong when he composed the first version of the *Libro* in 1330,[12] seems to have intensified in the following thirteen years. Diego Catalán and Suzy Petersen, developing a point made in passing by Menéndez Pidal, argue that the great majority of the passages added in the second version of the *Libro* were written to introduce or comment on lyrics (many of which are not preserved in MS *S*).[13]

---

[9] On Juan Ruiz's handling of topoi, see Impey, "Los *topoi* y los comentarios."

[10] His pride in his poetic skill is emphasized by Zahareas, *The Art*, pp. 64, 172-74, and Impey, pp. 292-93. Zahareas, pp. 67-68, notes that the Archpriest's comments belong to the literary tradition of autocommentary, but he stresses the ways in which they depart from that tradition. It is significant that they are not among the commonplaces of *clerecía* poetry which John K. Walsh finds (often in parodic form) in the *Libro*: "Juan Ruiz and the *mester de clerezía*: Lost Context and Lost Parody in the *Libro de buen amor*," *RPh*, 33 (1979-80), 62-86.

[11] Deyermond, "Some Aspects of Parody in the *Libro de Buen Amor*," in "*Libro de buen amor*" *Studies*, ed. G. B. Gybbon-Monypenny (London: Tamesis, 1970), pp. 53-78.

[12] Ramón Menéndez Pidal, *Poesía juglaresca y orígenes de las literaturas románicas: problemas de historia literaria y cultural*, 6th ed. [of *Poesía juglaresca y juglares*, 1924] (Madrid: Instituto de Estudios Políticos, 1957), pp. 211-12.

[13] "'Aunque omne non goste la pera del peral...' (Sobre la 'senten-

The list of poems that Juan Ruiz says he wrote, but that are missing from the extant manuscripts, is extensive, and is drawn from both the 1330 and the 1343 versions of the *Libro*. Some of the extant lyrics are introduced in this way:

d'ella primero fiz / cantar de sus gozos siete, que ansí diz (19)
Fiz con el grand pesar esta troba caçurra (114)
fiz de lo que ý passó las coplas deyuso puestas (958)

and a few more cases. Far more often, a poem is announced but none follows:

Enbiél' esta cantiga, que es deyuso puesta (80)
d'esto fize una troba de tristeza tan maña. (103)
Fiz luego estas cantigas de verdadera salva. (104)
Del escolar goloso...fize esta otra troba (122)
estas cantigas que son deyuso escritas (171)
Luego en el comienço fiz aquestos cantares (915)
diole aquestas cantigas (918)
con ello estas cantigas que vos aquí robré (1319)
diole aquestos viessos (1325)
Con el mucho quebranto fiz aquesta endecha (1507)
Dil' aquestos cantares (1625)

In addition, there are half a dozen cases in which poems are referred to, though without an explicit statement that they are included in the text. There is one comprehensive reference of this type:

Despés fiz muchas cánticas, de dança e troteras,
para judías e moras e para entenderas,

___

cia' de Juan Ruiz y la de su *Buen Amor*," HR, 38, Nº 5 (November 1970: *Studies in Memory of Ramón Menéndez Pidal*), 56-96. Menéndez Pidal, *Poesía juglaresca*, p. 210n. See also Raymond S. Willis' observations in his edition of the *Libro* (Princeton: University Press, 1972), p. xliii. Some early readers of the *Libro* were most powerfully impressed by this aspect, while others noticed the doctrinal content: the inventory of Argote de Molina's library includes "Cancionero del Arcipreste, de canciones antiquíssimas," but Alfonso Martínez de Toledo refers to "su tractado." Irma Césped, in her important reassessment of the extant lyrics, points out that some *cuaderna vía* passages, such as the lament for Trotaconventos, are lyric in tone ("Las composiciones líricas," p. 31).

para en instrumentos comunales maneras:
el cantar que non sabes, oilo a cantaderas.
Cantares fiz algunos, de los que dizen çiegos,
e para escolares que andan nocherniegos,
e para muchos otros por puertas andariegos,
caçurros e de burlas: non cabrién en diez pliegos. (1513-14)

Other references are to a single poem, for example:

Por conplir su mandado de aquesta mi señor,
fize cantar tan triste como este triste amor;
cantávalo la dueña, creo que con dolor,
más que yo, ella podría ser d'ello trobador. (92)[14]

We cannot dismiss these statements, despite their failure to assert categorically that the lyric is included in the text, because a reference of this kind to three poems (1021) is followed by one of the three, and a reference to four poems (1621) is followed by two. Jacques Joset argues that phrases like "estas cantigas" do not necessarily have a demonstrative value,[15] but even if he is right there is no explaining away "que es deyuso puesta" or "que son deyuso escritas." Juan Ruiz undeniably—at least, it seems undeniable to me—claims to include in his text many poems which are not now there.[16] Critics differ in their reactions to this claim. Some doubt

---

[14] See also the reference to a single lyric in 1498ab, and the more general allusions in 170a, 947, and 1508d. In addition, there is one lyric which has lost all but the first four lines (1684), but which is not preceded by any introductory reference.

[15] Note to stanza 915 in his edition, and "Le *Libro de buen amor* vu par Ramón Menéndez Pidal," *Marche Romane*, 20 (1970), 93-100, at pp. 97-98.

[16] It is not possible to state an accurate number, since most of the references are to lyrics in the plural. Willis says that "lyric poems numbering at least eleven, and maybe as many as two dozen, were explicitly promised by Juan Ruiz yet are not present in our manuscripts" (edition, pp. xl-xli), and Saralyn R. Daly agrees: "the eleven to twenty-four promised songs which appear in no manuscript" (*The Book of True Love*, trans. Daly, ed. Anthony N. L. Zahareas [University Park: Pennsylvania State University Press, 1978], p. 3). The number seems to me to be both higher and less precise: Juan Ruiz appears to promise a single lyric on three or four occasions, "viessos" (one poem?) once, and "cantigas" or "cantares" on six occasions. If we assume that each of these six plurals

whether the lyrics were included in the Archpriest's original manuscript: Willis, for instance, suggests that as they were not essential to the story line, they could be supplied from a large memorized stock by the performer (pp. xlii-xliii). Most critics, however, believe that the lyrics (or some of them) were originally included, but were suppressed by copyists who thought them frivolous or (if they were in Galician-Portuguese) incomprehensible, or, more persuasively, that these were the lyrics with musical notation and that a space was left in the archetype for a specialized music scribe to insert them.[17]

If the apparently missing poems were in Juan Ruiz's original manuscript and were omitted by copyists (whether of the archetype or of later manuscripts), then he must be taken with absolute seriousness when he says that he aims to set an example of poetic craft. It is necessary in that case to consider the state of cultured lyric poetry in Castile in the late 1320's and 1330's. There is little doubt that the traditional oral lyric, chiefly in the form of *villancicos*, existed long before it was committed to writing in the fifteenth century. Yet while Castilian was the natural vehicle for the oral lyric, the epic, the verse romance, and hagiographic, didactic, and devotional poems, there seems to have been no tradition of a cultured lyric in the Castilian language. The natural vehicle for such lyric was Galician-Portuguese. This is not merely a matter of infer-

---

represents the minimum of two lyrics, and that "viessos" refers to a single poem, these references give a total of at least sixteen or seventeen lyrics; no maximum can be deduced. The lyrics mentioned but not explicitly promised increase the number greatly, even if we do not take literally "non cabrién en diez pliegos" (1514d).

[17] An analogous process appears to have led to the omission of miniatures (*estorias*) from the extant manuscripts of the *Conde Lucanor*; this is the explanation of the words "Et la estoria deste exiemplo es ésta que se sigue" at the end of each *exemplum*, as several editors point out. G. B. Gybbon-Monypenny notes that in three cases (stanzas 80, 1021, and 1507) the reference to lyrics which are missing from the text occurs in both manuscript traditions of the *Libro* ("Estado actual de los estudios sobre el *Libro de buen amor*," *Anuario de Estudios Medievales*, 3 [1966], 575-609, at p. 597n) The problem thus goes back to the archetype. See also Gybbon-Monypenny, "Autobiography in the *Libro de buen amor* in the Light of Some Literary Comparisons," *BHS*, 34 (1957), 63-78, at pp. 76-77.

ence from the extreme scarcity of surviving texts (or even references to lost ones), though such an inference seems to me to be
wholly reasonable. We have, as is well known, the direct testimony
of the Marqués de Santillana, writing in the late 1440's:

> que non ha mucho tiempo qualesquier dezidores o trovadores
> destas partes, agora fuessen castellanos, andaluçes o de la
> Estremadura, todas sus obras componían en lengua gallega o
> portuguesa.[18]

Lyrical tone can certainly be found in some poems written in Castilian in the thirteenth century (for example, Berceo's *Loores de Nuestra
Señora*, or some sections of the *Libro de Alexandre*), but when we look
for cultured poems in Castilian which have the formal qualities of
lyric, we find very few, and even those are of questionable date.
There is a love poem generally attributed to Alfonso el Sabio, and
there are the lyrics of the *Historia troyana polimétrica*, but it is not
entirely certain that the former is by Alfonso X rather than
Alfonso XI, and Menéndez Pidal's date of circa 1270 for the latter
may be too early by half a century or more. Yet even if we accept
these as thirteenth-century poems, and assume that some others
of that period have been lost, there is still nothing like a settled
tradition of writing lyrics in Castilian—nothing comparable to the
contemporary tradition in Galician-Portuguese, or to the second
generation of poets represented in the *Cancionero de Baena*. It is clear
to us that the Galician-Portuguese courtly lyric was near the end
of its dominance when Juan Ruiz began to write, but it can hardly
have been clear to him. King Dinis died only five years before the
first version of the *Libro de Buen Amor*, and probably some years
after the composition of the Archpriest's earliest lyrics. Pedro,
Conde de Barcelos, poet, and compiler of a major *cancioneiro*, probably outlived the Archpriest by a few years.

In these circumstances, I think it reasonable to conclude that
the lesson in poetry which Juan Ruiz wished to teach his compatri-

---

[18] *Letter of the Marquis of Santillana to Don Peter, Constable of Portugal*, ed.
Antonio R. Pastor and Edgar Prestage (Oxford: Clarendon, 1927), p. 77.
See also Giuseppe Tavani, "Il problema della poesia lirica nel Duecento
letterario ispanico," in his *Poesia del Duecento nella Penisola iberica: problemi
della lirica galego-portoghese*, Officina Romanica, 12 (Roma: Ateneo, 1969),
pp. 9-50.

ots was probably the composition in Castilian of a wide range of cultured lyrics, both secular and religious. A few years ago I compared such an ambition with Santillana's determination to transplant Italian meters into Castilian, and suggested that it was equally unsuccessful.[19] I am now inclined to think that, if Juan Ruiz's aim really was to establish a Castilian tradition in the cultured lyric, a more satisfactory analogue would be Alfonso el Sabio's determination to make Castilian rather than Latin the natural language for historical, legal, and scientific prose. There is an obvious difference: Alfonso was backed by all the resources of his kingdom, but Juan Ruiz was alone. Such an ambition would therefore be extraordinarily presumptuous, but Juan Ruiz is an extraordinary poet. Moreover, I am no longer certain that, if he did attempt to create a Castilian cultured lyric, the attempt was unsuccessful. It is true that such a tradition did not take root until some forty years later, but it is now clear that when the early *Baena* poets were writing, the *Libro de Buen Amor* was widely diffused and its influence strong.[20] It is, of course, entirely possible to adduce reasons for the change from Galician to Castilian that have nothing to do with Juan Ruiz (just as Garcilaso's successful introduction of Italian meters seems to be wholly unconnected with Santillana's experiments). It would, however, be unwise to exclude the possibility that the example set by the *Libro de Buen Amor* was a contributory factor in the triumph of Castilian as a language for cultured lyric.

The preceding observations are based on the assumption that the apparently missing lyrics were at one time present in the *Libro*. If they were not, then the Archpriest is joking, he is misleading us,

---

[19] "Lyric Traditions in Non-Lyrical Genres," in *Studies in Honor of Lloyd A. Kasten* (Madison. Hispanic Seminary of Medieval Studies, 1975), pp. 39-52, at p. 48.

[20] Lucius G. Moffatt, "The Evidence of Early Mentions of the Arch-priest of Hita or of his Work," *MLN*, 75 (1960), 33-44. For recent evidence of the *Libro*'s influence even later, in the fifteenth century, see Samuel G. Armistead, "An Unnoticed Fifteenth-Century Citation of the *Libro de buen amor*," *HR*, 41 (1973), 88-91, and "Two Further Citations of the *Libro de buen amor* in Lope García de Salazar's *Bienandanzas y fortunas*," *La Corónica*, 5 (1976-77), 75-77; Charles B. Faulhaber, "The Date of Stanzas 553 and 1450 of the *Libro de buen amor* in MS 9589 of the Biblioteca Nacional, Madrid," *RPh*, 28 (1974-75), 31-34.

about his art and his literary ambition as well as everything else. Instead of a vastly presumptuous literary innovator, we have, on this alternative hypothesis, an obsessive joker and parodist. It is even possible that we have both at once. It is also possible that, even if Juan Ruiz's manifesto was a joke, the example of his lyrics had its effect a couple of generations later. That would be an irony unintended by the poet but in keeping with his deeply ironical work.

I have raised more questions than I can answer. The only things of which I am reasonably sure are that Juan Ruiz's interest in literary matters deserves more attention, and that the problem of the missing lyrics is central to any consideration of his artistic aims and of the seriousness with which he approaches them.[21]

WESTFIELD COLLEGE (UNIVERSITY OF LONDON)

AND PRINCETON UNIVERSITY

---

[21] A first version of this article was read in the special session on the *Libro de Buen Amor* at the MLA meeting in December 1979. I am very grateful to Gerald Gybbon-Monypenny, David Hook, and Julian Weiss for their comments on a second draft. They have saved me from a number of errors and oversights, but they have, of course, no responsibility for the opinions I express. Julian Weiss' discovery of important Provençal analogues for a number of Juan Ruiz's statements will, I hope, soon be published.

# El Cantar a la Ventura
# en el *Libro de Buen Amor*

MARGHERITA MORREALE

 NTRE LOS CANTARES AGREGADOS al final del *Libro* del Arcipreste de Hita en la parte representada exclusivamente por el MS de Salamanca (S) hay uno que empieza en la estrofa 1685, sin sobresrito, por lo que hasta época relativamente reciente se leía junto con la estrofa que precede, o sea con el fragmento, tal vez el estribillo, de una canción mariana, como si se tratara de una sola composición. Así en la edición de J. Cejador,[1] y aun en la fundamental monografía de F. Lecoy.[2] Solo desde que R. Menéndez Pidal señaló la diferencia formal y temática entre las dos composiciones,[3] el poema que aquí nos interesa ha sido deslindado; aparece con el sobrescrito "Cantiga contra Ventura" en la edición de J. Corominas,[4] y en las posteriores.

[1] Clásicos Castellanos, Nº 17 (Madrid, 1913; las ediciones llegan hasta 1970).

[2] Cf. *Recherches sur le Libro de buen amor* (Paris, 1938, reimpr. Farnborough, Hants, 1974).

[3] *Poesía juglaresca y juglares* (Madrid, 1957), p. 273, donde señala la posible pérdida de una hoja del MS.

[4] Madrid, 1967, p. 623. El título va entre corchetes, en letras mayúsculas.

El texto así marcado, no ha sido objeto, por lo que nos consta, de atención específica por parte de los estudiosos. El no habérsele encontrado un modelo directo, como sería la *Consultatio Sacerdotum* con respecto de los pormenorizados estudios que Lecoy y otros hacen de las fuentes. El no reconocerse el de la fortuna como un tema favorito de los *clerici vagantes* explica que apenas se le mencione en las páginas que Menéndez Pidal y otros han dedicado al "Arcipreste de Hita poeta goliárdico."[5] Su exigua extensión, por otra parte, y su univocidad, le sustraen al interés de los que analizan el *Libro* en su estructura y en sus varios "niveles de lectura."

En las menciones esporádicas lo vemos alienado con los otros pasajes en que los partidarios de identificar el *yo* del protagonista con el del autor ven una alusión autobiográfica. Una consideración un poco más extensa empareja a la Fortuna, por intermedio de la iconografía, con el Amor.[6] También se menciona a nuestro poeta en los estudios sobre el tema, o temas afines, como el del destino.[7] Mucho más interés ha suscitado el juicio del Arcipreste de Hita sobre la astrología, que el poeta agrega al apólogo del rey Alcárez (123-165), sobre cuya trascendencia o falta de trascendencia ideológica el Cantar a la Ventura echa alguna luz, según luego veremos.

La preeminencia de la invectiva en la poesía medieval latina sobre la Fortuna[8] posiblemente haya influido en el título que se le

---

[5] Véase, entre los más recientes, A. N. Zahareas, *The Art of Juan Ruiz, Archpriest of Hita* (Madrid, 1965), pp. 99-105.

[6] Cf. A. C. de Ferraresi, *De amor y poesía en la España medieval. Prólogo a Juan Ruiz* (México: El Colegio de México, 1976), p. 186 ss.

[7] El reciente ensayo de E. Guascón Vera, "Una nota sobre la fortuna en la vida y en las obras de Don Pedro, Condestable de Portugal," *Rev. de Archivos, Bibliotecas y Museos* 3 (1977), 531-44, me exime de indicar aquí la bibliografía sobre el tema de la Fortuna. Cabría agregar, para la iconografía, E. Kirschenbaum et al., *Lexikon des christlichen Ikonographie* (Roma-Friburgo, 1968-76), vol. II, col. 54 y ss., y sobre la rueda, que también entraba en otros temas, como el del tiempo y el de la justicia, pero que, en la Baja Edad Media, suele referirse a la Fortuna, vol. III, 492-94. Ensanchando la mirada a horizontes más amplios recordamos también la monografía de O. Rothe, *Studien zum Estrif de Fortuna et Vertu* (Berna, 1970), con amplia bibliografía (pp. 596-621).

[8] Cf. J. de Ghellinck, *Essor de la littérature latine au XIIe siècle* (2ª ed., París, 1955), p. 448 y los textos en A. Hilka, O. Schumann, *Carmina Burana* (Heidelberg, 1930), nn. 16-18.

ha dado, y que no cuadra a su conjunto, ya que el poeta, tras unos primeros versos quejumbrosos y recriminatorios, se dirige a la Ventura en son de súplica: ésta podía actuar para mal o para bien, para levantar o derribar, según el consabido símbolo de la rueda.

EL TEXTO. Éste consta de cinco estrofas de seis versos según el esquema *a a b a a b* (las rimas varían en cada estrofa). De los errores, cuya presencia puede suponerse de antemano en los textos líricos del *Libro*, dos son seguros; por contravenir a la rima el de "e mi grand tribulación" (1688c), donde los editores restablecen *tribulança*, más desusado a fines del siglo XIV; por haplología, el de *gasado* (1679f) por *gasajado* (Joset lee *gasajo*, pero sin explicar la "técnica" del error).

Por lo demás, nuestra lectura dependería de si consideramos el poemita anisosilábico, con Chiarini, o compuesto de estrofas de tres hexasílabos + tres heptasílabos, con Corominas, cuya reconstrucción siguen en parte R. Willis y J. Joset en sus enmiendas para salvar el ritmo, muy marcado, en la tradición goliárdica, y que ha llevado, por ejemplo, a Lecoy a asignar el poemita a la poesía rítmica o "acentual."[9]

La lectura de Corominas hace hincapié en las licencias poéticas: el hiato, no solo el etimológico normal en el interior de los lexemas (*crüel* 1685b, *desëo* 1686e), o restableciendo el sintagma (*buena ëstança* 1688f), sino entre vocablos de vocales no solo distintas (*coita ëstraña* 1686c, *damë alegría* 1687e, *coita ë* 1688b), + *më* + *ayudares* 1688e), sino iguales (*por qué ëres* 1685d, *Non sé ëscrevir* 1686a), y la sinalefa (*fasta oy* 1687a, *gasajadọ e* 1687f); atañe a la morfología con el restablecimiento de la forma apocopada del pronombre personal átono en "E si túm" (1688a) y de la forma plena en el imperativo *faze* (1687d); con la introducción de la forma *mucho*: "en mucho pocos días" (1689e) por "en muy pocos días"; interviene en la sintaxis, con la supresión de la preposición ante el infinitivo en "mis penas crecer" (1689c) tras *desviarse*; y en el léxico: "tener porfía" (1687b) por "mantener porfía"; afecta a éste, lindando con la estructura del idioma, en "e tan falsa vezina" (1685f) (por lo que veremos luego de *falso*), en "bien me ayudares (1688e), en cuanto al pronombre *me*,

---

[9] Cf. Lecoy, p. 91; entre los editores Corominas adopta sustancialmente los estudios de Hanssen; Chiarini, los de P. le Gentil.

intercalado, restablece el uso del verbo con complemento de término (normalmente *ayudar* lo lleva si no se emplea como neutro). Atañe al contenido con *podrían* 1689d, por *podrán* y "ya estas coitas mías" (1689c) por "ya las coitas mías." y en *tornar* "tribulança / en grand goço" (1688cd; Joset: "buen goço").

No todas estas enmiendas son justificadas. La que acabamos de señalar es innecessaria ya que bastaría el hiato en *coitas* para hacer hexasílabo el verso. El condicional *podrían* resta eficacia a la expresión en un lugar importante y conclusivo del poema. Hay desajuste rítmico en 1687d "faze ya cortesía" (*faz* es, además, la forma normal del imperativo en el *Libro*) y 1689e "en mucho pocos días" (aunque aquí no obstan razones morfológicas; cf. "escolar só mucho rudo" 1135a); desajuste sintáctico tras *desviar* (1689c), que más bien acusa vacilación entre uso reflexivo y neutro que en el uso con o sin preposición ante infinitivo[10]; desajuste semántico en 1685f ya que *falso* negando las cualidades que le son propias a *vezino*,[11] no puede ir modificado con *tan*. *Tener porfía* 1687b relega *mantener porfía* entre las intervenciones de *S*, aquí posible, pero no necesaria;[12] "si bien me ayudares" 1688e tiene todos los visos de ser una *lectio facilior*, por la consabida propensión de los copistas a restablecer formas más corrientes; además, en este caso tampoco el copista introduciría el pronombre *me* si ya había interpolado *mi* ante "gran tribulança"; ésta y no *mi tribulança*, ha de conservarse ha de conservarse porque, si bien en la lengua medieval el tipo *tornar X en Y* admitía modificación ponderativa del primer miembro, lo corriente era que se magnificase la necesidad del cambio por la ponderación del primero.

---

[10] Alternan más bien la forma reflexiva y la neutra; cf., por ejemplo, en *General Estoria* 4ª, donde *desviar* aparece con el sentido de 'apartarse': "que los sabios desvíen en sos estorias de no l llamar todos un nombre" Vat. lat. Urb. 539, 200r46.

[11] *Falso* se opone a *fiel*; el *falso malo* es el hipócrita (y por antonomasia, 'el diablo'), por ejemplo, en el *Arcipreste de Talavera*: "E comiença el falso malo por vía de bienfazer e en servicio de Dios," 159.3. En cuanto a *vezino* no estaría de más recordar que en castellano arcaico correspondía también el concepto de 'prójimo'.

[12] *Traer porfía* es la forma que puedo documentar como perífrasis verbal de *porfiar*, por ejemplo, en *General Estoria* 4ª, 203r46. *Mantener porfía*, a su vez, distribuye el sema 'perseverancia, obstinación' entre el verbo y el sustantivo.

Además en nuestro texto es la serie de los vocablos del campo semántico de la aflicción (o sea del estado) que aquí aparece representado tan abundantemente (cf. *coita* 1686c, 1688b, pl. 1689d, *tribulança* 1688c, *pesar* pl. 1688b, *pena* pl. 1689c, y, en caso oblicuo de complemento circunstancial, *tormenta* 1686f, ambiguo en cuanto al número,[13] amén del verbo *maltraher* 1687c, empleado aquí en la acepción de 'afligir'[14]), y no la representada en el polo opuesto por *alegría* 1687e, *gasajado* 1687f, *plazer* 1687f., *gozo* 1688d, la que lleva modificación de tipo ponderativo: *grand* 1688c, *tamaño* 1686f y también *estraño* 1686e (que más que un contenido propio indica que el nombre que modifica representa en sumo grado su contenido[15]). Advertimos también de paso, aunque ello no concierne al restablecimiento del metro, que de ningún modo puede enmendarse "con deseo" que también pertenece, con el afín *deseoso*, al vocabulario de la *coita* o aflicción,[16] en "non deseo," según sugiere Corominas en el comentario (lo que, además, destruiría la disposición paralelística repetitiva a que aludíamos antes).

Aun reconociendo la legitimidad de ciertos recursos fonéticos, disentimos, por las razones que acabamos de indicar, del restablecimiento de una secuencia regular de hexasílabos + heptasílabos, obligando la letra a doblegarse a un artificio que nos parece ajeno al poemilla (también las rimas, comprendiendo éstas el diptongo y dos

---

[13] En el siglo anterior, por ejemplo, en el romanceamiento bíblico contenido en el MS Esc. 1.l.6, hallo *tormenta* tanto por *tormentum* Sab. 2:19, 3:1, como por *tormenta* ib. 3:4, amén de *tormentas* 6:7, 11:10, 16:1 y *mucha tormenta* 12:23. Por lo demás, también *coita*, singular en 1686c, se alinea con *pesares* en 1688b.

[14] En los romanceamientos bíblicos *maltraer* sirve para traducir toda una gama de vocablos que expresan vejación tanto física como moral (así en el citado, cf. Sab. 18:22 *vexare*, Ecli. 3:14 *contristare*, 4:2 *exasperare*), amén de tener el sentido de 'reprender' (cf. ib. Ecli. 31:41 *arguere*).

[15] También tiene este sentido 'superlativo' cuando no modifica un lexema autosuficiente, sino un vocablo relativo, como *manera*, o la oración entera. En 222b *estraño* describe la manera de *arrastrar* o *enforcar* a los ladrones; en 621a, la ira de los señores; en 1722c, la crueldad de las reses para con el león.

[16] Cf. 1491a, donde leemos: "sodes monjas guardadas, deseosas, lozanas"; allí se ha explicado *deseoso* en el sentido de 'pobre, desgraciado'.

de las terminaciones del infinitivo, son de las más corrientes)[17].
La irregularidad en el cómputo de las sílabas no nos obliga a
aceptar, por otra parte, "e mi grand tribulança" (1688c); según ya
sugeríamos, el adjetivo posesivo *mi* tiene todos los visos de haber
sido introducido por el copista contra el ritmo. Tampoco leemos
con Chiarini, Corominas, Joset: "Fasta oy, todavía" (1687a), sino
"Fasta oy todavía" sin pausa, como lo exige el ritmo y la naturaleza
del sintagma.

Ni la sintaxis ni los recursos retóricos presentan problemas particulares, propios de la composición lírica. Para obedecer, pues al
ritmo y dar resalte a la rima, en un poema fuertemente marcado
por los apoyos acentuales, hacemos coincidir, siempre que sea posible, la pausa versal con la sintáctica: leemos a la manera tradicional
en 1685e "contra mí tan dañosa," a pesar de que *contra* era más
corriente con el adjetivo *sañosa* del verso anterior.[18] (El empezar el
verso con la preposición *contra* puede haber sido sugerido por el
adjetivo *contrario*, tan frecuente en relación con la ventura; cf. "a
muchos es contraria [la ventura]" 693b.) Ponemos una coma entre
los versos 1686ab y 1689ab (nuestros predecesores leen los versos
seguidos o con pausa solo uno de los dos pasajes), para marcar más
bien la repetición de la misma idea que el conjunto de conceptos
complementarios (*dezir* y *escribir* estaban más cerca uno de otro que
hoy). También hacemos una pausa, como de encabalgamiento
menor, entre 1685e y f.

Quedan, no obstante, los encabalgamientos más o menos fuertes de 1687bc, 1688ab (éste, amortiguado por la unión estrecha
entre los elementos léxicos del verso b), 1688cd, y 1689bc, que tal
vez se deban a contaminación con los versos largos de cuaderna vía
a los que Juan Ruiz estaba más acostumbrado, o al hecho de que
esta composición no está más lejos de los otros poemas líricos de lo

---

[17] Según Chiarini, *-ía* está representado en 113 estrofas, *-ir* en 33,
amén de *-año*, *-iño* en 30 y 20 respectivamente; *-er* falta en el recuento.

[18] *Dañoso* (aparte el hecho de encontrarse en el *Libro* referido tanto a
seres animados como a seres inanimados, mientras que el español actual
usa *dañoso* o más frecuentemente *dañino* de las cosas; de las personas se
dice que "hacen daño"), se construye normalmente con *a*; en 311e tenemos una referencia al león orgulloso, "que fue a todas bestias cruel e
muy dañoso"; ser *sañoso* (1685d) es perífrasis por *ensañarse*.

que haría suponer la comparación con el poemita goliárdico "O fortuna / sicut luna,"[19] con que a primera vista lo asemejaríamos, en cuanto al ritmo.

Sugerimos, pues, esta lectura:

1685    ¡Ventura astrosa,
crüel, enojosa,
captiva, mezquina,
por qué ëres sañosa,
contra mí tan dañosa
e falsa vezina?

1686    Non sé ëscrevir,
nin puedo dezir
la coïta estraña
que me fazes sofrir,
con desëo bevir
en tormenta tamaña.

1687    Fasta hoy todavía
mantoviste porfía
en me maltraher:
faz ya cortesía
e dame alegría
gasajado e plazer.

1688    E si tú m tirares
coïta e pasares,
e grand tribulança
en gozo tornares
e bien ayudares
farás buenestança,

1689    mas si tú porfías,
e non te desvías
de mis penas crecer,
ya las coïtas mías
en muy pocos días
podrán fenecer.

APOSTILLAS A LA LETRA. En primer lugar hemos de advertir que leemos *ventura astrosa* con el adjetivo como predicativo, aunque no vaya precedido de pausa ( o sea, leemos como en el *Arcipreste de*

---

[19] Cf. A. Hilka, S. Schumann, *Carmina Burana*, n. 17. versos 4-20.

*Talavera*: "Doña vil, suzia, vellaca..."[20]); del otro modo *(v)entura astrosa* se opondría a *buena ventura* (conmutable con *ventura*; compárense 697c y 988d), prejuzgando la bivalencia a la que aludíamos arriba.

Dando por descontado que Juan Ruiz se inscribe en una tradición literaria en la que el tema de la Fortuna estaba plenamente desarrollado, no podemos menos que notar que, a diferencia de su antecesor, el anónimo poeta del *Libro de Alexandre*,[21] y de otros autores expresamente didácticos,[22] no se refiere a la *Fortuna* sino a *(a)ventura*. En el resto de la obra se habla de ésta, buena o mala, como de un don de Dios ("a quien da Dios ventura e non la quier tomar..." 1391a) y también se apropia al individuo, según el uso romance: "quiso m Dios bien guiar e la ventura mía" (687d) (véase también en contextos negativos, en los que significativamente no entra la mención de Dios: "pensando en mi ventura sañudo e..." (181b), y "de tal ventura seo / que nunca puedo acabar lo medio que deseo" 180ab). Sería legítimo, por tanto, preguntarnos si, junto a una *Ventura* plenamente personificada (y vernácula solo en el nombre) del conjunto del poemita no afloran en la primera estrofa rasgos de la *ventura* como vivencia del poeta.

Pueden servir de indicio los adjetivos que se alinean junto a

---

[20] Cf. ed. M. de Riquer (Barcelona: Ediciones bibliófilas, 1949), p. 133.18.

[21] Véase especialmente la estrofa 877 (traducción de la *Alexandreis* de Gautier de Chatillon, IX 380), donde *Fortuna* aparece precedida de *doña*, y no falta el símbolo de la rueda; cf. I. Michael, *The Treatment of Classical Material in the "Libro de Alexandre*," (Manchester, 1970), pp. 94-273. También aparece en el *Poema de Fernán González*, estrofa 439, y en el *Libro del Caballero Zifar* (por ejemplo, en el Prólogo).

[22] Cf., por ejemplo, *Buenos proverbios*, ed. H. Knust (Tübingen, 1879), 29.20, y el *Libro de los exemplos por abc*, ed. J. E. Keller (Madrid: CSIC, 1961), p. 56. En otros muchos escritos aparece el término patrimonial *ventura*, el cual, sin embargo, no es incompatible con la personificación, y especialmente con el símbolo de la rueda, que tal vez se oculta tras el verso 692c de Juan Ruiz (aunque en ello puede haber confluencia de imágenes bíblicas); cf., entre otros, Berceo, *Sacrificio de la Misa*, 221b; luego la *Celestina* "yo estava quedo en título de alegre, si mi ventura quisiera tener quedos los ondosos vientos de mi perdición. ¡Oh fortuna, quánto e por quántas partes me has combatido!" ed. J. Cejador (Madrid, 1954), vol. II, p. 112.

(V)entura, por su solidaridad con uno u otro concepto. Modifican sin dejar lugar a duda la personificación sañosa d, dañoso e y falso vezino f, referidos, además, a la conducta, en función propiamente predicativa. Pueden predicarse tanto de la personificación como de la ventura-vivencia, astroso, como sinónimo tanto de malo como de feo,[23] cruel,[24] y enojoso;[25] y, por fin, tal vez cuadren mejor a la vivencia captivo[26] y mesquino.[27]

---

[23] Podríamos sentirnos tentados a atribuir a astroso un valor etimológico que cuadraría a la Ventura, voluble y caprichosa, y más en vista de la cercanía en los textos latinos y vernáculos entre fortuna y luna (v.s. n. 19); pero esto pudo darse a nivel de asociación más o menos consciente porque ni el uso contemporáneo ni el del propio Juan Ruiz (cf. 402c "al más astroso lobo, al enatío...''), nos permite desviarnos de las acepciones corrientes de 'feo', si Juan Ruiz describe el aspecto exterior (para las cualidades negativas, incluso físicas, que se le atribuyen a la Fortuna; cf. H. R. Patch, The Goddess Fortuna in Medieval Literature [Londres, 1967], p. 38), o de 'desgraciado', si se le quiere oponer, según decíamos arriba, a la "buena ventura" (cf. Berceo, SDom. 64d: "ca trae esta vida un astroso fallago"). También malfadado se deriva de malfado (empleado por Juan Ruiz en una maldición, estrofa 1625, que parece sacada del lenguaje coloquial), sin haber pasado por la conciencia explícita del concepto de hado. Por lo demás, las fronteras no están bien deslindadas. Sobre el desarrollo en las lenguas vernáculas de vocablos pertenecientes a la creencia en el hado y las estrellas, cf. M. Bambeck, Lateinromanische Wortstudien (Wiesbaden, s.v.

[24] Cruel, en los romanceamientos bíblicos medievales, es la traducción corriente de impius; cf., por ejemplo, Esc. 1.1.6, Ecli. 37:13.

[25] Enojo corresponde al latín eclesiástico tædium y significa 'molestia'; Juan Ruiz aplica el adjetivo a sí mismo, en el sentido correspondiente, cuando escribe: "e porque enojoso non vos querría ser." (1301c)

[26] Sobre captivo, pronunciado ca(v)tivo, cf. DCELC, y la ejempificación de M. R. Lida en RFH IV (1942), 152-54; su sentido aquí parece ser el de 'miserable', 'infeliz', que el autor podía aplicar a su propia suerte más bien que a la poderosa Ventura; cf. 1498a: "¿Do te esconderás, cativa?" v.q. 512c "Non a siervo cativo que l dinero non le aforre." Más sobre el término en R. Haerle, Captivos-Cattivo-Chétif. Zur Einwirkung des Christentums auf die Terminologie der Moralbegriffe (Berna, 1956).

[27] Me(z)quino, del ar. miskin, está documentado ya en las glosas emilianenses con el sentido de 'pobre': "qui pauberibus reddet: qui dat a los misquinos" 48; v.q. Elena y María, donde designa 'mendigo' (cf. RFE I [1916], 62), y la Disputa entre el alma y el cuerpo, donde se contrapone a rico: "que tú fueste tan rico, agora eres mesquino" v. 26; pero allí mismo

LA ELABORACIÓN. Los rasgos retóricos del poemita son de los más elementales, tanto en lo que se refiere a la forma como al contenido : apóstrofe, interrogación, acumulación de adjetivos, fórmula para ponderar declarando la propia incapacidad. La variedad que ya interviene en esta parte (nótese la unión de elementos desiguales *tan dañoso, falso vezino* por medio de conjunción copulativa, la alternancia entre la unión copulativa y la asindética en 1686ad y ef, con miembro creciente en el último verso), se manifiesta también en la parte narrativa, donde a una estrofa dividida por igual en dos partes siguen, en las estrofas siguientes, dos períodos largos, unidos por una conjunción disyuntiva, pero con distinta distribución, ya que el período hipotético de la estrofa 1689 está dividido por igual, mientras que la de 1688 contiene la apódosis en un solo verso, el final.

Huelga advertir que los versos del poemita han de compararse con los más ágiles de los de cuaderna vía (y aun así se diferencian en su distribución). Sirve de contraste, en cambio, el pasaje didáctico, de tono convencional, que Juan Ruiz dedica a la ventura en las coplas 692-93.[28] Pueden yuxtaponerse asimismo los versos 692b y

---

aparece con el sentido más genérico de 'desgraciado, miserable': "mesquino, malfadado, / tan mal ora fuest nado" v. 25; v.q. Berceo, *SDom.* 64a: "Yo pecador mezquino"; v.q. ib. 51a, 60c. Aún Alonso de Palencia en su *Universal Vocabulario* explica "*infelix* es desdichado y mesquino, que carece de toda buena ventura." p. 212. La acepción de 'miserable, escaso, avariento', que podría cuadrar únicamente a la Ventura personificada, se da desde el siglo XVI; por ejemplo, en el *Lazarillo.*

[28] Para mayor comodidad del lector los transcribimos aquí:

Muchas vezes la ventura, con su fuerza e poder,
a muchos omnes non dexa su propósito fazer:
por esto anda el mundo en levantar e en caer;
Dios e el trabajo grande pueden los fados vencer.

Ayuda la ventura al que bien quiere guiar,
e a muchos es contraria, puédelos malestorvar;
el trabajo e el fado suélense aconpañar,
pero sin trabajo todo esto non puede aprovechar.

Nótese el equilibrio pausado de estos versos de tono didáctico. A *fuerça e poder* (692a), más estáticos, se contraponen en nuestro trozo *porfía*, que aparece en una frase sustantiva verbal *mantener porfía* (1867b), amén del

693b con los versos 1685e y 1697abc, como buen ejemplo de trasvase de la forma impersonal (allí de cuaderna vía) a la personal del poemita lírico.

CONTENIDO. El yo del poetam se manifiesta, ya como narrador-protagonista ("non sé escrevir, / nin puedo dezir" 1686 ab), ya como protagonista sin más ) representado por el pronombre personal en los versos 1685e, 1687 ce, 1688 a, por las *penas* y *coitas* en 1689cd). Observamos que tras la apóstrofe a la (V)entura, con su curva ascendente, se empieza como *ex novo*, con otro exordio dedicado a las *cuitas*, realzadas así como segundo tema del poemita, que queda luego entretejido con el de la Ventura y emerge al primer plano en los versos finales.

La tercera estrofa está distribuida entre una mirada retrospectiva sobre la acción hostil de la Ventura y el ruego de sustituir el mal trato por la cortesía. En las dos últimas se explayan las alternativas que pesan en su balanza (la imagen, sin embargo, no aflora como tal): el poeta quedará librado o sucumbirá; en el *fenecer* de las cuitas está implícito el del sujeto que las padece.[29]

Interpretamos *buenestança* (1688f) como 'equidad'; el sentido de 'obra buena' (Chiarini) puede atribuirse solo si se considera como muy genérico su empleo, y más en cuanto se aplicó también a la acción benévola de la dama.[30] Lo que ello modifica no lo sabemos a ciencia cierta; más seguros estamos de que no se refiere a la prosperidad material (riqueza, honores), objeto de tantos poemas a la Fortuna. Tampoco podemos sumarnos a la tesis del encarcelamiento, aunque se sepa que el tema de la fortuna tuvo bastante difusión como para servir de desahogo en tales circunstancias.[31]

---

verbo *porfiar* (1689a), ambos más dinámicos; los cultismos *propósito* y *contrario* contrastan con el vocabulario patrimonial de nuestro poemita, destacándose, sin embargo, *malestorvar* como afín a *maltraher*.

[29] Ha de entenderse por la metonimia *cuitas* = yo poético, muy del estilo de las canciones de amor cortés, porque de otro modo el acabarse de las mismas sería signo de bonanza, contra el sentido.

[30] Cf. el poeta Macías: "E tú farás buenestança / e mesura," *Cancionero de Baena*, Nº 309, versos 13-14; ed. J. M. Azáceta (Madrid: CSIC, 1966), vol. II, p. 673.

[31] En el IV libro de *Amadís de Gaula* se cuenta como el malhechor Arcalao entretenía su cautiverio leyendo "un libro...de muy buenos

En cuanto al término *cortesía*, introducido también por el verbo concretizador *fazer*, que se halla al centro del poema como fiel de la balanza, lo más obvio sería relacionarlo con otros términos propios del "amor cortés," en particular con la muerte que el pretendiente espera, de no escucharse su petición (cf. Macías "en ti traigo la muerte / si me non vala tu vondat"[32]). Sin embargo no hay razón segura para afirmar que la gracia que el protagonista pide sea de índole amorosa. También la Virgen había de serle "alegre e pagada" (1641d). En cuanto a la propia Ventura, era natural que, después de increparla, el autor se dirigiera a ella en términos de cortesía (de *amistad*).

*Cortesía*, que tantos ríos de tinta ha hecho correr, se manifiesta también en dichos, como el que nos referirá un siglo más tarde el *Arcipreste de Talavera*: "Daño de cada día sufrir non es cortesía," de tono subjetivo y coloquial, más cónsono tal vez con la inmediatez familiar de nuestro poemita, leído *cum grano salis*.

EVALUACIÓN DOCTRINAL EN RELACIÓN CON OTROS VERSOS SOBRE EL TEMA. Volviendo al tema en su conjunto, nos atrevemos a sugerir que al evaluar las ideas sobre la fortuna o los hados, se han proyectado con demasiada facilidad los conceptos y las preocupaciones del siglo XV con sus vicisitudes políticas,[33] religiosas y raciales;[34] y demasiado fácilmente se ha dejado entender que Juan Ruiz tomaría una posición al lado de los "deterministas" en las controversias que atraviesan el siglo XV.[35]

En el nivel léxico y fraseológico en que el poeta mantiene su obra no habrá que buscar expresiones como la de *libre albedrío*; el

---

ejemplos y dotrinas contra las adversidades de fortuna," *BAE* 40, p. 39 (citado por A. Deyermond, *The Petrarchan Sources of La Celestina* (Oxford, 1961).

[32] *Baena*, vol. II, p. 673, versos 28-30.

[33] M. R. Lida, *Juan de Mena, poeta del prerrenacimiento español* (México: Colegio de México, 1950), pp. 20-21.

[34] Cf. S. Gilman, "The 'conversos' and the Fall of Fortune," *Studies in Honor of Américo Castro* (ed. M. J. Bernadete), pp. 127-136.

[35] J. Mendoza Negrillo, *Fortuna y Providencia en la literatura castellana del siglo XV* (Madrid: RAE, 1973).

"esfuerzo individual" que echan de menos A. Zahareas[36] y otros, se llama aquí *uso grande* (793d); "ayuno, e limosna e oración" (149a), la frecuentación de los sacramentos y las obras de misericordia (1579-1605) son los medios que el cristiano ha de utilizar para pertrecharse; pero, sobre todo, queda abierto el espacio para le intervención de Dios (cf. 140bc), cuando los hombres no acudan a los medios ordinarios.

Los versos ya aludidos, "Dios e la mi ventura que me fue guiador" (697c), "quiso m Dios bien guiar e la ventura mía" (687d), aúnan el consabido tópico de *fortuna dux* con la mención de Dios, [37] pero no podemos deducir de ello una postura doctrinal, y ni siquiera la conciencia por parte del autor de elucubraciones abstractas, aun de las más difundidas en la Edad Media, como la que hacía de la Fortuna un agente de la voluntad de Dios, compaginándola con la Providencia (idea avalada por Santo Tomás y que halló en Dante, *Infierno* VII 67-96, su más excelsa expresión poética).

El tema de la Ventura dejaba espacio para unos acentos de protesta que no cabían en el esquema religioso, por lo menos en la religiosidad que se inspira en el Nuevo Testamento. Se explica entonces cómo un motivo de origen docto pudiera confluir con impulsos enraizados en la vida de todo hombre, que se manifiestan también a nivel popular. En el *Arcipreste de Talavera* veremos el tema de la Fortuna en su formulación más literaria, con arrimo a Boccaccio, a la par que la condena de lo que el autor presenta como objeto de creencias—y aun terminologías—populares.[38]

En su *Libro*, Juan Ruiz dedica un pasaje explícito a la Ventura,

---

[36] Cf. su ensayo "The Stars: Worldly Love and Free Will in the *Libro de Buen Amor*," BHS 42 (1965), 85, y la obra ya citada, 188 y ss.

[37] Cf. el uso de *guiar* en 20ac: "¡Oh María / . . . / tú me guía!" (v.q. 1664, 1672).

[38] Cf. "Pues déxate de fablar de planetas e signos, fados e venturas e fortunas," *Talavera*, p. 264.15; "tema a Dios e déxese de fados e fortuna," p. 253.11; "non alegue ninguno ventura, signo, fortuna, fado nin planeta," p. 270.19. Si se objetare que tales palabras se parecen como una gota de agua a las correspondientes de San Agustín, tal vez podríamos recordar el cantarcillo popular: "Una es la rueda de la fortuna," que viene a coincidir, en cuanto a la voz *fortuna* con otro que he oído a los "grecianos" de Italia.

según vimos (cf. las estrofas 692-93 citadas en la nota 28), pero no hay que olvidar que en ellos amplifica su modelo latino, el *Pamphilus de amore*.[39] En el poemita que hemos comentado se dirige a la (V)entura, cuya personificación está aún enraizada en la experiencia individual.

La comparación con las principales composiciones, todas ellas posteriores, que se aducen para ilustrar el tratamiento poético del tema, además de demostrar que las eventuales analogías serán fruto de la utilización independiente de modelos accesibles o difundidos, destaca a Juan Ruiz como extraordinariamente esquivo de los lugares comunes y citas eruditas con que el asunto suele ir envuelto, y le revelan una vez más como caracterizado por la preeminencia del *yo*.

ISTITUTO DI LINGUE E LETTERATURE ROMANZE (PADOVA)

---

[39] Citamos aquí el pasaje para comodidad del lector, los versos 267-72, de la edición de G. Cohen, *La Comédie latine en France au XIIᵉ sîècle* (Paris, 1931), t. II:

Obstitit interdum factis fortuna uirorum
Propositumque suo, non sinit esse loco;
Sic multis nocuit, multos tamen illa beauit;
Viuit in hoc mundo taliter omnis homo.
Prouidet et tribuit deus et labor omnia nobis,
Proficit absque deo nullus in orbe labor.

# El Epílogo del

## *Libro de buen amor*

Nicolás Emilio Álvarez

 L AUTOR DEL *Libro de buen amor* se dirige directamente a su público en las coplas que van de la 1626 hasta la 1634, advirtiéndole que da por terminado su libro y que lo finalizará con cuatro cantares a la Virgen, puesto que ella "es comienço E fyn del bien" conforme a la fe católica que el profesa.[1] Estas nueve coplas marcan el epílogo, per se, del *Libro de buen amor*. La importancia del epílogo estriba en que el poeta se presenta a sí mismo como autor ("ffiz vos pequeno libro" (1631a) para puntualizar las características de su obra. En la copla inicial del epílogo se propone la conclusión inmediata del poema y en la final se data la obra; entre una y otra el autor dedicó cinco coplas a tratar el carácter didáctico-moral de su poema y otras dos coplas a su factu-

---

[1] Utilizo la edición de Manuel Criado de Val y Eric W. Naylor, *Arcipreste de Hita: Libro de buen amor*, edición crítica, 2da. ed. (Madrid: Consejo Superior de Investigaciones Científicas, 1972), p. 551, copla 1626b. Sigo la lectura del MS *S*, de lo contrario se citará la variante. Modernizo levemente la grafía. Prescindo de algunos signos diacríticos y de la puntuación añadida por esta edición, salvo para los puntos; por lo mismo en los casos necesarios mi puntuación seguirá a las comillas de las citas textuales.

ración poética. María Rosa Lida hizo hincapié en la importancia de
la copla final del epílogo (1634) como síntesis del Libro: "Moral,
relato, lírica son, pues, fines que presidieron a la ejecución del Libro
y no partes yuxtapuestas en él."[2] Entiéndase esto así o no, no cabe
duda de que en el epílogo se destacan tres rasgos primordiales: la
intención didáctico-moral, el arte poético y la unidad de la obra.

El didactismo moral está tratado explícitamente en las coplas
1627 y 1628 y en las 1630, 31 y 32. En la primera copla el autor
afirma que la lectura de su libro llevará a un resultado esencial:
"faser a dios seruiçio" (1627d) y a continuación determina cuál ha
de ser dicho servicio: "Desea oyr misas E faser oblaçones/desea dar
a pobres bodigos E rrasiones/faser mucha lymonsna E desir oraçiones (1628abc) y termina repitiendo "dios con esto se sirue" (1628d).
En realidad, el autor ha englobado bajo un sólo concepto los dos
resultados conexos que la "buena propiedad" de su libro ha de pro-
ducir en quien lo lea: Primero, rendir culto a Dios ("oyr misas E
faser oblaçones") y, segundo, hacer obras de caridad ("dar a pobres
. . . lymonsna"), pues, "desir oraçiones" puede pertenecer a una u
otra categoría. Esto es, el autor del *Libro de buen amor* está reprodu-
ciendo en orden cronológico los dos preceptos cardinales del cristianismo, estatuidos por Jesucristo en respuesta a la pregunta de un
fariseo: "Maestro, ¿cuál es el mandamiento más grande de la ley?
Él le dijo: Amarás al Señor, tu Dios, con todo tu corazón, con toda
tu alma y con toda tu mente. Éste es el más grande y el primer
mandamiento. El segundo, semejante a éste, es: Amarás al prójimo
como a ti mismo. De estos dos preceptos penden toda la Ley y los
Profetas" (Mateo 22:36-40).

Se entiende así que el poeta haya cerrado la cuarteta afirmando:
"dios con esto se sirue bien lo vedes varones" (d). Resulta extraña
pues la glosa que de este verso hizo un editor contemporáneo:
"Que J. Ruiz creía en las enseñanzas que predicaba no hay que
ponerlo en duda. Pero sería preciso ponerse anteojeras para no ver
que en este verso se está riendo."[3] Asimismo, los versos 1627bc

---

[2] María Rosa Lida, "Notas para la interpretación, influencia, fuentes
y texto del *Libro de buen amor*," en *Juan Ruiz: Selección del Libro de buen amor y
estudios críticos* (Buenos Aires: Eudeba, 1973), p. 153.

[3] *Juan Ruiz: Libro de buen amor*, edición crítica de Joan Corominas
(Madrid: Gredos, 1967), p. 600, glosa 1628d.

("que si lo oye alguno que tenga muger fea / o sy muger lo oye que
su marido vil sea") han hecho pensar en una intención paródica,
ambigua o irreverente del autor.[4] No dudamos que estos versos
ponen de manifiesto la vis humorística que está presente en la
obra, mas no creemos que desdicen o subvierten la doctrina teoló-
gica expresada en la copla 1628. Lo que el autor afirma en tales
versos, con la gracia y el chiste acostumbrados, es que en el caso de
desavenencias matrimoniales la lectura de su libro llevará a los cón-
yuges al amor de Dios.

La copla 1630 despliega el nombre del libro de forma inatacable.
Primero, el autor consigna el tema de la obra: "Pues es de buen
amor" (1630a). Luego, la titula conforme al tema: "non desminta-
des su nonbre" (1630b). Y, por último, reitera el título: "ca non ha
grado nin graçia buen amor el conplado" (1630d, *T*). Podrá obje-
tarse que en esta copla el concepto de "buen amor" no tiene un
significado inequívoco dado los varios significados de *"amor carnal*
(courtly love), *amor natural* (charity) and *amor celestial* 'que es el de
dios'" que Brian Dutton la ha trazado a dicho sintagma a lo largo
de la obra[5] y su conclusión de que "This last occurrence of the
term amounts to a superb *concepto* . . . implying each and every one
of the meanings the term *buen amor* could have" (p. 119). Creemos,
sin embargo, que el sintagma "buen amor" está inequívocamente
determinado en el epílogo por el propio autor al declarar que la
"buena propiedad" de su libro estriba en propiciar el amor de Dios
y al manifestar sucesivamente, como veremos, que es un libro
moralizante de acuerdo con la doctrina católica que él profesa ("tal

---

[4] Véase Corominas, ed. cit., glosa 1628d; A. D. Deyermond, "Some
Aspects of Parody in the *Libro de buen amor*," en *'Libro de buen amor' Studies*,
ed. G. B. Gybbon-Monypenny (Londres: Támesis, 1970), p. 73; Anthony
N. Zahareas, *The Art of Juan Ruiz, Archpriest of Hita* (Madrid: Estudios de
Literatura Española, 1965), p. 40-42. No vemos por qué ha de entenderse
"vil" (1627c) como "impotente" (V. Corominas, ed. cit., p. 528, 1627bc) a
la luz, por ejemplo, de su significado en los versos 463d, 1365c y 1690c.
Ver Margarita Morreale, "Más apuntes para un comentario literal del
'Libro de buen amor' con otras observaciones al margen de la reciente
edición de G. Chiarini," *BRAE* 47:432-33; *Arcipreste de Hita: Libro de buen
amor*, ed. Jacques Joset (Madrid: Espasa-Calpe, 1974), II, 273, glosa
1627bcd;

[5] Brian Dutton, "'Buen Amor', Its Meaning and Uses in Some Medieval Texts," en *LBAS*, ob. cit., p. 118.

es mi fe", 1626b). *Buen amor* es, según se define en el epílogo, libro de amor divino y de amor a nuestros semejantes, por lo cual el poeta desea que no se le desmienta o niegue su nombre por el chico breviario de burlas que contiene, y que en ningún momento se le entregue al mercadeo. (1630c).

La copla 1631 se inicia con una oposición ideológica y estilística fundamental: "ffiz vos pequeno libro de texto mas la glosa/non creo que es chica ante es byen grad prosa" (ab). Si omitimos varios pasos intermedios para abreviar, la oposición básica nos viene dada por texto/glosa. Según Spitzer: "Hay, pues, que explicar la referencia tanto de María de Francia como del Arcipreste de Hita al 'texto' que ha de ir acompañado de la 'glosa', por influjo de la exégesis bíblica."[6] Dentro de ese contexto teológico didáctico podrá entenderse el significado de la oposición; esto es, el *Buen amor* es breve por su doctrina explícita, mas su exégesis dará lugar a una extensa glosa doctrinal dado el sentido más profundo de cada situación poética (1631c). Tal entendimiento de la oposición anterior lo ha impuesto el mismo autor al afirmar que su libro "De la santidat mucha es byen grand lyçionario" (1632a) y añadiendo, para disipar cualquier duda, que "mas de juego E de burla es chico breuiario" (1632b). Por último, el autor añade en la copla final del epílogo que compuso el libro debido a los males que les ocasionan hombres y mujeres a "otras" (Ms. *S*) mujeres mediante el engaño (1634c). En suma, el autor dedica 22 versos de los 45 del epílogo a exponer la clave didáctico-moral dominante del poema.

El aspecto artístico de la obra se precisa en las coplas 1629 y 1633. El poeta exhorta en el verso 1629c a que su libro circule libremente y aprueba que lo sometan a revisión, pero solamente quien "bien trobar sopiere" (1629a) y "quien podiere" (1629d). Se dirige entonces cortésmente a sus lectores u oyentes en la copla siguiente utilizando el topos de *captatio benevolentiae*: "Señores he vos seruido con poca sabidoria" (1633a) y les dice que les habló "en jugleria" con la finalidad de darles esparcimiento y que por ello lo retribuyan rezando por él un Padrenuestro y un Ave María. Menéndez Pidal citó la copla 1629 y los versos 1626cd como prueba de que "El libro queda abierto para que todo el mundo quite y

---

6 Leo Spitzer, "En torno al arte del Arcipreste de Hita," en *Lingüística e Historia Literaria*, 2da. ed. (Madrid: Gredos, 1968), p. 98.

ponga en él las cosas que le dé le gana, como si fuera de todos."[7] En nuestra opinión, los sintagmas "bien trobar sopiere" y "quien podiere" le imponen serias limitaciones al juicio de Menéndez Pidal y nos hacen pensar que más que tratarse de una invitación a modificar el poema, tal parece que el poeta estuviera desanimando dicha participación. Y si bien declara: "E con tanto fare/punto a mi librete mas non lo çerrare" (1626cd), como apunta Menéndez Pidal, resulta igualmente cierto que agrega "por ende fago punto E çierro mi almario (1632c). En cualquier caso, el poema quedó abierto particularmente para su autor quien con toda probabilidad fue el que le adicionó a los poemas marianos el colofón satírico de la "Cántica de los Clérigos de Talavera" (1690-1709, S).

Por último, en la copla epilogal de cierre, junto al propósito moralizante (1634c), el poeta alega que también escribió el 'romance' "por mostrar a los synplex fablas e versos estraños" (1634d). El significado de este verso debe relacionarse con lo dicho en el Prefacio sobre el mismo tema, el cual también está precedido por una manifestación de intención moralizante: "E composelo otrosi a dar algunos leçion e muestra de metrificar E rrimar E de trobar Ca trobas E notas e rrimas e ditados e uersos que fiz conplid mente Segund que esta çiençia Requiere" (vii, 19-22). Se comprueba, luego, que 'synplex' no hay que entenderse peyorativamente, sino como esos 'algunos' que desconocen la 'ciencia' poética, y 'fablas e versos estraños' son los compuestos conforme a dicha ciencia los cuales podrán parecer extraños para los que no están familiarizados con las reglas poéticas. Lo anterior no pretende fijarle un significado único al verso 1634d, sino proponerle una interpretación que, además, se justifica dentro del epílogo porque esos 'synplex' se contraponen a quien "bien trobar sopiere" y a "quien podiere" para quienes el poeta autoriza, *nolens volens,* la ingerencia en su obra. Es difícil concebir que el poema haya quedado abierto para tales 'synplex'. No cabe duda, sin embargo, que tanto en el Prefacio como en el Epílogo el poeta estima que sus versos y su arte poético en general son dignos de la mayor atención. En suma, creemos que el aspecto artístico del poema tal y como lo comenta su autor en el epílogo está más en consonancia con esta opinión de Corominas:

---

[7] *Poesía juglaresca y juglares: Aspectos de la historia literaria y cultural de España,* 5ta. ed. (Madrid: Espasa-Calpe, 1965), p. 145; véase p. 166.

"El Arcipreste podía escribir ajuglaradamente, pero no era un juglar: era un literato" (ed. cit., p. 602).

Las manifestaciones de unidad que están presentes en el epílogo provienen esencialmente de la firme conciencia del autor del *Libro de buen amor* de haber compuesto un todo unitario. El epílogo en sí mismo es ya señal de esa unidad y representa una comunicación directa del autor a su público con la finalidad de comentar su obra terminada y expresar su última voluntad en cuanto autor. Versos como "ffiz vos pequeno libro" (1631a), "Señores he vos seruido" (1633a), "yo un gualardon vos pido" (1633c) y otros muchos (1828d, 1630abc, 1632cd, 1633bd) subrayan la conexión bilateral autor-público, que en rigor se manifiesta desde los dos primeros versos del epílogo: "Por que santa maria Segund que dicho he/es comienço E fyn del bien tal es mi fe" (1626ab), porque a quién la ha dicho y a quién le sigue diciendo que no sea a ese público. Es lógico que el lector, personal o colectivo, reaccione preguntándose cuándo se lo dijo y halle le respuesta en la copla 19 (*G*) en que, en efecto, le había dicho: "Por que de todo el bien es comienço e rrays/la virgen santa maria por ende yo juan rruys/açipreste de fita dello primero fis/Cantar de los sus gosos siete que asy dis". El autor se propuso así entroncar artística e ideológicamente el comienzo con el final a fin de proveerle un movimiento circular y unitario a su obra y de paso recordarle a ese lector su nombre y su cargo ahora cuando se despide de él. Tal movimiento uniformante viene consignado por la representatión de la Virgen como símbolo del Bien según la fe católica expresamente declarada por el autor.

Estas determinaciones le brindan un significado trascendente al sintagma "comienço E fyn del bien" puesto que, efectivamente, el poema comienza con esa alusión-invocación a la Virgen y concluye de manera parecida. El Bien ha presidido, por tanto, la trayectoria del libro y éste se ha plasmado bajo su advocación, de donde se enlazan ideológicamente el *Libro* y el *Bien*.[8] Se comprende entonces que el autor proponga en el epílogo que el tema cardinal de su libro lo es el *Bien*; esto es el *Buen Amor* (1630a). La acepción específica del

---

[8] Una concepción de que el *Libro de buen amor* es una obra sobre el Bien y asimismo de carácter didáctico-moral ya está presente en el Prefacio. Esto lo hemos expuesto en "Análisis estructuralista del Prefacio del *Libro de buen amor*" cuyo estudio se publicará en *KRQ*, en el Vol. XXVIII, No. 3, del año 1981.

sintagma 'buen amor' viene dada en el epílogo por la copla 1628 según ya vimos.[9] Que 'buen amor' es el amor de Dios concuerda además con la definición explícita del Prefacio: "el buen Amor que es el de dios" (iv, 10-11); así como el amor del prójimo está representado en el epílogo por la declaración del autor de que escribió el poema para prevenir algunos de los males que se infligen los seres humanos.

Forma parte también de tal concepción unitaria del libro el hecho de que el autor le asigne características generales a *toda* la composición. Primeramente, subraya su carácter didáctico-moral a lo largo de más de cinco coplas. Segundo, declara la polisemia del texto, cifrándola especialmente en la oposición texto/glosa. Tercero, afirma el aspecto artístico del poema como composición "de jugleria" y hace hincapié en la calidad de su versificación y de su composición. En suma, resulta patente en el epílogo la presencia de un yo artístico inconfundible que se sabe creador de una obra unitaria y totalmente suya ("mi librete"). Este yo creador le confiere un carácter unitario al poema al dotarlo de un epílogo (el cual él enlazó ex profeso con el preámbulo), al designarle un tema central y, por extensión, un título, al estipular los rasgos ideológicos y estéticos de su arte y al datar su obra en una copla magistral de síntesis.

Ahora bien, existe un paralelismo numérico entre las nueve coplas del epílogo, seguidas por poemas marianos, y las nueve que van de la copla 11 a la 19, seguidas igualmente por poesías dedicadas a la Virgen, que hace que estructuralmente el *Libro* presente un comienzo y un fin semejantes. Todo esto parece convenir, de cierto modo, con la teoría de la doble redacción sentada por Menéndez Pidal, según la cual el *Libro de buen amor* se iniciaba originalmente en la copla que hoy numeramos como once, en tanto que su súplica inicial (1-10) y el Prefacio pertenecen a la segunda redacción representada por el MS S.[10] No parece ser tampoco casual las correspondencias ideológicas que se constatan entre uno y otro pasaje, algunas de las cuales presentaremos poniendo en primer lugar los

---

[9] *Cf.* G. B. Gybbon-Monypenny, "Lo que buen amor dize con rrazon te lo pruevo," *BHS* 38:14-16.

[10] *Poesía árabe y poesía europea*, 5ta. ed. (Madrid: Espasa-Calpe, 1963), p. 149s.

versos del comienzo, luego los del epílogo y separándolos por una raya:

CONEXIÓN PRIMARIA

19 (G)     Por que de todo el bien es comienço e rrays
           la virgen santa maria por ende yo juan rruys
           açipreste de fita dello primero fis
           Cantar de los sus gosos siete que asy dis

1626       Por que santa maria segund que dicho he
           es comienço E fyn del bien tal es mi fe
           fiz le quatr o cantares E con tanto fare
           punto a mi librete mas non lo çerrare

DIOS

11abc      Dyos padre dios fijo dios spiritu santo
           el que nasçio de la virgen esfuerçe nos de tanto
           que sienpre lo loemos en prosa E en canto

13b        enforma e ayuda a mi el tu açipreste

1633cd     yo vn gualardon vos pido que por dios en rromeria
           digades vn pater noster por mi E ave maria

LIBRO

a) TEMA E IDIOLOGÍA

13c        que pueda fazer vn libro de buen amor aqueste

18d        ansi so el mal tabardo esta buen amor

18d (G)    asy so mal tratado yase el buen amor

1628       Desea oyr misas E faser oblaçones
           desea dar a pobres bodigos E rrasiones
           faser mucha lymonsna E desir oraçiones
           dios con esto se sirue bien lo vedes varones

1630ad     Pues es de buen amor enprestadlo de grado
           ca non ha grado nin graçias nin buen amor conplado

d (T)      ca non ha grado nin graçia buen amor el conplado

b) Utile/Dulci

| | |
|---|---|
| 13d | que los cuerpos alegre |
| 14a | Sy queredes senores oyr vn buen solaz |

| | |
|---|---|
| 1632bd | mas de juego E de burla es chico breuario<br>Sea vos chica fabla solas E letuario |
| d (T) | sea vos chica burla solas e letuario |
| 1633b | por vos dar solas a todos fable vos en jugleria |

| | |
|---|---|
| 13d | e a las almas preste |
| 16ab | Non tengades que es libro neçio de devaneo<br>nin creades que es chufa algo que en el leo |

| | |
|---|---|
| 1627 | buena propiedat ha do quier que sea/. . ./. . ./. . . |
| 1628 | Desea oyr misas E faser oblaçones/. . ./. . ./. . . |
| 1632ab | De la santidat mucha es byen grand lyçionario<br>mas de juego E de burla es chico breuiario |

c) Polisemia

| | |
|---|---|
| 14cd | non vos dire mentira en quanto en el yaz<br>Ca por todo el mundo se vsa E se faz |
| 16cd | Ca segund buen dinero yaze en vil correo<br>ansi en feo libro esta saber non feo |

| | |
|---|---|
| 1631cd | que sobra cada fabla se entyende otra cosa<br>syn la que se alega en la Rason fermosa |
| 1634bc | fue conpuesto el rromançe por muchos males e daños<br>que fasen muchos e muchas a otras con sus engaños |

d) Arte poético

| | |
|---|---|
| 11c | que sienpre lo loemos en prosa E en canto |
| 15b | fablar vos he por tobras e cuanto rrimado |

| | |
|---|---|
| 1634d | E por mostrar a los synplex fablas e versos estraños |

Nos hemos limitado a reproducir sólo las concordancias anteriores porque ellas representan las unidades ideológicas esenciales. Existen, sin embargo, otros puntos de contacto textuales. Así en el verso 14b se anuncia la apertura de la obra usando el vocablo 'rromance' ("ascuchad el rromance") y en el epílogo se declara su clausura usando igual término ("fue compuesto el rromance," 1634b) Tanto a un extremo como al otro del poema el autor califica su obra de "librete" (12c, 1626d) y alude a la virtud de la sentencia: "rrazon mas plazentera" (15d)/"Razon fermosa" (1631d). En fin, en ambos extremos del *Libro*, el poeta se dirige directamente al público como autor ("senores" [14a]/"varones" [1628d]) con la finalidad de sentarle pautas a la lectura y al entendimiento de su *Libro de 'Buen Amor'*, manifestando su tema esencial y su título y encareciendo su intención didáctico-moral, la cualidad y la calidad de su arte poético y la unidad de la obra.

WAYNE STATE UNIVERSITY

# The Singer of Tales
# and the
## Siete Infantes de Lara

THOMAS A. LATHROP

N 1896, WHEN MENÉNDEZ PIDAL published his famous *La leyenda de los Infantes de Lara*, he told us that this lost epic existed in two different *cantares*, the work of two individual poets, separated in time by over a century.[1] The contents of the first *cantar*, which Menéndez Pidal tells us dates from the 1200's, comes from the prose rendering found in the *Primera crónica general*, finished at the end of the 13th century. Menéndez Pidal says that the second *cantar* was composed in about 1320, more than a hundred years later than the first, and our knowledge of this version comes mostly from the *Crónica de 1344*. The second *cantar* is quite a bit longer than the first, largely due to an extended chase scene at the end. In comparing the two *cantares*, we see that when the second *cantar* relates events told in the first, its details are often different. In addition, the second *cantar* contains

---

[1] This is a revised version of a paper that John invited me to give at the Kentucky Foreign Language Conference in April 1978. I would like to thank Alan Deyermond for commenting on an early draft of the paper. He graciously made a number of good suggestions, but I am solely responsible for any lingering infelicities.

a number of events not found in the first. Menéndez Pidal was able to extract and reconstruct 559 epic verses from the *Crónica de 1344* and other chronicles of the period, yet he was able to see only a very few assonances from the early version found in the *Primera crónica general.*

In 1934, just as Menéndez Pidal was coming out with the second edition of his *Infantes de Lara*, the Italian hispanist Angelo Monteverdi published an article which disagreed with don Ramón's TWO *cantar* theory. Monteverdi proposes that there was only ONE *cantar*, saying that the differences between the two chronicle versions are due to different attitudes of two chroniclers towards one and the same *cantar*, the work of a single poet, and not due to two different *cantares*, as Menéndez Pidal had proposed. The writer of the version found in the *Primera crónica general*, Monteverdi tells us, had a notable tendency to summarize and recast the *cantar*, the proof being in the fact mentioned by Menéndez Pidal, that there were only very few assonances found in this version. The reason that the *Primera crónica general* does not contain elements found in the later version is simple, according to Monteverdi, "*É la fretta*"— It's haste. Our chronicle writer was in too much of a hurry to include certain episodes that the *cantar* made available to him. Because of the author's haste we do not witness the lament of the anguished father over the heads of his seven sons; because of haste we don't see the prophetic dream of Doña Sancha, in which the death of her sons is avenged, because of haste, he elimantes the scene where Mudarra is baptized, and because of haste, there is no long chase scene at he end of the *cantar*, when Mudarra tracks down the treacherous uncle of the *infantes*, the man who caused their death. According to Monteverdi, the 1344 writer, who includes *all* of the scenes just mentioned, took full advantage of the *cantar* and used the complete version.

Monteverdi's thesis has been questioned by some scholars, a recent example being Louis Chalon in his *L'Histoire et l'épopée castillane du moyen âge*.[2] Chalon first states that in comparing other epics with their versions in the *Primera crónica general*, there is no evidence that the Alphonsine writers had a tendency to summarize their poetic material. He goes on to say that since Menéndez Pidal had convin-

---

[2] Paris: Champion, 1975, pp. 507-09.

cingly shown that the *Poema de mio Cid*, as we know it, derived from eariler versions which are now lost, we should not refuse to acknowledge the existence of successive versions of the *Siete infantes*. Chalon further cannot believe that the *dénouements* of the two chronicle versions can derive from one and the same source.

I would like to suggest a theory different from those of Menéndez Pidal and Monteverdi. I propose that once the *Cantar de los siete infantes de Lara* was composed, in about the year 1000, it was sung *continuously* throughout the Middle Ages by innumerable *juglares*, and thus underwent continuous evolution and revision as it passed from mouth to mouth and from generation to generation, some *juglares* adding to the epic, some editing from it, some changing the order of events from the way they learned it, some expanding what they learned, and still others adding elements from folklore. The version of the legend seen in the *Primera crónica general* would then be an accurate representation of an early stage of the *cantar*, taken directly from the oral tradition at that point in its evolution and prosified by the Alphonsine writers, and the version seen in the *Crónica de 1344* would represent a more evolved, more mature stage of the development of the epic, transcribed from the oral tradition a hundred or so years later. Other chronicle versions, such as the *Interpolación de la tercera crónica general*, dating from about the year 1400, and the *Refundición toledana de la Crónica de 1344*, dating from around 1460, show even further developments.

My continuous evolution theory derives from Albert B. Lord's book, *The Singer of Tales*,[3] which deals with the ways in which the oral epic poets of modern Yugoslavia learn and compose their songs. The principal goal of his book was to provide a new tool for Homeric scholarship, which it has done rather well, but the conclusions of the book are universal enough to be applied to any European literature which has epic poetry. Lord himself devotes a final chapter to the the medieval epic in Britain, France and Greece.

In our field, just three years after the publication of the *Singer of Tales*, L. P. Harvey applied Lord's principles to the *Poema de mio Cid*,[4] and in 1965, Alan Deyermond followed with a more encompassing

---

[3] Cambridge: Harvard University Press, 1960.

[4] "The Metrical Irregularities in the *Cantar de mio Cid*," BHS 40 (1963), 137-43.

article entitled "*The Singer of Tales* and Medieval Spanish Epic,"[5] in which he suggested that other Spanish epics might be fruitfully approached using Lord's research. Since then, a number of our colleagues, such as Edmund de Chasca, J. M. Aguirre, Stephen Gilman, Joseph Duggan, Adrián Montoro, Charles Faulhaber, and others, have dealt with the Spanish epic in this light,[6] but no one has yet looked in detail at the ways in which the *Siete infantes* may illustrate Lord's points.

We learn in *The Singer of Tales* that every time an epic song is sung, it is done differently; that any particular song is different in the mouth of each of its singers, and that every time the same song is sung by the same singer it is composed differently; yet through all the changes, revisions, and personal touches, the story itself is carefully preserved. Such is indeed the case with our lost epic in its two major versions. Lord lists the various types of changes that songs undergo as they pass from singer to singer, from teacher to learner, and these fall into a half dozen clear-cut categories. In the pages that follow, I shall give Lord's list of changes, and shall show how they apply to our epic. If Lord's and my reasoning are convincing, then a good case can be made for my continuous evolution theory.

Lord says one change that we see from one version of an epic to another is: "expansion or ornamentation, the adding of details or description (that may not be without significance)."[7] In our epic, a number of important details are added to the later version to make it more dramatic than the first. Let me begin by discussing

---

[5] *BHS* 42 (1965), 1-8.

[6] Edmund de Chasca, "Toward a Redefinition of Epic Formula in the Light of the *Cantar de mio Cid,*" *HR* 38 (1970), 251-63; J. M. Aguirre, "Épica oral y épica castellana," *RFor.* 80 (1968). 13-43; Joseph Duggan, "Formulaic Diction in the *Cantar de mio Cid* and the Old French Epic," *FMLS* 10 (1974), 260-69; Stephen Gilman, "The Poetry of the *Poema* and the Music of the *cantar,*" *PQ* 51 (1972), 1-11; Adrián Montoro, "Le épica medieval española y la »estructura trifuncional» de los indoeuropeos," *CHA* (1974), 554-71; Charles Faulhaber, "Neo-traditionalism, Formulism, Individualism, and Recent Studies on the Spanish Epic," *RPh* XXX (1976), 82-101.

[7] This reference, and the others which discuss characteristics of the oral epic, are to Lord, p. 123.

the episode where omens indicate that the *infantes* should not go to meet their treacherous uncle. In the first version, Nuño Salido, the the *infantes'* governor, sees only one set of unspecified omens, and he tells the *infantes* to return home until the omens pass. In the second version, Nuño sees two set of very specific omens; first, he sees a crow on both the left and the right side, and he warns the *infantes* of danger. When another omen appears in the form of an eagle killing itself with its own claws, he tells his charges that they are being led to their death. He then dismounts and draws a line on the ground in front of the *infantes*, and tells them not to cross it; but if they insist, he warns, they should send word home to cover seven beds with mourning in order to counter the bad omens.

We see another example of added detail when Ruy Velázquez witnesses the decapitation of his nephews. In the early version, he is merely a spectator. But in the later version, he is a participant, for he tells the Moors how to decapitate them, and while the young men are being beheaded, he relates how they were born.

Later, when the heads are brought to Cordova, Gonzalo Gustioz, the *infantes'* father, who happens to be in custody there, is asked if he would try to identify them, for no one knows who they are. In the first version, the heads have already been cleaned and lined up, so he recognizes them immediately. In the second version, however, the heads are covered with dirt and blood, and Gonzalo Gustioz has to clean them himself; at first, he has no idea who they are, but as his cleaning progresses, he begins to get a grim suspicion, and finally realizes the gruesome reality that he is wiping blood from the faces of his sons.

These added details have certainly heightened the drama in the second version and have greatly increased the emotional effect.

The next item that Lord mentions is: "changes in order in a sequence, [which] may arise from a different sense of balance of the learner."

In its order of events, the second version differs in a very important way from the first. Some details which in the early version are undramatic and even lacking in *raison d'être*, become very dramatic in the later version merely by changing their location— and not by very much.

A striking example of this is found in the episode where Mudarra is engendered. In the first version, soon after Gonzalo

Gustioz is put into custody with the Moorish lady serving him, they make love and Mudarra is engendered. This conception takes place some time *before* the seven *infantes* are killed, so at the time, the future child has little heroic significance. In the second version, on the other hand, *after* Gonzalo Gustioz has seen the heads of his sons, Almanzor's sister comforts him by saying that he is not so old that he cannot have more children to avenge his sons, at which point he can only agree, so he rapes her and the conception takes place. The engendering of a Mudarra *vengador* at this point makes dramatic sense.

Next on Professor Lord's list is: the "addition of material not in a given text of a teacher but found in texts of other singers of the same district." It is impossible to speak with certainty about variant texts from the same district in this situation, but the second of our versions does show added material which does increase the drama of the story.

Much of the new material seems to have its origin in folklore, and could have been included in bits and pieces as the epic traveled back and forth across Spain. For example, in the second version, Doña Sancha, the *infantes'* mother, has a dream on the eve of young Mudarra's arrival in which a great hawk flies from Cordova, attacks her brother, Ruy Velázquez, and she herself drinks blood from the resulting wound. There is nothing of this in the first version.

Another event that the later version contains in the scene where Sancha adopts Mudarra as her own son, an act in which she gives him symbolic birth; she is wearing a tentlike garment, and Mudarra crawls through one sleeve and out the other. This folk ritual was actually pan-European in the Middle Ages, and its inclusion here serves to legitimize even further Mudarra's rightful quest for vengeance.

The most notable difference between the two versions is seen in their *dénouements*. In the first chronicle version, the story ends two short chapters after the *infantes* are decapitated, but in the second chronicle, it takes four long chapters to finish the story. Why would the two versions differ so much in their endings? Lord provides an answer, as Alan Deyermond pointed out in 1965, saying that the length of the song is most affected by the audience's restlessness. "... If his listeners are propitious and his mood heightened by their interest, he may lengthen his tale, savoring each descriptive passage. But it is more likely that...the singer will realize...that his audience is not receptive [at the end] and hence will shorten his song...." (Lord, p. 17) It seems fair to assume that the first minstrel gave the short version to a restless Alphonsine author, but that the minstrel whose song was used by the 1344 writer was able to take time and develop a fuller ending.

In the first version, the tale ends this way: Mudarra and Ruy Velázquez to to the court of Garci Fernández, where Ruy Velázquez requests a three day truce. While Ruy Velázquez is going home that night, he in ambushed by Mudarra who kills him with a sword. Not a very poetic way to mete out justice.

In the second version they do not go to court; Mudarra just takes off after his rival in a chase that lasts some days and ends after about 350 kilometers, through eleven towns (all of which exist today) and over two rivers. When Mudarra catches Ruy Velázquez, he merely wounds and doesn't kill him; in this way, doña Sancha, the bereft mother of the *infantes*, picks the way to execute her evil brother, and he is killed very cruelly.

Another catrgory which applies to the variants of this epic is "omission of material." One notable example of this is that in the first version, young Mudarra is made a knight when he is only ten years old. In the later version his knighting has been omitted.

There are two Lordian categories which do not apply to our epic, and, of course, it would be unusual if *all* of the types of changes were to be found in two variants of *any* song. Since our texts derive from chronicle sources, the first of which appears to be quite prosified, it would be impossible to apply Lord's category which deals with "saying the same thing in more or fewer lines." His final category, having to do with "substitution of one theme for another," also does not apply to our case, given the nature of the sources.

In conclusion, problems concerning the composition, transmission and evolution of the *Cantar de los Infantes de Lara* are obviously extremely complicated, and many of the questions arising about it have answers that faded away centuries ago. How many major variants were there? and what were they like? How much of the existing versions was influenced by cultured poets? Did the epic become more memorized with the passage of time? Were there any written versions of the poetic texts? The list of questions can go on and on, yet through it all, Professor Lord's conclusions seem to apply, and it seems reasonable, at least to me, that we are dealing with a single epic song in constant evolution rather than two separate *cantares*, as Menéndez Pidal thinks; or one basic text which was reworked according to the exegencies of two chronicle writers, as Professor Monterverdi thinks.

University of Delaware

# Epic Imagery in the
# *Laberinto de Fortuna*:
# Some Notes on Juan de Mena
# and Homer

HARLAN STURM

HE POETIC IMAGERY of Juan de Mena in the *Laberinto de Fortuna* is of course a worthy topic of scholarly inquiry. As the poet who gave to the Hispanic world such expressions as the "no me mueve" which became the main device in Spain's most famous sonnet[1] as well as the figure of the extended labyrinth, he has stimulated commentary ever since his works were first published in the fifteenth century and discussed in complete *explication de texte* fashion by Hernán Núñez.[2] Juan del Encina and Antonio de Nebrija used his poetry as examples of lan-

---

[1] Mena, in "Claro escuro" has "No me mueue la gran disciplina / de la poesia moderna abusiva...mas causa me mueue del daño que passo / que fuerças y seso y bienes me priua." in *Cancionero castellano del siglo XV* (Madrid, 1915) ed. R. Foulché-Delbosc, vol. II, p. 184. compared to "A Cristo Crucificado."

[2] The Núñez commentary, first published in 1499 in Seville went through fourteen sixteenth century editions. Hernán Núñez was known as the Comendador Griego and was an active scholar until his death in

159

guage and expression in their studies of grammar.[3] Recent scholarship has contributed a great deal to our understanding of Mena's poetry, especially of the *Laberinto de Fortuna*, and it seems that his works are about to receive long needed attention in the years to come.[4] What needs to be done is to focus on the imagery itself and place it in its proper tradition to see just what it is about his poetry which caused it to be such a model for future poets, and to be considered the Spanish classic throughout much of the Golden Age.

The study of the element of time in imagery is central to the inner workings of metaphor in general, and can show a great deal about the ability of the artist. The study of time in Mena's imagery leads to profitable conclusions about him as an innovator and a pre-renaissance poet. Most of the images which stand out in the work do so because of the special nature of their relationship to time, and the use of time in their development. Although the time sequence itself in the *Laberinto* is another topic in need of further exploration, this study is limited to a much more local use of time in specific images.

The images discussed here are of two types, those in which time plays an important role either in the narration or in the poetic device, and those which can be said to be epic similes, or extended similes for which the element of time is essential. The principal images which fall into these categories are those at the beginning of the *ficción*, or stanzas 11-13, and the description of the throne of Juan II beginning in stanza 143.[5]

---

1556. See Paul Groussac, "Le Commentateur de *Laberinto*" in *Revue Hispanique* 11 (1904), 164-224.

[3] See Antonio de Nebrija, *Gramatica Castellana*, ed. Romeo and Múñoz, (Madrid, 1946) pp. 96-104.

[4] See Luis Beltrán's excellent analysis of the *Laberinto de Fortuna* in *Speculum* (1972). More recently, Margaret Parker has studied the Ovidian material in Mena in the *Bulletin of Hispanic Studies* 55 (1978), 5-17.

[5] Both the Blecua edition in Clasicos Castellanos (Madrid, 1960) and the edition of John G. Cummins in Anaya (Salamanca, 1968) have been used. Citations are from the Cummins edition, which takes into account more recent deliberations on the editing of the text. Stanza numbers are only found in Blecua, whereas Cummins unfortunately uses line numbers.

Although the basic definitions of epic or Homeric simile do not seem to mention the peculiar function of time, examples show its importance, and in fact it is one of the logical results of the amplification of the basic comparison. That Juan de Mena was indebted to the classics and to Homer specifically is undeniable in that he himself translated the *Iliad*. Whether or not one agrees with the assertion that the *Laberinto* is a classical epic as proposed by Professor Clarke,[6] it is still easy to see that the work is written in the spirit of epic poetry. It was Clarke's insistence on considering the work consciously Aristotelian which caused her to be easily refuted. However it should be possible to say that the work was written to create for Spain the type of poem which Homer created for the Greeks and Virgil for the Romans. Mena's influence on the future course of national and renaissance epic is important, flowing through Camões to Milton. The fact that his poem is also based on more medieval forms, that of an allegorical voyage, has beclouded the main issue, that it is a poem which has as its basic intent the glorification of Spain in comparison to Antiquity.

To what extent could it be said that Juan de Mena intended to imitate specific Homeric techniques in his use of extended similes in the *Laberinto*? Unfortunately, his translation of the *Iliad*, or of the versions available to him do not include many of the extended similes quoted here. In fact, the accounts he was responsible for translating are much more narrative than poetic, and the principal focus seems to be the transmission of knowledge of the wars of Troy, or the *materia* of the *Iliad*, rather than the poetic expression used to create it in the first place. His attitude toward Homer is clearly stated in his prologue to his translation of the *Yliada*:

> "dispuse de no interpretar de veynte y quatro libros, que son en el volumen de la Yliada, salvo la suma brevemente dellos no como Homero palabra por palabra lo cuenta, ni con aquellas poéticas estensiones ni ornación de materias; ca, si assí se oviese de escrevir, gran aparato y compendio se hiziera. Mas escrive Homero de las esculturas solas y varias figuras que eran en el escudo de Achiles de compendio, que ay en aqueste todo volumen."[7]

    6 Dorothy C. Clarke, *Juan de Mena's* Laberinto de Fortuna: *Classic Epic and Mester de Clerecía* (University, Mississippi, 1973).

    7 Juan de Mena, *La Yliada en romance*. Edited from the Valladolid print-

He seems aware of both the importance and the strength of the Homeric simile which he terms the *"poéticas estensiones"* and *"ornación de materias"* and is specifically aware of the scene describing the shield of Achilles, which, as will be seen, he translated quite extensively.

Epic simile has been defined simply as a simile which is "more involved, more ornate, and a conscious imitation of the Homeric manner."[8] Epic similes are comparisons between something within the narration, the primary object, or tenor, and something without the narration, secondary object, or vehicle. The specific nature of the extended simile is that the vehicle nearly becomes a narration in itself. Readers are familiar with the manner used by Homer to zoom from the battlefield to the mundane to elucidate something more abstract or obscure. Typically, the vehicles are "developed into independent esthetic objects, an image which for the moment excludes the primary object or tenor with which it is compared."[9] An example from Book XVII of the *Iliad*:

> "He was like a lion retreating from a farmyard when he is tired of pitting himself against the dogs and men who have stayed awake all night to save the fattest of their heifers from his jaw. In his hunger for meat he has charged them, but without success. Showers of darts and burning faggots hurled by strong hands have scared him away, for all his eagerness; and at dawn he slinks off disappointed. Thus Menelaus of the loud war-cry retired from the body of Patroclus."[10]

The tenor, or primary object, is the way Menelaus moved from the body of Patroclus. The secondary, or vehicle, is the lion retreating.

---

ing of 1519 by Martín de Riquer (Barcelona, 1949) p. 37.

8 C. Hugh Holman, *A Handbook to Literature* (Indianapolis, 1972), 195. The *Princeton Encyclopedia of Poetry and Poetics* says "The true epic simile involves the comparison of one composite action or relation with another composite action or relation.... It is to Homer's epic simile that the whole European tradition of extended simile may be traced." (pp. 767-68)

9 Holman, *Handbook* p. 196.

10 Homer, The *Iliad*, translation E. V. Rieu (Penguin Books, Middlesex, 1964), p. 333. Page references in the text will be to this edition.

But the basic simile could have been something like "Menelaus moved from the body of Patroclus like a tired lion from its prey." What Homer has added is time—we learn the background behind his vehicle and are thus equipped with the emotional foundation giving it much more poetic impact and meaning. The understanding of the primary object has been enhanced by the secondary object which in turn has been elaborated by the addition of elements of time. If one were to characterize Homeric simile in this way, one could say that the vehicle takes on life and becomes a story in itself. Another example, this time from the Odyssey:

> "(Odysseus) wept as a woman weeps when she throws her arms round the body of her beloved husband, fallen in battle before his city and his comrades, fighting to save his home town and his children from disaster. She has found him gasping in the throes of death; she clings to him and lifts her back and shoulders with spears, as they lead her off into slavery and a life of miserable toil, with her cheeks wasted by her pitiful grief. Equally pitiful were the tears that now welled up in Odysseus' eyes..."[11]

It is indeed easy to lose the thread, and become absorbed in the vehicle. In both these examples, however, there is at least one unifying factor—the addition of time. The woman's history, past and future, are part of her emotion and we must understand it if we are to comprehend fully the strength of the basic simile.

Juan de Mena's first extended simile in the *Laberinto* comes in the eleventh and twelfth stanzas in a description of the nature of Fortune:

> Como las nautas que van en poniente
> fallan en Calis la mar sin repunta,
> Europa por pocas con Libia que junta,
> quando Boreas se muestra valiente;
> pero si el Austro comueve al tridente,
> corren en contra de como vinieron
> las aguas, que nunca ternán nin tuvieron
> allí donde digo reposo patente;

---

[11] Homer, the *Odyssey*, translation E. V. Rieu (Penguin Books, Middlesex, 1964) p. 136.

> Assí fluctuosa Fortuna aborrida,
> tus casos inciertos semejan atales,
> que corren por ondas de bienes e males,
> faziendo non cierta ninguna corrida. (ll. 81-92)

Fortune in life here is compared to the ships which meet the uncertain waters of the Straights of Gibraltar. When the North wind blows the waters are favorable for a westward bound ship, but if the East wind blows the tide is contrary and the ships are met with turbulence. Although not as elaborate nor as endearing as the similes of Homer, it shares with the great Bard the necessity of seeing things in more than a fixed time reference. As was the habit in the fifteenth century when editions were made of works of poetry, these sections were simply labeled "comparación".[12] In this comparison, the secondary object is the ships, the vehicle, which is expanded without reference to the primary object, or the tenor (Fortune's "cases") in order to amplify our understanding of the primary object. Mena's primary object is abstract, the way Fortune affects our lives which is elaborated as something which travels on both good and bad "waves." His vehicle is heroic and classical, the ships in uncertain waters, yet easily associated with everyday experience. It is not, as in Homer, a complete narration in itself, but begins to approach it.

The *Laberinto*'s transition stanza is one of the more important in the work for its special relationship to time, although it is not an extended simile. This stanza or passage is a necessary tool in any variant of dream or voyage literature, for it solves special problems and asks us to suspend our own sense of time and space:

> "Non bien formadas mis bozes serían
> quando robada sentí mi persona
> e llena de furia la madre Belona
> me tomó en su carro que dragos traían,
> e quando las alas non bien remecían
> feríalos ésta con duro flagello,
> tanto que fizo fazerles tal buelo
> que presto me dexan adonde querían. (ll. 97-104)

---

[12] Milton Buchanan, in *Spanish Poetry of the Golden Age* (Toronto, 1947) says "Long epic or homeric similes, called 'comparaciones,' occur frequently in *la poesía culta* of the time." (p. 198). It is an error to call all *comparaciones* Homeric.

The device here is to distract the reader with the flurry of activity of the mythical Belona and the flagellation of her dragons. By means of the spectacle created, we may not be aware that this is the change from introduction to dream or voyage, when the narrator passes from the real world, or at least an expression of it, into the world of the poetic, where time and space are now but poetry. What is disguised here is the psychological entrance into the dream, "sentí robada mi persona" which Núñez paraphrases as "quando sentí mi persona enagenada de mi mismo,"[13] since he found the passage in need of clarification. It is this stanza which delivers him to his crowded desert (gran desierto do vi multitud) which is his expression of what Dante found as a *selva oscura*. He has made this entry into his fiction palatable by distraction and allowed us to go with him unquestioningly into another time where the narrator can observe the world in past, present, and future.

Where time and movement become the central poetic device in Mena is in his description of the carvings and paintings on the throne of the King, Juan II, in the circle of Mars. This passage has always been recognized as one of the finest of the period, and it was often chosen for modern anthologies as an example of fifteenth-century form and tone.[14] The description includes the history of the deeds of the Alfonsos, Fernandos, Enriques, the story of the battle of Las Navas de Tolosa, the famous battle of the Higuera, the civil wars with the Infantes de Aragón, and much more. Mena himself recognized his debt to Homer in the narration of this particular scene, for there is an obvious comparison between the throne of the King and the famous shield of Achilles. Critics have similarly pointed out this debt, but our attention is first drawn by the author himself:

> Nunca el escudo que fizo Vulcano
> en los etneos ardientes fornaces,
> con que fazía temor a las hazes
> Archiles delante del campo troyano,

---

[13] *El Laberinto de Fortuna*, ed. Hernán Núñez, Seville, 1499 fol. vi.

[14] See M. Menéndez y Pelayo, *Antología de poetas líricos castellanos* (Santander, 1944) vol. II, pp. 175-76; and Buchanan, *Spanish Poetry*, pp. 2-3.

se falla tuviesse pintadas de mano
nin menos escultas entretaladuras
de obras mayores en tales figuras
como en la silla yo vi que desplano. (ll. 1145-52)

Mena, always conscious of the debt to the classics never tried to
conceal it. To do so would have been contrary to one of his
purposes—to point out Spain's artistic and historical place with
respect to Greece and Rome. Even Villena is seen as a poet in a line
of poets begun by Homer and followed immediately by Virgil, a
line of which Mena surely saw himself a part.[15]

In the *Iliad* the shield of Achilles forged by Hephaestus is famous as the earliest example of the double perspective of art within
art—a description in one form of narration of another form of narration. It carries with it a double impact—that of the information
contained in the description, as well as the symbolic meaning as all
the history Achilles carries into battle with him. But one of the
principal narrative aspects of the shield and what must have been
observed by Juan de Mena himself, is its addition of time and
movement in the narration. The shield and what must have been
observed by Juan de Mena himself, is its addition of time and
movement in the narration. The shield is made up of five layers
decorated with designs which represent Earth, Sky, Sea and the
Sun and Moon as well as the Constellations. A short citation
shows this movement:

> "...two beautiful cities full of people. In one of them wed-
> dings and banquets were afoot. They were bringing the
> brides through the streets from their homes, to the loud
> music of the wedding hymn and the light of blazing torches.
> Youths accompanied by flute and lyre were whirling in the
> dance, and the women had come to the doors of their houses
> to enjoy the show. But the men had flocked to the meeting-
> place, where a case had come up between two litigants, about

---

15 "Vimos a Omero tener en las manos / la dulce Ilíada con el Odisía.
/ El alto Virgilio vi que lo seguía; / Eneo, con otro monton de roma-
nos..." (ll. 976-79). He says that he is not mentioning current poets lest
he be accused of favoring his contemporaries along with himself, but he
has done it by simply mentioning the names of the famous before he
mentions Villena in l. 1010.

the payment of compensation for a man who had been killed. The defendant claimed..." (p. 351)

Obviously, Homer has let the narration run clearly beyond the confines of time, space, and perspective to allow us to know even what the litigation was about, but also to allow us to see time perspective. Loud music, as well as the reason for the litigation would not be easily depicted in the medium used even given the expressiveness of Greek art. In one passage, Homer mentions a field which was being plowed for the third time, and again in another he mentions that this artist depicted some things as well as Daedalus had done for Ariadne. Mena picks up on the last reference saying that his throne was "tan rica labrada como si Dedalo bien la fiziera." (l. 1136)[16]

In Mena's translation of the *Iliad*, in spite of the fact that he had said that he was not going to include many of the "poéticas estensiones ni ornación de materias"[17] the description of the shield is one of the more complete passages treated, lasting approximately four pages in the Riquer edition.[18] Although not as extensive as the versions we now have from the original Greek texts, it does incorporate some of the aspects of time which must have interested the translator. In the scene of the litigation, for example, "E allí entallara al ygual juez como se assienta entre las partes amas et como difine et concluye la question con serena cara;[19] and later, after the sounds of the young playing instruments, "canciones introduziendo et firiendo con la diestra las cuerdas de la lirial harpa, et con pulgar estendido corriendolas todas et modulando por siete riendas los modos todos, e componiendo los cantares que al mundo fazen razonar con aquexado movimiento."[20]

---

[16] Daidalos, in H. J. Rose, *Gods and Heroes of the Greeks* (New York, 1959) was a skillful craftsman whose art was responsible for the existence of the Minotaur which he captured by creating a labyrinth. (pp. 95-96), a fact which did not escape Núñez who notes it in his commentary (*Laberinto*, fol. xli).

[17] See note 11.

[18] *Yliada*, pp. 171-77.

[19] *Yliada*, p. 175.

[20] *Yliada*, p. 175.

Homer's description is obviously one of extensive movement, activity, and time sequences, and it was admired by Mena as proven by his mention of it in the introduction to his translation, the translation itself, and the beginning stanza of his own description of the throne. Mena's use, as always, is more historical. He uses the description of the sculptures and paintings on the throne to show us history, showing the reigns with deliberate distortion of times, "faziendo mas largos sus reinos estrechos" (l. 1156). The suspension of belief required of the reader is great and has confused readers and critics alike. The description of what the narrator sees in the art of the throne lasts until stanza 158 and the beginning of the Conde de Niebla episode.[21] This section includes the oft anthologized Batalla de la Higuera with all its action, movement, and poetic force. Stanza 148 is one in which the relationship to time and movement in the Homeric manner is easily seen:

> "Con dos quarentenas e más de millares
> le vimos de gentes armadas a punto,
> sin otro más pueblo inherme allí junto
> entrar por la vega talando olivares,
> tomando castillos, ganando lugares,
> faziendo por miedo de tanta mesnada
> con toda su tierra tenblar a Granada,
> tenblar las arenas fondón de los mares."
> (ll. 1177-84)

His narration of what he saw on the throne is punctuated with his narrative presence (le vimos) and his own reaction to the emotionally moving scene. The activity he manages to bring to the scene with the repetition of the verbs and the use of the present participle sets up the hyperbole of the fear which causes the territory of Granada to tremble even to the sands at the bottom of the sea.[22]

---

[21] Buchanan, *Spanish Poetry*, p. 108, misreads this, saying that the author was an eye witness of the battle and can therefore say that he saw the action. Núñez feels the suspension is worth the following comment (*Laberinto*, fol. xli). "Todo lo que el auctor dize que vio en las coplas siguientes fasta que comiença a tratar de la muerte del Conde de Niebla todo avemos de entender que estava entretallada y esculpido en la silla del rey don Juan.

[22] The term hyperbole here belongs to Núñez as a footnote to "temblar las arenas...." He says "Hiperbole es figura usitada entre los poetas como aquello."

The element of sound present in Homer is also here in one of the *comparaciones* found in this part of the work:

"Como en Cecilia resuena Tifeo,
o las ferrerías de los milaneses,
o como gradavan los sus entremeses
las sacerdotiças del tiemplo lieo
tal vi la buelta daquesta torneo;
en tantas de bozes prorrompe la gente"
(ll. 1193-98)

Even that which is difficult to portray in art or sculpture, like sound, is aided by both Homer and Mena. Homer has a field being plowed for the third time, and Mena has a pile of bodies in the shade of the famous fig tree (l. 1203). In the words of Homer, who calls our attention to the skill needed, "The artist had achieved a miracle."[23]

Mena's use of time in imagery, if it is indeed learned from Homer, helps us to consider the *Laberinto de Fortuna*'s role in the development of poetry in the period just preceeding the Renaissance. Mena was clearly a student of Homer, and has incorporated into his poetry one of the aspects which made up the classical spirit. Time is, in effect, what gives it life and causes the throne of Juan II to be immortal in Spanish letters.

University of Massachusetts

# La poesía y la prosa del
## *Siervo libre de amor*:

### ¿"aferramiento" a la tradición
### del *prosimetrum* y de la convención lírica?

OLGA TUDORICĂ IMPEY

A MÁS NOTABLE caraterística del *Siervo libre de amor* es su hechura proteica: lo sentimental se transfigura en lo caballeresco, el amor se convierte en piedad, Venus en Vesta; el tiempo vacila indeciso entre presente y futuro y la voz narrativa se sutiliza dando lugar a la lírica. Este último aspecto, de la alternancia entre prosa y verso, salta a la vista desde la primera lectura, pero las razones que guiaron a Juan Rodríguez del Padrón a usar el "prosimetrum" son menos visibles. Para sacarlas a luz es imprescindible hallar respuestas a varias cuestiones. ¿Qué relación hay, por ejemplo, entre los versos y el relato prosístico del *Siervo libre*? ¿Qué función desempeñan las canciones? ¿Son mera diversión, mero intermezzo lírico destinado a quebrar la monotonía de la prosa? ¿Se limitan a reiterar retóricamente el sentido de la narración o lo complementan contribueyendo a su desarrollo? ¿Brota la combinación de la prosa con la poesía de una tradición literaria española, de una influencia francesa e italiana, o del impulso creador de Juan Rodríguez?

Siete son las canciones que se integran en el texto del primer

libro sentimental español.[1] Tres de ellas—"Sy syn error puedo
dezir," "Pas a pas entil señor," y "Recebyd alegre mente"—se inter-
calan en la primera parte; sólo una, "Alegre del que vos viese," se
inserta en la segunda; en la tercera se incorporan tres: "Avunque
me vedes asy," "Çerca el alua" y "Pues que Dios y mi ventura."[2] La
fecha de su composición, que puede ser anterior o posterior a la
prosa, no es importante. Tampoco merecen una atención especial,
por lo estudiados que fueron, su pertenencia a la tradición proven-
zal y gallega[3] y el empleo de los obligados lugares comunes cancio-
neriles: el cautiverio amoroso, la maldición contra el amor, la
exhortación e imprecación de la amada, etc. Más interesante sería
destacar aquellos versos que, tal vez, llevan el sello individual de la
mentalidad de Juan Rodríguez con respecto a la convención erótica
en voga, mentalidad que contribuiría a la mejor comprensión de su
libro.

---

[1] Aunque el término "novela," aplicado al *Siervo libre de amor* es
impropio, lo empleo porque es el que predomina en la crítica española.
Para las dificultades terminológicas relacionadas con la prosa sentimental
española, v. Keith Whinnom, *Diego de San Pedro* (New York: Twayne
Publishers, Inc., 1974), p. 145, n. 1 y Alan Deyermond, "The Lost Genre
of Medieval Spanish Literature," *HR*, XLIII (1975), 142-149.

[2] A primera vista se pueden contar sólo seis canciones, pero la más
superficial lectura descubre que la sexta poesía contiene dos canciones. El
papel de la poesía en la trama del *Siervo libre* fue poco estudiado. En su
tesis doctoral, "Siervo libre de amor," (Valladolid: Universidad de Vallo-
dolid, 1970) pp. 43-56, César Hernández Alonso dedica su atención sobre
todo a los aspectos de métrica. Con una o dos excepciones (p. 49), la
relación entre la poesía y la prosa se despacha rápidamente, tal vez porque las canciones de la novela se consideran inferiores a las independien-
tes. Unas interesantes referencias a las poesías del *Siervo libre* se hallan en
la monografía de María Rosa Lida de Malkiel, "Juan Rodríguez del
Padrón: Vida y obras" y "Juan Rodríguez de Padrón: influencia," publica-
das respectivamente en *NRFH*, VI (1952), 313-357 y *NRFH*, VIII (1954),
1-38. En el siguiente cito de la reimpresión hecha por Yakov Malkiel en
*Estudios de literatura española del siglo XVI*, Madrid: Porrúa-Turanzas, 1977,
pp. 21-144. Las poesías del Siervo libre fueron también el objeto de interés de la ponencia de Gregory Andrachuk, leída en el VIª Congreso de la
AIS, Toronto, 1977.

[3] María Rosa Lida, p. 31: Juan Rodríguez "no altera en lo más mínimo
las convenciones externas de la lírica cortesana tradicional" por lo cual el
poeta muestra gran "aferramiento" (p. 64).

Tanto la prosa como la poesía del *Siervo libre* versan sobre el mismo asunto: el amor desgraciado por una "grand señora." A pesar de ello, desde el principio es evidente una diferencia de tratamiento y perspectiva. Así, la prosa que rodea la primera conción, "Sy syn error puedo dezir," escudriña y pormenoriza los sentimientos del *yo* ante la inminencia de un solo amor y de una servidumbre única. En cambio, la poesía, por los sintetizadores versos iniciales, "leal seruir a ty, amor, / es perdiçion," (p. 41),[4] amplía desmesuradamente la dimensión temporal, de modo que abarca tanto el amor pasado como el futuro y sirve a la vez de *memento* para una desgracia remota del protagonista y de *caveat* para la infelicidad en que está a punto de incurrir. En la prosa se aclara que este indirecto rechazo del servicio amoroso lo canta la Discreçion. La segunda canción, puesta en boca del Coraçon, sanctifica el pacto con el amor. La presencia de estas figuras alegóricas y sobre todo la proximidad de sus canciones, que están separadas sólo por algunas insignificantes frases, hacen hincapié en la contienda anímica provocada por la intención del amante de servir a la "grand señora." La canción tercera, "Recebyd alegremente," condensa en una trillada imagen concreta, del "coraçon en cadenas," y en una auto-caracterización del amante como sirviente, la gama de los torturados sentimientos que la prosa detalla profusamente. En líneas generales, las tres poesías insertadas en la primera parte del *Siervo libre*, en la que el protagonista "bien amo y fue amado" (p. 37), cumplen el papel de sintetizar el contenido de la prosa, y por tanto concuerdan en el significado con ella.

La primera discrepancia de sentido entre la poesía y la prosa se observa en la segunda parte del libro, en la cual se describe la desaforada pesadumbre del *yo*-amante, ya abandonado por la "grand señora." Es significativo que en esta parte, que coincide con el tiempo cuando el protagonista "bien amo y fue desamado" (p. 37) se da cabida solamente a la canción "alegre del que vos viese." Juan Rodríguez, como poeta, parece compartir la creencia del Arcipreste de Hita que "con pesar y tristeza" la fuerza creadora merma. Esta canción marca una nota disonante con el relato que la precede y

---

4 Para esta cita y las siguiente me sirvo de la edición de Antonio Paz y Mélia, *Obras de Juan Rodríguez de la Cámara* (Madrid: Sociedad de bibliófilos españoles, 1884) pp. 3-80. Sólo para las últimas poesías recurriré a la lección de César Hernández Alonso.

con la mentalidad tradicional del amante cortés. En el relato el *yo* contempla su propia muerte; en lugar de reflejar la luctuosa contemplación, la canción "Alegre del que vos viese" expresa una acerba maldición contra la "grand señora": "ninguno vos quisiese." Siendo un lugar común, la maldición no llama la atención por sí misma sino por contener un insólito múcleo de cuatro versos, en el cual se entrecruzan varias insinuaciones:

> "Mal quisto de vos y cuanto
> paso por la desierta via
> amadores con espanto
> fueyen de mi compania." (p. 52)

Se insinúa primero que el *yo*—Siervo de un amor desesperado toma conciencia de su desolada condición sólo al verse evitado por sus "amigos... en bien amar" (p. 39). Se insinúa después una pregunta: si la tristeza y el sufrimiento continuos son los rasgos inherentes del amor cortés ¿por qué rehuyen los amadores al Siervo, cuyo inmenso sufrir fue capaz de trastornar la vida de las plantas, de las aves y de los animales? Dos respuestas se perfilan: por ser "malquisto" por la "grand señora" o por la desmesura de su sufrimiento. Ambas posibilidades están lejos de concordar con la ideología de la lírica trovadoresca y de la *fin'amors*. Claramente, los amadores mencionados en la canción de Juan Rodríguez no son provenzales, sino castellanos. Con esta procedencia se relaciona tanto la implícita condena del amante "malquisto," es decir, del amante que no es capaz de hacerse amado, como la del amante que siente y ostenta una tristeza desmesurada. En lugar de provocar simpatía y admiración, la desesperación y el "mal querer" excesivos causan espanto. La última insinuación contenida en los versos citados, quizá la más importante, es que el Siervo, al llegar a esta etapa del proceso erótico, rechaza su soledad y busca la compañía de sus pares.

Con respecto a la prosa circundante los cuatro versos de la canción-desempeñan una función complementaria. En la narración se describe el atolladero en que se halla el Siervo, quien, deseando morir, recorre la "descendiente via" (p. 48) solamente para descubrir que el reino de la muerte y de los amadores famosos le rechazan. Si en la prosa se le "veda el paso" al mundo sobrenatural y a la compañía de los amantes muertos (p. 50), en la poesía se le niega la entrada en el mundo social, en la esfera de los amadores vivos, que en el pasado fue suya.

Las poesías incluidas en la tercera parte del libro, que corresponde "al tiempo que no amo ni fue amado" (p. 38) adquieren una importancia singular, ya que sobrepasan en extensión y sentido a la prosa que las rodea y en fuerza sintetizadora a las canciones anteriores: sus versos condensan la materia de todo el libro. Además en ellos se hace patente el hilo de no-conformismo del *Siervo de amor*, el cual es todavía tenue en la canción-maldición. El deseo de compañía que se perfila en ésta, se concretiza precisamente en las canciones de la tercera parte, cuyo punto de partida es el súbito silencio de las aves cantadoras, provocado por el errar del yo-amante. Es un silencio acusador, al cual el yo contesta con su canción de autodefensa, "Aunque me vedes asy / catyvo, libre naçy."[5] Después de sumar las transformaciones padecidas por el Siervo en su tortuoso proceso erótico—de libre a sandío, de sandío a cativo, de cativo a siervo—la canción plantea unas interesantes preguntas con respecto a la alienación del Siervo—amante de su propio ser, con respecto a su humildad y a la cualidad de su servicio. Lo hace, además, de manera muy insistente,[6] entrelazando las estrofas por la repetición de un verso. Así, al final de la primera estrofa, el Siervo-amante se pregunta "¿Cómo diré que soy mío?" para contestarse en la segunda con una interrogación insólita y socarrona: "¿Como dire que soy mio, / pues no soy enteramente?" Por una sola palabra, el adverbio *enteramente*, Juan Rodríguez se desvía de la convención poética del amor predominante en su época[7] y, al mismo tiempo, tuerce el sentido de su libro. Hasta este pasaje, el protagonista, de acuerdo con

---

[5] Hernández Alonso, p. 49, la considera "una de las mejores y más distintivas poesías de Juan Rodríguez," que "alude a la naturaleza misma del Siervo."

[6] María Rosa Lida, *Influencia*, p. 91, apunta que ningún otro poeta de cancionero insistió tanto en la dictomia *siervo-sirviente* como Juan Rodríguez.

[7] Completamente dentro de esta tradición poética se halla la poesía de los contemporáneos de Juan Rodríguez; por ejemplo, el Marqués de Santillana, en la "carta que embió a su amiga" hace alarde de que "mio no / mas todo vuestro / soy despues que me prendiste" *Cancionero general de H. del Castillo* (Madrid: Sociedad de bibliófilos españoles, 1882), I, P. 105 p.18.

los preceptos del amor cortés,[8] ha insistido en voz alta en la integridad y firmeza de su servidumbre. Al contrario, en los versos citados insinúa *sotto voce* que su enajenación no es total: si no es suyo enteramente tampoco lo es de la amada. Para que esta insinuación, que pone en duda tanto el servicio amoroso del Siervo como su obediencia a las prescripciones del amor cortós, no quede inadvertida, Juan Rodríguez la subraya en los versos siguientes por una extraña división de los servidores del amor en dos categorias:

> Avnque dyxesse otra mente,
> diria vn gran desuario.
> Por ende, digo y porfyo
> que por servir leal mente,
> no soy syervo, mas syrviente.
>
> No soy syervo, mas syrviente,
> pues que libre fuy llamado
> en el tiempo ya passado,
> que no puede ser presente." (76)

La primera categoria, de los siervos, apunta hacia una servidumbre anclada en el pasado e independiente de la voluntad; una servidumbre esencial, ineluctable, sin esperanza de rescate. La segunda categoría, de los sirvientes, se relaciona con el presente,[9] con una condición circunstancial, transitoria, que no excluye la vuelta al estado de libertad. Semejante distinción concuerda con la auto-caracterización del *yo* protagonista, como sirviente, en la carta-canción que envía a la grand señora al principio de su servicio amoroso. Es interesante observar que la dicotomía *siervo-sirviente* tal como aparece en el texto de Juan Rodríguez está atestiguada, siglo y medio después, en el diccionario de Covarrubias: "Servir... vale obedecer a otro y hazer su voluntad, y *unos sirven libremente dando gusto a otros, y otros sirven con su voluntad;* otros sirven forçados como los esclavos y otros en una medianía alquilándose o haziendo con-

---

[8] Para la utilidad y necesidad de este término, que empleo a pesar de sus defectos y limitaciones, v. Alicia C. de Ferraresi, *De amor y poesía en la España medieval. Prólogo a Juan Ruiz,* (México: Colegio de México, 1976) pp. 53-58.

[9] A un escritor versado en latín, como lo era Juan Rodríguez, traductor de las *Heroidas,* no se le escapó el valor de "sirviente" como participio presente.

cierto con la persona a quien sirven, como son los criados a los señores." (mi subrayado).[10] Estas líneas ayudan, además, a comprender el título de la "novela" de Juan Rodríguez: *Siervo libre de amor* es el que sirve libremente, con su voluntad, al amor.[11]

Los siervos de amor abundan en la poesía cancioneril.[12] En este contexto, el hecho de que ni una sola vez se designa Juan Rodríguez a sí mismo como siervo en su obra poética adquiere una significación especial. Por ejemplo, el amante de "Siete gozos de amor" se presenta a sí mismo como sirviente, y no como siervo.[13] Además, que yo sepa, sólo a Juan Rodríguez se le ocurre contraponer las dos caracterizaciones en el mismo texto poético. Es muy posible, por lo tanto, que esta relación antitética entre *siervo* y *sirviente* sea una creación suya, inventada[14] para expresar su despego hacia el amor cortés. Idéntico propósito expresa la serie de interrogaciones y exclamaciones de la canción "Aunque me vedes asy," que tratan con ironía los más importantes requisitos impuestos por la tradición al amante cortés. Así, el padecer identificado con "el verdadero ser / de cualquier enamorado," tan encarecido por la "grand señora" está acompañado de una exclamación, "Vereys do syrvo, cuytado!" (p. 76), en que el desdén se mezcla con la compasión por sí mismo; la paradójica relación entre los sentimientos de la dama y los del Siervo—el desamor de aquella aumenta el amor de éste—se comenta mediante otra exclamación irónica: "¿Llamais ventura la mia?" (p. 77) Acordándose de las maldiciones proferidas contra el

---

[10] Sebastián de Covarrubias, *Tesoro de la lengua castellana o española* Ed. Martín de Riquer (Barcelona: S. A. Horta, 1945) p. 935.

[11] La ambigüedad del título fue acertadamente interpretada por Hernández Alonso, p. 23.

[12] El amado como *sirviente* es poco frecuente en la poesía cancioneril. Macías lo emplea en la canción "Ay, señora, en que fiança": "e non dexes tu sirviente / perder su olvidança" *Le chansonnier espagnol d'Herberay des Essarts* ed. Charles V. Auburn (Bordeaux: Férét et fils, 1951) p. 157. Para Lope de Stúñiga v. la canción "Donzella cuya belleza." (*Cancionero general*, I, p. 200).

[13] En el gozo seteno el poeta escribe: "Si voluntad no consiente / virtud la debe forçar / amar tu leal sirviente." (Paz y Méliz, p. 12).

[14] Con respecto a la *inuentio* en la obra de Juan Rodríguez v. María Rosa Lida, *Vida*, pp. 43, 101.

amor mientras estaba libre, el *yo*-Siervo se pregunta: "¿Qué diré, syendo forçado / del sentido que avia?" (p. 77) La implicación es que en este estado las maldiciones deberían ser, con razón, aún más enconadas. La reflexiva auto-justificación que el *yo* adopta ante los "auzeles" testigos, su insistencia en que él es únicamente sirviente, la ironía en que envuelve su experiencia erótica, manifestada en las exclamaciones, presentan su amor cortés como una convención de dudoso valor.

El comentario del yo-amante sobre su cautiverio y el amor cortés continúa en las canciones siguientes, "Cerca el alua" y "Pues que Dios y mi ventura."[15] Las dos arrancan del mismo deseo de comunicar con los "auzeles silenciosos y esquivos que le movió a decir "Avnque me vedes asy". A diferencia de ésta, la canción "Cerca el alua" gira en torno a los motivos del cantar, esquivez y silencio de los pájaros. Por esto el ambiente ("una rybera verde") y el tiempo (el alba primaveral) son típicamente trovadorescos e invitan a amar. También los cantantes—el gayo, la calandría, el ruyseñor—son pájaros característicos del amor. Sin embargo, su canto, "Servid al Señor / pobres en andança" nada tiene de erótico, pero sí mucho de ironía, porque relaciona burlonamente "la pobreza en andança" con el servicio de Dios. Y "buena o mala andanza" tal como lo atestiguan el contexto de la canción y otras poesías concioneriles significa recompensa o pena de amor.[16] Se infiere que precisamente por ser "pobre de andança" tacha el protagonista sus amores de disparatados: "Y yo por locura / canté por amores / pobre de favores, / mas no de tristura." Esta compungida reflexión de nuevo sitúa sus amores en el pasado. En el presente, la angustia del *yo* no es el amor, sino la total incomunicación. Por esto quiere quebrar el silencio de los "auzeles": "E por los mas atraher / a me querer responder, / en señal de alegria / cantava con gran afan / la antygua cançion mia." La antigua canción, "Pues que Dios y mi ventura," gira en torno a dos leit-motivs: el cautiverio y el cantar con amargura. El motivo del cautiverio se expresa mediante el verso de Macías, "cativo de minha tristura," que sella el final de

---

[15] Cito estas canciones en la transcripción de Hernández Alonso, p. 48-55, más correcta que la de Paz y Mélia.

[16] Véase, por ejemplo, la canción "Mi querer y vuestro oluido" de Costana en *Cancionero general*, I, p. 324.

las estrofas. Juan Rodríguez incorporó este verso ajeno en la creación propia no tanto por atender a una práctica medieval corriente, sino porque encierra la esencia de su libro: "cativo de mi tristura" es la clave que aclara que el *yo* está encadenado, no por el amor sino por su propia pesadumbre. Es natural por lo tanto que en lo siguiente el objeto de su cantar sean los "cuydados y maginança y la contemplación de un futuro inseguro: "No se que postremeria / ayan buena los mis dias." La canción acaba con dos versos sacados de la poesía de Macías: "Ya, señora, en quien fiança / cativo de mi tristura." Es, desde luego, un final ambiguo del que trataré cuando venga el caso.

Las canciones y la prosa de la tercera parte guardan una relación complementaria. Por una parte, en la poesía "Avnque me vedes asy" la experiencia de la servidumbre erótica se da por pasada ya que el *yo* elige el pretérito indefinido para describir la pérdida de identidad, y el profundo efecto de la transformación erótica: "perdi mi libre 'albedrio' " (p. 75), "par Dios, no me *conoci*: / tan turbado me *senty* / del semblante que traya." (p. 77; mi subrayado). El presente lo reserva para la descripción de su servidumbre parcial y para las irónicas exclamaciones. En este presente, el sirviente alcanza la sabiduría que le permite caracterizar su estado pasado como "sandío," lo que le sería imposible si no se hubiera librado de su sandez. Por otra parte, en la alegoría prosística se describe al *yo* yendo tras las huellas de su extraviado entendimiento. En su búsqueda se aleja primero de "la deçiente via de perdicion," toma después "la muy agra senda de Minerva," y finalmente pasa "los grandes Alpes de mis pensamientos, deçendiendo a los sombrosos valles de mis primeros motus, arribando a las faldas de mi esquiva contemplaçion" (p. 75). En la geografía erótica de la "novelita" las altas montañas representan el máximo aislamiento contemplativo y la "deçiente via" corresponde a la mayor desesperación (pp. 47-48). La alegórica posición del yo en la tercera parte "a las faldas" de su contemplación, "en los... valles de los primeros motus" es equivalente a la baja del dolor, de la locura y al final de su aislamiento. El *yo*, que ya recorrió todo el círculo de la servidumbre erótica, vuelve a la indecisión de sus "primeros motus" amorosos cuando la Discreción se oponía al amor y el Coraçon lo defendía. Tanto la poesía como la prosa indica que la furia del amor se ha calmado y apuntan, por lo tanto, hacia una salud incipiente.[17]

Porque por sí solo no es capaz de hallar a su entendimiento, el *yo* "preguntava alos montañeros, e burlavan de mi; alos fyeros saluajes, y no me respondían; alos auzeles que dulçe mente cantavan, e luego entravan en silençio; e quanto mas los aquejava, mas se esquivavan de mi, que por çelar mi tristura, e ser dubdoso en triste vía, les dizia." Una profunda transformación se ha operado en la conducta del *yo*: las quejas angustiadas de la segunda parte quedan reemplazadas por las preguntas con finalidad exacta. Su persistente interrogar, que recuerda al de la desposada en el "Cantar de los cantares" bíblico, indican claramente la voluntad del Siervo de abandonar su "esquiva contemplación" y de reestablecer, por "la muy agra senda" de Minerva (p. 75) la comunicación con el mundo exterior, interrumpida por su servidumbre y aislamiento. Por otra parte, el silencio con que se chocan sus preguntas, subraya el tercer rechazo del *yo*: esta vez lo rehuyen aun los más huraños seres humanos (los "fyeros saluajes") y los pájaros. Parece que esta última exclusión, esta vez del mundo natural, le resulta al *yo* más insufrible que la del mundo sobrenatural (de la muerte) y del erótico (de los amigos). Tal como la prosa deja inferirse, del acuciante deseo de comunicar con el mundo de alrededor depende el recobrar del entendimiento y la existencia de las canciones "Avnque me vedes asy," "Cerca el alua" y "Pues que Dios y mi ventura." Los últimos versos de esta canción, como ya he mencionado, son muy ambiguos. ¿Quién es la señora "en quien fiança," es decir, pone su esperanza, el "cativo de la tristura?" Desde luego, no puede ser aquella "grand señora" culpable de su desesperación y "perdición." De nuevo, la combinación de la prosa con el verso contribuye a resolver el enigma. Inmediatamente después de los últimos versos, que aluden a la "señora en quien fiança" el *yo*, la prosa atestigua la llegada de "una señora mastresa," "dueña ançiana," acompañada de siete doncellas. Ella aparece de repente, justamente cuando el *yo* se esfuerza a "devisar algun poblado." (p. 79). La búsqueda del poblado subraya el anhelo de comunicación expresado por la poe-

---

[17] Resulta raro que Hernández Alonso, p. 50, afirme: "aunque la canción está incluída en la tercera vía su contenido concuerda más con la segunda."

sía; sin duda, por esta frase alegórica se indica la decisión del *yo* de integrarse de nuevo en el orden de la sociedad, de la cual le aisló el amor y su tristeza. Como guía se le ofrece esta "dueña ançiana," que llega en el más oportuno momento para sacarle del yermo y del error. Su identidad es tan misteriosa como su aparición. No obstante, en su presencia se pueden vislumbrar por lo menos tres figuras medievales: la Filosofía, la Discreción y Syndéresis. La Filosofía se representa en la iconografía de la baja Edad Media como una imponente mujer rodeada de siete jóvenes—las artes liberales o las virtudes.[18] Además, según la vigorosa tradición que arranca en la obra de Boecio, la Filosofía, figurada como una grave señora, acude a la salvación de los que tienen el alma lánguida. La identificación de la "ançiana dueña" con la Discreción se insinúa en la introducción al *Siervo libre*, en la cual se aclara que el entendimiento del *yo* "siguio despues de libre, en compañia de la discrecion" la vía de Minerva. Hacia semejante identificación apunta también una glosa del texto en la que el protagonista describe a la Discreción como a la "madre de las virtudes" y, significativamente, como "parte de su salud" o salvación. Las últimas líneas del libro ofrecen otra posibilidad de identificación: la de Syndéresis. De acuerdo con el *Diccionario de autoridades*, Syndéresis es la "virtud y capacidad natural del alma para la noticia e inteligencia de los principios morales que dictan vivir justa y arregladamente." Según la Madre María de Jesús de Agreda, Syndéresis es "la virtud fundamental," que "nace en nosotros con la misma naturaleza racional."[19] Tal vez la presencia de este nombre en el pasaje final del *Siervo libre* indique que su protagonista pudo hallar su congénita virtud que le ayudaría a vivir "arregladamente." Conocido el apego de Juan Rodríguez a los cambios bruscos y a los juegos metamórficos, bien podría ser que la enigmática "señora mastresa," "dueña ançiana," representara por turno a la Filosofía, la Discreción y la Sindéresis.

En resumen, todas las canciones del *Siervo libre* son partes inte-

---

[18] Herrade de Landsberg, láminas del f. 32 de *Hortus deliciarum*, y del ms. del s. XIII de la Biblioteca de la Universidad de Leipzig, reproducidas por Pierre Courcelle en *La Consolation de la Philosophie dans la tradition littéraire*. (Paris: Centre de la Recherche Scientifique, 1967).

[19] Para ambas citas, v. el *Diccionario de autoridades*, ed. facsímil (Madrid: Gredos, 1963, II), p. 297.

grantes, inseparables de la prosa. Las primeras tres canciones sinte-
tizan el relato de la aventura sentimental del *yo*, mientras que las
demás lo complementan y, de esta manera, contribuyen a su desarrollo. Las poesías incorporadas en la segunda y tercera parte de la
novela ofrecen una clave para la comprensión del proceso amoroso
del amante que de siervo de amor se convierte en sirviente, y de
sirviente en siervo libre de amor; que pertenece a la amada, pero
no del todo; que es cativo, pero no del amor sino de su propia "tristura." Esta cautelosa e insólita conducta del amante puede expli-
carse por la resistencia de Juan Rodríguez al amor convencional
impuesto por la tradición cortesana.[20]

Las canciones del *Siervo libre* insinúan que la soledad y la
incomunicación—fomentadas por el amor cortés—son impropias a
la naturaleza humana y, por lo tanto, nocivas. Estas insinuaciones
están corroboradas por la poesía suelta de Juan Rodríguez. Huir de
la soledad, vivir en alegría y buscar compañía es la materia de uno
de los diez mandamientos recomendados por el poeta gallego, porque "De beuir solo recrescen / grandes males sin medida, / y la
fama destruyda / D'aquellos que lo padescen" (p. 20). La soledad
genera la tristeza, que todo lo invade, incluso al amor. La cárcel del
Siervo no es de amor sino de "desolación". La figura del amante,
meditabundo desesperado no parece gozar de mucho halago: de un
espanta-amadores, y espanta-muerte llega a ser un espantapájaros.
Tanto en el poema "Siete gozos de amor," como en "Diez mandamientos de amor,"[21] Juan Rodríguez recomienda sólo el amor
correspondido, lo cual elimina la angustia que es la base del amor

---

[20] Gilderman, *Juan Rodríguez del Padrón* (Boston: Twayne Publishers,
1977) p. 40, encuentra otra explicación para la reticencia del amante:
"This was the case for many Castilian poets, who deemed it unmanly to
subordinate themselves to a woman."

[21] En el seteno gozo, el *yo* poético exclama con ansia: "Solo fin de mis
dolores / es amar y ser amado, / qu'es la gloria d'amadores (Paz y Mélia,
p. 12). En el mandamiento noveno (p. 21) el desafío de las normas del
amor cortés es todavía más explícita: "el que ama lealmente / nunca sigue
en otra parte / si no donde amor prospera." En su libro, *Juan Rodríguez del
Padrón*, p. 55, Martin S. Gilderman considera que la actitud cínica manifestada por el poeta gallego en "Diez mandamientos" no apunta al amor
cortés sino a la sociedad cortesana de Castilla, "as being fit not for true
courtly love, but for the courtier, the hypocrite and social climber interested only in the appearance of courtly love."

cortés. No disfrutar el amor cuando se tiene la oportunidad se convierte en motivo de burla: "tener la niña en el campo / y catarle cortesía" se ríe la hija del Rey de Francia en un romance atribuido al poeta gallego.[22] La prosa no hace sino corroborar esta mentalidad que contraviene a la *fin'amors*. En el *Triunfo de las donas*, Cardiana la ninfa, que siente no haber amado a Aliso, viviendo todavía éste, perdona a las dueñas que por piedad amorosa hacia el amante, "por le saluar la vida, son vistas errar, *si yerro se deue decir... ¡O ligero, yerro aquel del qual es prinçipio virtud, e perdonable culpa la que se vee de sola humanidat proceder!*" (p. 96, subrayo yo). Este error, que a los ojos de Juan Rodríguez es ligero resulta imperdonable de acuerdo con el código del amor cortés. Sus leyes se infringen varias veces también en la prosa del *Siervo libre de amor*. El *yo* protagonista no guarda el secreto de su amor por "la grand señora;" abandonado por ésta, no se echa la culpa a sí mismo por la transgresión cometida, sino a la amada cruel y al amigo desleal. En la "estoria de dos amadores,"— relato intercalado en el del Siervo—Juan Rodríguez se rebela contra el precepto que sitúa a la amada en una posición superior a la del amante: Liessa es solamente hija de un "grand señor" mientras que Ardanlier, quien la ama, es hijo de rey. Cuando se enciende la chispa de otro amor, el de la infanta Yrena, se atropella otra ley del amor cortés, ya que es Yrena—hija del famoso rey de Francia— quien "requiere de amores" a Ardanlier y se declara prisionera de él, invirtiendo así el orden establecido por la tradición.

La suma de estas contravenciones forma un anti-código, o por lo menos un código erótico nuevo, castellano, más flexible y humano. Un código que proclama la igualdad de los amantes, que rechaza el amor secreto, la soledad, el sufrimiento y la tristeza; un código que recomienda en lugar del deseo insatisfecho el *amor mixtus*. Desde luego, en el siglo XV español este código coexiste con el más antiguo del amor cortés.[23] Es difícil determinar cuál fue el papel de Juan Rodríguez en la invención y difusión de las nuevas leyes de amor. Lo seguro—y en esto consiste su mérito—es que su

---

[22] "De la hija del rey de Francia," ed. de Hugo A. Rennert, *ZrPh* XVII (1893), p. 55.

[23] Para el tratamiento de los varios rasgos del amor cortés en la poesía concioneril, v. Otis H. Green, "Courtly Love in the Spanish Cancioneros," *PMLA*, 64 (1949), 247-301.

obra aúna las nuevas leyes que andaban dispersas por la poesía
lírica y la novela caballeresca y que en lugar de promover el amor
cortés, de ser su Mesías—como se ha afirmado—lo socava.[24]

El aferramiento de Juan Rodríguez a la convención de la lírica
trovadoresca fue exagerado por todos los críticos que siguieron a
Mercelino Menéndez Pelayo.[25] Más de lo debido se ha exagerado
también la diferencia lingüística y estilística que separa la prosa del
*Siervo libre* de la poesía; de acuerdo con María Rosa Lida, ésta
ostenta "el más límpido castellano," mientras que aquélla se carac-
teriza por abundantes "innovaciones lexicológicas y sintácticas."[26]
En realidad, las canciones incluidas en el *Siervo libre* y sobre todo las
de la tercera parte, no tienen la transparencia que se les atribuye.
Las alusiones vagas, la sintaxis elíptica de la cual a menudo faltan
las partículas de relación, la técnica "sincopada," compendial, que
caracterizan la prosa, aparecen también en la poesía. Incluso la
enigmática "bimembración" del relato en dos "estorias,"—la del
Siervo y la del Ardalier—tiene como paralelo la composición bipar-
tita de la canción "Cerca el alua."

En una obra como el *Siervo libre*, la poesía y la prosa convergen
en el mismo género, el sentimental; ni Juan Rodríguez, ni sus
seguidores, las conciben aisladamente; el origen de su separación

---

[24] Gilderman, p. 60, toma en serio las licencias poéticas de Juan
Rodríguez y en consecuencia le atribuye el papel de "Mesías del amor
cortés."

[25] María Rosa Lida, *Vida*, pp. 31 y 64; Antonio Prieto, introducción a
la edición del *Siervo libre de amor* (Madrid: Castalia, 1976), p. 35; Gilderman, pp. 22-24. Resulta interesante la observación de María Rosa Lida
de que la poesía de Juan Rodríguez "no altera no lo más mínimo las
*convenciones externas* de la lírica cortesana" (p. 31, mi subrayado); se insinúa
así que en lo íntimo esta poesía "personal y apasionada" no respeta
dichas convenciones. Tal vez la mencionada observación es una de las
paradojas en que incurre a veces la investigadora argentina, a las que
Yakov Malkiel se refiere—con tanta objetividad—en la introducción a la
monografía, p. 6.

[26] María Rosa Lida, *Vida*, p. 63. Una opinión discordante expresa
Charles Auburn en la introducción de *Le chansonnier espagnol d'Herberay*, p.
cxv: "Juan Rodríguez de la Cámara gagne à être comme dans son *Siervo
libre de amor*. Ses poésies temoignent d'une téchnique littéraire assez
savante."

es, por lo general, la crítica de índole decimonónica,[27] que, además, concedió a veces una importancia exagerada a la participación de las fuentes en la composición de una obra literaria. Por ejemplo, el entrelazamiento de la prosa con los versos en el *Siervo libre* se ha asociado frecuentemente con el que aparece en otras obras medievales latinas o vernáculas.[28] Sin embargo, el acoplamiento entre el relato y la poesía en la "novela" sentimental española tiene poco en común con el de *De nuptiis Philosophiae* con *De Consolatione Philosophiae* con *Vita nuova*. Martianus Capella, por ejemplo, emplea la poesía sólo en las introducciones y conclusiones de los *libri* y en el lenguaje directo de los dioses.[29] En Boecio los poemas—invocaciones y oraciones a Dios, variaciones sobre un tema dado, relatos versificados de mitos—guardan una relación muy tenue con la grave prosa, tal vez porque la Filosofía había tachado a la poesía de "meretricula." Tampoco se refleja la finalidad de la combinación dantesca de prosa y verso en el libro de Juan Rodríguez. Para el poeta florentino la prosa es explicativa; gira en torno a la lírica con el propósito de glosar los poemas, analizar sus divisiones y exponer detallada y objetivamente las circunstancias que los inspiraron. En el texto de la *Vita nuova*—pero no en la cronología real—la poesía aparece como mera recapitulación, como una variación sobre algún motivo presentado en la prosa.[30] En este aspecto, tal vez Juan Rodríguez coin-

---

[27] Keith Whinnom puntualiza en Diego de San Pedro, *Obras completas*, (Madrid, Castalia, 1973, II) p. 48, el error de la crítica moderna de "insistir en la distinción entre la prosa y el verso, separándolas habitualmente en las historias de literatura como 'géneros distintos' ". En la introducción al libro de Juan de Flores, *Grimalte y Gradissa*, (London: Tamesis, 1971) p. xviii y en "Love and Honour in the *Novelas sentimentales* of Diego de San Pedro and Juan de Flores," *BHS*, XLIII, 1966, pp. 253-275, Pamela Waley destaca la afinidad entre poesía y prosa en la obra sentimental de Diego de San Pedro. El parentesco entre la prosa sentimental española y la poesía cancioneril fue señalada también por Dinko Cvitanović en *La novela sentimental española* (Madrid: Ed. Prensa Española, 1973) pp. 40 y 118.

[28] María Rosa Lida, *Vida*, p. 34; Antonio Prieto, p. 35.

[29] William Harris Stahl, en *Martianus Capella and the Seven Liberal Arts* (New York: Columbia University Press, 1971) p. 30, subraya el contraste entre la poesía de Martianus compuesta con "high regards for classical models" y la prosa, caracterizada por su "florid style" (p. 32), con "rococo propensities" (p. 39).

[30] Para la relación entre la poesía y la prosa de *Vita Nuova*, v. Mark

cida más con Guillaume de Machaut, cuyas *complaintes* se enlazan estrechamente con la narración y las cartas de *Voir-dit*, por ejemplo. Se han mencionado también algunos remotos antecedentes hispánicos: *De consolatione rationis* de Pedro de Compostella, la anónima *Chronica Adelphonsi Imperator*, *El collar de la paloma* de Ibn Hazm, pero su lectura por Juan Rodríguez es poco probable y, de haberlos leído, poco habrán tenido que ofrecerle. Los antecedentes más próximos, las canciones de la emperatriz Nobleza y de Roboán insertadas en el *Libro del Cauallero Zifar*[31] y las de Aquiles, Casandra, Briseida y Troylo, Andromaca, que avivan la monótona relación de la *Historia troyana polimétrica* tampoco sirvieron de modelo para la combinación de la poesía y prosa en el *Siervo libre de amor*. Todas estas canciones no hacen sino bordar detalles en torno a los dolidos sentimientos de los personajes, frecuentemente amenazados por la separación; la lírica ni sintetiza ni complementa a la narración como ocurre en el *Siervo libre de amor*. Por esto, con razón se puede decir que la combinación de poesía y prosa en esta novela tiene sus raices en el afán de Juan Rodríguez de experimentar con formas y técnicas nuevas. El valor de la simbiosis del relato y el verso—aunque imperfecta—aparece claramente si se eliminan las canciones: La narración se queda enclenque, pobre de sentido y lirismo.[32] La técnica del *prosimetrum*, renovada por Juan Rodríguez en tierras hispánicas, gozó de gran éxito en los siglos XV y XVI, siendo imitada entre otros por el Comendador Escrivá en *La Quexa que da de su amiga ante el dios de Amor*, en *Triste Deleytacion*, por Diego de San Pedro en el *Tractado de amores de Arnalte y Lucenda*, y por Juan de Flores en *Grimalte y Gradissa*. Sin embargo, ninguna de estas obras logra un entrelazamiento tan estrecho entre la poesía y la prosa como la tercera parte del *Siervo libre de amor*.

Tres conclusiones se imponen. a) Juan Rodríguez no sigue a

---

Musa, *Dante's Vita Nuova. An essay on Vita Buova* (Bloomington: Indiana University Press) p. ix y sigs., 91.

[31] Para estas canciones v. Brian Dutton y Roger Walker, "*El Libro del Cauallero Zifar* y la lírica castellana", *Fil*, 9 (1963) pp. 53-67.

[32] Disiento de la opinión de Hernández Alonso, p. 56, quien escribe que "la unión de prosa y verso es una elemental yuxtaposición como cita textual."

pies juntillos la tradición de la lírica trovadoresca en su obra, que sólo aparentemente está regida por la convención. Como otros tantos poetas castellanos, anteriores y posteriores, Juan Rodríguez goza en someter dicha convención a experimentos, goza en tantear su resistencia para introducir en los puntos débiles unas notas si no individuales, por lo menos autóctonas, castellanas. Como otros coétaneos suyos—y antes de Jorge Manrique-el poeta gallego cultiva la dictomía de la tradición e individualidad.[33] b) Con respecto al prosimetrum, por usarlo Juan Rodríguez se relaciona con una tradición europea preestablecida; por usarlo a su manera—integrando orgánicamente el verso en la prosa—se aparta de ella. c) Para comprender la primera "novela" sentimental castellana y para apreciar su papel experimental, al que debió la fama que tuvo en el siglo XV, es necesario sacarla de la horma en que la fijó la crítica del siglo pasado y leerla, analizarla en sí misma y por sí misma. En una palabra es necesario revalorizarla en todos sus aspectos.

INDIANA UNIVERSITY

---

[33] Sobre la presencia de tal dicotomía en las obras de los escritores del siglo XV llamó la atención fugazmente, Carmelo Samoná, en *Studi sul romanzo sentimentale e cortese nella letteratura spagnola del quattrocento* (Roma: Carucci, 1960) pp. 17-19. Una reacción semejante a la de Juan Rodríguez en cuanto al amor cortés manifiesta Juan del Encina en la *Egloga de Plácida y Vitoriano* (V. Antony van Beysterveldt, *La poesía amatoria del siglo XV y el teatro profano de Juan del Encina* [Madrid: Insula, 1972], pp. 271 y ss).

# Prehumanismo del siglo XV:
# La *Letra* de los escitas
# a Alejandro

Del cancionero de Herberay des Essarts
y las formulaciones utópicas en la edad media

FRANCISCO LÓPEZ ESTRADA

STOY RECOGIENDO los datos dispersos por la literatura medieval española en lengua vernácula que impliquen una cierta relación con algún aspecto de los que pudieran servir para una formulación utópica.[1] Si consideramos que la *Utopía* de Moro es la que reúne en forma armónica los elementos que indican el grupo genérico de la literatura utópica, en estas obrillas medievales que examino se encuentran algunos de estos elementos, a veces sólo en forma de esbozos o apuntes, pero constituyendo una pieza completa en sí misma en cuanto a su constitución literaria.

---

[1] Así mi colaboración en el Homenaje al Profesor Franco Meregalli, "Por los caminos medievales hacia la Utopía: *Libro de los Ejemplos*, núm. 6", y otros más que preparo. Un resumen de este artículo fue leído como ponencia en el VII Congreso de la Asociación Internacional de Hispanistas, celebrado en Venecia del 25 al 30 de agosto de 1980.

Aquí examinaré una pieza en prosa que se encuentra entre las siete que se hallan al comienzo del Cancionero de Herberay des Essarts.[2] Cada una de las piezas en cuestión posee por sí unidad de obra, y así se la asigno a esta *Letra* o carta, a pesar de que los elementos que la componen pueden en gran parte identificarse con fragmentos de otras obras, al menos en este caso de una predominante. Su editor, Ch. Aubrun, la califica de "epístola moral" e indica que la suya es la primera edición de la pieza.[3]

La obra es una breve exposición de índole moral y política sobre un asunto que sería conocido de muchos de los oyentes o lectores; tanto esto es así, que, por el número de obras que contienen un texto muy cercano, me atrevo a considerarla como un ejercicio retórico sobre el caso. Se trata de las razones que los escitas manifiestan a Alejandro para evitar dignamente la guerra con el conquistador.

Como ocurre en estos casos, la procedencia de los materiales puede presumirse: en nuestra *Letra*, como el asunto había obtenido una cierta difusión literaria, la exploración de las fuentes debe ser cautelosa. Para mostrar estos antecedentes he reunido los siguientes textos:

a) PRIMERA LÍNEA (en cursiva): el texto del Cancionero de Herberay según la edición de Ch. Aubrun (que menciono CHE y la línea de la edición).

b) SEGUNDA LÍNEA: el texto de la *Historia de Alejandro* de Quinto Curcio según aparece en la edición de "Les Belles Lettres", Paris, 1948; pertenece al Libro VII, Cap. viii y el número citado es del párrafo según las ediciones modernas más autorizadas.

---

[2] Cito por *Le Chansonnier espagnol d'Herberay des Essarts (XVe siècle)* (Burdeos: Féret et fils, 1951), edición de Charles Aubrun, fascículo XXV de la Bibliothèque de l'École des Hautes Études Hispaniques. Las siete piezas en prosa son: una Declamación de Lucrecia, procedente de un trozo retórico de Coluccio Salutato; una epístola de Madreselva a Mausoleo, libre interpretación de las *Heroidas* ovidianas y la *Crónica Troyana*; la *Letra* de los escitas que aquí comento; la Complaynta de Pere Torrella sobre Agnès de Clèves; una *Lamentación de España* del Marqués de Santillana; unas *Leyes de amor*, dirigidas probablemente a Mossén Hugo de Urríes; y el más conocido *Razonamiento* de Pere Torrella en defensa de las damas.

[3] El comentario de esta pieza, en idem., pég. 207.

c) TERCERA LÍNEA: el texto del *Alexendreis* o *Gesta Alexandri Magni* de Gautier de Châtillon (libro VII) según la edición de la *Patrología latina* de J. P. Migne, Vol. 209, cols. 459-74; el número citado es el del verso.

## LETRA QUE FUE EMBIADA POR LOS CITAS
## A ALEXANDRE

CHE, 1    *Si los dioses quisieran fazer el tu cuerpo formado segunt la*
QC, 12    "Si di habitum corporis tui auiditat*i* animi parem
Al., 4260    Vel si, quanta cupis, tantum tibi corporis esset,

CHE, 2    *grant desordenada cobdicia de tu voluntat, una redondeza de*
QC, 12    esse uoluissent, orbis te non caperet: altera manu
Al., 4261    Non tibi sufficeret capiendo maximus orbis,

CHE, 3    *mundo non te cabria. La una mano ternias en oriente e la otra*
QC, 12    Orientem, altera Occidentem contingeres; et hoc
Al., 4262    Sed tua mundanas mensura excederet oras;
Al., 4263    Ortum dextra manus, occasum laeva teneret,

CHE, 4    *en occidente e, tuuiendo entre tus manos toda la grandeza del*
QC, 12    adsecutus scire uelles ubi tanti numinis fulgor conde-
Al., 4264    Nec contentus eo, scrutari et quaerere votis
Al., 4265    Omnibus auderes, ubi se mirabile lumen

CHE, 5    *cielo, saber querrias donde salle tanta claror de lumbre con*
QC, 12    retur.
Al., 4266    Conderet, et solis auderes scandere currus

CHE, 6    *el sol e adonde se asconde o que esta allende del cielo. Loco*
QC, 14    Stultus est, qui fructus
Al., 4267    Et vaga depulso moderari lumina Phoebo:
Al., 4277    Stultus, qui fructum dum suspicit, arboris altum

CHE, 7    *es el que considera la fermosura del fruto e non piensa la*
QC, 14    earum spectat, altitudinem non metitur. Vide ne,
Al., 4278    Non vult metiri; videas, sublime cacumen

CHE, 8    *altura e peligro del arbol. Guarda que quando hayas puyado*
QC, 14    dum ad cacumen peruenire contendis, cum ipsis
Al., 4279    Prendere dum tendis (postquam comprenderis illud)

CHE, 9   *suso non cayas con las ramas delgadas. Que tu no vees*
QC, 14   ramis quos conprehenderis, decidas.  Quid?
Al., 4280  Cum ramis ne forte cadas. [...]
Al., 4274  An nescis longo quod provocat aethera ramo

CHE, 10  *grandes hedifficios e arboles durar tanto tiempo en crescer, ser*
QC, 14   tu ignoras arbores magnas diu
Al., 4275  Arboreum robur, firma radice, superbum,

CHE, 11  *en un punto desfechos? Non hay ninguna cosa tan firme en*
QC, 14   crescere, una hora extirpari?
QC, 15                Nihil tam firmum est cui
Al., 4276  Quoque diu crevit, hora extirparier una?
Al., 4284  Tam firmum nihil est, cui non metus esse ruinae

CHE, 12  *la natura que non tenga peligro contrario que lo destruye. Al*
QC, 14   periculum non sit etiam ab inualido
QC, 15                  Leo quoque
Al., 4285  possit, ab invalido. [...]
Al., 4280           [...]Avium fuit esca

CHE, 13  *leon quantas vezes lo comieron animales pequeños, el coco-*
QC, 15   aliquando minimarum auium pabulum fuit; et
Al., 4281  Parvarum quandoque leo, rex ante ferarum
Al., 4282   Ferrum cuncta domans, atque omni durius aere

CHE, 14  *drillo pequeña aue le mata y el fierro se corrompe por orín.*
QC, 15   ferrum robigo consumit.
Al., 4283  Consumit rubigo vorax;

CHE, 15  *Que tenemos merecido a ti porque nos deuas hacer guerra?*
QC, 16   Quid nobis tecum est?
Al., 4287  Quid nobis tecum? Non infestavimus armis.

CHE, 16  *Nunca pisamos tu tierra. Ca ni podemos seruir alguno ni*
QC, 16   numquam terram tuam attigimus. ...nec seruire ulli pos-
         simus nec imperare
Al., 4288  Contigimusve tuam, facturi praelia, terram.

CHE, 17  *desseamos ser señores. Pues dizes que vienes a perseguir*
QC, 16   desideramus.
QC, 19   At tu, qui te gloriaris ad latrones

CHE, 18  *los ladrones, entre nosotros no ay hombres que rompan los*
QC, 19   persequendos uenire,...

CHE, 19  *drechos de naturaleza ni rompen la ignoçençia ni falsan uno*

CHE, 20  *a otro la verdat. Non contendemos en juizio sobre las agenas*

CHE, 21  *possessiones, non fabricamos moneda de metal espulsiua de*

CHE, 22  *virtudes, no enchimos los vientres de los tributos de las gentes,*

CHE, 23  *no cortamos la mar spantosa por visitar las agenas nationes*

CHE, 24  *e trattar engañosas permutaciones e fraudulentas juras, non*

CHE, 25  *fazemos por ganar, no alçamos los palacios con bigas moradas*

CHE, 26  *en el ayre, non es nuestra fin en las piedras de las minas ni*

CHE, 27  *en las labores de los gusanos tenyidas son sangre de animales*

CHE, 28  *por cobrirnos los corporales carnes. Los cuerpos tenemos por*

CHE, 29  *sieruos, las almas inchimos e ornamos de virtudes, las quales*

CHE, 30  *son durables de inmortal bienauenturanças, nin nos delectamos*

CHE, 31  *en las voluntades bestiales, mas nuestro fin es saber por el*

CHE, 32  *qual differemos de los animales brutos e somos semeiables a*

CHE, 33  *los dioses biuientes. Mas tu que te alabas de perseguir la-*

CHE, 34  *drones, todas las tierras por do vienes dexas llenas de ladron-*
QC, 19  ...omnium gentium quas adisti latro es.

CHE, 35  *icios, e aun no eres farto, que aun tienes guardadas las manos*
QC, 19  ...iam etiam ad pecora
Al., 4307  [ ... ] ad nostras pecudes extendis avaras

CHE, 36  *avarientas para robar la nuestra tierra. ¿Que diablo has*
QC, 19  nostra auaras et insatiabiles manus porrigis.
QC, 20  Quid
Al., 4308  Instabilesque manus [ ... ]
Al., 4310  Quid tibi divitiis opus est? quae semper avaris

CHE, 37  *menester tu riquezas, las quales cobrando te faze mayor cob-*
QC, 20  tibi diuitiis opus est, quae esurire te cogunt? Primus
omnium satietate
Al., 4311  Esuriem pariunt, quanto tibi plura parasti,
Al., 4312  Tanto plura petis, et habendis acrius ardes.

CHE, 38  *dicia? Contra natura es la fambre que nasçe de mucha fartura.*
QC, 20  parasti famen, ut, quo plura haberes, acrius quae non
habes cuperes.
Al., 4313  Sicque famem faciens, defectum copia nutrit.

CHE, 39  *Los otros fazen batalla por aver paz, tu fazes batalla por*

CHE, 40  *hauer mas guerra. E la victoria que a los otros es causa de*
QC, 21  ...bellum tibi ex uictoria nascitur.
Al., 4316  Nascitur ex bello victoria, rursus as illa,
Al. 4317  Surgunt bella tibi [ ... ]

CHE, 41  *folgança, a ti es causa de mayor trabajo, pues batallas despues*

CHE, 42     *de la victoria. Guardate de las reboluçiones de fortuna, non*
QC, 24       Proinde fortunam tuam pressis manibus tene:
Al., 4330      Proinde manu pressa digitisque tenere recurvis

CHE, 43     *te venga el peligro de donde menos piensas. Quantas cosas veemos*
QC, 24      lubrica est, nec inuita teneri potest.
Al., 4331     Fortunam memor esto tuam, quia lubrica semper
Al., 4332     Et levis est, nunquam poterit invita teneri.

CHE, 44     *perdidas donde se pensauan ganar. Despues del dia muy*

CHE, 45     *claro ya vimos cielo anublado. Los fuertes deuen morir por*

CHE, 46     *la libertat, la / qual Dios e natura les dieron. Si nos vençes,*

CHE, 47     *non somos por ende en numero de las batallosas gentes porque*

CHE, 48     *te recrezca fama. Pues ¡quanta infamia te seria ser vencido!*

CHE, 49     *Si dios eres, da beneficios a las gentes. Ca tal es la condicion*
QC, 26      Denique, si deus est, tribuere mortalibus beneficia debes,
            non sua eripere sin
Al., 4242     Denique si Deus es, mortalibus esse benignus
Al., 4243     Et dare quae tua sunt, nunquam sua demere debes.

CHE, 50     *de Dios. Hombre eres, acuerdate de las miserias humanas en*
QC, 26      autem homo es, id quod es, semper te cogita:
Al., 4344     Si similis nobis homo, te debes reminisci
Al., 4345     Semper id esse quod es; stultum est, horum meminisse

CHE, 51     *las quales con nosotros eres ygual. La otra es acordarte de*
QC, 26      stultum est eorum meminisse, propter quae tui
Al., 4346     Ex quibus ipse tui es oblitus; habebis amicos,

CHE, 52     *las cosas que te fazen oluidar a ti mesmo. Si tu nos das*
QC, 26      obliuiscaris
QC, 27            Quibus bellum
Al., 4247     Bella quibus non intuleris: fortissimus inter

CHE, 53     *batalla podernos has tractar como amigos. Ca entre los*
QC, 27      non intuleris, bonis amicis poteris uti. Nam et firmissima
            est inter pares
Al., 4348     Aequales, interque pares, est nodus amoris.

CHE, 54     *yguales es la amistança verdadera e yguales son los que no*
QC, 27      amicitia, et uidentur pares qui non fecerunt inter se
Al., 4349     Aequales sunt sive pares, qui nec tibi cedant
Al., 4350     Nec sese excedunt, hi sunt, qui nulla cruentis.

CHE, 55     *han prouado las fuerças. A los que vençieres, guardate de*
QC, 27      periculum uirium.
QC, 28           Quos uiceres, amicos tibi esse
Al., 4351     Viribus inter se fecere pericula Martis.
Al., 4352     Esse tibi carone putes, quos vincis amicos?

CHE, 56  *creer que sean amigos tuyos. Ca el hombre no ama a aquel*
QC, 28  caue credas: inter dominum et seruum nulla amicitia est.
Al., 4335  Quam servi ad dominum sit veri nodus amoris
Al., 4356  Inter eos nulla est concordia [...]

CHE, 57  *el quel teme. Por benefiçios ha de començar l'amistat.*

El resultado de esta comparación es que el *Alexandreis* se basa en este caso, como en tantos otros,[4] en la obra de Quinto Curcio; la Historia romana en este episodio presenta un texto relativamente uniforme en los manuscritos tanto en lengua original como en las traducciones. Este episodio, a su vez, pasa a otros libros que sirvieron para aprovisionar de ejemplos a un gran número de obras medievales, como el tan conocido *Speculum historiale* de Vincent de Beauvais[5] y otros más. Sin embargo, no puedo aún señalar si la redacción del Cancionero se hizo de manera directa sobre Curcio (o sobre el *Alexandreis*) o si existe otra pieza intermediaria a través de la cual se haya verificado ya esta labor de traducción y glosa amplificatoria. De todas maneras, aun en la situación acual de la investigación, cabe establecer un comentario provisional.

a) La pieza del Cancionero ofrece una disposición genérica diferente de la Historia del Curcio, del *Alexandreis* de Gualterio "el de las escuelas," del *Speculum historiale* de Vincent de Beauvais y del Libro de Alexandre.[6] En estas obras el trozo en cuestión es un par-

---

[4] El libro básico es el de George Cary, *The Medieval Alexander* (Cambridge: Cambridge University Press, [1956] 1967); debe completarse con la amplia reseña de María Rosa Lida, "La leyenda de Alejandro" (1962), en *La tradición clásica en España* (Barcelona: Ariel, 1975), págs. 165-97, en donde se encuentra la más extensa referencia de las menciones y citas anecdóticas de Alejandro en la literatura medieval castellana. La mención de M. R. Lida a la *Letra*, en la pág. 193, y la considera como paráfrasis del trozo Curcio. Cary trata de este episodio de los escitas en la pág. 149 y señala de la tradición literaria en la que Alejandro se enfrenta con un filósofo que no es su maestro Aristóteles, tal como ocurre en la anécdota de Diógenes y en la de los gimnosofistas, a las que añade esta de los escitas en la que el emisario es "unum ex his maximum natu" (VI, viii, 12); lo mismo se reitera en Gautier de Châtillon (pág. 173).

[5] El texto de Vincent de Beauvais puede leerse en la *Bibliotheca Mundi* (Duaci: B. Bellero, 1624), págs. 135-36 del *Speculum historiale*. Otros textos medievales con la anécdota en Cary, págs. 298-99.

[6] En el libro de *Alexandre* (edición de Dana Arthur Nelson [Madrid: Gre-

lamento del más anciano de entre los embajadores escitas, mientras que en el Cancionero se trata de una *Letra* o carta. Los textos precedentes guardan su propia entidad genérica: el de Curcio, como historia, el *Alexandreis* y el *Libro de Alexandre* como poemas épicos adecuados para la exaltación medieval del héroe, y el *Speculum* como ejemplario moral. En cada estos textos suponen la base de Curcio, y cada uno el trozo se interpreta en forma acorde con el contexto.

En nuestro caso hay una evidente diferencia: lo que son discursos del guerrero de más edad (y por eso de mayor experiencia) de convierte en una *Letra* o carta, epístola en prosa en tono elevado. La nueva interpretación está acorde con con el gran desarrollo que ha tomado el grupo genérico epistolar en el siglo XV. La *Letra* es aquí un breve tratado moral y político, y aparece aislada del resto de la historia de Alejandro que el autor del arreglo supone que ya conocen los nobles oyentes o lectores; la cáustica y cínica réplica de Alejandro[7] se ha suprimido y no importa que lo que el viejo guerrero escita haya dicho o escrito no produjera en la historia ningún efecto. La lección persiste más allá de la circunstancia a que pertenece en la Historia de Curcio y se convierte en exposición moral aplicable a cualquier hombre, antiguo o moderno. Y éste es el valor más importante que se desprende de este replanteamiento genérico.[8] La *Letra* se sitúa en un punto crítico; es una pieza que está en los comienzos del Humanismo en cierto modo militante, que ha buscado la base de una mejor lección textual (Curcio, aunque no se limita a ella ni la declara), dejando atrás el Humanismo medieval, sosteniendo por la clerecía, que tanto se había valido de la figura de

---

dos, 1979]) el episodio análogo se encuentra en las estrofas 1918-39 en una versión más libre que las precedentes y que no puede relacionarse con nuestra *Letra*.

[7] La respuesta es breve y en discurso indirecto: "Contra rex fortuna sua et consiliis eorum ursum esse respondet; nam et fortunam, cui confidat et consilium suadentium ne quid temere et audacter faciat, secuturum." (VII, ix, 1) ("En respuesta de lo que se la había dicho, el Rey les responde que él haría caso tanto a su fortuna, a la que se confía, como al consejo que le persuade de que no lleve a cabo nada que resulte temerario o audaz.")

[8] No olvidemos tampoco el gran número de cartas dirigidas a escritas por Alejandro que existen en la literatura medieval, por lo que añadir una más no fue nada extraordinario en esta tradición epistolar.

Alejandro, incluso tomándola del mismo Curcio. Reúne también el
tema de la Fortuna con el de la exposición de un buen gobierno
natural, basado en una limitación consciente y disciplinada de los
medios de vida; esto resulta diferente de la pobreza de índole religiosa que expone, por ejemplo, el fraile agustino Martín de Córdoba en su *Compendio de la Fortuna*. Cabe, pues, situar la *Letra* en estos
límites de transición que son propios de la corriente prehumanista.

b) Esta *Letra* representa también una innovación con respecto a
la consideración de esta parte de la Historia de Curcio como ejemplo medieval, según muestra G. Cary en varios casos. Sin embargo,
el parlamento de los escitas a Alejandro en Curcio resulta ser también una "tradición" que él ha recogido para incluirla en su Historia; esto lo declara diciendo que las palabras del escita pueden
parecer extrañas para el tiempo y el ingenio cultivado de los roma-
nos, pero su fidelidad de historidor no puede rechazarlas y así
recoge lo que le ha contado o ha sabido (la tradición) sin alterarlo.
La *Letra* del Cancionero de Herberay, compilado probablemente
entre 1461 y 1464, aísla la materia mencionada con un propósito
más complejo. Ch. Aubrun sitúa esta parte inicial del Cancionero,
escrita en prosa, en la Corte de doña Leonor, condesa de Foix,
regente del reino de Navarra y propone a Hugo de Urríes como
complidor del mismo. Resulta, pues, una novedad que entre la lírica
cancioneril vernácula (castellana, navarra y aragonesa en unos límites difíciles de precisar) aparezca esta *Letra* en prosa. Si bien en el
Cancionero predomina la poesía amorosa, también hay piezas que
se acercan al contenido de esta prosa, sobre todo en lo tocante al
asunto común de la fortuna: la pieza CCI "Dezir de la Fortuna,"
anónima, con una fuerte contenido anticlerical, se refiere a los
casos de la misma, y en una estrofa alude, sin nombres, al contenido de la *Letra*:

> De los reyes e monarchas
> que mucho triumpharon
> en el mundo conquistando [ ... ]
> quiçá conmemoraría,
> s[i] fuesse necessidat,
> relatando sus caýdas.
> Mas entiendo que sería

extrema prolijidat
para quien las ha oýdas.[9]

El anónimo autor de la poesía no cita a Alejandro, el mejor
modelo de conquistador, sino a los casos que son contemporáneos
de los oyentes: el de don Álvaro de Luna y del duque de Sofolech (o
Suffolk), ejecutado en Inglaterra en 1450. Sin embargo, en la *Letra*,
con una nueva presentación, el caso de Alejandro con los escitas
aparece como el motivo fundamental para establecer las reflexiones
morales en las que la fortuna interviene esta vez mediante un
texto procedente del latino antiguo Curcio. El tópico reaparece una
vez más, procedente de un libro romano que se ofrece directamente (en parte del texto y sin la mención del autor, pero un maestro podría declararlo se era oportuno) a los nobles oyentes o
lectores de la corte navarra. Podemos, pues, afirmar que no se trata
en esta ocasión de exaltar otra vez al héroe conquistador, sino de
ofrecer la opinión de los que, frente a él, defienden con la razón
humana la dignidad de una paz amistosa como preferible a la
odiosa guerra. El ropaje clásico de la presentación es evidente, y así
la exposición de la causa y su defensa sobrepasan los límites de las
moralidades precedentes (sobre todo, el conodico tópico de la fortuna y la mención de los "vicios" de Alejandro, en este caso la ambición y la soberbia) para dar en un asunto político como es la
demostración de un pueblo que expone las bases de su buen
gobierno y que en los términos en que se presenta sólo ha podido
ponerse de manifiesto en donde haya un público capaz de percibir
la intención en que se apoya la virtualidad de la pieza retórica. Su
situación en las primeras páginas de un códice que reúne obras líricas de tan diferentes procedencias resulta sintomática para probar
que el asunto planteado en la pieza se asegura un lugar en las páginas de una obra destinada a la nobleza cortesana y no sólo a un
grupo reducido de entendidos en las cuestiones de la Antigüedad.

c) La *Letra* puede considerarse como un ejercicio retórico que
replantea un tema muy conocido en los círculos cortesanos aficiona-
dos a la poesía pues se había puesto de manifiesto en grandes obras
(*Alexandreis*, *Speculum* o *Libro de Alexandre*) y en los menudos ejem-

---

9 Cancionero citado, poesía, CCI, pág. 199.

plos.[10] En este caso el traductor-glosador ha reducido la dimensión
de la pieza pues el texto original de Curcio es más amplio, y en la
nueva constitución literaria han desaparecido las menciones de
Europa, Asia, persas, medos, tracios, bactrianos, sogdianos, indios y
sus lugares, y también la cuestión del cruce del río Tánais (que es
causa última del discurso o de la *Letra*, pues era la frontera de los
escitas). Solos frente a frente, escitas y Alejandro, representan dos
concepciones opuestas de la vida, aplicadas al examen de la codicia
o apetencia de poder político y en relación con las mudanzas de la
fortuna.

La exposición de los escitas ante Alejandro es clara: ellos le avi-
san de su condición humana y que no tiente a la Fortuna hasta la
exasperación pretendiendo alcanzar el dominio del mundo pues él
es hombre como los demás. La *Letra* expresa la opinión del pueblo
escita de acuerdo con sus elementales pero justas normas políticas.
En esta *Letra* no se dice nada del Alejandro como héroe de los poemas y paradigma de virtudes; pertenece en esto a la tradición
estoica medieval en que un filósofo insiste frente al hombre de
acción en los límites de la condición humana que es común a los
grandes y a los menudos. En este época—siglo XV—se apaga el
brillo del Alejandro medieval, esplendente en medio de las maravillas que de él se contaron. La progresiva difusión de la Historia de
Curcio a través de la copia de los manuscritos latinos y de las versiones a las lenguas vernáculas devuelve al gran conquistador estos
límites humanos. Vasco de Lucena[11] traduce al francés la Historia
de Curcio en 1468 y dedica su labor a Carlos el Temerario; en un
ambiente cortesano paralelo al que rodea nuestra *Letra*, Lucena,
rechazando los aspectos fantásticos del Alejandro medieval proce-
dentes del Pseudo-Calístenes y otras obras, quiere restituir "au
vray comment Alexandre conqcuist tout Orient," y esto lo hizo
"sans voller en aer, sans aller soubz mer, sans enchantemens, sans

---

[10] En el tratado *Liber de vita et moribus philosophorum de Gulterio Burleus (Walter Burley)* (edición de Hermann Knust [Tübingen, 1886], págs. 278-81; versión castellana, *La vida y las costumbres de los viejos filósofos*, Ms. H-iii-1 de la Biblioteca del Escorial), se atribuye a Calístenes un fragmento del trozo que aquí trato, en otra versión; y otros más, como estudiaré.

[11] Véase Robert Bossuat, "Vasque de Lucène, traducteur de Quinte-Curce," en le *Bibliothèque* d'Humanisme et Renaissance. Travaux et Documents, VIII (Paris: Droz, 1946), págs. 197-245.

estre sy fort comme Raignault de Montaubain, comme Lancelot,
comme Tristan...;" Lucena indica que la conquista la hizo "avec
gens de tels forces que nous sommes aujourd'hui."[12] Este paralelo
de los hombres de ayer con los de hoy mueve también el propósito
de la *Letra* del Cancionero, de una evidente modernidad en la exposición. Los escitas ya no aparecen mezclados con la irracionalidad
salvaje o con los poderes maléficos de Gog y Magog,[13] y recobren
su identidad colectiva como pueblo "bárbaro" pero poseedor de una
filosofía de la vida basada en la naturaleza humana primigenia que
los conduce a obrar con justicia y verdad. Sobre esta base, que se
da como presupuesta en la *Letra* y desde la que los escitas funda-
mentan sus razones, se atreven a formular su opinión ante el conquistador, y poco importa que los oyentes o lectores conozcan el
aciago destino del pueblo que sería derrotado por Alejandro.

El héroe medieval aparece, pues, desmitificado en esta breve
pieza del siglo XV y no es ya el vencedor liberal y magnánimo, sino
la representación de cualquier poder que sobrepase el respecto que
se debe al hombre y al pueblo constituido; atentar contra la libertad
es ir contra Dios y contra la Naturaleza y oponerse a los principios
que genera el alma humana como base de la conducta civil.

d) Esta vía conduce la pieza en cuestión hacia el dominio que
me interesa comentar. Por una parte el traductor sigue a Curcio en
el planteamiento topístico que tanto atrajo la imaginación medieval: Alejandro con el mundo en la mano, sujeto desde Oriente a
Occidente. Esta grandeza enunciada se contapesa con los peligros
de la mudable Fortuna. Pero luego el traductor-glosador abre una
extensa amplificación (líneas 15-34) en la que los escitas describen
su vida, y esto sí que importa para nuestro fin, pues tal vida es un
programa que ofrece coindidencias con el ideal utópico:

---

[12] Bossuat, pág. 213. Paralelamente a Vasco de Lucena, Pier Candido
Decembri tradujo la Historia de Curcio y le ofreció al Duque de Milán en
1438 (Bossuat, pág. 201); esta versión estaba en castellano en la Biblioteca
del Marqués de Santillana (Mario Schiff, *La Bibliothèque du Marquis de Santillana* [Paris: E. Bouillon, 1905], págs. 146-49.) en un manuscrito que hoy se
concerva en la Biblioteca Nacional de Madrid (Ms. 10140, el trozo del que nos
ocupamos en el cap. 21, libro VI, fols. 197v-181v).

[13] Cary, *The Medieval Alexander*, pág. 130.

1. Los hombres viven según naturaleza en la inocencia y la verdad.

2. Su organización social desconoce la propiedad y el dinero, no navegan para cambiar o negociar, no construyen palacios y no visten con lujos.

3. Se dedican al cultivo del alma despreciando los apetitos del cuerpo, pues el alma los hace semejantes a dioses y el cuerpo a bestias.

La cuestión está en averiguar de dónde pudo proceder esta amplificación. Una hiptótesis es que el traductor glosó en esta parte una referencia que el propio Curcio había hecho, de una manera muy condensada, a unos escitas llamados abienos: "Se les considera-raba como a los más justos de entre los bárbaros; se abstenían de las armas como no fuesen para defenderse. Por el uso moderno de la libertad y de la igualdad, ellos habían hecho iguales a los más elevados con los más humildes."[14] Este trozo pudo servir como punto de partida para describir la situación social que se nos des-cribe en la *Letra*. Pudiera añadirse que el Epítome de Justino[15] acaso fuese otra fuente de noticias; en él aparece una descripción de la vida de los escitas en donde hay algunos rasgos, incluso más acusa-dos, de lo que se nos dice en el Cancionero; la gran difusión del Epítome de Justino hizo que esta imagen del pueblo escita pudiera ser conocida en los medios clericales y de estos pasar a los cortesa-

---

[14] "Iustissimos Barbarorum constabat: armas abstinebat, nisi iacessiti. Libertatis modico et aequali usu principibus humiliores pares fecerent," Curcio, VII, vii, 11.

[15] El trozo de Justino se encuentra en la rama general de los textos, que recoge, por ejemplo, le edición de la Colección francesa de Nisard, en el tomo encábezado por C. Nepote (p. 394, Cap. II, iii) y que recojo en una traducción castellana del siglo XVI: "Son gente que mantienen mucha justi-cia y esto más por su condición y buen natural que no por leyes. [ ... ] El oro y la plata tanto lo menosprecian, como nosotros lo deseamos . [ ... ] De aquí procede que, por ser tan continentes en sus usos augmentan en tanto grado la justicia y rectitud en que biven, porque no desean nada de lo ajeno..." (*Justino claríssimo abreuiador de la historia general del famoso y excellente historiador Trogo Pompeyo...* [Alcalá de Henares: Brócar, 1540]). Se trata de la parte en que describe el país de Escitia y sus gentes, cuyas características coinciden en parte con lo que de dice en la *Letra*, si bien en este caso se atribuye al nomadismo del pueblo.

nos. También cabe indicar otras resonancias de los textos medievales de la familia de la *Historia de Preliis*, en especial de las cartas entre Alejandro y Díndimo, rey de los bragmanos, que ofrecen un contenido parecido al de la *Letra*l, sólo que establecido con mucha mayor amplitud; la confusión inadvertida o la mezcla consiente de los rasgos de los bragmanos con los de los escitas pudo ser fácil, aunque en este caso no hubiese una relación inmediata con esta rama de la difusión del Alejandro medieval.

f) El autor de la *Letra* en el ambiente cortesano de la corte de Navarra, valiéndose de la lengua vernácula (en castellano con ligeros aragonesismos) abrió paso a la consideración de un pueblo que vive en un régimen de justicia política conducente al cultivo de las virtudes "durables de inmortal bienaventuranza" (Cancionero, línea 30). El traductor y glosador acerca el texto antiguo a la modernidad religiosa con este leve toque de cristianismo. La exposición de las virtudes antiguas resulta válida para el hombre moderno. Y con esto la *Letra* se aproxima al propósito que había de servir a Moro para su *Utopía* en la que establece este paralelo de una manera sistemática y constitucional. Alejandro, que de tan conocido ya no cuenta, queda sólo con la función de destinatario de la epístola moral. El propósito espiritual de la *Letra* queda manifiesto: un pueblo expone su constitución política, basada en la justicia, aunque sea extranjero, fuera de los límites de la cultura griega, esto es "bárbaro". También para él, el traductor defiende la amistad basada en la paz y el mutuo respeto.

Evidentemente la *Letra* es una preciosa pieza del humanismo preliminar del siglo XV. Cercana al texto histórico de Curcio, establecida sobre una glosa amplificatoria, inclina el desarrollo del asunto hacia cuestiones que tocan a la organización social, la justicia y la libertad humanas. Se trata de un episodio más de lo que R. Trousson llama los "genres apparentés"[16] que preceden y acompañan a las utopías propiamente dichas y sin los cuales éstas no pudieran haberse establecido; en este caso es evidente un propósito literario, aunque se trate, como me parece, de un ejercicio retórico. La figura de Alejandro, que ha servido para establecer la exaltación del imperio medieval, vale también para su rechazo por motivos de

---

16 Raymond Trousson, *Voyages aux pays de nulle part. Histoire littéraire de la pensée utopique* (Bruselas: Éditions de l'Université, 1979) 2ª ed., págs. 25-28.

orden moral que se convierten en políticos al referirse al caso de un pueblo entero. Así el bárbaro tiene la ocasión de ofrecer su lección al griego o al romano o al hombre clerical de estas raíces; el humanismo, remodelando las viejas cuestiones, realza estos exámenes de conciencia preparando la modernidad. La Literatura española recoge esta corriente, y así en esta *Letra* sobrepasa las formas medievales de los ejemplos y performula ya la de los tratados más complejos, si bien en este caso la pieza literaria examinada resulta de breve dimensión y escaso valor creativo pero intensamente sintomática para el proveso que pretendo ilustrar: la participación española en este movimiento espiritual europeo que anuncia la aparición de la *Utopía* de Moro, impresa por vez primera en 1516. Importa mencionar, como colofón, que en 1527 fray Antonio de Guevara había obtenido un privilegio de impresión para Castilla de su *Relox de Príncipes*, impreso en 1529, en donde figura el extenso episodio del discurso de los garamantes que vuelve a ofrecer en forma extensa (y probablemente con la misma base en Curcio) este propósito de exponer el ideal de une justa vida colectiva.[17]

UNIVERSIDAD COMPLUTENSE, MADRID

---

[17] Véase Augustin Redondo, *Antonio de Guevara (1480?-1585) et l'Espagne de son temps* (Ginebra: Droz, 1976), págs. 661 y 667; y Asunción Rallo, *Antonio de Guevara en su contexto renacentista* (Madrid: Cupsa, 1979), págs. 130-33; y sobre su conexión con T. Moro, en Francisco López Estrada, *Tomás Moro en España (sus relaciones hasta el siglo XVIII)* (Madrid: Universidad Complutense, 1980).

# The Tale of the Helpful Dolphin
# in Lope García de Salazar's
## Libro de las bienandanzas e fortunas

HE TENTH BOOK of Lope García de Salazar's *Libro de las bienandanzas e fortunas*, written between 1471 and 1476, is a heterogeneous mixture of history and pseudohistory concerning various dukedoms, counties and cities in France, the Low Countries and northern Italy.[1] The book opens with a curious tale of the origins of the dukedom of Dauphiné: how the name Dauphiné was derived from the incident of a dolphin coming to the rescue of a young French prince, the sole survivor of a sunken flotilla that had been led by the boy's pagan father who was bent upon invading and destroying England, despite his son's strong moral opposition.

---

[1] For the full text of Book X, see *Las bienandanzas e fortunas*, ed. Angel Rodríguez Herrero (Bilbao: Diputación de Vizcaya, 1967), II, 195-219, and "folios" 106, col. 2-120, col. 2 (a photographic reproduction of fols. 172c-179d of the so-called Cristóbal de Mieres codex, Madrid, Real Academia de la Historia, MS. 9-10-2/2100, the earliest surviving copy of the *Bienandanzas e fortunas*, dated 1492). Short extracts from Book X are also included in my edition *The Legendary History of Britain in Lope García de Salazar's* Libro de las bienandanzas e fortunas (Philadelphia: Univ. of Pennsylvania Press, 1979), pp. 47-49.

## THE TEXT[2]

[fol. 172d] En el reyno de Françia reynaba vn rey de quien non se dize su nonbre, tornandole voluntad de yr en el reyno de Ynguelaterra para la dañar e destroyr. E avia vn fijo mançebo e mucho noble cauallero e deuoto en su criador, cavn en aquel tienpo no eran christianos. E pesandole de aquel mal proposito quel rey su padre avia[3] tomado, trabaxose en lo sacar dello, mostrandole como las cosas contra Dios eran de poco fruto quanto mas a los reyes que eran logartenientes en la tierra. E quando mas no pudo, fuese con el en su nao mesma en vno con grande flota que leuaban consigo. E entrados en la mar nabegando, somieronse algunas naos de fuerte tormenta. Entre las quales fue una dellas aquella en quel el rey e su fijo yban; e pereçidas todas, andando este fijo del rey medio afogado e quisiendose yr al suelo, pusosele vn toyno asaz grande entre las piernas; e como el lo sintio, apetrose[4] en el como es estilo de los que pereçen en la mar o en rios de se apretar con lo que fallan e suele conteçer perderse el que sabe nadando trabandole el que no sabe [fol. 173a][5] e caerse anbos al suelo. E commo las cosas que Dios quiere guardar son breuemente saluas, sacolo aquel toyno de la mar e pusole en la orilla de la tierra casi desacordado del trabaxo e de la agua salada que avia vebido. E salido en tierra e a cabo[6] de ser tornado en su sano sentido e reynando en su reyno en Françia e menbrandosele deste milagro quel Señor Dios avia fecho, por el trabaxose en lo serbir e ovedeçer en todas las cosas quel pudo en toda su vida;

---

[2] I give my own reading of MS. 9-10-2/2100, fols. 172d-173a, since the Rodríguez Herrero edition should be used with caution due to its many errors in transcription. I preserve the original orthography, modernizing only the Tironian sign to e and regularizing the use of i and j (except in roman numerals); I generally follow modern norms of capitalization and punctuation. In the notes below I include variants from a sixteenth-century copy, Madrid, Biblioteca Nacional, MS. 1634, which at times tends to correct scribal errors in MS. 9-10-2/2100.

[3] MS. 1634, le avia.

[4] MS. 1634, apretose.

[5] Scribal repetition of sabe at beginning of fol. 173a.

[6] MS. 1634, acabado.

e menbrandosele del miraglo que Dios mostro por el con
aquel toyno, que era pescado tan señalado e el mas allegado a
la natura del ome de todas las animalias brabas e mansas, no
fuendo el puerco, e avn aquel no tanto en el amor, ca dizen
los mareantes que cada que los topan en la mar siguen los
nabios e peganseles mucho por oyrlos fablar e van sienpre a
lo verde[7] del nabio faziendo entre si bueltas a manera de solaz
mostrando alegrias e a las vezes saltando aRiba. E dio este rey
por remenbrança deste toyno a vn su fijo mayor la tierra que
estonçes se llamaba de los albroges,[8] que comarca[9] con el
ducado de Saboya, e llamolo dolfinazgo por el nonbre e
remenbrança de aquel toyno a que los françeses llaman
dolfin. E diole por armas con aquel dolfinado quatro toynos
entre una ✠. E ordeno que todos reyes que reynasen despues
del en Françia eredasen a sus primeros fijos mayores en aquel
dolfinado e que se llamasen dolfines; e asi paso en grandes
tienpos en Françia.

## COMMENTARY

The helpful dolphin is found in folklore and numerous stories
and iconographic representations of helpful dolphins survive from
antiquity, some of the ancient stories continuing to be recounted
during the Middle Ages,[10] but in my research on the history and
legend of dolphins and the early history of the territory of Dauphiné, I have uncovered no other account quite like that told by
García de Salazar. While it is clear that the greater part of the *Libro
de las bienandanzas e fortunas* was derived from written sources, from

---

[7] MS. 1634, *verdes.*

[8] Within his history of the Romans, Salazar narrates Hannibal's journey to Italy (Book VII, Chapter 12) and states that Hannibal "llego a vna
ysla que vebian vnas gentes que se llamaban los alogres que se llaman
agora del Dolfinat e de Saboya de Vergoña" (Rodríguez Herrero, II, 15,
"folio" 6).

[9] MS. 1634, *comarcaua.*

[10] See Stith Thompson, *Motif-Index of Folk Literature* (rpt. Bloomington:
Indiana Univ. Press, 1975), I, B473; Eunice Burr Stebbins, *The Dolphin in
the Literature and Art of Greece and Rome* (Menasha, Wis.: The George Banta
Publishing Co., 1929); and Anthony Alpers, *Dolphins: The Myth and the
Mammal* (Boston: Houghton Mifflin, 1960).

books in the personal libraty of García de Salazar,[11] the work also
includes material taken presumably from oral tradition, as Ramón
Menéndez Pidal, S. G. Armistead, and I have pointed out elsewhere.[12] Whether García de Salazar's helpful dolphin tale was
based primarily on a written source or was built upon hearsay and
legend remains a mystery, but it reveals a remarkable combination
of pseudohistory, marine lore, heraldic tradition, and moral didacti-
cism, as well as the use of the word *toyno* for 'dolphin' in García de
Salazar's native province of Vizcaya.

The García de Salazar text does share a feature with some of
the ancient dolphin stories: the belief that dolphins come to the aid
of the shipwrecked and carry the victims to safety. For example,
Telemachus, son of Ulysses, is said to have been rescued at sea by
dolphins and brought safely to shore;[13] Arion, the semilegendary
poet-musician of Lesbos was supposedly led ashore by a dolphin
after jumping overboard from a pirates' ship;[14] and Coeranus, who
once saved some dolphins caught by fishermen, is said to have
been rescued by a dolphin when his boat overturned and was
taken to a cave.[15] In the Middle Ages such stories are used to illustrate virtue and sin: Nicole Bozon's *Contes moralisés* attributes to
Pliny the story of the gratitude of dolphins toward humans who
have earlier befriended them by not eating dolphin meat;[16] in the
*Gesta Romanorum* we find a story, attributed to Aulus Gellius, of
greedy sailors who are condemned to death after throwing overboard a rich shipbuilder whom they first allowed to sing in honor
of dolphins, thus prompting the shipbuilder's rescue by a dol-

---

[11] See the summary of my unpublished paper, "A Scrutiny of the
Library of Lope García de Salazar," presented to the 1976 conference of
the Association of Hispanists of Great Britain and Ireland, in *La Corónica*,
4 (1975-76), 99.

[12] See *The Legendary History of Britain*, pp. 6, 10-11, 18, 49, 72-73, 126-
29.

[13] William Berry, *Encyclopaedia Heraldica or Complete Dictionary of Heraldry*
(London: Sherwood, Gilbert and Piper, 1828), I, Aa3.

[14] Stebbins, pp. 66-70.

[15] Stebbins, pp. 62-63.

[16] *Les Contes moralisés de Nicole Bozon*, ed. Lucy Toulmin Smith and Paul
Meyer (Paris: Librairie de Firmin Didot, 1889), p. 67.

phin.[17] From China there also comes the story of a drowning princess saved by a river dolphin.[18] While the possibility of conscious or instinctive rescue by dolphins is generally discounted by modern scientists, for centuries sailors believed that dolphins possessed humanlike intelligence and that dolphins could save them from drowning in case of shipwreck. As recently as 1943 a report appeared in the magazine *Natural History* of a woman pushed to shore by a dolphin after being caught in a riptide along the Florida coast, thus revealing the persistence of the ancient belief in our own times.[19] In response to the report, a letter to the Editor of the magazine and an editorial comment discount the likelihood of the dolphin deliberately helping the woman in distress in favor of the general "sporty" behavior of dolphins around humans.[20]

Although I am not aware of any other medieval account placing the helpful dolphin motif within a historically medieval framework,[21] the dolphin did become an obejct of medieval heraldry (it also appeared on shields in antiquity)[22] and it, from an early date, associated with the dukedom of Dauphiné, although there are conflicting explanations for the origin of the name. According to William Berry, the early nineteenth-century historian of heraldry, the sovereign rulers of the territory known as Dauphiné took the dolphin for their arms, and, when the line came to an end, the last ruler turned the territory over to the king of France with the stipulation that the heir to the French throne should be called *Dauphin* and always use the dolphin for his arms.[23] As Berry points out, the

[17] *Gesta Romanorum*, trans. by Charles Swan, revised and corrected by Wynnard Hooper (rpt. New York: Dover Publications, 1959), pp. 254-55 (Tale CXLVIII).

[18] Alpers, p. 156.

[19] "Saved by a Porpoise," *Natural History*, 56 (1947), 337, 383.

[20] *Natural History*, 58 (1949), 385-86; see also remarks by Alpers, pp. 107-10.

[21] But cf. the story of the helpful stags (Stith Thompson motif B443.1) that rescue Oliveros de Castilla and a companion knight from a shipwreck, in the romance *Oliveros de Castilla y Artús de Algarbe*, in *Libros de caballería*, ed. Alberto Blecua (Barcelona: Editorial Juventud, 1969), pp. 60-62.

[22] Stebbins, pp. 95-96.

[23] Berry, I, Aa3.

arms of the Dauphin consist of a cross diadem with four dolphins, just as García de Salazar describes them, except for the diadem, at the end of his tale.[24] Modern literature on Dauphiné shows that historians have now probed further into the origin of the name. The volume dedicated to Dauphiné in the popular *Les Guides bleus* series (Paris, 1971, p. 45, n. 1) states that *Dauphin* was derived from the Christian name Dolphin, or Adolphe, which the English wife of Guigues III gave to their son, Guigues IV, as a surname, at the beginning of the twelfth century, but that the emblem on the arms did not appear until much later. In a study published in 1972, Paul Dreyfus also states that Guigues IV was the first to bear the name Dauphin (before assuming the throne) and cites as evidence a document of 1110 containing the name "Guigo Dalphinus."[25] But concerning the origin of Dauphin as a name, Dreyfus is unable to provide an explanation other than what others have proposed, "selon les uns, ce surnom aurait été donné à l'enfant en souvenir du poisson qui impressionait tant les navigateurs de l'époque; selon d'autres, il lui aurait été attribué sur le désir de sa mère, dont un cousin germain se prénommait Dolfin. Il s'agirait donc d'un surnom d'origine britannique."[26] As for the name Dauphiné, Dreyfus and other historians find its origin in the word *Dalphinatus*, which first appeares in 1293.

García de Salazar's heraldic references are to the arms of the eldest son of the French king, the one holding the *dolfinazgo* or exclusive right to inheritance as Dauphin (Bk. X, ch. 2, continues with the history of the Dauphin as heir to the kingdom of France), but his account of the origin of dolphins on the arms may be a unique survival of a now lost, contemporary fifteenth-century (or possibly earlier) explanation for the names Dauphin and Dauphiné.[27]

---

[24] On various uses of the arms of Dauphiné, see John Woodward and Geroge Burnett, *A Treatise on Heraldry, British and Foreign, with English and French Glossaries*, revised by J. Woodward (rpt., with new Introduction by L. G. Pine, Rutland, Vt.: C. E. Tuttle, 1969), I, 424, 429, 463, 572, 629, 632, 636.

[25] Paul Dreyfus, *Histoire du Dauphiné* (Paris: Presses Universitaires de France, 1972), p. 23.

[26] Dreyfus, p. 24.

[27] Dreyfus, p. 24; Bernard Bligny, *Histoire du Dauphiné* (Toulouse: Privat, 1973), p. 9.

As a proud Vizcayan nobleman, Salazar had a keen interest in heraldry and makes many references to shields and coats-of-arms throughout the *Bienandanzas e fortunas*. Elsewhere I have commented upon his strange reference to King Arthur's arms;[28] among other heraldic references we find the shield of Hector of Troy ("e traya en su escudo dorado tres leones colorados,"[29] "lleuaba en vn escudo dorado pintado vn leon vermejo"[30]), the flag of the kings of France ("fue echado del çielo la vandera que llaman oriflama con tres flores de lises, e aquellas tomo el por armas para si e para los que del suçedieron, ca de primero .iiij. sapos avian por armas los Reyes de Françia"),[31] and, of course, the arms and shield of the Salazar family ("e dexo las armas de Salazar, que eran vna torre almenada con su cortijo e las armas de la Çerca, que eran quatro almenas con su pitel blanqueçido; e tomo aquellas .xiiij. estrellas doradas en vn escudo el campo colorado").[32] Is it possible that Salazar, being familiar with the arms of the Dauphin, attached the story of the helpful dolphin to explain the appearance of dolphins on the arms and thus the etymology of Dauphiné? The suspicions of some modern French historians that the popularity of the dolphin may have given rise to the names Dauphin and subsequently Dauphiné would seem to discount such originality on Salazar's part, yet I know of no other surviving medieval explanation for the names. Elsewhere in the *Bienandanzas e fortunas* Salazar makes use of the common device of eponomy to explain place names, and he frequently combines information derived from disparate sources to produce his own version of history.[33] The same Book X is replete with curious amalgamations of varied materials and moralistic teaching similar to the poetic justice underscored in the story of the sinking of the pagan king of France's flotilla and the survival of his God-fearing, righteous son. For example, after the chapters on

---

[28] *The Legendary History of Britain*, pp. 118-19.

[29] Rodríguez Herrero, I, 177 ("folio" 104, col. 2).

[30] Rodríguez Herrero, I, 180 ("folio" 106, col. 2).

[31] Rodríguez Herrero, II, 148 ("folio" 83, col. 2).

[32] Rodríguez Herrero, IV, 113 ("folio" 46, col. 2).

[33] For examples of Salazar's use of eponomy, see *The Legendary History of Britain*, pp. 56, 57; on his concept of historiography, pp. 5-6.

the origin of Dauphiné and the Dauphin of France, we find a story of cannibalistic Flemings living in the time of King Arthur and the Knights of the Round Table,[34] the story of the descent into hell by a squire of a cruel count of Flanders and Lucifer's gift to the count of a casket which when opened spews forth fire burning the whole land,[35] a summary of the romance *Mélusine* set in Flanders,[36] and illusions to the story of Tristan and Iseut within the genealogical history of Brittany.[37]

Other texts may yet be brought to light showing that Salazar was not all that inventive in his telling of the helpful dolphin story, but his inclusion of sailors' observations of dolphin behavior would definitely seem to be his own contribution. Bits of marine lore and knowledge of seafaring activities in other countries are introduced at scattered points in the *Bienandanzas e fortunas*. Elsewhere I have singled out Salazar's knowledge of cartography, of North Atlantic voyages out of Bristol in search of the mythical Island of Brasil, and of trade between England and the northern ports of Spain.[38] Because Salazar lived in the Valley of Somorrostro, not far from the port of Bilbao, he undoubtedly had frequent contact with both

[34] Rodríguez Herrero, II, 197-98 ("folios" 107, col. 2-108, col. 1); *The Legendary History of Britain*, pp. 48, 92-94.

[35] Rodríguez Herrero, II, 198-201 ("folios" 108-10, col. 1).

[36] Rodríguez Herrero, II, 201-02 ("folios" 110-11, col. 1). In an unpublished paper presented to the annual Kentucky Foreign Language Conference in 1977, I pointed out that Salazar's summary seems to derive from a variant version of the French romance. On the Spanish translations, also different from the Salazar summary, see A. D. Deyermond, "*La historia de la linda Melusina*: Two Spanish Versions of a French Romance," in *Medieval Hispanic Studies Presented to Rita Hamilton*, ed. A. D. Deyermond (London: Tamesis, 1976), 57-65.

[37] Rodríguez Herrero, II, 210-11 ("folio" 115, col. 2); *The Legendary History of Britain*, pp. 48-49, 94-95. In addition to Salazar's use of Arthurian romances and the romance *Mérusine*, he also seems to have incorporated an Alexander romance into his history of Alexander the Great (Book V). See Dorothy Sherman Severin and Harvey L. Sharrer, "Fifteenth-Century Spanish Fragments of a Lost Prose Alexander," *Medium Aevum*, 48 (1979), 205-11.

[38] "The Passing of King Arthur to the Island of Brasil in a Fifteenth-century Spanish Version of the Post-Vulgate *Roman du Graal*," *Romania*, 92 (1971), 65-74; *The Legendary History of Britain*, pp. 18, 126-29.

Spanish and foreign seamen and ship captains. The behavior attributed to dolphins in the Salazar text—their humanlike qualities, their pattern of following ships and leaping out of the water in playful merriment—is, of course, also testified to in the literature of Greece and Rome and is certainly familiar to the modern reader through publicity given to scientific studies of dolphins in captivity.[39]

Throughout the narrative Salazar uses the word *toyno* for "dolphin" and explains only toward the end that the French call the animal *dolfin* (cf. Fr. *dauphin*, It. *delfino*, and the unusual OSp. form *dalfyn* in the *Cancionero de Baena*). For "dolphin" in the Iberian Peninsula, the more common form is *tonina* or *tonino*, and it is the masculine form that is used along the Cantabrian coast and in the Castilian of the Basque Country, in the same sense as the Fr. *dauphin*.[40] I find no other recorded use of *toyno*; it would seem to be an acceptable phonological variant of *tonino* rather than a scribal error. The statement that the pig resembles man perhaps more than the dolphin may seem a strange observation, but in the Middle Ages man's behavior was frequently compared to that of the pig or boar, usually in terms of sin (gluttony, sensuality, lust, bestiality, rath, madness) or as a symbol of the Jew as persecutor of Christ, but the boar also had its positive features and frequently appears in such light in medieval heraldry.[41]

UNIVERSITY OF CALIFORNIA, SANTA BARBARA

---

[39] Stebbins, p. 93; J. R. Norman and F. C. Fraser, *Giant Fishes, Whales and Dolphins* (New York: W. W. Norton, 1938), pp. 329, 330; Ronald M. Lockley, *Whales, Dolphins and Porpoises* (New York: W. W. Norton, 1979), pp. 18-43, 167-85.

[40] See J. Corominas, *DCELC*, I, 328*b*, and especially the expanded entry for *atún* in Joan Corominas and José Pascual, *Diccionario crítico etimológico castellano e hispánico*, I (Madrid: Gredos, 1980), 408.

[41] Beryl Rowland, *Animals with Human Faces: A Guide to Animal Symbolism* (Knoxville: Univ. of Tennessee Press, 1973), pp. 37-43.

# Mito y realidad
# en el mundo medieval español

RICHARD P. KINKADE

L CONTACTO que tuvo España con la antigua civilización talásica de los celtas señalaba nuevos e importantes derroteros para la literatura hispánica, abriéndole la puerta a novedosos elementos novelescos que, con el tiempo, habían de aleajarle bastante de su antigua dependencia sobre el mundo mitológico greco-romano del Mediterráneo. La Europa medieval nunca se sentía del todo cómoda con los viejos mitos clásicos a pesar de haber aceptado las teorías de Evémero que creía ver en los dioses greco-romanos una raza de gigantes cuyas hazañas en los albores de la historia se habían transformado en las legendarias bases de una religión pagana.

Por otro lado, la mitología celta surgía en un ambiente de avanzada cristianización, siendo absorbida en gran medida por el cristianismo en un fenómeno que se repite una y otra vez en el Nuevo Mundo. He aquí por qué la mitología celta o bretona no lleve el estigma que había caracterizado a los antiguos mitos del mundo mediterráneo, y por consiguiente fueron adoptadas estas nuevas leyendas y empleadas al servicio de la Iglesia sin la menor resistencia. Sirva aquí de ejemplo el ciclo arturiano y el del Santo Grial donde el elemento espiritual parece dominar e incluso deformar nuestra visión de la realidad. Es aquí donde los endriagos, jayanes, y otros vestiglos del mal cobran el más legítimo sentido de su existencia, o sea, el de contraponerse como representantes del mal a las fuerzas del bien, en una constante lucha maniquea que se va alternando entre la luz de la razón y las tinieblas de la confusión.

Otro aspecto importante de la nueva mitología celta se realza en la preponderancia del papel que juega el mar. Como la civilización celta dependía en gran parte del comercio marítimo sobre el Atlántico, éste desplazaba en importancia al mar Mediterráneo. Al mismo tiempo, esta civilización marítima cristiana dio reiterado ímpetu a las leyendas que situaban en las islas del Atlántico al Paraíso Terrenal, tema explotado hasta lo máximo en los viajes marítimos del irlandés San Brendán, que desde entonces sale como el dechado superlativo de las historias en este género.

Esto es lo que ocurre en el pequeño relato de *La Vida de San Amaro* en que Amaro, avisado por una nocturna voz angélica, emprende un viaje en busca del Paraíso Terrenal. La leyenda de San Amaro, como lo hemos comentado muy extensamente en otras ocasiones,[1] es una conflación de la *Navigatio Sancti Brendani* con otros cinco *immrama*, o épicas celtas del mar, que forman un núcleo de las más antiguas obras conocidas en la literatura irlandesa.[2] El nombre de San Amaro es una corrupción de San Machuto o Saint Maclaw, fiel compañero de San Brendán en sus varios viajes marítimos en busca del Paraíso Terrenal. Por casualidad, estos viajes de San Brendán fueron atribuidos en varios manuscritos a su amigo, conocido en francés como San Malo, nombre que en español resulta un poco inverosímil por lo que habrá sido en alguna oportunidad sustituido por el de Maro o Amaro, tal como lo atestigua un códice portugués del siglo catorce que le llama San Mauro.[3]

Pero no vayamos a pensar que fuesen los celtas los primeros en

---

[1] Cf. R. P. Kinkade, "La evidencia para los antiguos *immrama* irlandeses en la literatura medieval española," *Actas del V Congreso Internacional de Hispanistas* (Bordeaux, 1977), II, págs. 511-25.

[2] *Navigatio Sancti Brendani Abbatis*, ed. Carl Selmer (University of Notre Dame, 1959); Sérgio Buarque de Holanda, *Visão do Paraíso* (São Paulo: Editôra da Universidade de São Paulo, 1969).

situar al Paraíso Terrestre en el Atlántico. Hesiodo (fl. s. IX A. DE J.
C.) en *Los trabajos y los días* habla de los guerreros que caían en
defensa de Tebas y Troya que ya fueron a vivir en las Islas Bienaventuradas del Océano mientras que Homero en la *Odisea* hace
comentar a Proteo que los Campos Eliseos están en el Océano
donde les da el aire suave de Occidente.[4] Platón (427?-347 A. DE J.
C.), contando una historia que le fue transmitida por Solón, que a
su vez la había oído en Egipto, relata en los diálogos de *Critias* y
*Timeo* que existía en tiempos remotos toda una civilización, en le Isla
de Atlántida, más allá de las Columnas de Hércules.[5] Y así segui-
mos a través de la antigüedad greco-latina, en las obras de Teo-
pompo de Quios (fl. 350 A. DE J. C.), Diodoro Sículo (fl. s. I A. DE J.
C.), Pausanias (fl. s. II A.D.), y Plutarco (c. 46-c.120 A.D.), juntamente
con las geografías de Estrabón (fl. s. I A. DE J. C.) y Claudio Tolomeo
(fl. s. II A. DE J. C.) que tratan el tema de las islas Afortunadas,
atribuyendo su descubrimiento a los cartagineses.[6]

Es notable que estamos en una época cuando los sabios eran a la
vez expertos en la filosofía, la literatura y la ciencia sin que existie-
ran entre esas disciplinas claras líneas divisorias. Y para el hombre
medieval, los escritores de esta edad constituían una autoridad
indiscutible e inexpugnable, cuyas palabras deberían de someterse a
un cuidadoso escrutinio con el fin de descubrir todos los esotéricos
sentidos que yacían por debajo de un exterior engañosamente senci-
llo. Por lo tanto, el cordobés Séneca podría escribir en su tragedia
*Medea* unos versos que tendrían fuertes repercusiones en la edad
media siendo interpretados como un pronóstico cierto de futuros
acontecimientos cuando hace decir al coro: "Vendrá un día en que el
Océano aflojará los vínculos y cuando la ingente Tierra se abrirá,
cuando la diosa marina Tifis descubrirá nuevos orbes y Tule no será

---

[3] Cf. Otto Klob, "*A vida de Sancto Amaro*, texte du XIVe siècle," *Romania*
XX (1901), 504-18.

[4] Hesiodo, *Los trabajos y los días*, 11. 170-73; *Odisea*, IV, 563 et seq.

[5] *Critias*, 108-19; *Timeo*, págs. 21-25.

[6] Max Carey y E. H. Warmington, *The Ancient Explorers* (New York:
Dodd, Mead & Co., 1929); John N. L. Baker, *A History of Geographical Discovery and Exploration* (New York: Cooper Square Publishers, 1967).

más el último extremo."[7] Este caso de bibliomancia corre parejo con
otro de la *Eneida* de Virgilio en un pasaje del libro sexto apuntando
el advenimiento de un salvador del mundo que la edad media acep-
taba como una legítima profecía mesiánica del nacimiento de
Cristo.[8]
     Así seguía cada vez más fuerte y acreditada la leyenda de las
islas paradisíacas del Océano, alentado las esperanzas de una civilización que soñaba con encontrarlas algún día. Ya en el siglo V de
nuestra era, el enciclopedista africano, Marcelo Capella, hace eco de
Plinio (23-79A.D.) repitiendo la leyenda que había encontrado en su
*Historia natural* sino que ahora declara que las islas Afortunadas son
en realidad el Jardín de las Hespéridea, dándoles el nombre de las
islas Górgades o Gorgonas.[9] Jordanes, escribiendo hacia la mitad del
siglo VI en su *Historia de los godos*, nos dice que "en las regiones occi-
dentales del Océano hay ciertas islas conocidas por todos en virtud
de los muchos viajeros que allí van y vienen" (I, 4, 7). En el siglo
noveno, el monje irlandés, Duicil (fl. 825), nos dice que las Hespéri-
des están más allá de las Górgades,[10] con lo que podemos comprender que la mente del hombre parece estar siempre inclinada a
extender su concepto de la realidad un poco más allá de lo que se
puede comprobar por datos empíricos recogidos de la observación,
sin que por esto haya sustraído nada a la totalidad de esta existencia. De lo que hemos dicho hasta ahora, es evidente que la realidad
coexiste en dos planos distintos, en un mundo visible regido por las
leyes naturales de la física y en otra esfera invisible como extensión
del mundo real sino que en este mundo metafísico, algo se deforma

---

[7]    Venient annis secula seris
     Quibus Oceanus vincula rerum
     Laxet, et ingens pateat tellus,
     Tiphysque novos detegat orbes
     Nec sit terris ultima Thyle. (Acto II, 371)

[8] Cf. D. Comparetti, *Virgilio nel medio evo*, 2 tomos (Livorno, 1872) y
John W. Spargo, *Virgil the Necromancer* (Cambridge. Harvard University
Press, 1934).

[9] *De Nuptiis Philologiae et Mercurii*, ed. Adolfus Dick (Leipzig: B.G.
Teubneri, 1925), VI, pág. 349.

[10] Cf. Antoine J. Letronne, *Recherches géographiques et critiques sur le livre*
De Mensura Orbis Terrae (Paris. G. Mathiot, 1814), VII.1.5.

la realidad para adaptarse a la realidad personal del individuo. De nuevo, lo que más nos interesa es la manera en que esta segunda realidad mental y abstracta haya sido informada por la literatura. En el siglo XII, el geógrafo Al Idrisí, conocido por el sobrenombre de "el Estrabón árabe," relata un extenso viaje emprendido con el fin de explorar el oeste del mar Océano, contándonos una serie de aventuras en un estilo típicamente medieval, entre burlas y veras.[11] Es posible que Al Idrisí conociera las obras del erudito francés y contempóraneo suyo, Honoré d'Autun, autor del famoso *Imago mundi* que tantos hechos y cifras había encontrado en las *Etimologías* del sevillano San Isidoro. Por más señas, la primera geografía en lengua castellana, la *Semiança del mundo*, una conflación de las obras del santo sevillano y Honorio, fue compuesta en el siglo XIII. Es este un curioso compendio donde encontramos por vez primera una referencia a la leyenda de San Brendán y las islas Bienaventuradas en las cuales logró el intrépido protagonista su visión del Paraíso Terrenal. Es notable que esta misma obra trae a colación el mito de Faetón y el carro del sol con respecto a varios fenónemos meteorológicos, aunque es obvio que el anónimo autor no ha querido prestarle mayor importancia que la de ser una actitud de los hombres de otra época frente a sus observaciones atmosféricas.

Al llegar al siglo XIII, con el ímpetu económico de la competencia por las rutas al Oriente con su rico comercio de especias, entraba el mundo medieval en una nueva fase de vida en que existían fuertes motivos económicos para comprobar la exactitud de las leyendas que hasta ahora no se habían puesto en tela de juicio. Impulsado por el deseo de lucro y aventuras, salió el joven Marco Polo de Venecia en el año 1271, volviendo unos 25 años más tarde con grandes riquezas que dieron pábulo a muchos rumores y, con el tiempo la composición en 1298 de la narración de su expedición al Oriente. Medio siglo después, aprovechándose de la gran popularidad del libro de viajes que había escrito el veneciano, se compuso en 1356 otro libro de semejante índole que declaraba ser el relato de los viajes emprendidos por un inglés errante, John Mandeville.[12]

---

[11] *Description de l'Afrique et de l'Espagne*, edd. R. Dozy y M. J. de Goeje (Leipzig: E. L. Brill, 1866), págs. 223-25.

[12] Hoy se sabe que el autor era un médico belga, Jean de Bourgogne (fl. 1350).

Esta obra extravagante, llena de lo que Cervantes hubiera calificado de "trufas paladinas," no fue ni más ni menos que el compendio y resumen de todo lo que la edad media había recibido del mundo clásico entre geografías, bestiarios, lapidarios y cosmografías. Pueblan sus páginas descripciones de toda suerte que hoy nos divierten por lo ridículas e ingenuas que son, no sospechando que la mayoría se sus lectores medievales las tragaban enteras, tomándolas por experiencias personales de un testigo ocular. Y éste fue el punto de vista de D. Cristóbal Colón, cartógrafo, navegante, descubridor de un nuevo mundo y Almirante del mar Océano.

Nos cuenta Fernando Colón, hijo del descubridor, que su padre había leído las obras de Marco Polo y Mandeville entre otras y que de allí se había confirmado en la convicción de que era del todo posible encontrar una ruta marítima por donde llegar al Nuevo Mundo.[13] Al mismo tiempo, otro biógrafo de Colón, el padre Bartolomé de las Casas en su *Historia de las Indias*,[14] no menciona siquiera a Mandeville en este contexto cuando nos habla de las obras y hombres que más influencia tenían sobre Colón. La historia de Colón y las fuentes de su inspiración revelan datos que nos pueden proporcionar una nueva perspectiva sobre el tópico que hemos abordado aquí hoy porque recalcan el hecho de que Colón, en la mayoría de los casos donde tenía libre elección de fuentes, prefería escoger y creer no en las obras científicas de su día sino en el fárrago de leyendas que había heredado ya por oídas, ya por lecturas, y una de estas leyendas, la que versa sobre la fabulosa isla de Antilla, resulta ser nada más ni menos que una extensión de las leyendas que surgían a raíz de la invasión árabe y la caída de Rodrigo, el último rey godo.[15]

Esta leyenda era muy corriente durante el siglo XV, según nos

---

[13] *Histoire*, ed. y trad. B. Keen (Rutgers University Press, 1959), cap. 8. Véase también, A. Cioranescu, "Christophe Colomb: sources de sa biographie," en *La Découverte de l'Amérique*, por M. Ballasteros-Gaibrois et al. (Paris, 1971), págs. 39-50.

[14] ed. Agustín Millares Carlo con una intro. de Lewis Hanke (México-Buenos Aires: Fondo de Cultura Económica, 1951).

[15] He encontrado una referencia pasajera a una leyenda vasca que parece contener los mismos elementos narrativos si bien no he logrado hasta el momento precisar la fuente del mito éuscaro mencionado en C. Raymond Beazley, *The Dawn of Modern Geography* (Oxford: Clarendon Press, 1897; rep. New York: P. Smith, 1949), 3 vols., cf. págs. 230-31.

informa el padre Bartolomé de las Casas, afirmando que Colón conocía la historia y que le había inspirado en su decisión de buscar una nueva ruta al Oriente. En el capítulo XIII de su *Historia de las Indias*, las Casas relata lo siguiente en lo que a la isla de Antilla se refiere:

> Mas dice Cristóbal Colón que el año de 1404 vido en Portugal que un vecino de la isla de la Madera fue a pedir al rey una carabela para ir a descubrir cierta tierra, que juraba que vía cada año y siempre de una manera, concordando con los de las islas de los Azores. De aquí sucedió, que en las cartas de marear que los tiempos pasados de hacían, se pintaban algunas islas por aquellos mares y comarcas, especialmente la isla que decían de Antilla, y poníanla poco más de 200 leguas al Poniente de las islas de Canaria y de los Azores. Ésta estimaban los portugueses, y hoy no dejan de tener opinión que sea la isla de las Siete Ciudades, cuya fama y apetito aun ha llegado hasta nos, y a muchos ha hecho por su codicia desvariar y gastar muchos dineros sin provecho y con grandes daños, como placiendo a Dios, en el discurso desta historia parecerá. Esta isla de las Siete Ciudades, dicen según se suena, los portugueses, que fue poblada dellos al tiempo que se perdió España reinando el rey D. Rodrigo; y dicen que por huir de aquella persecución se embarcaron siete obispos y mucha gente y con sus navíos fueron a aportar a la dicha isla, donde cada uno hizo su pueblo, y porque la gente no pensase tornar, pusieron fuego a los navíos; y dícese que en tiempo del infante D. Enrique de Portugal, con tormenta corrió un navío que había salido del puerto de Portugal y no paró hasta dar en ella, y saltando en tierra, los de la isla los llevaron a la iglesia por ver si eran cristianos y hacían las ceremonias romanas, y visto que lo eran, rogáronles que estuviesen allí hasta que viniese su señor, que estaba de allí apartado; pero los marineros, temiendo que no les quemasen el navío y los detuviesen allí, sospechando que no querían ser sabidos de nadie, volviéronse a Portugal muy alegres, esperando recibir mercedes del infante; a los cuales diz que maltrató y mandó que volviesen, pero el maestre y ellos no lo osaron hacer, por cuya causa, del reino salidos, nunca más a él volvieron: dicen más, que los grumetes cogieron cierta tierra o arena para su fogón, y que

hallaron que mucha parte della era oro. Algunos salieron de Portugal a buscar esta misma, que, por común vocablo, la llamaban Antilla, entre los cuales salió uno que se decía Diego Detiene, cuyo piloto [que se llamó Pedro de Velasco, vecino de Palos], afirmó al mismo Cristóbal Colón, en el monasterio de Santa María de la Rábida, que habían partido de la isla del Fayal, y anduvieron 150 leguas por el viento de lebechio, que es el viento Norueste, y a la vuelta descubrieron la isla de las Flores,... (ed. cit., págs. 67-68)

Añade las Casas que esta expedición concluyó sin hallar la isla, "porque era ya agosto y temieron el invierno," y que esto "fue cuarenta años antes que Cristóbal Colón descubriese nuestras Indias."

Ahora bien, los portugueses durante el reinado de D. Enrique el Navegante habían establecido desde el año 1420 un centro de exploración situado en Sagres, en el Cabo de San Vicente. Desde allí salieron un busca de nuevas rutas al Oriente.[16] En la colección de cartas marinas del Infante, figura un mapa catalán del año 1375 en que anda la famosa isla de San Brendán, ubicada a unas doscientas millas al oeste de los Estrechos de Gibraltar. Hoy es sabido que el nombre del Brasil se deriva, no de la madera roja proveniente de este país, sino del nombre céltico para la isla de San Brendán, "Hy Brasil," que significaba "Isla Afortunada." En el año 1431, D. Enrique mandó una expedición capitaneada por Gonçalo Velho Cabral a fin de encontrar la isla de San Brendán y un año más tarde, en una segunda expedición con el mismo objeto, descubrió el capitán Velho las islas Azores. En el año 1452, D. Henrique envió a un residente de Madeira, un tal Diogo de Tieve con un amigo suyo, Pedro de Velasco, a descubrir la mítica isla de Antilla, pero no lograron encontrarla, aunque sí hallaron otras dos islitas de las Azores a las que daban nombres tomados de la leyenda de San Brendán, Corvo y Flores. En el año 1474, Fernão Teles recibió unas *cartas de doação* o cartas de donación, en las que el sucesor del Infante D. Enrique, Alfonso V, le concede cualesquiera islas descubriera en el Atlántico, renovando las cartas al año siguiente, pero este vez con una mención específica de la isla de las Siete Ciudades. A pesar de que esta isla nunca se halló, continuaba figurando en casi todas las cartas marítimas de la época, menos en las cartas portuguesas, lo que

---

16 Cf. Damião Peres, *História dos descobrimentos portugueses*, 2a. ed. (Coimbra, 1960); Jaime Cortesão, *Os descobrimentos portugueses*, 2 tomos (Lisboa, 1959-60); Eduardo Brazão, *A descoberta da Terra Nova* (Lisboa, 1964).

extraña porque eran ellos los que con más ahinco y tesón la busca-
ban. De hecho, uno de los pilotos más respetados de su época, João
de Lisboa, publica en el año 1514 su *Livro da Marinharia*[17] en que
consagra un capítulo a las "Islas aún no descubiertas" y en el que
figura la de "Antilha."

Hemos visto por lo que nos cuenta las Casas que los portugueses decían haber colonizado la isla y, de hecho, el nombre Antilla,
en portugués *Anti Ilha = Antilha*, significa "isla opuesta a Portugal"
aunque hay otros que creen con poco fundamento podría ser una
corrupción de la antigua Atlántida. Sea de esto lo que fuere, lo
cierto es que figura la Antilla en la mayoría de las cartas marinas a
partir de la carta náutica de Zaune Pizzigano,[18] creada en el año
1424, en la que el cartógrafo nos ha dado hasta los nombres de cada
una de las siete ciudades. Estos nombres, entre raros e incomprensi-
bles, son *Asay, Ary, Vra, Jaysos, Marnlio, Ansuly* y *Cyodne.*

La historia de la isla de Antilla, recogida por las Casas en una
versión bastante aumentada, aprece escrita por vez primera en el
mapamundi del alemán, Martín Behaim, en el año 1492, donde
pone al lado de la etiqueta "Insula antilia septe citade,"

> En el año 734 A. D., cuando toda España había sido conquis-
> tada por los paganos africanos, la isla de Antilla, llamada de las
> Siete Ciudades, fue ocupada por seis obispos y otros cristianos
> entre hombres y mujeres, que habían salido de España en bar-
> co, junto con su ganado y otros bienes. En el año 1414 un barco
> español se le acercó a esta isla sin correr peligro.[19]

Fernando Colón, en su *Historia*, nos da una fecha de 714, unos 20
años antes, para el éxodo del grupo, pero lo que más importa es
saber que Colón fue convencido de la existencia de esta isla con que
esperaba llegar finalmente a las Indias. Hemos visto que las antiguas
leyendas tenían la tendencia de extender las islas desconocidas cada
vez más lejos de las orillas del continente europeo a la medida de que
se iban descubriendo islas nuevas que no correspondían a los mitos.

---

[17] ed. Jacinto Ignacio de Brito Rebello (Lisboa: Imprenta de L. da
Silva, 1903).

[18] Armando Cortesão, *The Nautical Chart of 1424* (Coimbra, 1954).

[19] Citado por Samuel Eliot Morison, *The European Discovery of America,
The Northern Voyages A. D. 500-1600* (New York: Oxford University Press,
1971), pág. 99; y por el mismo autor, *Portuguese Voyages to America in the
Fifteenth Century* (Cambridge, Mass., 1941); E. G. Ravenstein, *Martin
Behaim, His Life and His Globe* (London, 1907).

Así es que Colón creía que él Oriente se podría alcanzar a través de
una serie de islas que el pensaba utilizar en calidad de puertos de
escala, forjando de esta manera una sólida cadena de estriberones
insulares entre las Azores y las Indias.[20]

En el año 1474, se enteró Colón de una carta escrita por el
famoso doctor florentino, Paolo dal Pozzo Toscanelli, al canónigo
Fray Fernão Martins, que a su vez había correspondido con este
sabio italiano a instancias del rey Alfonso V. En la carta se hablaba
de Antilla y otras maravillas del Oriente con las teorías de Toscanelli sobre la mejor ruta para alcanzarlas. Colón le escribió con su plan
y le contestó Toscanelli en 1475, dibujando de nuevo un mapa en
que figura prominente la isla de Antilla, entre otras.[21] Las Casas
publica la carta en el capítulo XII de su *Historia*:

> E de la isla de Antilla, que vosotros llamáis de Siete Ciudades,
> de la cual tenemos noticia, hasta la nobilísima isla de Cipango,
> hay 10 espacios, que son 2,500 millas, es a saber, 225 leguas,
> la cual isla es fertilísima de oro y de perlas y piedras preciosas.
> Sabed que de oro puro cobijan los templos y las casas reales;
> así que por no ser conocido el camino están todas estas cosas
> encubiertas, y a ella se puede ir muy seguramente (ed. cit.,
> pág. 64).

De nuevo, en 1549, Pedro de Medina en su *Grandeza de España*,[22]
señala la importancia de la fabulosa ínsula de Antilla aunque no se
había encontrado todavía. Luego en 1563, Antonio Galvão en su
*Tratado*, trae otra relación de una nave portuguesa llevada por la
consabida tormenta al oeste donde la tripulación encuentra una isla
con siete ciudades pobladas por sus compatriotas quienes les piden
noticias sobre la guerra con los moros. Galvão repite la historia ya

---

[20] William H. Babcock, *Legendary Islands of the Atlantic* (New York. Ame-
rican Geographical Society, 1922); Florentino Pérez Embid, *Los descubri-
mientos en el Atlántico hasta el Tratado de Tordesillas* (Sevilla, 1948); Vincent H.
Cassidy, *The Sea Around Them* (Baton Rouge, 1968); T. Bentley Duncan,
*Atlantic Islands* (Chicago, 1972); David B. Quinn, *North America from Earliest
Discovery to First Settlement* (New York: Harper & Row, 1975).

[21] Cf. Hanry Vignaud, *Toscanelli and Columbus: The letter and Chart of
Toscanelli* (London, 1902, rep. 1971); S. E. Morison, *Journals and Other Documents on the Life and Voyages of Christopher Columbus* (New York, 1963).

[22] Citada en Henry Harrisse, *The Discovery of North America* (London-
Paris, 1872), pág. 656.

contada por las Casas sobre la arena aurífera recogida por los marineros para sus fogones de cocina en que se encontró granos de este precioso metal.[23]

Si Colón, hombre netamente medieval, creía en la leyenda de Antilla y las Siete Ciudades, le podemos perdonar porque al fin y al cabo, utilizaba la información a su manera y descubrió un nuevo mundo. Mas ¿qué podemos decir del cartógrafo, E. M. Blunt, que en el año 1841 publicó su *Chart of the Atlantic* en la que coloca a 46 grados de longitud norte y 20 grados de latitud oeste nuestra isla fantasma de Antilla, casi 400 años después de que salió por vez primera en el mapa de Pizzigano?[24]

Pero no nos detenemos aquí por falta de más datos al respecto, al contrario, Colón era, como decíamos, un hombre medieval y como tal demostraba no sólo un apego a la antigua leyenda de Antilla, sino que creía firmemente en otras muchas que hoy nos excitan a la risa. Por las páginas del *Imago mundi*, escrito entre 1410 y 1415 por el cardenal francés, Pierre d'Ailly,[25] la Biblia, y las glosas del Antiguo Testamento de Nicolás de Lira,[26] sabemos que Colón se había persuadido de que iba a descubrir la mina de Ofir de Salomón y de allí, fue convencido que sería poca cosa encontrar el país vecino que en los días de antaño había sido de la opulenta amiga de Salomón, la reina de Sebá.[27]

No podemos dejar de puntualizar que otra de las fuentes que orientan a Colón fue el mismo Eneas Silvio Piccolomini, el papa Pío II, conocido por su famosísimo *De duibus amantibus*, que tanta influencia ha tenido en la esfera de la novela sentimental, pero esta vez, en el caso de Colón, fue otra obra, la *Historia rerum*, la que le aseguró que cerca de Cipango, o Japón, habría de encontrar la isla de las perlas, la isla de las mujeres, prototipo de las amazonas, y otros seres entre raros y extraños como antropófagos, monóculos y monópedes.

---

[23] Citado por Morison, *European Voyages*, pág. 99.

[24] Citado por S. E. Morison, *The European Discovery of America*, pág. 102, donde se le refiere al mapa como el de "Pizzi."

[25] ed. y trad. Edmond Buron, 3 tomos (Paris, 1930).

[26] Cf. Juan Manzano, *Colón y su secreto* (Madrid: Ediciones Cultura Hispánica, 1976), pág. 206.

[27] Manzano, págs. 214-16.

Lo cierto es que Colón, frente a fenónemos naturales para los que él carecía de modelos más que los que había leído en sus fuentes fabulosas, los compara lógicamente con los patrones que ha heredado. El suyo es un mundo aristotélico, de cosas concretas, ya descubiertas y descritas por las mayores autoridades de la antigüedad. Por consiguiente, al llegar en su tercer viaje al golfo de Paria donde desemboca el río Orinoco, escribe en la *Relación* que envía a los reyes católicos:

> La Sacra Escriptura testifica que Nuestro Señor hizo el Paraíso Terrenal y en el puso el árbol de la vida, y d'el sale una fuente de donde resultan en este mundo quatro ríos principales: Ganges, Tygris, Eufrates...y el Nilo.... Sant Isidro y Beda y Strabo, y el maestro de la Hystoria Scolástica, y Sant Ambrosio, y Scoto, y todos los sanos theólogos conciertan qu'el Paraýso Terrenal es en el Oriente &c.... Yo no tomo qu'el Paraýso Terrenal sea en forma de montaña áspera, como el escrevir d'ello nos amuestra, salvo qu'el sea en el colmo...y creo que pueda salir de allí esa agua, bien que sea lexos, y venga a parar allí donde yo vengo, y faga este lago. Grandes indicios son estos del Paraýso Terrenal, porqu'el sitio es conforme a la opinión d'estos sanctos & sanos theólogos. Y asimismo las señales son muy conformes, que yo jamás leý ni oý que tanta cantidad de agua dulce fuese así adentro & vezina con la salada. Y en ello ayuda asimismo la suavíssima temperancia.... Torno a mi propósito de la tierra de Gracia y río y lago que allí fallé, a tan grande, que más se puede llamar mar que lago...y digo que si no procede del Paraýso Terrenal, que viene este río y procede de tierra infinita, ques al Austro, de la qual fasta agora no se a avido noticia. Mas yo muy assentado tengo en el ánima que allí, adonde dixe, es el Paraýso Terrenal, y descanso sobre las razones y auctoridades sobre escriptas.[28]

Todo lo que hemos dicho hasta ahora subraya lo que venimos intentando demostrar desde un principio en este ensayo, que hay dos realidades, una ideal y perfecta y otra real e imperfecta. Colón tenía varios motivos por persistir en la creencia de que había descu-

---

[28] Manzano, págs. 223-24.

bierto no un nuevo continente sino una nueva ruta al Oriente. Primero, pensaba que era la suya una misión divina, que Dios le había dado el nombre de Cristóforo o Cristóbal por ser el que llevaría, si no a cuestas por lo menos en barco, a Cristo sobre las aguas del mar donde los masas paganas le habían de aceptar como su salvador. En este contexto, hay gente poco caritativa que quisiera imputarle a Colón motivos de lucro, de haber negado que descubriera un nuevo mundo porque los Reyes Católicos la habían concedido su almirantazgo en virtud de haber hallado una nueva ruta a las Indias y que de ser de otro modo, pudiera haber perdido Colón sus títulos y concesiones reales.

Aun y con todo, lo cierto es que en su empresa Colón encarnaba las antiguas leyendas hagiográficas y tal vez en uno que otro aspecto de sus aventuras, las habrá sobrepasado, comprobando la veracidad del dicho que reza que la verdad es aun más extraña que la ficción. Además, se sabe que si Colón hubiese prestado atención a los escépticos científicos de su día, no habría nunca emprendido el viaje que le llevó a América, pues parece que por una serie de errores garrafales de cálculo, suponía la distancia por tierra entre Europa y China ser de unos 177 grados en vez de 131, lo que producía el efecto de cortar bastante la distancia de su viaje en el otro sentido, por el mar Atlántico.[29] Por otro lado, seguía creyendo Colón en lo que había leído en la introducción al *De quaestionibus naturalibus* de Séneca, donde el sabio cordobés declaraba que las orillas del otro lado del Océano se podrían alcanzar en *paucis diebus.*

Pero este análisis revela algo más, y es que refuerza el concepto de la literatura española como concebida dentro del realismo y del que aprece recibir sus mayores y más originales estímulos.[30] España no parece haber dudado nunca de la realidad de los héroes, ya clásicos, ya medievales, como San Brendán, sólo que nadie podría hacer entonces más que leer sus aventuras, o sea experienciarlas indirec-

---

[29] George E. Nun, *The Geographical Conceptions of Columbus* (New York, 1924).

[30] Cf. Irving A. Leonard, *Books of the Brave* (Cambridge: Harvard University Press, 1949); Agustín Zapata Gollán, *Mito y superstición en la conquista de América* (Buenos Aires: Eudeba, 1963); Demetrio Ramos Pérez, *El mito del Dorado, su génesis y proceso* (Caracas: Biblioteca de la Academia Nacional de la Historia, 1973); Edmondo O'Gorman, *La idea del descubrimiento de América* (México: Centro de Estudios Filológicos, 1951).

tamente. Ahora en una edad en que se habían descubierto muevos mundos, existía la gloriosa posibilidad de que un hombre cualquiera pudiera hacer y ver lo que antes había sido reservado estrictamente para los santos. Ya un hombre como Colón podía ver las maravillas de Cipango, visitar al Paraíso Terrenal, enriquecerse con el oro de Salomón o soñar con cristianizar a los indios. Mientras los científicos dudaban, los rudos aventureros, más susceptibles a la seducción de los mitos, confiaban aunque hemos de admitir que en su mayoría fueron impulsados por motivos económicos cuando no frenados por motivos racionales. Sea de esto lo que fuere, estamos en una época cuando la historia y la historiografía se confunden, cuando los mitos coinciden con la realidad, en un período que se puede comparar favorablemente con el momento de hoy en que estamos en los umbrales de la exploración espacial, cuando la ciencia y la ciencia ficción coexisten sin claros límites que las dividan.

Lo que sí podemos afirmar es que a medida que se les aproxime un conflicto a la ciencia y la ciencia ficción, la historiografía y la historia, ceden los elementos fictivos a los científicos y las metas de los exploradores se van alejando del alcance de los que los buscan. De esta manera, las Siete Ciudades de Antilla se perdían paulatinamente en la distancia del nuevo continente, siempre en dirección al oeste, llegando a ser ahora las Siete Ciudades de Cíbola, ahora Quivira, ahora Copal. Lo cual significa que el hombre irá siempre en busca de sus mitos, y éstos estarán siempre un poco más allá del horizonte, como el suplicio de Tántalo, o la perfecta "donna che non si trova" de los "stilnovisti" del siglo XIII. Pero esto no puede impedir la búsqueda ni enfriar el ánimo de los aventureros, sino que servirá como siempre para estimular el apetito y aguzar la pesquisa. Y los descubridores, sin encontrar los mitos soñados, se contentarán con vivir en su propio mundo, rodeados de los nombres fantasmas de sus Californias, sus Floridas, una Argentina o un Potosí, reflejos todos de sus lecturas, de sus ensueños, de sus imaginaciones, mundos de posibilidades, mundos perfectos que estarán siempre al otro lado del mar.

UNIVERSITY OF CONNECTICUT

# An Early Censor:
# Alejo Venegas

DANIEL EISENBERG

 HE JOB OF CENSOR, as we understand it today,
is a product of the Renaissance and a pheno-
menon of the age of printed books. The deliberate destruction of books and manuscripts
—which cannot compete with their gradual
loss through deterioration, accident, or obsolescence[1]—has existed over almost as long a
period as books themselves. However, this
has been more an *ad hoc* than a systematic practice: for example,
Lope de Barrientos' famous examination and partial destruction of

---

[1] By "obsolescence" I mean the changes in style of writing or from
writing to printing, all of which led to the destruction of books and
manuscripts, but for reasons unrelated to their subject matter. The classic
statement on the topic, although biased by the author's position on "missing" Spanish epic texts, is that of Menéndez Pidal, *Reliquias de la poesía épica
española* (Madrid: n.p., 1951), pp. xvi-xx. The conservation of an old book or
manuscript from antiquarian interest, as a curiosity to be collected, was
virtually unknown even in the sixteenth century, as I mentioned briefly in
my "Who Read the Romances of Chivalry?" *KRQ*, 20 (1973), 219, note 23
(now being reprinted in updated form in *The Romances of Chivalry of the Spanish Golden Age* [Newark, Delaware: Juan de la Cuesta, in press]). Even when
early Humanists, preparing new, scholarly or semi-scholarly editions of
Classical texts, realized the value of old manuscripts and sought out and
used the same, they frequently did not conserve them after finishing the
new editions (see the comments of L. D. Reynolds and N. G. Wilson,
*Scribes and Scholars. A Guide to the Transmission of Greek and Latin Literature*, 2nd
ed. [Oxford: Clarendon, 1974], p. 124).

the books of Enrique de Villena.[2] Censorship prior to publication, considering the private and slow nature of medieval book production, seldom existed other than in the mind of the person choosing the work he was about to copy or have copied.[3]

More than the invention itself, it was the rapid spread of printing and the decreasing cost of book publication, combined with the nearly simultaneous emergence of new ideas to be circulated through this new technology, that made systematic, organized, and official censorship a logical development. In Spain, this "boom" of publication is commonly and correctly associated with the *Reyes Católicos*, who—one of their most enlightened and long-lasting policies[4]—legally and economically supported the fledgling industry, without any known interference with the contents of books published (Norton, pp. 119-20). Censorship in Spain, in fact, is

---

[2] Emilio Cotarelo y Mori, *Don Enrique de Villena. Su vida y obras* (Madrid, 1896), p. 110.

[3] One exception are the books produced commercially for students' use (H. J. Chaytor, *From Script to Print* [Cambridge, England: W. Heffer, 1950 reprint of 1945 ed.], pp. 136-37), in which some outside authority chose, like today's textbook, the books which were, and which were not, to be produced. However, this choice was primarily in the field of law, secondarily in theology, and never in literature. The examination of an individual book referred to by Chaytor (p. 136) was to verify its "correctness" in the most literal sense, and it is greatly to Spain's credit that this salutory practice was followed over quite some period of time (F. J. Norton, *Printing in Spain, 1501-1520* [Cambridge, England: Cambridge University Press, 1966], p. 119; Agustín G. de Amezúa y Mayo, "Cómo se hacía un libro en nuestro Siglo de Oro," first published Madrid: Magisterio Español, 1946, included in his *Opúsculos histórico-literarios*, I [Madrid: CSIC, 1951], 331-73, at 355).

[4] More permanent than the unification of Castile and Aragón, more effective than the mostly symbolic conclusion of the *reconquista*, and more beneficial than the expulsion of the Jews. Almost certainly we can attribute this idea to Isabel, by all accounts the more intellectual of the pair, and the owner of a significant private library (the contents of which are itemized by Diego Clemencín in *Elogio de la reina Católica Doña Isabel*, Memorias de la Real Academia de la Historia, 6 [Madrid, 1821, and reprint by Kraus Reprint, Liechtenstein, 1968 on the title page, and 1969, apparently the correct date, on the title page *verso*], pp. 431-81; see also Francisco Javier Sánchez Cantón, *Libros, tapices y cuadros que coleccionó Isabel la Católica* [Madrid: CSIC, 1950]).

commonly dated from the publication of the first two lists of prohibited books, in 1551,[5] two generations later, creating the mistaken
impression that censorship was subsequent to the Council of
Trent and to most of the reign of Carlos V.

Yet this dating of censorship in Spain is incorrect; a more accurate staring date might be the first prohibition of a specific work or
works, those of Luther, prohibited in 1521 by Carlos V's enor-
mously unpopular regent and inquisitor Hadrian.[6] This misconcep-
tion has come to be simply because "es bien poco lo que de eso [la
censura] sabemos en la primera mitad del siglo XVI."[7] Therefore,

---

[5] Most handily available together with much other useful material, in
*Die Indices Librorum Prohibitorum des sechzehnten Jahrhunderts*, ed. Fr[anz] Hein-
rich Reusch, Bibliothek des Literarischen Vereins in Stuttgart, 176 (1886;
rpt. Nieuwkoop: B. de Graaf, 1961), a companion to the editor's *Der Index
der verbotenen Bücher. Ein Beitrag zur Kirchen- und Litteraturgeschichte* (Bonn: M.
Cohen and Son, 1883-85). Archer Huntington subsidized the reproduction
in facsimile (by the De Vinne Press, New York, 1896) of these two indices,
as well as the related *Censura generalis contra errores, quibus recentes haeretici
sacram scripturam asperserunt* (Valladolid: Francisco Fernández de Córdoba,
1554) and the *Mandament der Keyserlijcker Maiesteit* [Carlos V] (Louvain: Ser-
vaes van Sassen, 1546) the same year, and the much more serious index of
1559 in 1902. Since all of these were in editions of 100 copies, and are now
rarities of themselves, the two lists of 1551 and that of 1559 were reproduced also in facsimile by the Real Academia Española in 1952 as the
volume *Tres índices expurgatorios de la Inquisición española en el siglo XVI*.

[6] To my knowledge, it has escaped the attention of nationalistic crtics
and students of the *comunero* revolt that the Spanish people, to whom
Luther was, at this time, more a distant figure than an immediate peril,
saw the prohibition of books as yet another unwanted Flemish innovation.
The removal of Hadrian, Carlos' regent during his absence from Spain,
was a main goal of the *comuneros*. (His former student Carlos then played a
major role in his obtaining the position of Pope Hadrian VI.) The Prohibition of Hadrian was reaffirmed in 1530 by Alonso Manrique de Lara, later
*Inquisitor General*, another defender of Carlos during his time of difficulty.
And the model for the Spanish indices of 1551 was that which Carlos had
requested in 1546 of the University of Louvain (reproduced in *Die Indices*,
cited in the previous note).

[7] Antonio Sierra Corella, *La censura de libros y papeles en España y los índices y
catálogos españoles de los prohibidos y expurgados* (Madrid: Cuerpo facultativo de
archivos, bibliotecarios y arqueólogos, 1947), pp. 93-94. The most recent
comments on Spanish censorship with which I am familiar, those of Keith
Whinnom, in "The Problem of the 'Best-Seller' in Spanish Golden Age
Literature," *BHS*, 57 (1980), 189-98, at p. 190, similarly suggest that censorship was a port-Tridentine phenomenon.

this article will present some hitherto little-known information about one of the first Spanish censors, one whose intellectual career falls largely between 1521 and 1551: Alejo Venegas del Busto (1498/99-1652).[8]

Venegas is a particluarly interesting figure to examine because of his associations with the city of Toledo and later that of Madrid. Venegas was born, educated, and worked for a good part of his life in Toledo, in constant and close contact with the ecclesiastical authorities of this religious center.[9] Rather than an unimportant person in a small town, we have in Venegas a person of considerable scholarly reputation in a major Castilian city; parallel with Toledo's dwindling intellectual importance during this period,[10] as it lost ground to the new centers of Madrid and Alcalá, Venegas moved about 1544 to Madrid, in which city he continued his censorial activities. He is therefore, not only a person about whom some significant information is known, but he is at least geographically a representative figure; for reasons to be explained shortly, he can be taken as representative of early Spanish censorship, and perhaps of all censorship, at its best.

Venegas was born to a noble but undistinguished Toledan fam-

---

[8] Also spelled "Vanegas." On his name, see Juan Bautista Avalle-Arce, "Los testamentos de Alejo Venegas," in *Dintorno de una época dorada* (Madrid: José Porrúa Turanzas, 1978), 137-72, at. p. 143. (this article was originally published in *Anuario de Letras*, 6 [1966-67], 135-62).

[9] I have discussed this to some extent in my introduction to a facsimile edition of Venegas' *Primera parte de las Diferencias de libros que ay en el universo* (Barcelona: Puhvill, in press). For another piece of evidence, note his references to the "muchas pláticas y conversaciones particulares" with Pedro de Campo, *canónigo de Toledo* and professor of theology, in NBAE, 16, 109b, and Campo's comment on 107b.

[10] There is no single accurate and up-to-date source from which to obtain an appreciation of Toledo's role in the early sixteenth century. The inaugural speech in the Real Academia de la Historia of the Conde de Cedillo, Jerónimo López de Ayala, *Toledo en el siglo XVI después del vencimiento de las comunidades* (Madrid, 1901), is uncritical as well as dated. Sounder scholarship, to some degree relevant to the sixteenth century, may be found in Eloy Benito Ruano, *Toledo en el siglo XV. Vida política* (Madrid: CSIC, 1961). The ringing words of his introduction (pp. 9-10) set forth well Toledo's special importance for Castile as a whole.

ily.[11] Although never wealthy—more to the contrary—he was able to study at the "estudio" (after 1520, University) of Toledo. Presumably his studies were extensive, because he achieved considerable competence in Greek, Latin and Hebrew, to the point that he could write a treatise on the orthography of these languages,[12] and because those who knew him in Toldeo write unanimously in favorable terms about his learning. His studies continued at least until obtaining the degree of *maestro* sometime between 1531 and 1537.

An ecclesiastical career would have been a likely one for such a talented young man, but became impossible after his marriage, whose date and circumstances are unknown to us. However, a career as professor, which he was to follow throughout the rest of his life, was also in harmony with his knowledge and the methodical, organizing, and expository approach we find in all his works. In Toledo, Nicolás Antonio tells us he founded a Latin school,[13] and he was to teach in the university where he had studied. Later, he was invited to occupy the Cátedra de Gramática del Estudio de Madrid, the same position subsequently held by Cervantes' teacher, López de Hoyos. Among Venegas' students are counted Francisco Cervantes de Salazar, whom Venegas called "mi discipulo,"[14] and Rivadeneyra.

In addition to his professorial activities, Venegas is the author of several important books; Besides the orthographical treatise already mentioned, he is the author of *Agonía del tránsito de la muerte*,

---

[11] For documentation and a fuller summary of Venegas' life, see my introduction cited in note 9.

[12] *Tractado de orthographía y accentos en las tres lenguas principales* (Toledo: Lázaro Salvago, 1531), discussed briefly by Conde de la Viñaza, *Biblioteca histórica de la filología castellana* (Madrid, 1893), cols. 1099-1101, used extensively by Amado Alonso, *De la pronunciación medieval a la moderna en español*, ultimado y despuesto para la imprenta por Rafael Lapesa (Madrid: Gredos, 1967 [2nd ed. of Vol. I]-69), and analyzed by myself in my introduction, already referred to.

[13] *Bibliotheca hispana nova*, 1 (Madrid: Sancha, 1783), 8-9.

[14] In the final (unpaginated) page of Venegas' prologue to the second work (*Appólogo* [sic] *de la ociosidad y el trabajo...compuesto por... Luis Mexía*) of the *Obras* of Cervantes de Salazar (Alcalá: Juan de Brocar, 1546).

called by Marcel Bataillon "la obra maestra de la literatura ascética española en la época de Carlos V."[15] It is a handbook on death and dying for the use of the living who should always be ready, spiritually and temporally, for that event which awaits all of us and all of our loved ones. The *Agonía* was first published in 1537, added to by the author in 1543, and gained reputation as a classic; twelve editions were published between 1537 and 1682. It is available to modern readers in the edition of Miguel Mir (*Escritores místicos españoles*, I—though Venegas is not a mystic, as Mir admits on p. xxvii—, NBAE, 16 [Madrid: Bailly-Baillière, 1911], 105-318), and there have been some fragmentary editions based on this one[16].

Venegas is also the author of a much less well-known work, the *Primera parte de las diferencias de libros que ay en el universo*, of which five editions were published, from 1540 to 1583. Conceived of as a work of bibliographical guidance, the part which was published, and which apparently is the only part Venegas completed, deals with metaphorical "books": an archetypal book (the term is Venegas'), which only God and those in heaven can read, and three imperfect copies of it, a book of the natural world, a book of reason, and a book of revelation or holy writings. "Books" as we understand them would be copies of these three books, or second copies—full of errors—of the original, master book.[17]

Venegas' activities as censor are known to us primarily through his own words, found in preliminary matter of his own works, those of his friends, and those sent to him for examination. The best and almost the only known of these is the brief note at the beginning of Antonio de Torquemada's *Coloquios satíricos* (reproduced in *Orígines de la Novela*, II, NBAE, 7 [Madrid: Bailly-Ballière, 1907], 486), in which Venegas states that he ordered changes before publication. At greater length, Venegas discusses the corrections necessary in Agustín de Almazán's translation of León Baptista Alberti's *Moral e muy graciosa historia del dios Momo* (Alcalá, 1553): "Yo he visto estos quatro libros del Momo, que debaxo de poesía

---

[15] *Erasmo y España* trans. Antonio Alatorre, 2nd Spanish edition (Mexico: El Colegio de México, 1966), p. 565.

[16] M[anuel] A[ltolaguirre] (Santiago de Chile: Cruz del Sur, 1948), and of Rafael Fiol (Madrid: Rialp, 1969).

[17] See note 9.

juglar, tratan alta philosophía moral. E digo que con las emiendas que yo en él tengo hechas, es un libro muy útil y provechoso, no menos a los príncipes que a los subditos. Las emendaciones no son faltas del intérprete, que muy bien e fielmente trasladó estos libros, mas fueron incurias del autor, cuyas emiendas fueron necessarias al libro." Similarly, at the beginning of the *Rissa y planto de Demócrito y Heráclito* of Antonio Fregoso, translated by Alonso de Lobera (Valladolid, 1554), there is found a "Carta del maestro Alexio de Venegas vezino de Madrid, a quien por el Consejo Real fue encomendado el examen deste libro." In it, Venegas says: "Yo el maestro Alexio Venegas digo, que e visto y examinado todo este libro, y aun que el trasladador se uvo en él fielmente, por trasladar el sentido del auctor, digo que porque algunos italianos son en algo platónicos, con las emiendas y censuras que yo en él tengo hechas, assí como van en este original, queda libro sano y de buena y moral doctrina."[18] Also, though he does not discuss any changes, we have evidence of his examination of numerous manuscripts in his words at the beginning of the *Arismética práctica y especulativa* of Juan Pérez de Moya (Salamanca, 1562, but I quote from the edition of 1609): "Alguna razón tengo yo de dar testimonio deste presente libro, porque entre otros libros que nuestro muy alto rey Don Felipe el segundo, monarca del orbe nuevo, quando por cámara despachava su Magestad la impressión de los libros, me mandó que viesse y examinasse, para que dellos diesse mi parecer, fue este libro, el qual yo vi y con diligencia examiné."

However, Venegas' original job, later to be continued in Madrid[19] and to lead to his pre-publication examination of manuscripts, was the "oficio de visitar los libros que vienen a esta ciudad de Toledo."[20] He was, then, employed by the ecclesiastical authori-

---

[18] Since Venegas states the translations are accurate, a comparison of the originals with the translations—something possible in no American Library—could permit a better understanding of Venegas' *emiendas* in these works. A topic for a future researcher.

[19] In a late document, dated by Antonio Paz y Melia (*Papeles de inquisición. Catálogo y extractos*, 2nd ed. by Ramón Paz [Madrid, 1947], p. 459) in 1560, Venegas asks for "algún socorro... [por] lo que a servido en la visita de las librerías públicas y particulares" (Archivo Histórico Nacional, Papeles de Inquisición, legajo 4442, número 25).

[20] Prologue to the *Harpa de David* of Fray Benito Villa (Burgos: Juan de

ties of Toledo to examine the *novedades*, presumably about the time they arrived and were put on sale, in order to confirm that no works were being sold which had not been submitted for approval of the archbishop (Norton, p. 119). His words suggest more concern with books imported from other cities or abroad than with those produced in the city of Toledo itself.

These pieces of information are most incomplete. We cannot tell from them whether Venegas vetoed the publication or sale of certain books, or which they were, though considering his statement (in the 1545 edition of the *Diferencias de libros*, fol. 2r) that it is insufficient merely to declare books "inútiles y dañosos," it would not be out of keeping with his outlook for him to have done so. Similarly, we do not know what corrections he ordered in the works whose publication he permitted. Yet even when this information is lacking, there are illuminating questions to be asked and answered concerning Venegas' activities as censor, and we can provide, indirectly, information relative to the above.

There are at least two important questions that we can respond to concerning Venegas' employment as censor. These are: first, why was he, rather than another, asked to take on this important job? Secondly, why did he accept it, and what did he hope to accomplish? Related to this, of course, is the question of his censorial practices.

On the first question, why was he offered this position, there is a superficial answer: that the Inquisitorial authorities were aware of his difficult financial situation,[21] and wished to help him with

Junta, a costa de Juan de Medina, 1548). Ironically, and testimony of Venegas' reasonable outlook, this book itself was to be prohibited, in the *Index* of 1559 (see note 5 above).

[21] See the famous passage to this effect in NBAE, 16, 317-18. Later in his life, Venegas gives us direct information about his economic difficulties in the document cited in note 19, in a petition to the Consejo de Madrid (Eulogio Varela Hervías, "Sobre Alejo de Vanegas [1554]," *Correo Erudito*, 1 [1940], 83, and also in Varela's book, *Un aspecto de la labor cultural del Ayuntamiento de Madrid* [Madrid, 1949], pp. 17-18), and in his will, in which he complains "es poca la sustancia de mi poure ['proue," en el artículo de Avalle-Arce] hacienda para repartir entre tantos hijos como Dios Nuestro Señor fue seruido de darme" (first published by J. R. Cabezalí, "Tránsito de la muerte del maestro Alejo Venegas," *Revista Bibliográfica y Documental*, 3 (1949), 291-301; I cite from the reprint by Juan Bautista Avalle-Arce in *Dintorno de una época dorada*, p. 157.)

this part-time and probably irregular employment. Yet surely this reason counted little compared with the inquisitors' concern for the proper exercise of the job, and with their knowledge of Venegas' qualifications.

In striking contrast with modern censorship, ususally carried out by persons of limited education and uncertain esthetic principles, Venegas was widely held to be one of the smartest, best-educated, and wisest men to be found in the city of Toledo. Besides being, in the words of his professor and friend Alonso Cedillo, "en si muy virtuoso, y zeloso del servicio de Dios" letter to Venegas' *Tractado de orthographía*), numerous sources concur in his considerable learning. In the words of Juan Ginés de Sepúlveda, he was a "varón muy versado en Humanidades y en Sagrada Teología":[22] Alfonso García similarly praises him in his *De adserenda Hispanorum eruditione*,[23] and Pedro de Campo, canon of Toledo, praises his learning in a prefatory letter to the *Agonía del tránsito de la muerte* (NBAE, 16, 107).

If one must have a censor, then better by far that it be a man of learning than the general's wife who, folklore has it, often carries out such a function in the modern military dictatorships[24] where extensive censorship exists or has existed. In one sense, rather than a censor, Venegas resembles more what we would call an editor or *asesor literario*, persons who today decide what will and

---

[22] P. 224 of the edition of Ángel Losada of Sepúldeva's letters (Madrid: Cultura Hispánica, 1966).

[23] P. 229 of the edition of José López de Toro, Anejo 28 of the *RFE* (Madrid, 1943).

[24] As a curiosity, it is worth citing, as an example of the yet-unstudied scholarship of the Franco period, the opening words of the study of Sierra Corella cited in note 7: "Sólo algún pobre escritor, contagiado, desgraciadamente, de un liberalismo trasnochado, podrá ya en lo sucesivo combatir, con apariencias de convencimiento, el ejercicio legal de la censura científica y literaria, como si esta función vital de la sociedad en general fuese una enojosa e injusta intromisión del poder" (p. 17). And later: "Lutero y sus partidarios no tardaron en difundir sus errores, recurriendo no solamente a la palabra hablada, sino principalmente a la siembra de folletos y libros en todos los pueblos, vecinos o lejanos, y por medios más ingeniosos y audaces" (p. 92). Similarly, at about the same time, we can find Amezúa ("Cómo," p. 339) praising the fact that censorship prevented the original publication of Quevedo's first *Sueño*.

will not be published, specifying, at times, the *enimendas y correcciones* necessary before publication is permitted.

A person of equivalent learning, prestige, and conscience would probably not accept, today, the sort of position which Venegas held. What are the reasons which led him to carry out this function? There are, again, superficial answers: economic need on the one hand, and the different value system of an intensely religious, fervently Catholic, and recently unified peninsula. Yet we can add three key points to these reasons.

The first of these is Venegas' personality, of which his Catholicism was an integral part. His religious outlook, bringing with it a respect for authority as well as willingness to exercise it upon request, is as deep as can be found in any author of this period. His contemporaries, such as Cedillo, speak of his virtuous and Christian life; from his wills and his *Agonía* we receive the image of a thoughtful and Catholic, as well as a learned, man. From the prefatory letters of his own which were published with his works, we can see how he sent his books to religious figures with an apparently sincere plea for their evaluations and possible corrections.

Related to this is Venegas' outlook as *maestro*. This was both his profession and his highest degree, a title which he apparently preferred be used in referring to him (the term is always found with his name in his writings subsequent to 1537, the *terminus ante quem* for his receipt of the degree). Throughout Venegas' writings—both in the selection of topics and in the presentation of the material within them—his didactic orientation is clear. Rather than a scholar who theorized or sought old manuscripts, Venegas was an author who organized, structured, defined, and explained: a teacher, in short, by disposition. Determining what people should read—a widespread if less official activity in today's academic world—is a form of instruction, and would have seemed a sensible enterprise to him.

Finally, we must mention Venegas' love of books and reading. His most ambitious authorial project, so ambitious that it was never completed, was that familiar product of poor bibliophiles, a bibliography (the *Diferencias de libros*), and one, moreover, whose explicit purpose was to classify books so as to help the reader choose the appropriate ones for himself or for persons under his care. Like the regular book reviewer of today, to be paid to examine texts which one therefore did not have to buy must have been an opportunity not to be missed.

However, Venegas' interest in censorship, like his plan to write a work of bibliographical guidance, may reflect some personal observation of a link between improper reading and un-Christian, dissolute living. Specifically, I refer to the activities in the house of the Duque del Infantado, Diego Hurtado de Mendoza.[25] Mendoza's licentious and later ludicrous lifestyle was fairly widely known,[26] but there are two avenues through which Venegas could have had direct information. The first of these is through the Mélito house of Toledo, another branch of the large Mendoza family, with which, we can tell from the dedication to the *Agonía del tránsito de la muerte*, Venegas had close contact. The second is via one of the persons Venegas most admired, Álvar Gómez de Ciudad Real, a significant Toledan humanist of exemplary life, who was married to one of the several illegitimate daughters of the Duque del Infantado.[27]

The interest of the Duque del Infantado in romances of chivalry, at that point at the peak of their popularity, is known.[28] Could it be a coincidence that Venegas is virtually the initiator of the tradition of learned attacks on romances of chivalry, which was to last for a century and find ample reflection in the *Quijote*?[29]

---

[25] A popular name. This Diego Hurtado de Mendoza, who died in 1531 and lived in Guadalajara, should not be confused with the Toledan Diego Hurtado de Mendoza, Count of Mélito, after whose death in 1536 Venegas began the *Agonía del tránsito de la muerte*, dedicated to his widow, nor with the Granadine Diego Hurtado de Mendoza (1503?-1575), the poet, diplomat, and author of the *Guerra de Granada*.

[26] See my "Two Problems of Identification in a Parody of Juan de Mena," *Oelschläger Festschrift*, Estudios de Hispanófila, 36 (Chapel Hill, 1976), pp. 155-60.

[27] For information on Gómez and on Venegas' interest in him, see my introduction cited in note 9.

[28] I have mentioned it in my article cited in note 26, as well as in "Who Read the Romances of Chivalry?" cited in note 1.

[29] For references to these criticisms, see notes 4 and 5 to Chapter II of my *Romances of Chivalry in the Spanish Golden Age*. The best discussions of these criticisms, placing them in the context of Renaissance literary theory, remains that of Alban Forcione, *Cervantes, Aristotle, and the* Persiles (Princeton University Press, 1970), Parts One and Two.

Two writers often cited as antecessors are only partly that. Juan de Valdés's *Diálogo de la lengua*, which is not particularly hostile to the romances, was virtually unknown until its publication in the eighteenth century, and had no influence on the later critics. Vives was hostile, to be sure, but for him the romances were merely one part of a broader spectrum of objectionable literature, particularly literature in the vernacular; Vives' translator Cervantes de Salazar, who amplified his comments on romances of chivalry, was, as has already been mentioned, Venegas' student.[30] The identification of the romances with the antithesis of good literature scarcely antedates Venegas' comment in an epilogue to the *Theológica descriptión de los misterios sagrados* of Álvar Gómez de Ciudad Real (Toledo, 1541; facsimile, Cieza, 1965), a work with whose publication Venegas was associated: "Dízese milesia de la ciudad de Mileto.... En esta fábula escrivió Apuleyo su *Asno dorado*, y Mahoma escrivió su *Alcorán*, y todos los milesios escrivieron sus cavallerías Amadísicas y Esplandiánicas hervoladas."[31]

It is well known that romances of chivalry—secular ones, at any rate[32]—were never censored. While this fact reflects well on the practice of censorship in sixteenth-century Castile, it is worth pointing out that Venegas may have set a model by himself declining to act against any of them. There are two possible explanations for this inaction: first, Venegas' statements about the romances strongly suggest that he had never read one, and they contrast with his comments on the works he censored, which he had

---

[30] Vives and his translator are both cited by Henry Thomas, *Spanish and Portuguese Romances of Chivalry* (1920: rpt. New York: Kraus Reprint, 1969), pp. 161-66.

[31] Although the above is posed as a question, what is certain is Venegas' initiation of the identification of the mysterious Milesian fables with the Spanish romances of chivalry (see my introduction, already cited), although such identification is frequently credited to such later authors as Cervantes' source, López Pinciano. On the Milesian fables, whose alleged relationship to Spanish literature I hope to discuss more fully on another occasion, see Alexander Scobie, *Apuleius Metamorphoses, I: A Commentary* (Meisenheim am Glan: Anton Hain, 1975), pp. 66-67, and for their context, Arthur Heiserman, *The Novel before the Novel* (Chicago and London: University of Chicago Press, 1977), in which they are discussed in Chapter 8.

[32] On the romances of chivalry *a lo divino*, see my book cited in note 1.

indeed read. Secondly, perhaps more likely, is the fact that whatever the social effects of the romances, their religious orientation, basically that of the Crusaders, was very unexceptional. Whatever Venegas' feelings as a private scholar, his official function was to eliminate religious error.

Beyond the above I am not going to defend Spanish censorship, just as I would not defend the expulsion of the Jews, the execution of heretics, the blood laws, or any one of a number of similar measures which are offensive to us moderns, no matter how laudable they seemed to contemporaries. But I would suggest that the picture is not exclusively black. The choice, first in Toledo and later in Madrid, of such an educated, Christian, and modest man suggests that censorship, at least during this early period, was being intelligently and carefully exercised.

FLORIDA STATE UNIVERSITY

# Three Hispano-Jewish
# *romances* from Amsterdam

SAMUEL G. ARMISTEAD

JOSEPH H. SILVERMAN

 HOSE OF US who have been concerned with the Judeo-Spanish *Romancero* have tended to neglect some geographic branches of the Hispano-Judaic disapora, where, in earlier centuries, the *Romancero* might have been cultivated. Being thoroughly Hispanic in their culture and intensely proud of their Iberian heritage, it seems quite likely that the Marrano settlers of such areas as Holland, England, Bordeaux and numerous communities of the New World, must, not unlike their coreligionists in Salonika, Istanbul or Tetuán, have cultivated a ballad tradition of their own. In the present article, we would like to call attention to some concrete documentary evidence in support of such a possibility.[1]

---

[1] We discussed the Ms. treated in the present article in an earlier study published in *Études...offertes à Jules Horrent*. At that time, we had not yet seen the London Ms., which is the counterpart of the recently discovered Brussels codex. Our earlier publication offers only a transcription of the Brussels text of the *Testamento de Felipe II*. The present article was read in a preliminary form by S. G. A. at the 94th Annual Convention of the Modern Language Association of America, in San Francisco, December 28, 1979.

From the end of the sixteenth century, when Hispano-Portuguese Jews established their community in Amsterdam, the so-called "Dutch Jerusalem" was to become the most important and the most distinguished western European center of the Marrano diaspora. In Amsterdam, during the next two and a half centuries, not only would Spanish and Portuguese be the everyday languages of the Sephardic community, but a rich and abundant literature was to be cultivated in both these languages, exemplified in a great variety of genres: Prose, drama, and poetic writings, in both Spanish and Portuguese, were to be produced in great abundance in the Dutch Sephardic community. Until the middle of the nineteenth century, Portuguese continued to be spoken as a home language by the Amsterdam Sephardim. Though Dutch was eventually to become their native language, an extensive vocabulary of Hispanic words and expressions continued to be used in Dutch Sephardic speech, in both familiar and ritual terminology, almost down to the present day.[2]

In regard to the presence of *romances* in this eminently Hispanic community, certain compositions of a semi-popular nature are well known: A *romance* of *Jacob y Raquel*, for instance, was printed as an appendix to the *Comedia famosa de Adán y Mordochai*, by Ishack Cohen de Lara, published in Leiden, in 1699.[3] The erudite *romancero nuevo* also seems to have been cultivated by the Dutch Sephardim, as is attested in the anonynmous collection: *Romances varios de differentes authores nuevamente impressos por un curioso*, published in Amsterdam, in 1688, and offered for sale, as specified on the title page, "en caza de Ishaq Coen Faro."[4] On the other hand, the possibility of the exist-

---

[2] Concerning the history of the Amsterdam community, its literary activities, and the survival of Hispanisms in Dutch Sephardic usage, see our article, "El Romancero entre los sefardíes de Holanda," *Études... offertes à Jules Horrent* (Liège, 1980), nn. 1-4.

[3] See J. A. van Praag, "Dos comedias sefarditas," *Neoph*, 25 (1940), 12-24, 93-101: 23-24.On the ballad of *Jacob y Raquel*, see the perceptive commentary of Edward Glaser, "Un patriarca bíblico en el Romancero," *Sef*, 16 (1956), 113-23.

[4] Biblioteca Nacional (Madrid), R3237. See E. M. Wilson, "Miguel de Barrios and Spanish Religious Poetry," *BHS*, 40 (1963), 176-80: p. 179, where editions of 1677 and 1688 are mentioned. For more detailed bib-

ence of *romances* in oral tradition among the Amsterdam Sephardim has, until now, been largely neglected.[5] In 1913, José Leite de Vasconcellos consulted, in London, a certain "miscelânea judaica do século XVII." From this manuscript, Leite edited in 1922 two ballads under the somewhat deceptive title of "Dois romances peninsulares."[6] The great Portugeuse scholar had described British Library Ms. Add. 18:155 (= RD 7950534) in detail in his book *De Campolide a Melrose*,[7] but his better known article of 1922 contained no information on the character or the geographic origin of the ballad texts and they were, consequently, not taken into account as being representative of a Sephardic tradition. The poems edited by Leite consist, on one hand, of an abbreviated and ill-remembered version of *El sacrificio de Isaac*, which was probably learned from a written source and does not reflect the variation characteristic of an oral text.[8] On the other hand, Leite also published a version of *La infantina* (contaminated with *El caballero burlado*), which is quite traditional in character and whose language is a complex mixture of Spanish and Portuguese, similar to that found in modern oral tradition in the frontier repertoire of Trás-os-Montes.

In a recent article, published in *Les Lettres Romanes*, Dirk Van der Cruyse pointed out the existence of a second and until now unknown Ms. of the same London miscellany studied by Leite.[9] The copy discovered by Van der Cruyse is Ms. II-93 of the Biblio-

---

liographical data on these editons, see Antonio Rodríguez-Moñino, *Manual bibliográfico de Cancioneros y Romanceros*, I. *Impresos durante el siglo XVII*, ed. Arthur L.-F. Askins (Madrid: Castalia, 1977), pp. 673-75 (ed. 1677), 677-80 (ed. 1688).

[5] Concerning the liturgical and art music of the Dutch Sephardim, see the exhaustive study by Israel Adler, *Musical Life and Traditions of the Portuguese Jewish Community of Amsterdam in the XVIIIth Century* (Jerusalem: Hebrew University, The Magnes Press, 1974).

[6] *RFE*, 9 (1922), 395-98.

[7] (Lisbon: Imprensa Nacional, 1915), pp. 7 and 159-64.

[8] See Diego Catalán's comments in *Por Campos del Romancero* (Madrid: Gredos, 1970), pp. 68-69.

[9] "Un témoignage de rancune et de *saudadismo* judéo-portugais au XVIIe siècle," *LR*, 27 (1973), 16-36.

thèque Royale Albert I$^{er}$ in Brussels. Van der Cruyse's article also gave notice of the presence, in the same Ms., of a third *romance* with traditional connections. Without mentioning Leite's London Ms. and without recognizing the *romance*, Van der Cruyse cites two verses of a version of *El testamento del rey Felipe*, along with references to the already familiar *Sacrificio de Isaac* and *Infantina*.[10] The Ms. discovered by Van der Cruyse, just like Leite's London codex, is entitled *Relações, cantigas, adeuinhações, e outras corisidades, trasladadas de papeis velhos e juntados neste caderno.* The title page is dated "Amsterdam, 1683." On fol. 39r. there is another title page, in Hebrew, which specifies the name of the mansucript's compiler: he was the famous Sephardic scholar and author, Isaac ben-Matitia Aboab (1631-1707). The London Ms. and the new Brussels Ms. are very similar in their content. They are obviously two copies of essentially the same miscellany. Yet, as far as the three *romances* we have mentioned are concerned, the two copies are not identical. Each offers readings which, in minor details, correct and supplement the other. It is, moreover, not without interest that the London text of *El sacrificio de Isaac* has been slightly emended by at least one subsequent reader, indicating a particular interest and perhaps familiarity—oral or bookish we cannot know—with a narrative of particular significance in Judaic tradition. It is worth noting that one of the emendations (v. 4*b*) agrees with the version printed in the *Silva de romances* (Zaragoza, 1550-51): "yua ysaac muy fati-

---

10 For essential bibliography of early and modern traditional versions of *El testamento*, see our *Romances judeo-españoles de Tánger* (recogidos por Zarita Nahón) (Madrid: Cátedra Seminario Menéndez Pidal, 1977), núm. 9, and Diego Catalán, "El romancero de tradición oral en el último cuarto del siglo XX," *El Romancero hoy: Nuevas fronteras,* ed. Antonio Sánchez Romeralo, D. Catalán, and S. G. Armistead (Madrid: Cátedra Seminario Menéndez Pidal-Univeristy of California, 1979), pp. 217-56: 246, nn. 83-84, 86. For *El sacrificio,* see our *Judeo-Spanish Ballads from New York* (collected by Maír José Benardete) (Berkeley-Los Angeles: University of Calfornia Press [in press]), no. 11. Catalán's study (*Por campos,* pp. 56-75) is fundamental. Note also the existence of a lone "Crypto-Jewish" version from Portugal: Amílcar Paulo, "Os Marranos em Trás-os-Montes (Reminiscências Judio-Portuguesas)," *Douro-Litoral,* 7:v-vi, vii-viii (1956), 523-60, 627-60: pp. 556-57. For *La infantina* and *El caballero burlado,* see *Romances . . . de Tánger,* nos. 60 and 54.

gado."[11] The other changes, which do not improve the text, probably reflect arbitrary alterations or may perhaps respond to traditional variations which have not been recorded elsewhere. On the following pages we offer a transcription of the three *romances* according to the Brussels Ms., with differences present in the London MS. recorded as variants:[12]

[I. *La infantina*]
.1.
Acasar Vay Caualheero.
aCasar Como solia.
2   los perros lheua Cansados.
o falcão pirdido auia.

.2.
Debaxo de Vn aruoredo.
muy alto en marauilha.
4   que el pie tenia de oro.
y la Rama de plata fina.

.3.
Yno mas alto rincon /
Vi estar huna donz.[a]
6   oCabelho desu Cabesa /
todo su Cuerpo cobria.
os olhos da sua Cara todo.
arboledo Resplandisia.

.4.
8   Apontoulhe Coalança.
para Ver oque dezia.
tate tate Caualhero.
no fagais tal Vilania.

---

[11] *Silva de romances (Zaragoza, 1550-1551)*, ed. Antonio Rodríguez-Moñino (Zaragoza: Cátedra de Zaragoza, 1970), p. 292 (v. 20); Catalán, *Por campos*, p. 65.

[12] We wish to thank Mr. Pierre Cockshaw of the Bibliothèque Royale for granting us permission to publish the Brussels texts.

.5.

10  Que sou hija.
del Rey de fransia.
de la Reina.
Costantina.

.6.

sete fadas me fadaram.
nos brasos da madre minha.
12  que andase aquy sete annos.
sete annos Emais um dia.

.7.

Oje se acabam os sete.
amanhã se aCaba odia.
14  Sete plugier Caualhero.
lheuame Entu Companhia.

.8.

Home lheua por mujer.
home lheua por amiga.
16  home lheua por Esclaua.
que muy bien te Seruiria.

.9.

Deixame hauer Conselho.
Conselho da madre mia.
18  que elha Era muger Viega.
bon Conselho me daria.

.10.

Fuese el Caualhero /
asu madre lo dezia.
20  muy Cobarde fueste hijo
de muy g.<sup>de</sup>
Cobardia se troxeras la infanta.
yo por hija la queria.

.11.

22  Bolue el Caualhero.
ainifanta ya es seida.
que su Padre la buscara.
y en su Companhia es hida.

.12.
24 Yseyo fuera alcalde.
yo por mi me julgaria.
matarme con mis manos.
pues la infanta perdia.
[fols. 10v.-11r.]

Variants from British Library Ms. 18:155, fols. 12r.-12v.:

| | |
|---|---|
| 1 *a* | Caualhero |
| 2 *b* | aVia |
| 5 *b* | donze.ᵃ |
| 7 *b* | Resplandesia |
| 10 *b* | Constantina |
| 11 *a* | fadaron |
| 11 *b* | Braços |
| 12 *a* | que andais aqui Sete Annos |
| 12 *b* | hum |
| 13 *a* | acabão |
| 13 *b* | amanha |
| 16 *b* | seruira |
| 21 *a* | ynfanta |
| 22 *b* | aynfanta ya Es es seida |

[II. *El sacrificio de Isaac*]

Ya se parte Abraham:
2 partese para los montes:
donde Dios le ha Enbiado:
asacrificar su hijo/
Ishack q̃ era nombra.º
4 Abraham hiua por el monte arriba:
Ishack hiua fatigado:
mucho mas lo hiua Abraham:
por ser ja Viejo pezado:
6 Hijo mio hijo mio:
descanso de mi Cuidado:
para mi plazer nacido:
para mi dolor Criado:
8 Desto que Vos quiero dezir:
no Cuideis destar torbado:
que Dios manda y ordena:
que seais sacrificado:
10 Pues que Dios assi lo quiere
que se Cumpla su mandado

ala querida my madre:
Embiaredes de grado:
12 Dezilde que no se afliga:
En perder su hijo amado:
que el que muere por Dios:
Enel Cielo Esta Coronado:
14 Ja le hiua dar el golpe:
con su braso muy ayrado:
deciende del Cielo un Angel:
de la mano lo ha quitado:
16 Tate Tate Abraham:

tate tate Viejo honrado:
q̃ Dios Esta de ty/
Contente y pago:
18 decierto tu Coraçon/
ya le tiene bien prou.º
Toma dally Vn Cordero:
Entre las sarças atado:
20 q̃ manda q̃ le den/
aŝ. sacreficado:
fuese Abraham asu Caza
con suhijo mui Consolado:
Finis

[fol. 24r.]

Variants from British Library Ms. 18:155, fol. 25r.:

2b    Embiado

3a    Ijo

3b    nomb.º

4a    ariba

4b    Ishack hiua <mui> fatigado (mui *supplied above the line by another hand*).

8b    no Cuideis destar turbado (cuideis *is crossed out and* penseis *supplied above the line by another hand*).

13b   <p> que el que muere por Dios (por *supplied in the margin by another hand*).

15a   hun

18a   decierto (?) *has been crossed out and* le *altered to* lo; *the emended verse reads:* <y> tu Coraçon ya l<o> tiene bien prou.º

20a   *The second* que (*spelled out here*) *has been crossed out and* a *has been changed to* al; *the emended verse reads:* q̃ manda que le den a<l> señor sacreficado.

## [III. El testamento de Felipe II]

### .1.

El gran monarca del mundo.
arima Corona y Setro.
2   tiene la muerte Sercana.
azer quiere Testamiento.

### .2.

Por que lagota y la piedra.
lo tiene ya quazi muerto.
4   Con otros diuersos males.
de lepra Cubierto el Cuerpo.

### .3.

No por falta de dotores.
que tiene muchos y buenos.
6   pero es mal de la muerte.
que solo el morir es Remedio.

### .4.

No quiere mudar de Ropa.
por que muda el pensamiento.
8   de las baxezas del mundo.
alas alturas del Cielo.

### .5.

Mando hazer un altar.
delante sus hojos puesto.
10   Con mil Reliquias de santos.
que muchos Papas le dieron.

### .6.

Mando Sacar de una Tumba.
tres Cabesas de hombres muertos.
12   al pie del diemo las puzo.
que es Voluntad del enfermo.

### .7.

Hijos Veis Estas Cabesas.
sin barba y sin Cabelho.
14   que paresem ala muerte.
pues Reys ansido primeros.

### .8.

Vistieron Ricos borcados.
limpias Espadas sinieron.
16   ansy la muerte anos otros.
trastornara Como aelhos.

.9.
Miralde bien si aCazo.
la aueis algun parentesco.
18 que ahy Esta el Emperador.
my Padre y Vuestro aguelo.

.10.
Los guerfanos saboyanos.
Razon Es fauoreserlos
20 que si son Vuestros Sobrinos.
bien sabeis que son mis nietos.

.11.
Mi hija Dona Yzabel. Vuestra
hermana Vos encomiendo.
22 que mireis muy bien por elha.
y tomedes sus Consegos.

.12.
Que elha era mi moger.
my Regalo y mi Contento.
24 que siento mas Enperderla.
que perder la Vida y Reyno.

.13.
Toda la Corte lhoraua.
hazian gran sintimiento.
26 no lhoreis queridos mios.
que me dais muy gran tormento.

.14.
My hija Dona Iyzabel.
Vuestra hermana Vos Encomiendo.
28 que Encomendarla dos Vezes.
no es mucho aun que fueran Ciento.

Finis

[fols. 9v.-10r.]

Variants from British Library Ms. 18:155, fol. 11r-11v.

| 8 b | de Cielo |
| 9 b | ojos |
| 11 a | huna |
| 11 b, 13 a | Cabezas |
| 17 b | Le aVeis algum |
| 20 b | q̃ |
| 24 a | Emperderla |
| 27 a | Izabel |
| 28 b | aVnque |

Two of these ballad texts are not really traditional. Both *El sacri-ficio de Isaac* and *El testamento del rey Felipe* are, in effect, poorly remem-bered memorizations of written texts. *La infantina*, on the other hand, does represent oral tradition. But despite these limitations, it is worthy of note that all three of these *romances* are still current today in the oral tradition of the Moroccan Sephardim. The three ballads of our 1683 miscellany allow us to perceive something—very little, we must admit, but little is better than nothing—of what the ballad repertoire of the Dutch Sephardim may have been like in the second half of the seventeenth century. Some of these Sephardim, at least, seem to have had a ballad repertoire not unlike that of their North African coreligionists. The thematic agreement with the Moroccan repertoire is, we believe, significant. And, like ballad singers elsewhere in the Sephardic and the Pan-Hispanic traditions, the Amsterdam Sephardim reveal an interest in *romances* of a variety of different sub-types: Here we have a nove-lesque ballad (*La infantina*), a Biblical narrative (*El sacrificio de Isaac*), and yet another *romance* on the recent history of Spain (*El testamento de Felipe II*). Thus, the *Romancero's* characteristic diversity, as to orig-ins, themes, and content, clearly emerges, even from this minus-cule three-text collection. Still, it must be granted that the London and Brussels Mss. offer very limited testimony. Their *romances*, in fact, may well have been brought to Holland by some late immi-grant of Peninsular origin. (Matatías Abobab, Isaac's father, arrived in Amsterdam only in 1626.) It is, therefore, possible that by 1683 these ballads were little more than a nostalgic memory, copied with antiquarian affection from "papeis velhos." Yet all the same, their basic significance remains: the Hispano-Portuguese Jews of Amsterdam, like all other Hispanic peoples, were acquain-ted—however tenuously—with the *romance* of oral tradition.

Our three Dutch Sephardic ballads constitute, then, yet another testimony to the Pan-Hispanic character and diffusion of the *Romancero* in its constant correlation to the Hispanic languages. Menéndez Pidal's theory has, once again, been proved correct.[13] Hopefully, the evidence embodied in the London and Brussels Mss. may provide an incentive for the archival exploration of other

[13] See *Romancero hispánico*, 2 vols. (Madrid: Espasa-Calpe, 1953), II, 358-59.

Sephardic communities in both Europe and America. And, if we are lucky, still other testimonies to the *Romancero's* Pan-Hispanic diffusion may yet come to light.

University of Pennsylvania

University of California, Santa Cruz

# Toward a Conjectural Model of
# The *Corral del Príncipe*

JOHN J. ALLEN

OME OF JOHN KELLER'S most original contributions to American hispanism have resulted
from his realization that the visual possibilities inherent in the materials we work with
have been neglected. To think of illustrated
lectures, of the ways in which word and picture can illuminate one another as well as the
age that produced them, is to remember
John's lectures on Alfonso el Sabio's *Cantigas* and other medieval
texts. With this "visual" perspective in mind, I have been engaged
for some months in the construction of a conjectural model of
Madrid's *Corral del Príncipe*, the theater of Lope, Tirso, and Calderón, and what follows is offered in gratitude to John.

If something of the inspiration for my work with the *Príncipe*
came from John Keller, virtually everything in this study is based
upon the years of precise, patient work by N. D. Shergold and J. E.
Varey in the Municipal Archives of Madrid. Their publications
over the past thirty years have provided material for generations
of future *comedia* scholars, and as will be clear from my notes, only
a fraction of the information in this piece comes from my own
brief examination of the as-yet-unpublished eighteenth-century
documents in the Archives. We are all very much in their debt.

1983 will mark the four-hundredth anniversary of the inauguration of the *Corral del Príncipe*, four hundred years of theater on the spot where the *Teatro Español* stands today. This is a remarkable record, and it is regrettable that the volumes published on Shakespeare's original Globe playhouse—which burned to the ground after only fourteen years—have as yet no counterpart for the *corrales* of Madrid, which stood for over a hundred and fifty years. The *Príncipe* and its near twin, the *Corral de la Cruz*, were *the* public theaters in Madrid, from the time of Cervantes' early plays, when Lope was in his teens, until around 1745, when they were finally pulled down and replaced by the new *coliseos*.

The *Cruz* was the first, built in 1579, and the *Príncipe* second, with its first performance in 1583. I have chosen the *Príncipe* because its overall configuration is a little more regular, and because we have slightly more information about it, but they were very nearly identical in their overall disposition.

The theaters both came into existence as projects of charitable brotherhoods, to finance their hospitals for the poor, but they came under the supervision of the *Ayuntamiento de Madrid*. Certain administrative changes in 1615 and 1638 brought them even more directly under its control, and these changes generated most of the documents on which conjectural reconstruction must be based today: leasing documents, repair contracts awarded on the basis of competitive bids, and subsequent official inspections.[1] So, although we have almost no records of the initial construction, we can watch the theater being put back together piece by piece, as it slowly deteriorated over the decades. In what follows I will discuss briefly two of the many perplexing and controversial aspects of the *Príncipe*: the relationship between the *gradas*, or stands, and the stage, and the interpretation of the Armona box assignment sketch (see Fig. 4), the only graphic representation we have of the arrangements for the spectators.

Our basic knowledge of the dimensions and disposition of the

---

[1] For a concise account of what is known of the construction and earliest years of the Madrid *corrales*, see N. D. Shergold, "The First Public Theatres," in *A History of the Spanish Stage from Medieval Times until the End of the Seventeenth Century* (Oxford: Clarendon, 1967), pp. 177-208. For the administrative arrangements, see pp. 383-84.

*corrales* comes from the ground plans for each drawn up in 1735 by Don Pedro de Ribera.[2] Although they, like the Armona sketch, are from the final years of the life of the *corrales*, there is every indication that there were no major changes in the basic ground plan during the century and a half of their existence.[3] Hemmed in on all sides by preexisting buildings, the only way for the *corral* to expand was up.

I

There are some puzzling anomalies in the information we have as to the relationship between the *gradas*, or stands, and the stage in both *corrales*. First of all, the Ribera plans of the *Cruz* and the *Príncipe* are radically different in this respect (see Figure 1):

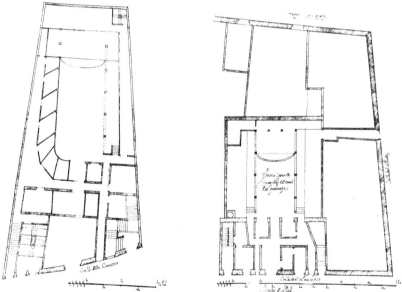

FIGURE 1. Ground plan of the *Cruz* (left) and *Príncipe* by Pedro de Ribera (1735)    Archivo del Ayuntamiento de Madrid

[2] First published by J. E. Varey and N. D. Shergold, "Tres dibujos inéditos de los antiguos corrales de comedias de Madrid," *Revista de la Biblioteca, Archivo y Museo del Ayuntamiento de Madrid* 20 (1951), figuras 2 and 3, following p. 320.

[3] Shergold, *A History*, p. 400.

As Othón Arróniz says: "Otra interrogante de gran significación es que el tablado, en dicho plano [Ribera's *Cruz*], ocupa toda
la parte frontal del patio y ni los aposentos ni las galerías [= *gradas*]
lo abrazan como sucede en el Corral del Príncipe. ¿Quiso el dibu-
jante indicar transformaciones que se operaron en el siglo XVIII?"⁴
Shergold says simply that "at first sight the stage [of the *Cruz*]
appears to be 42 feet wide, but a closer examination of the drawing suggests that as in the Príncipe 'gradas' ran along the side . . . .
The repair document of 1641 confirms that the 'gradas' in the
Cruz did in fact reach to the back of the stage, for in that year
partition walls were put up 'en los testeros de las gradas que arriman al vestuario.' In effect both corrales were equipped with huge
apron stages with spectators sitting along the stage sides, both at
stage level . . . "⁵ Well, yes, something like that must have been the
case, and it squares with a comment by López Pinciano about the
commotion caused "cuando uno atraviesa el teatro [the stage] para
ir a su asiento."⁶
But the stage was nine feet high, and the four or five steps up
to the *gradas* indicate that they cannot have been more than four
feet off the ground at the level next to the yard, and hence, if they
ran along its sides, next to the stage itself. There must have been
something like a five-foot difference between the lowest platform
of the *gradas* and the stage. And there are other problems. Shergold says: "It seems probable that the 'gradas' may have been used"
for stairways down to the stage from the corridor above;⁷ the difference in level between stage and stands would certainly compli-
cate this procedure. It is not entirely clear either that the reference
from 1641, cited above, to "los testeros de las gradas que arriman
al vestuario" necessarily means that the *gradas* reached to the back
of the stage, since it is in that same document that we discover
that the *Cruz* stage was nine feet high, and that there was a second
*vestuario* under it, in addition to the one at stage level rear: "se

---

⁴ *Teatros y escenarios del siglo de oro* (Madrid: Gredos, 1977), pp. 72-73.

⁵ *A History*, p. 401. In the Armona sketch (Figure 4), the stage of the
*Príncipe* appears in its turn to occupy the entire width of the theater.

⁶ Alonso López Pinciano, *Philosophía antigua poética*, ed. A. Carballo Picazo
(Madrid: CSIC, 1973), III, 290-91.

⁷ *A History*, p. 407.

metieron en el vestuario bajo del corral de la Cruz cinco pies dere-
chos...que cada uno tiene nueve pies...."[8]

To approach the problem from another angle, let us return to
the examination of the stage itself, and begin with Shergold's description of Juan Comba's drawing (Figure 2) of the *Príncipe* (1888):

FIGURE 2. The *Corral del Príncipe* (Juan Comba, 1888)
Biblioteca Nacional de Madrid

---

[8] N. D. Shergold, "Nuevos documentos sobre los corrales de comedias
de Madrid en el siglo XVII," *Revista de la Biblioteca, Archivo y Museo del Ayuntamiento de Madrid* 20 (1951), 409, henceforth referred to as "Nuevos docs." 1.
The height of the below-stage area might of course have been achieved by
excavation, thus diminishing the distance between the levels of the yard

Sur la scène Comba a esquissé deux acteurs, qui se battent en duel, tandis qu'à gauche un homme et une femme les observent bien paisiblement. A droite, on voit un autre homme assis, avec un long bâton à la main, et, derrière lui, deux autres, debout. Ces trois personnages ne sont pas des acteurs. Pour maintenir, ou chercher à maintenir, le bon ordre dans la corral, c'est devenue la coutume, au Siècle d'Or, qu'un magistrat, ou *alcalde*, soit assis sur la scène pour surveiller la représentation et pour y imposer la gravité de sa présence. Plus tard, l'alcalde cessa d'occuper cette place pour se retirer dans la pièce de l'*alojero* . . . [9]

In *A History*, Shergold quotes the standing orders of the *Sala de Alcaldes y Corte* (c. 1630) with regard to this practice: "Entra [el alcalde] al vestuario y junto a él en el tablado ponen silla y se sienta y sin hacerle esperar salen luego los músicos y ha de estar con gran mesura y autoridad cuidando de lo que le toca" (p. 391 n.). Riccoboni's second-hand account of 1738 describes it as follows, speaking of the two *alojeros*, or lower boxes, facing the stage:

. . . dans l'une desquelles un *Alcalde de Corte* qui est un Juge Royal, se place, ayant tout son cortège devant lui dans une petite enceinte qui est dans le Parterre. Ce Magistrat ne s'y met cependant pas ordinairement, mais seulement lorsque la Scène est embarassée par les Décorations; car dans la Comédie simple, que l'on appelle *de Capa y Spada*, il occupe une chaise sur un des côtés du théâtre, avec deux ou trois Archers de sa suite placés derrière lui.[10]

---

and the stage. Although I think this is probably not the case, it is a very complex problem, and one which I have chosen not to explore here, since a decision as to the elevation of the stage is not crucial to the hypothesis I am developing. Arróniz, at any rate, puts the elevation of the *Cruz* stage at 2.5 meters "cuando menos" (*Teatros y escenarios*, p. 67)

[9] N. D. Shergold, "Le Dessin de Comba et l'ancien théâtre espagnol," in *Le Lieu théâtral à la Renaissance*, ed. J. Jacquot (Paris: Centre National de la Recherche Scientifique, 1964), pp. 261-62.

[10] Louis Riccoboni, *Réflexions historiques et critiques sur les différents Théâtres de l'Europe* (Paris, 1738), p. 48. See also the Italian account cited by Arróniz, *Teatros y escenarios*, p. 68. There is another Spanish reference from 1736, among the unpublished documents in the Archivo del Ayuntamiento de Madrid. Materials in the Archivo are represented by three separate cata-

A quaint practice indeed, if this *tablado* is the stage itself, as has been supposed, and perhaps that is really the way it was. But if so, the situation was more complicated than that, or at least more crowded, since the documents from 1632 mention "el banco que está encima del tablado a la mano derecha arrimado al primer poste [que] está pagado por una vez a Francisco de Alegría [the lessee] por todo el tiempo de su arrendamiento.... [L]os comisarios de la Villa con la nueva administración han quitado los bancos mudando la forma sin reparar que éste tiene diferencia de los demás por estar dado el dinero desde el primer día...."[11] There are clearly several benches on this *tablado*, and if it is really the stage, the benches would constitute a radical departure from the ruling in 1608: "que no se consienta...que en el teatro donde se hace la representación [the stage] haya silla, ni banco, ni persona alguna."[12]

That the same or a very similar situation of seating on the *tablado(s)* prevailed one hundred years later is clear from Riccoboni's account:

> On y mont [the *gradas*] par cinq petites marches de bois: ils sont entourés d'une espèce de balustrade, et *vont se joindre à deux rangs de bancs qui sont sur la scène où les Acteurs représentent*. (p. 49, emphasis mine)

Arróniz' perplexity is understandable: "¿A qué se refieren estas últimas palabras del viajero anónimo? No alcanzamos a descubrirlo" (p. 76). It seems clear that we are dealing with an ambiguous area, which can be used flexibly, now for seating (the *alcalde* and his men, the man with a hired bench, the two rows of benches), now for staging (portable staircases., elaborate scenery which requires that the *alcalde* move to the back of the yard). These

---

logues: "Cuentas," "Secretaría," and "Corregimiento." Subsequent parenthetical references in the text will indicate the catalogue and *legajo* designation necessary for retrieval—*Corr.* for Corregimiento, and *Sec.* for Secretaría—, in this case: *Corr.* 1-131-24. I have modernized the Spanish of all of the documents, published and unpublished.

[11] Shergold, "Nuevos docs." 1, p. 396.

[12] J. E. Varey and N. D. Shergold, *Fuentes para la historia del teatro en España* (London: Tamesis 1971-79). Volumes III-IV have been published, and subsequent citations will indicate volume and page, in this case: III, 49.

corner areas, then, seem to be distinct from both the stage proper and from the *gradas*, and yet are associated with and at times confused with both.[13] The difference between the two Ribera ground plans reflects this ambivalence graphically.

The history of the development of the *corral* in Madrid suggests what I believe is a plausible soultion to the dilemma. All of the predecessors of the *Cruz* and the *Príncipe* in Madrid had platforms at the sides of the stage—the *Pacheca*, the *Valdivieso*, and the *Puente*—, and with respect to the *Puente*, mention is made of "los tabladillos colaterales del teatro [= the stage]"[14] Shergold comments that "the exact meaning of this phrase is not clear, but these 'tabladillos' or 'small platforms', may have accommodated spectators who sat along the sides of the stage itself."[15] In the new *Corral de la Cruz* the accounts from December 20, 1579, "mention the takings from 'both platforms' ('entramos tablados') just as they do in the Pacheca and the Puente, and indeed these platforms were fairly certainly the same ones that had been brought across from the latter corral...."[16] At the first performance in the new *Príncipe*, on September 21, 1583, "hubo de dos tablados con la representación 70 reales, porque no estén hechas gradas ni ventanas ni corredor."[17]

The most plausible assumption, in the face of all of the apparent contradictions we have reviewed here, seems to me to be that

---

13 In *A History* (p. 206), Shergold says that "along either side [of the stage] ran platforms, generally called 'tablados' in the documents, on which were seats for spectators. These later came to be known as 'gradas', and are a permanent feature of theatre buildings throughout the period covered by this study." But the *gradas* proper are "*scalinate*" in an Italian account from 1668-69 (Shergold, *A History*, p. 409); the men are seated there "comme on l'étoit dans les Amphithéâtres des Anciens," according to Riccoboni (p. 49), and a distinction between these lateral *tablados* and the *gradas* existed from the beginning, as indicated by Pellicer, below.

14 Shergold, *A History*, pp. 181-82.

15 Ibid.

16 Ibid. p. 184.

17 Casiano Pellicer, *Tratado histórico sobre el origen y progresos de la comedia y del histrionismo en España* (Madrid: Administración del Real Arbitrio de Beneficencia, 1804), I, 69.

these *tablados* or *tabladillos colaterales* persisted throughout the history of the *Príncipe* and the *Cruz*, in the corners between the *gradas* proper and the stage. A clear distinction in 1652 between the *gradas* and the "floor where the benches are," supports it:

> En *el suelo adonde están los bancos* se contaron catorce tablas nuevas de a nueve pies de largo deshiladas y clavadas que a cinco reales cada una montan setenta reales.
>
> De muchos aderezos que se han hecho *en este dicho suelo y en las gradas*.... [18]

This "*suelo*" is clearly neither the stage nor the *gradas*. Figure 3

This "*suelo*" is clearly neither the stage nor the *gradas*. Figure 3 embodies my understanding of how the *Príncipe* stage and adjacent platforms might have looked, with the platforms of my model here arranged for seating, not scenery. I have gone on at some length on this point because it seems to me that instead of the naive staging which has been universally accepted as characteristic of the *corral*—the *alcalde* on the

FIGURE 3 Reconstruction of the ground floor of the *Príncipe*, with four benches on each lateral platform (outlined in white). J. J. Allen

stage among the actors—, we are dealing with what was probably the most flexible and in a sense "modern" stage in Renaissance Europe.

---

[18] N. D. Shergold, "Nuevos documentos sobre los corrales de comedias de Madrid, 1652-1700," *Boletín de la Biblioteca de Menéndez Pelayo* 35 (1959), 219, henceforth referred to as "Nuevos docs." 2. Emphasis mine.

## II

The second aspect of the *Príncipe* of interest here is the interpretation of the invaluable box assignment sketch form among the *borradores* for the *Memorias cronológicas sobre el origen de la representación de comedias en España. Año de 1785*, by the Corregidor Armona, which purports to depict the *Príncipe* in the early eighteenth century.[19] In what follows I will interpret the Armona sketch in the light of other seventeenth- and eighteenth-century documents in an attempt to relate the *Príncipe* to the buildings which adjoin it and the balconies and windows attached to and within them, and thus dispel some of its mystery. Figure 4 reproduces the Armona sketch without alteration, and Figure 5 with the insertion of the alphabetical box designations that I will use in my subsequent discussion. I hope it will be clear that the determination of the chain of ownership of individual boxes which occupies much of these remaining pages is important in establishing the distinctions between the buildings adjoining the *corral* and at times in ascertaining the characteristics and dates of inauguration of the boxes. All references to the right and left sides of the façade assume that one is standing on the Calle del Príncipe facing the theater. References to the north and south sides of the yard (*patio*) require one to remember that the *corral* faced west. I will begin this tour through the theater on the right, proceeding along the south side of the yard. The Calle del Príncipe, with its series of entrances to the *corral* would be along the top of the sketch.

A box assignment list, undated, but probably from 1736 (*Corr.* 1-131-24), which corresponds rather closely to the Armona sketch, identifies five boxes (A, B, C, D, and H) as having belonged to Don Pedro Antonio Dávila y Aragón, Marqués de Povar (or Pobar). Aragón seems first to have opened a single box (Box A) at the *Príncipe*. He bought a room "cinco varas y media de largo y cinco y cuarto de ancho," above the owners' bedroom, in a house said to adjoin the *corral* on one side and the house of Gabriela Peña on the other (*Sec.* 3-134-51). There was a box, probably—although not

---

[19] The sketch is in the Biblioteca Nacional de Madrid, *Ms.* 18474, *legajo* 1.

necessarily—this one, associated with his name as early as 1615,[20] and Box A is associated with his name in 1542,[21] and again in 1722.[22] He subsequently bought three houses, located on the Calle del Príncipe adjoining the theater and continuing around the corner on the Calle del Prado, which are said to provide three more boxes, "y el uno de los tres aposentos es un balcón grande de hierro [Box H] y encima dél caen los desvanes y los otros dos caen en bajo con dos rejas del corral [Boxes C and D, called respectively, "reja grande" and "Protectora" on the Armona sketch] en el sitio de las gradas" (*Sec.* 3-134-51).

The "reja nueva" (B) was so called because it was opened in 1697, "en tiempo de [el recaudador] Socueva" (*Sec.* 3-135-19). Aragón had sought permission as early as 1656 to modify one of his houses, "en la cual tenía dos aposentos [A and C] con vistas al corral de las comedias, [y] quiere agora abrir en medio de los dos otra ventana [B]...,"[23] but permission was not granted until after his death, to the Almirante de Castilla, second husband of Ara-

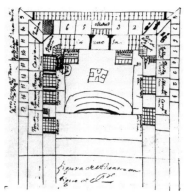

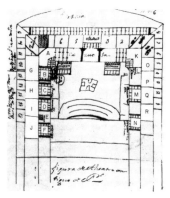

FIGURE 4. The Armona sketch of the *Príncipe*
    Biblioteca Nacional de Madrid

FIGURE 5. The Armona sketch of the *Príncipe* with box designations added.

[20] J. E. Varey and N. D. Shergold, "Datos históricos sobre los primeros teatros de Madrid: contratos de arriendo, 1587-1615," *Bulletin Hispanique* 60 (1958), 92.

[21] Shergold, "Nuevos docs." 1, p. 415.

[22] *Fuentes* V, 169.

[23] Shergold, "Nuevos docs." 2, p. 330.

gón's widow, Doña Ana Catalina de la Cerda, now Duquesa de Medina de las Torres de Rioseco.

All five of these boxes became, by bequest, "bienes de las niñas," a phrase which can be understood in the light of *Sec.* 3-131-51 as indicating that the proceeds from their rent went to the Colegio de las Niñas de [Nuestra Señora de] la Paz.

Box A is referred to in *Corr.* 1-131-24 as one of two *faltriqueras*, or corner boxes, and is described elsewhere[24] as "un balcón que hace esquina a la cazuela, que se llama de Povar." This, I believe, is the corner balcony shown in the Armona sketch which Shergold took for stairs.[25] The position of Box A, and of Box K (see below), with respect to the *gradas*, is indicated in the following terms, from 1698:

> Por los cuatro balcones que están arrimados a las cazuelas de los dos corrales [two in each *corral*] se bajan diferentes personas a la grada que a cada uno le corresponde, de que resulta daño..., pues se entran sin pagar puerta ni gradas... y para... que no resulten mayores inconvenientes, lo pongo en noticia de Madrid para que se sirva de mandar que en cada uno de dichos balcones se ponga una reja del ancho de una vara hacia el lado que coge la grada, que es el vacío por donde se reconoce el daño.... [26]

That Box B, and presumably boxes C, D, E, and F, were located at the same level is indicated by the request that "Sebastián de Pineda, maestro que fue quien abrió la dicha reja, declare con distinción y claridad los asientos que se han quitado de la grada primera sobre que está puesta, y cuántos hubo menester para disponer y formar la dicha reja."[27] This was exactly the situation with respect to Box L, its counterpart on the opposite side of the *corral*, when it was opened in 1635 (see below). The grilles all along the lower level on both sides were clearly functional, then, and not simply the charming ornaments of Comba's drawing.

---

[24] *Fuentes* V, 169.

[25] *A History*, p. 411.

[26] *Fuentes* VI, 260-61. The same situation obtained a hundred years earlier. See Pellicer, *Tratado histórico*, p. 84.

[27] *Fuentes* VI, 242.

The case against Shergold's interpretation of the corner balconies as stairs is as follows: (1) Boxes A and K are balconies, and
each "hace esquina con la cazuela." (2) A close look at the mysterious little structures drawn just inside the representations of
Boxes A and K on the Armona sketch reveals that the one next to
Box A has tiny cross marks perpendicular to the bars, analogous to
those at the sides of the *cazuela* opening and all across the *tertulia-
cazuela alta* area on the top floor of the façade, indicating some sort
of *celosía* or *reja*, not stairs. Perhaps they represent the two lower
boxes under the *cazuela* and behind the two railed enclosures
(marked *aloxero* on the Armona sketch, and used, in part, as vend-
ors' stalls), which were raised a little off the ground. (3) Stairs to
what? Access to Boxes A, B, C, D, E, F, H, I, J, and K, and apparently to *desvanes* 14-17 (see below), is through the adjoining houses
at the side. Access to G is by a special staircase on the *corral*
property—almost certainly the one which gives onto the last door
of the *corral* on the left. The remaining *desvanes* (9-13) formed part
of the *tertulia* on the façade.

Above Box B was the "balcón grande" of the Marqués del Carpio (G), which later belonged to the Marqués de Heliche. It was
apparently not part of the adjoining houses; at any rate it was
reached by a *corral* staircase, as mentioned above.

A new women's entrance to the *cazuela baja* was built in 1642 on
the Calle del Prado through the property of Francisco Garro de
Alegría, lessee of the *corrales* for a time, and owner of the next
house up the street.[28] "La casa de Doña Juana González Carpio
[Alegría's widow] tenía dos balcones [Boxes I and J] y una reja
[F]...[que] llaman de Molina" (*Sec.* 3-135-19). It had also the "reja
chica" (E) shown on the Ribera plan, as indicated in *Sec.* 3-135-19,
where it is said that the Molina window was sold to the Conde de
Torrehermosa, "y había una rejilla pequeña que también pertenecía
a Torrehermosa..." the new passageway on the Alegría property
constituted a corridor through which the women entered the *corral*
proper to the point where they turned left and proceeded behind
or beneath the *gradas* to the stairway built for them under that of
the Marqués del Carpio.

Five *desvanes* on the south side (nos. 13-17) are designated on

---

[28] Shergold, "Nuevos docs." 1, pp. 423-26.

the Armona sketch as belonging to Don Martín Marcelino de Ver-
gara, and the remaining four to the "*casa*," which leads one to suspect that in this case the ownership and access to the boxes carries
right through to the top floor. Thus the house that once belonged
to Francisco de Alegría and now to Don Martín Marcelino must
have housed or given access to the Molina box (F) and the "reja
chica" (E) on the first level behind the *gradas*, to the Pastrana (I) and
Rincón (J) boxes on the second, and to *desvanes* 13-17 on the third.
Another document from *Corr.* 1-131-24 supports this hypothesis,
and it seems to refer to the Marcelino house. The administrator of
the estate of Don Joseph García Ramón, Secretario de la Villa at
the turn of the century, sought compensation in 1739 for a period
of time when construction blocked the view of the boxes in his
house, which is referred to as follows: "una casa en la calle del
Prado, y pertenécenla las vistas de dos balcones y cuatro desvanes
que caen al Corral del Príncipe." Four *desvanes*, and not five?

It is difficult to imagine what house on the Calle del Prado this
could be, other than the Marcelino house, and other evidence leads
to the conclusion that the Armona sketcher simply drew the divid-
ing line between the *desvanes* which belonged to Don Martín Marcelino and those belonging to the theater itself on the wrong side of
*desván* 13, since we find elsewhere that the *tertulia* took up the space
of five *desvanes* on this side,[29] which would be nos. 9-13, leaving
nos. 14-17 for the Alegría/Remón/Marcelino house.

This assumption would seem to be conclusively corroborated
by the box assignment list from *Corr.* 1-131-24, which indicates
that *desvanes* 1-13 belonged to the theater, and that 14 (not 13)
through 17 "son de sisas [proceeds to the management] domingo,
lunes y martes, y los demás días de los herederos de don Martín
Marcelino."

On the left of the façade, adjoining the theater itself was a
house said in 1744 to have been bought by (or for) Lope de Ve-
ga (!) in May of 1613 (*Sec.* 3-134-38), and to have belonged subsequently to Don Rodrigo de Herrera, who opened a balcony
there—the other *faltriquera*, which corresponds to balcony A on the
opposite side: "Labró a su costa [un aposento] desde una casa que
compró sin tomar sitio al corral ni quitarle aprovechamiento sino

---

[29] Shergold, "Nuevos docs." 2, p. 329.

sobre lo claro por donde se entra debajo de las gradas."[30] This is Box K, which is elsewhere described as "un balcón a las gradas junto a la cazuela."[31] Herrera obtained permission in 1635 to open another window from the same room (Box L), having agreed to pay for two seats on the *gradas* taken up by the window, which was a yard wide and protruded one foot into the *corral*.[32] This house belonged subsequently to the ubiquitous Don Pedro Antonio de Aragón, and then, by inheritance, to Don Juan Thomás Gueri, and, finally, to Don Pedro de Yermo (*Sec.* 3-134-38), which confirms the suspicion that the "esquina de Yermo" on the Armona sketch, which Shergold took to be a stair-tower roof, is in fact the *faltriquera* box.

Next there was a house or houses with six boxes, four above, designated on the Armona sketch as: Tablas (O), Uceda (P), Almirante (Q), and Compañero (R); and two below: Puñonrostro (M) and Orejón (N). These are evidently the six referred to in a document of 1708 cited in 1744 (*Sec.* 3-135-19), where it is noted that the Conde de Puñonrostro owned all six, of which three were at least partially handled by the lessee: Almirante, Compañero, and Orejón. This property was described in 1692 as follows: "son hacienda de [doña Isabel de Mendoza y Aragón, Condesa de Grajal y Marquesa de Mirallo]...el valor y tasación del sitio y fábrica de unas casas...en la Calle del Príncipe con seis aposentos al patio de comedias del Corral del Príncipe..., linde casas de las memorias de don Rodrigo Herrera de dicho corral...."[33]

The box assignment list referred to above (*Corr.* 1-131-24) helps clear up some of the remaining mystery of the Armona sketch. The upper level boxes on both sides of the theater in the sketch have two names or designations each, as follows, proceeding first from the stage along the south side:

| (J) | (I) | (H) | (G) |
|---|---|---|---|
| Rincón | Pastrana | Aragón | Carpio |
| Marcelino | Marcelino | Niñas | casa |

---

[30] Shergold, "Nuevos docs." 1, p. 398-99.

[31] *Fuentes* V, 169-70.

[32] Shergold, "Nuevos docs." 1, p. 400.

[33] *Fuentes* VI, 153.

Proceeding from the stage along the north side, we find:

| (R) | (Q) | (P) | (O) |
|-----|-----|-----|-----|
| Compañero | Almirante | Uceda | Tablas |
| casa | casa | Ynteresados | Ynteresados |

From the assignment list we learn that the proceeds from the boxes were apportioned as follows, keeping the same order as before. On the south: "el rincón le toca a las sisas domingo, y lo[s] demás días al dicho Don Marcelino" (J), "Pastrana el domingo y lunes [es de las sisas] y los demás días de los herederos de Don Martín Marcelino" (I), "el aposento que llaman de Aragón las propias niñas" (i.e., the Colegio de las Niñas de la Paz) (H), "el Carpio lo propio [en cuanto a ser sisas]" (G). On the north: Uceda (P), Tablas (O), and the "reja de Puñonrostro" (M) all belong jointly to a group of "*ynteresados*" whose administrator is Don Francisco Durán.

And so it becomes clear that the Armona designations are indications of both the traditional name of each box and its current (1736) owner. Shergold has suggested that Box H, which both of the later versions of the Armona sketch (1785 and 1881) label Aragón/Peñas, actually reads Aragón/añal on the Armona original, indicating that the box was rented out by the year.[34] The box was not treated differently from the others in that respect, however, and the use of two names throughout as indicated above, leads one to conclude that the barely legible word is "Niñas," for the Colegio de las Niñas de Nuestra Señora de la Paz, which was in fact the beneficiary.

It seems clear that there are, indeed, four floors to the *corral*, as Arróniz says,[35] and not three, as Shergold would have it.[36] On the ground floor are the lower *alojero* boxes and the entrances to the yard facing the stage, and the *gradas* on each side. On the next level is the *cazuela*, facing the stage, and the two corner balconies (A and K) and the series of grilled windows set just above and behind the *gradas* on either side (B, C, D, E, F, and L, M, N). That these boxes

---

34 "Le Dessin," p. 271, and *A History*, p. 411.

35 *Teatros y escenarios*, p. 91.

36 "Le Dessin," p. 270.

were "upstairs" from the street level is indicated by the rise needed to accommodate at least three levels of *gradas* below and in front of them, by their apparent correspondence in level with the *cazuela*, at second-floor level, by the description of Box K as located "sobre lo claro por donde se entra debajo de las gradas" —i.e., at second-floor level—, and by the following text from 1698, establishing the fact that the Almirante had padlocked two of his boxes, one in each *corral*:

> ...pasé al Corral de la Cruz..., *habiendo subido por una escalera* de las casas de la Exma. Sra. doña Ana Catalina de la Cerda por donde se sube a los cuatro aposentos que da de vistas en dicho Corral de la Cruz, y en una puerta del aposento que llaman la puerta del Protector había un candado grande; y habiendo pasado al Corral del Príncipe,... *subí* por las casas de la dicha Señora que caen a la Calle del Prado, y en una puerta de un aposento que es una reja [C] pegada al aposento nuevo [B] había un candado grande en la puerta dél...."[37]

On the third floor are the boxes handled by the lessee (8, 1, 2, 3, 5, 6, 7) and the Madrid box (4) facing the stage, and the rather regularly spaced balconies on either side (G, H, I, J, and O, P, Q, R). On the fourth are the *desvanes*, the *cazuela alta*, and the *tertulia*. The stage itself, remember, was nine feet high, and thus well up toward the second-floor level.

The foregoing exposition has been limited to only two aspects, though relatively fundamental ones, of the reconstruction of the *Príncipe*, It has been implacably verbal and only marginally pictorial. But it is a necessary step toward the full application of John Keller's insight to the *corral*.

University of Florida

---

[37] *Fuentes* VI, p. 237. Emphasis mine.

# Don Quixote II / 60-61:
# Some Observations
# on Roque Guinart

KARL-LUDWIG SELIG

F THE MANY episodes in *Don Quixote*, it seems rather surprising that the narrative segment of the text devoted to Don Quixote's encounter with Roque Guinart has received relatively little attention. Although he figures and appears only in chapter 60 and the beginning of chapter 61 of Part II, Roque Guinart is one of the more memorable secondary characters in *Don Quixote*; he is a wanderer and is one of a group of important outsiders and in a way in affinity to other outsiders whose "biography" and wanderings are also portrayed in *Don Quixote*, such as Ginés de Pasamonte and Ricote. And all this pertains also to certain aspects of correspondences in a text which very much depends on a system of correspondences and to shared feelings between Don Quixote and other outsiders and wanderers in the text.

The principal thrust of scholars to date has been to identify Roque Guinart and to elucidate his biography outside the text and in history.[1] While I am quite aware of the biographical background

---

[1] I cite from the edition of Luis Andrés Murillo (Madrid: Castalia, 1978), with ample bibliographical notes. See also the edition of Martín de Riquer (Barcelona: Juventud, 1968) for further bibliography.

273

and historical setting which resonate in the episode—we are dealing with a text which is anchored in reality and in history and are
analyzing a narrative area of the text where there is a concerted
effort to close the gap between the time of the fiction and historical time—I should, however, like to make some observations on
the episode as to what is operative contextually; to put it into
other words, I should like to start from within the text and fathom
how the episode reaches out to history.

Let us see how the episode is set up in the text, how it is
posited, and how it is unraveled sequentially. After an encounter
pertaining to the validation and authentication of the text, Don
Quixote and Sancho Panza are on their way to Barcelona. It is
night; they are out in the open; Sancho Panza is asleep and the
Don in a quandary as to the disenchantment of Dulcinea, a predicament he hopes to resolve by referring to Alexander the Great and
the Gordian knot, an allusion which serves to anticipate the comparison later of Roque Guinart to *Alejandro Magno*. Don Quixote
tries to whip Sancho Panza; there is a brief but tense confrontation—and rebellion—between master and squire; the refusal per-
tains to a matter of *voluntad* and *albedrío*, as Sancho refuses to do
anything against his free will.[2] As he, having promised to whip
himself at his pleasure, is going to a tree or from tree to tree, he
notices some feet and legs dangling from the trees, causing him
tremblings and fear. Don Quixote in this instance recognizes the
physical phenomena for what they are:

> ...sin duda son de algunos forajidos y bandoleros que en
> estos árboles están ahorcados; que por aquí los suele ahorcar
> la justicia...por donde me doy a entender que debo de estar
> cerca de Barcelona. (493)

He *is* aware of the social and historical reality. And it is a reality
confirmed or attested by an authorial voice: "y así era la verdad
como él lo había imaginado." Their surprise if not astonishment is
increased at dawn by the sudden appearance of *cuarenta bandoleros
vivos*, who surround them *de improviso*. Not only their actions ("acu-

---

2 It should be noted that Sancho in defending himself refers to a
proverb, his habitual sphere of reference, and to a slightly more literary
text, a ballad, a popular text from which a citation is quoted which has
become proverbial.

dieron los bandoleros a espulgar al rucio, y a no dejarle ninguna cosa de cuantas en las alforjas y la maleta traía ... "), but also their speech in Catalan add to the state of confusion depicted in the scene; a certain emphasis on and occurrence of expressions of time, such as *en esto* and *de improviso* are at the service of the textual situation; they underline a certain precariousness, an atmosphere of insecurity, and which anticipate another (formal) facet or device which can be observed in the episode, similarly emphasized and at the service of the textual situation, namely disjuncture and constant interruption, and again indicative of instability—people are on the run. The sudden appearance of Roque Guinart begins—but only begins—to clarify the situation; he, in addressing Don Quixote, commits the malapropism *Osiris* for *Busiris* (495). It may be to indicate that Roque Guinart is "unlettered," but on another track of the text and as a strategem of a polydimensional text, it may be an authorial manipulation to presage a / the resolution of the total episode with a ray of hope and reconciliation, since Osiris, in contrast to Busiris (who stands for cruelty), is associated with fertility, renewal, resurrection, and hope.[3] And this is supportive of the references to and comparison to Alexander the Great which surround the episode and which are associated with Don Quixote and with Roque Guinart and their particular and individual predicament for a final spiritual reaffirmation.

There is a certain vagueness hovering about the encounter and meeting of Roque Guinart and Don Quixote and the way they greet each other. Don Quixote seems to know and to have heard of Roque Guinart's fame, and the latter has heard of Don Quixote:

> ...aunque algunas veces le había oído nombrar, nunca tuvo por verdad sus hechos, ni se pudo persuadir a que semejante humor reinase en corazón de hombre; y holgóse en estremo de haberle encontrado, para tocar de cerca lo que de lejos dél había oído. (495-96)[4]

---

[3] Cf. Mozart, *Die Zauberflöte*, Zweiter Aufzug, Chor:
     O Isis und Orisis, schenket
     Der Weisheit Geist dem neuen Paar!

[4] Cf. also Roque's statement: "...no os despechéis ni tengáis a siniestra fortuna esta en que os halláis; que podía ser que en estos tropiezos vuestra torcida suerte se enderazase; que el cielo, por estraños y nunca

In this area of the text, where the gap between life and letters, history and fiction becomes closer and closer, the boundary is indeed very vague and nebulous, and so is the boundary between the identity of personage(s) inside and outside the/their text.

Roque Guinart is interrupted (*de tropel*) by the appearance of Claudia Jerónima, whose family is involved in a feud. She tells her *cuento* with some (literary) traits, conventions or facets often associated with a novella structure (here very much in mini- or microform), and she is linked to history, since Roque Guinart, historical character that he is, knows her family and is a partisan or has taken a position in the feud. It is Don Quixote and Sancho Panza who interrupt her account, with Sancho Panza alluding to one of the episodes which took place at the domain of the Duke and Duchess, barely able to distinguish between fiction and reality, between contrivance/make-believe/artifice and fact:

> ...mi señor tiene muy buena mano para casamentero, pues no ha muchos días que hizo casar a otro que también negaba a otra doncella su palabra; y si no fuera porque los encantadores que le persiguen le mudaron su verdadera figura en la de un lacayo, ésta fuera la hora que ya la tal doncella no lo fuera. (497)

It is "la fuerza rabiosa de los celos" which is the cause of the tragic events narrated by Claudia and also witnessed by Roque who sheds tears: "sacaron las lágrimas de los ojos de Roque, no acostumbrados a verterlas en ninguna ocasión" (499).[5] This act—I should like to call it an emblematic act—adds a special touch to a sympathetic portrait; it may be indicative of his humanity and that there is still some hope; that in spite of many wanderings, insecurity, and restlessness, this man, pursued and harassed and on the

---

vistos rodeos, de los hombres no imaginados, suele levantar los caídos y enriquecer los pobres" (496). It is the language of "literature" or fiction rather than the language of "history." There is even something formulaic in the statement (e.g., *rodeos*).

[5] This show of emotion and emblematic act merit comparison to the tears shed by Eugène de Rastignac in *Père Goriot*. Of course, in the case of de Rastignac, there are so many and no more, and then he takes on Paris.

run, is not totally hardened and made hard and insensitive by life. As Claudia Jerónima so to speak fades out of the text and an authorial voice asserting itself and commenting on *celos* states:

> ... ¿qué mucho, si tejieron la trama de su lamentable historia las fuerzas invencibles y rigurosas de los celos?

Roque Guinart assembles his troops and orders that all that has been taken from Sancho be given back to him. It is an atmosphere which is tense, explosive, filled with irritation, suspicion, mistrust, and danger. Sancho will "no descoser los labios en tanto que entre aquella gente estuviese" (500).

At this point (*en esto*) sentinels announce the appearance of travelers on the road, victims to be robbed, but before their arrival, there is again significantly an interruption, a disjuncture: one notes again an acceleration of *cantus interruptus*. It is at this moment that Roque Guinart relates to and shares with Don Quixote his account and explanation, the mystery of his life, his *condition humaine*, in fact, his hell.

Although he is compassionate and endowed with good intentions, and his feelings are expresed *con concertadas razones* and with a hope "de salir del [laberinto] a puerto seguro" (501), his life-style and life can only be described as restless, labyrinthine, and filled with chaos, disorder, and confusion. There is a reason for his *abismo*, his *laberinto*, his struggle and enigmatic situation: *deseos de venganza*,[6] and this is all the more intensified and made more enigmatic, for when giving an account of his condition and state (also made more emphatic by the repetition of *nueva... nuevas... nuevos*) this reason or cause is underpinned, as it is qualified by *"no sé qué deseos de venganza"* (my italics), the *no sé qué* reverberating and resonating enigma, mystery, personal and universal drama.[7]

Don Quixote is willing to give advice, but by this time the tra-

---

6 As in the case of Ginés de Pasamonte, the specific deeds and acts are not spelled out.

7 For the *no sé qué*, see Dámaso Alonso, *Poesía española*, 5ª ed. (Madrid, 1966), pp. 238 ff., pp. 282 ff; Erich Köhler, *Esprit und arkadische Freiheit. Aufsätze aus der Welt der Romania* (Frankfurt, 1966), pp. 230-86 and pp. 328-62; Alberto Porqueras-Mayo, *Temas y formas de la literatura española* (Madrid, 1972), pp. 11-59.

velers appear. It will be the moment of exemplariness. *El gran Roque* will impose his authority in the presence of his (own) men and squires whom he cannot trust and who are greedy, ruthless, and brutal; he will assert himself by way of an exemplary act of magnanimity in the treatment of the travelers; he wil reveal his personal code (his *Lebenskodex*) and his utopian spirit[8] and display his *cortesía*, his *nobleza*, his *gallarda disposición*. He will be praised and compared to a paragonic figure in Antiquity "teniéndole más por un Alejandro Magno que por ladrón conocido" (503-04). He is also in contact with Don Antonio Moreno, *caballero rico y discreto* (508), and to whom by way of a letter he recommends Don Quixote. Roque reveals a great spirit of humanity and an appreciation of art, a work of art, which is the representation of an order. He is human and humane: while he would like to reserve Don Quixote for his friends and deprive his enemies of the pleasure of Don Quixote's and Sancho Panza's company, he is truly generous. He is aware of the possibilities of a work of art, of the possible (exemplary) functions and mission of a work of art. Roque is in the presence of a work of art, of a very special work of art and it should be shared by all: "que las locuras y discreciones de don Quijote y los donaires de Sancho Panza no podían dejar de dar gusto general a todo el mundo" (505). It can express the hopes and yearnings of man; it can serve to reconcile enemies and resolve feuds and to bind mankind and be a model and instrument for brotherhood, friendship and peace.

There is an epilogue, so to speak, to the episode and to the portrait of Roque Guinart. After it is stated that Don Quixote spent three days and three nights with Roque and before they embrace and bid farewell to each other on the Strand of Barcelona, an authorial voice once more summarizes and comments on Roque's life. With its powerful stacatto tone and abrupt rhythm and with its emphasis on constant movement, it reinforces the depiction of a life and atmosphere dominated by instability, mistrust, suspicion, and fear. With its reference to authority in a social institution and in history ("el visorrey de Barcelona"), it seems to serve as a warning and admonition and seems to subvert and

---

[8] Cf. the utopian ideas and ideals presented in *La gitanilla*, and again by outsiders.

undercut the hopes and yearnings expressed by Roque, a character from history in fiction:

> ...aquí amanecían, acullá comían, unas veces huían, sin saber de quién.... Dormían en pie, interrompiendo el sueño, mudándose de un lugar a otro. Todo era poner espías, escuchar centinelas, soplar las cuerdas de los arcabuces, aunque traían pocos, porque todos se servían de pedreñales. Roque pasaba la noche apartado de los suyos, en partes y lugares donde ellos no pudiesen saber dónde estaba; porque los muchos bandos que el visorrey de Barcelona había echado sobre su vida le traían inquieto y temeroso, y no se osaba fiar de ninguno, temiendo que los mismos suyos, o le habían de matar, o entregar a la justicia: vida, por cierto, miserable y enfadosa. (505)

Even if one allows for certain ironies and what one might like to call protective camouflage—the episode deals with an outlaw—, the text (and/or subtext) is a statement and plea pertaining to a person, a very special person,[9] and his condition, his isolation and solitude in a rather unstable and precarious and distrustful world.

COLUMBIA UNIVERSITY

---

[9] Cf. Herman Meyer, *Der Typus des Sonderlings in der deutschen Literatur* (Amsterdam, 1943) and his *Der Sonderling in der deutschen Dichtung* (München, 1963).

# Has Tirso Satirized the Conde-Duque de Olivares in Nineucio of
## *Tanto es lo de más como lo de menos?*

 N TIRSO'S LOATHSOME NINEUCIO of *Tanto es lo de más como lo de menos*, do we have a satirical portrait of the Conde-Duque de Olivares? J. C. J. Metford,[1] having accepted with minor reservations my conclusion that *Tanto es lo de más* was written in 1620 (though retouched in 1622-23), put forth in 1959 his belief that Gabriel Téllez (i.e., Tirso) had painted in this play a satirical portrait of Philip IV's minister-favorite, the Conde-Duque de Olivares. I am inclined to believe that Dr. Metford is right in his thesis, but if we accept as accurate the assessments that Dr. Gregorio Marañón and Professor John H. Elliott have made of this historical figure, we must set beside the very, very vivid figure of Nineucio the judgment of history and, by such a comparison, take note not only of the many similarities that

---

[1] "Tirso de Molina and the Conde-Duque de Olivares," *BHS*, 36 (1959), 15-27.

undoubtedly exist between the dramatic portrait and the historical one but also of a few striking discrepancies between them.

Before beginning our comparison of these two figures, we must give our readers some background essential to their understanding of this tragicomedy. *Tanto es lo de más* represents a fusion of the two Biblical parables of the rich miser and the prodigal son.[2] To this fusion Tirso has added the love story of Felicia,[3] who is courted by the three men of the Bibilcal parables, i.e., by Nineucio,[4] the rich miser; by Liberio, the prodigal son; and by Lázaro, the beggar who, as Tirso would have it, starts off, as the play opens, in comfortable financial circumstances, but quickly becomes a beggar as a result of his charity toward any and all who ask him for financial help.

The very vivid portrait of the rich miser, as portrayed by Tirso, early includes one of his physical appearance. Nineucio has just outlined the immense riches that he is willing to lay at Felicia's feet. Liberio scoffs at Nineucio's offer, reminding him that (I. 1, p. 78):

> No quita el oro los años
> que ya han mediado tu edad;
> ya en la tela de tu vida
> teje la vejez ingrata
> hilos de peinada plata
> que traen la muerte escondida:

---

[2] Luke XV:11-21 and XVI:22-32.

[3] The love-story of Felicia was borrowed from Mira de Amescua's *El rico avariento*, which Vern G. Williamsen dates "before 1619." See his "The Versification of Mira de Amescua's Comedias," in *Studies in Honor of Ruth Lee Kennedy*, edited by Vern G. Williamsen and A. F. Michael Atlee, pp. 151-76, in particular p. 165.

[4] Tirso carried over the very unusual name of "Nineucio" from an *auto* by Juan Valencia, a Jesuit, who had written two *autos* (precisely those of the rich miser and the prodigal son). In the one of the rich miser, the protagonist is "Nineusis." J. López Navío has convinced me, in his "Una comedia de Tirso que no está perdida" (in *Estudios*, XVI [1960], 331-47) that *El saber guardar su hacienda*, an unfinished *auto* in Juan Acacio's hands in September, 1612, would become *Tanto es lo de más como lo de menos* when it was converted into a *tragicomedia*. I believe the transformation took place in 1621-23. Later, in 1626-27, the play was again altered.

> ya con arrugas procura
> tu cara desengañarte,
> pues te dobla por guardarte
> el tiempo en la sepultura.
> Disforme estás para amante
> que la gula corpulenta
> en fe que en ti se aposenta
> te hizo su semejante.
> Si amor se pinta con alas,
> porque siempre es ágil ¿cómo,
> siendo tú un monstruo de plomo,
> a mi agilidad te igualas?

Before analysing the passage just cited, let us quote two *seguidillas* of the second act (ii) in which Dr. Metford believes Tirso is referring to Olivares. The first of these reads:

> ¿Qué parecen valonas que adornan calvas?
> Los hornazos de huevos que dan por Pascua.

The second is as follows:

> Corcobados amantes, di ¿qué parecen?
> Hijos engendrados de muchas veces.
> Mas, si hay dinero,
> es como un pino de oro todo camello.

No one has studied in detail these *seguidillas*—the only ones found in Tirso's entire theatre—and so we can not be entirely certain that Dr. Metford is right in thinking that the dramatist had Nineucio in mind when he wrote them. The general themes of the six *seguidillas* is the importance of money in all human relationships: for instance, the third *seguidilla*, which certainly seems to refer to Nineucio, is:

> Los ricos avarientos son como cardos
> que a ninguno aprovechan, sino enterrados.

And the concluding lines are:

> Todo dinero
> es redondo por causa que es rodadero.

Let us fuse the complaints of Liberio and the satire of the *seguidillas*. Nineucio's life is half over: his golden hair already numbers some gray ones and his face has wrinkles. He is, as a result of his over-eating, fat: is, in fact, a monster of lead. And love [he should remember] is always painted with wings because it is agile. What is more, Olivares is hump-backed and bald, if the *seguidillas* refer to him.

Let us now see how history paints Olivares. When in 1615 Olivares became "gentil-hombre" to Prince Philip, he was nearing 38 years of age, whereas young Philip was only 10. Certainly at 38, his life would have been half over, and his hair (black, according to Siri) could well have had gray in it and his face could have had wrinkles. That he was partly bald and wore a toupée is in keeping with history.[5] And though he was not in reality hump-backed, Siri[6] tells us "tenía los hombros lo bastante elevados para que *se le haya tomado por jorobado sin haberlo sido.*" Another Italian,[7] the author of *La Relación política* (del gobierno de Olivares), agrees that he was "cargado y encorvado de espaldas."

He was undoubtedly fat. Marañón[8] tells us (op.cit., pp. 66-67):

> Lo que físicamente llamaba más la atención era la corpulencia ... ya a los veinte años, nos dice Novoa, que era grueso y corpulento ... y todos los demás que le conocieron en otras edades, es a su masa a lo que se refieren de preferencia

John H. Elliott[9] has given us an unforgettable picture of Olivares in his *Imperial Spain*:

> A restless figure, never fully at ease either with others or with himself, Olivares was less one personality than a whole succession of personalities, coexisting, competing and conflicting within a single frame. By turns ebullient and dejected, humble and arrogant, shrewd and gullible, impetuous and cautious, he dazzled contemporaries with the versatility of his performance and bewildered them with his chameleon

---

[5] See G. Marañón, *El Conde-Duque de Olivares*, Madrid, 1936, p. 67. Marañón says his portraits of 1626-27 indicate he had no "arrugas," but in his Leningrad picture (N⁰ 15) his "rostro" is "desfigurado por las arrugas." They would, I should think, depend largely on the caprice of the painter. Marañón speaks repeatedly of his *peluca*. For instance, the *Relación política* (del gobierno de Olivares) by an Italian, mentions his *caballera postiza*.

[6] See G. Marañón, op.cit., p. 67.

[7] See *Relación política* (quoted by Marañón), p. 67.

[8] See Marañón, op.cit., pp. 66-67.

[9] *Imperial Spain, 1469-1716*, p. 320 of "Mentor" edition.

changes of mood. Somehow he always seemed larger than life-size, bestriding the court like a colossus.

But he ends his paragraph, stressing not his size but his super-activity:

> With state papers stuck in his hat[10] and bulging in his pockets, [he seemed] always in a flurry of activity, surrounded by scurrying secretaries, ordering, hectoring, cajoling, his voice booming down the corridors of the Palace.No man worked harder or slept less.

Marañón confirms Olivares' tremendous activity. He speaks at one point (p. 73) of his "exaltación hipomaníaca;" at another point (op.cit., p. 74) he says, "Toda la actividad del nuevo valido da, por entonces, sensación de frenesí." Such "hipervirilidad ['hiperpituitary' = excessive hormones] es típica de los hombres pícnicos ['stocky and florid'] y mucho más si son, como nuestro personaje, hiperhipofisarios." (p. 66). This picture of a tremendous activist is, of course, miles distant from Felicia's characterization of her husband's daily routine (II, v):

> Desde la cama a la mesa,
> y de la mesa a la cama

The portrait of history and that of the drama coincide in other directions: for instance, in regard to the love of power that characterized both Olivares and Nineucio and of the "fausto" with which each surrounded himself. Marañón, in an early chapter of his biography, entitled "Los impulsos," has written of Olivares' love of power and of his emulation of young Philip, his king (p. 100):

> Y Olivares sentía, desde lo más hondo de su organismo, como uno de los impulsos más eficaces, el afán de mando por el mando mismo y a esto sacrificaba él todo lo demás.

He continues (p. 100):

> Uno de los grandes defectos del Valido de Felipe IV fue, pues, el ser mucho más mandarín que gobernante... se le iba a Olivares toda la energía en las apariencias del mando... El ansia de mandar y de grandeza adquirió en él formas delirantes, a

---

[10] In *El dueño de las estrellas* (I, 1), Ruiz de Alarcón gives us a very similar picture of the *privado*. This play is Alarcón's tribute to Olivares, though it has not been recognized as such.

veces de extravagante aparato, a veces trágicas. Entre las primeras citaremos la solemnidad de que rodeaba su persona..., en el famoso retrato ecuestre de Veláquez...parece escrito aquello de que 'la vanidad le reventaba por la cincha del caballo.' Verdad o leyenda...se dijo que había hecho por fruición de su poder, caballero de Calatrava al hijo del pregonero de Medina del Campo, que acababa de entrar a su servicio, sólo por haber soportado con maliciosa mansedumbre uno de los raptos de iracundia de don Gaspar."

Commenting on the same episode (p. 100), Marañón observes, "Subir a los hombres de la nada es lo que más acerca a un hombre a la condición de Rey, meta subconsciente del Conde-Duque."

With these acute sentences from his fine biographers, let us now see how Tirso painted Nineucio, the rich miser of his play. Gabriel Téllez makes much of Nineucio's great delight in the display of his power and even more of his "royal emulation." The long first scene of Act I is given over to painting the miser's pride of possession, his baronial arrogance over the power he wields: indeed Nineucio's power knows no measure; his pride in it, no limits. Tirso has caught admirably his spirit of royal emulation. Nineucio states in this same opening scene, when boasting of his fine food and wines (I, 1): "Para *rey* me sobra mucho." When in the third act (xii) the miser is dining, the stage directions are, "Descúbrase una mesa muy esplédida...tocan chirimías y *sírvenle con majestad*." He at one point (I, iii) orders his servants to bring him "el ave fénix, si Arabia / se atreve a ponerle en precio." When he drinks (III, xii), it is "al son de chirimías e híncanse de rodillas sus criados mientras bebe." He even dresses to the sound of *chirimías*: the stage directions of the first act read as follows (x): "Nineucio, vistiéndose y lavándose *con música de chirimías*, criados dándole de vestir y Dina se hinca de rodillas..." In a later scene of the same act, Felicia is serving him breakfast with her own fair hands to the end that his food should taste even better to him. Nineucio's comment is (I, xii).

> Envídieme el aparato
> el Monarca que hay mejor,
> pues ninguno mereció
> el banquete que hoy recibo
> en fuentes de cristal vivo.

Felicia we remember had married her rich miser precisely because (I, ii):

en la casa de Nineucio
desde el retrete al zaguán
*todo huele a ostentación,*
*todo sabe a majestad.*

She goes ahead to ask (I, ii):

¿qué invención el apetito
ha levantado, qué manjar
que no registre su mesa?
¿qué licor tan cordial
que su sed no satisfaga...?

Nineucio himself had already boasted of that same regal table (I, i):

Mi mesa es la cifra y suma
donde el gusto no preserva
desde el árbol a la hierba,
desde la escama a la pluma.
Brindo a la sed que desprecia
vides que poda Tesalia,
ya con Falernos de Italia
y ya con Candías de Grecia.

Marañón, having first described a meal which the royal cook gave his monarch (op.cit., p. 384)—one consisting of "perniles, capones, olla de carnero, pasteles, pollos con habas, truchas, gigote de carnero, torreznos asados, criadillas de carnero, cazula de natas, tartaletas de ternera y lechuga, empanadillas con masa dulce, aves en alfilete frío, alcachofas con jamón, frutas, pastos, queso, conservas, confites, suplicaciones y requesones"—grants that the Conde-Duque in his younger days had likewise set a famous table (op.cit., p. 385):

El Conde-Duque en los años de fausto y licencia que precedieron a la privanza, tuvo una mesa famosa; de ella dice Roca que 'el saber servirla era ciencia,' y entonces fue cuando se hizo gotoso.

In his later years, he ate and drank moderately, according to Marañón, as far as quantity was concerned, but the food was "muy picante." As to drink in these later years (p. 385) it was "muy corta y en lugar de ella tomaba *quintaesencias* de cosas aromáticas." But Tirso was writing his play in those *first* years of the new reign when, as royal *valido*, either Olivares' habits of over-eating still lin-

gered, or when the bad reputation that he had gained in that direction was still pursuing him.

I can find no specific mention to the effect that Olivares' every
move was to the sound of music. This may possibly be a detail thet
Gabriel Téllez carried over from the gossip of Lerma's reign.[11]
Cabrera, for instance, tells us of Philip III's *privado*: "se le hacían
músicas a las comidas y cenas para aliviarle las melancolías." Olivares, too, suffered from profound fits of melancholia and well
may have felt the need of music, but the blare of the bagpipes,
referred to over and over in *Tanto es lo de más*, gives pause for
thought. *Chirimías*, it should be realized, were normally used in the
theatre to hail a divine apparition. Is Tirso perhaps suggesting sar-
castically, with his repeated insistence on them, that Nineucio was
striving to raise himself to the level of a god? At one point (I, 1)
the rich miser even states: "para Dios me falta poco." In truth his
stomach was his god as he declares: "Mi vientre es mi Dios" (II, vi).
And the table where he ate was his "altar" (III, xii).

Nineucio, like Olivares, appears to enjoy raising men out of the
nothing ("subir a los hombres de la nada"). For no better reason
than the caprice of the moment, he takes the "corpulent poet" into
his household (I, x)—and with *gajes* that are to begin immediately,
merely because the theme of the poet's song happened to be in
consonance with his own materialistic outlook. Something similar
happens when Liberio and his servant Gulín come into Nineucio's
presence (III, i). Nineucio capriciously takes on Gulín as his *mayordomo* because Gulín was addicted to gluttony as was he. He does
not even ask what are his qualifications for the place. As for Liberio, Gulín makes him "porquero," warning him, however, as to the
acorns (III, iv): "No las golosméis."

The position of *mayordomo* was open because the official who had
held it, a relative of Nineucio's, was in prison for embezzlement of
funds. It was that situation which leads Dina to implore Nineucio's
mercy. It is, interestingly enough, one which recalls, in a fashion,
an event that took place in Olivares' own household sometime

---

[11] Quoted from the introductory pages of *Tanto es lo de más*, written
by Doña Blanca, I, p. 925. She believed that Tirso was satirizing Lerma,
not Olivares, in the figure of Nineucio. Quotations in this study are
taken from her edition.

before October 14, 1621. Almansa y Mendoza,[12] the chatty chronicler of events who early hitched his wagon to Olivares' star, recounts in a letter of that date the following bit of news.

Al sol de la justicia distributiva no le vencen exhalaciones ni nieblas, pues el señor Conde de Olivares hizo prender y proceder contra su maestresala *por haber recibido mil ducados,* (my emphasis) por la negociación de una canongía de Málaga: llevóle a la cárcel D. Luis de Paredes, Alcalde de la casa y corte de su Majestad. Estuvo muchos días encerrado en la cámara del tormento con pena de la vida a quien le hablase sin orden particular; dióle el Conde una libranza de cien ducados para sustentarse; dicen que le sentenciarán vigorosamente.

Olivares' broom of justice was still new in those days, and it was sweeping very, very clean, possibly with the thought on Olivares' part of preparing public opinion for the very severe justice that would be meted out shortly to don Rodrigo Calderón, whose wife and children in those same days[13] were making vain appeals for don Rodrigo's life. Tirso needed only to fuse the two episodes of "distributive justice" in order to fashion the scene of Dina, who, accompanied by her children, pleads in vain with Nineucio for mercy for her husband. The sum of money involved, it should be noted, both in the case of Olivares' *maestresala* and of Tirso's *mayordomo* was 1000 ducats. It was a scene that must have been included in the play when Tirso expanded his *auto*[14] (in 1621 to early 1623) to a full-length *comedia.*

Cruelty was one of the early charges that Tirso (and others) brought against the Conde-Duque de Olivares. In his *La prudencia en la mujer* (III, vi) of 1622, we remember, don Juan had insinuated to his young King, Fernando IV, that he should "leave off his chase of animals *(fieras)* in the mountains and go in search of others in the city" (i.e., his political enemies). Marañón has defended the *valido* against this particular charge of cruelty. In doing so, his biographer cites Cánovas (p. 117), who wrote: "Si fue violento, no fue

---

12 Andrés Almansa y Mendoza, *Cartas,* pp. 77-78.

13 Almansa y Mendoza, *Cartas,* pp. 60-61.

14 J. López Navío believed (with Doña Blanca) that this transformation must have happened early—possibly around 1612—but the play of *Tanto es lo de más* could not have been written before the 1620's.

nunca cruel." Marañón agrees with Cánovas completely (op.cit., p. 117): "La fama de cruel del Conde-Duque se inaugura con las medidas violentas que tomó al comenzar su privanza y sobre todo con la dramática sentencia de don Rodrigo Calderón...." Yet Olivares' reputation among his contemporaries was on the whole that of cruel. As Marañón points out (op.cit., p. 118): "Novoa refiérese al genio duro con que trataba a los ayudas de cámara de Palacio, que acabaron por estar 'más rendidos a la servidumbre y al imperio saña del Privado que en las mazmorras de Argel.'" That Tirso, along with Novoa, was one of the many who thought Olivares cruel there can be no doubt: he makes it clear in *La prudencia* that for him the King should be the father of his people and, as such, he should be clement toward his children. His *privado* should not be permitted to give him the reputation of being harsh and unfeeling.

    With this same episode of Nineucio and Dina—and with various others—Tirso raises the question of Olivares' *codicia*. This is another charge which Marañón (op.cit., p. 113) refutes as a calumny: "una de estas acusaciones arbitrarias ha sido el de codicia e inmoralidad en el atesoramiento de riquezas." In view of the fact that greed had been the principal charge levelled against Lerma and those of his clan such as don Rodrigo Calderón, it was inevitable that Olivares' behavior in matters of nepotism—once he took the reins of power—should be under the very closest scrutiny from Lerma's friends. Dr. Marañón excuses Olivares, saying of his nepotism p. 115). "no parecían inmoralidades actos que hoy nos lo parecen... como el colocar en públicos empleos a todos sus parientes y el percibir los pingües beneficios económicos que le valiera su oficio de ministro único y todos los demás que ejercía"— which he grants were "very, very many." But by the same token, Dr. Marañón would have to grant that he should have shown more pity towards his predecessors, Lerma and Calderón. It could only be Tirso's point of view, as well as that of those who held to the same yardstick of values, that Lerma's favorite had lost his life on the scaffold at the orders of a minister who began forthwith to sin in the same direction as the man he was sending to death. It should surprise no one, therefore, that those whose sympathy lay with the "outs" should have deemed Olivares *codicioso*.

    Tirso, for one, certainly did not doubt that Olivares was just that! As early as *Privar contra su gusto*, written in mid-1621,[15] the Mercedarian was begging his young king to give his *privado* fewer *mercedes*. In this play, don Juan, the saintly figure who is clearly spokesman for Tirso, gives the King this advice with regard to his *privado* (II, xxv):

> La segunda es que reprimas
> el curso a mercedes tantas
> como le haces, pues siempre
> fue prudente la templanza.
> Aborrecible es a todos
> después que tanto le ensalzas,
> y ocasionando a la envidia
> le expones a mil desgracias.
> El privado es inferior
> a su rey; pues si le igualas
> a tu grandeza ¿qué intentas,
> siendo forzoso que caiga.
> No tiene tanto talento
> don Juan, puesto que le alabas,
> para gobernarlo todo;
> alíviale de la carga
> con que sus fuerzas oprimes.
> Mediano estado le basta;
> pues cuanto menos le dieres,
> facilitas más la causa
> de su conservación noble;
> y cumpliendo tu palabra,
> él vivirá quieto y tú
> conservarás su privanza

This sage recommandation is the real burden of Tirso's advice to the King; the other two bits, while to the point, do not together require as much space as does this advice concerning the *mercedes* that young Philip was giving his favorite.

Just how close this matter was to his heart may be seen also in *La prudencia*. Ths Queen Regent María is handing over the reins of government to her weakling son, Fernando. Before retiring to her

---

[15] I have a long study in my files on *Privar contra su gusto*, which, I believe, proves with reasonable certainty that this play was written in the late summer of 1621, or else the early fall.

estate in the little town of Becerril, she gives him some pointed advice. Having first told him that "no hay razón de estado como es el servir a Dios," she launches then into what she most fears (III, i):

> Nunca os dejéis gobernar
> de privados de manera
> que salgáis de vuestra esfera.
> *Ni les lleguéis tanto a dar*
> *que se arrojen de tal modo*
> *al cebo del interés,*
> que os fuercen, hijo, después
> a que se lo quitéis todo.

In the *Cigarrales de Toledo*, Tirso addresses in apparently jocular tone—he is, in reality, deadly serious—the pygmy river, Manzanares, which in summer is reduced to a mere trickle. Nevertheless, Tirso maintains that the river should allege its many *services* to Philip IV. Why, says he, "no os dan siquiera un estado que os pague en agua alimento." He then urges the Manzanares (ed., Espasa-Calpe, II, p. 93):

> Pedidle al Cuarto mercedes,
> que otros han servido menos
> y gozan ya de más *estados*
> que cuatro pozos manchegos.

I believe these bits of advice from Tirso were written in the order in which I have taken them up. That of *Privar contra su gusto* was done with real comprehension of the danger that such *mercedes* had represented historically for a *privado, any privado*. There is no political blame implied for the *privado*. The second, that of *La prudencia en la mujer*, recognizes, as did the passage in *Privar contra su gusto*, the King's responsibility in the matter, but also takes into account the covetousness of the *valido*. The last, that of the *Cigarrales*, is frankly contemptuous of the very slight services of his minister-favorite.[16]

While listing the earthly possessions with which he can endow Felicia, Nineucio mentions not only his jewels, of which we shall speak later, but also his far-flung lands, covered with cattle, his crops, his rents (I, i):

---

[16] See just above.

No hay caudal ni posesión
que en Palestina pretenda
ser réditos de mi hacienda;
casi mis vasallos son
cuantos en Jerusalén
saben mis bienes inmensos;
sus casas me pagan censos;
sus posesiones también.
Desde el Nilo hasta el Jordán
Ceres me rinde tributo;
cada año a Baco disfruto
desde Bersabé hasta Dan.

One gets glimpses here of Nineucio's great expanse of lands, lands covered with sheep, with horses, and with cattle.[17] His estates extend to Alexandria and, as he states later (I, xx), his power to Memphis.   Now, as Dr. Metford has pointed out, Tirso has identified Memphis with Sevilla: "a Nuestro Menfis español," he calls that southern city—and, as it happens, in a play that was written in 1626,[18] [i.e., in *El amor médico*]. I remember—or seem to remember—a document[19] of 1620, which lists the "censos" that Olivares received from his southern estates. They were impressive even in that year. Yet Philip was clearly giving him further estates during his reign, as is evident in the quotation from the *Cigarrales* (cited above) concerning others who have served less than the Manzanares, yet "*gozan ya más estados que cuatro pozos manchegos.*"[20]

It was not only that Nineucio had amassed tremendous riches, but that he showed no human compassion whatsoever to the poor. This play, is first and last, a plea for charity, one made in a year of

---

[17] The passage is reminiscent of Don Tello's boasts in *El rey don Pedro en Madrid.*

[18] The comparison of Sevilla to Memphis is made not only in *El amor médico* (I, ii) but in *No hay peor sordo* (III, viii). For the date of *El amor médico,* see my study, "The Dates of *El amor médico* and *Escarmientos para el cuerdo, Reflexión 2,* num. 1, vol. 1.

[19] It probably is in Marañón's biography, though search has not enabled me to find it. On p. 115 of the biography, it is stated: "...le dejaron sus clarísimos ascendentes 60.000 ducados de mayorazgo."

[20] See above.

hunger.[21] The rich miser, in accordance with the Biblical parable, denies the crumbs from his table to Lázaro, preferring to give what is left from the abundance of that table to his hounds rather than to the starving beggars who were pleading for them. Liberio had told Nineucio early within the play (I, i):

> Arrogante, a Dios te igualas,
> y a nadie te comunicas;
> caudaloso te publicas,
> y a ti sólo te regalas;
> el bien es comunicable;
> Dios es bien universal;
> tú para ti liberal,
> para todos, miserable...

Lázaro. on the other hand, seeks to build up his credit in heaven with acts of charity in this world. The poor are, he says (I, xiii):

> ...del crédito de Dios
> ...abondas libranzas

All nature, says he, *if it receives, also gives* (I, xiii):

> No fuera augusto planeta
> el sol, si su luz negara,
> pues no se alumbra a sí mismo
> y alumbra a todos de gracia.
> Si sutileza vapores,
> que le da la tierra, paga
> en nubes que fertilizan
> sus verdes campos con agua.

He even tries in vain to appeal to Nineucio's sense of royal emulation: "el dar es de reyes."

At the close of the play, Clemente, father to Liberio, gives his stamp of approval to Lázaro's charity. He points out to his prodigal son what has happened to Nineucio after death. Having watched the punishment meted out in hell to this gluttonous miser, Clemente then urges Liberio to eschew the life of Nineucio and follow that of Lázaro (III, xxi):

---

[21] The years 1621, 1622, and 1623 were all years of drought. Escudero y Perosso, Francisco, *Tipografía hispalense* (Madrid, 1894; under the year 1622) shows that the year 1622 was unusually bad.

Hijo, a Lázaro imitando
y escarmentando en Nineucio,
restaurarás lo perdido
y escusarás tus tormentos.
*Vicioso pródigo fuiste*
*y aquél, mísero avariento;*
*tanto en ti fue lo de más*
*como en él fue lo de menos.*
En medio está la virtud;
si son vicios los extremos,
de Lázaro el medio escoge,
y tendrás a Dios por premio.

I cannot say how Olivares in general treated "the little man" of his day. We do have documental proof that at his death Olivares felt that he had not made proper provision for servants who had, throughout the years, served him loyally and well. In his will, as Marañón points out, he begs the king to look after them (op.cit, p. 116):

Al Rey, nuestro Señor, le suplico se sirva de honrar así y favorezca a los criados que dejo, *porque voy con algún desconsuelo de lo poco que les he ayudado y valido y con pena de su descomodidad; y* déboles cuanto he podido en entender el amor y cuidado con que me han servido *y el gusto que me han dado de no haberse valido en el puesto que he tenido y ocasiones que se suelen ofrecer.*"

The complaint of Calvo in *Privar contra su gusto* is precisely that his master, recently elevated to the role of *privado*, is not willing to share his good fortune with his servants. The *gracioso* has been promised a position by the Infanta. Don Juan has, however, yet to approve the appointment, something he is unwilling to do. He tells Calvo impatiently (II, xii):

Calvo, no bufonicéis;
ese oficio ya está dado;
bástaos ser vos mi criado.

Calvo parodies his master's words in an *aparte*:

"Bástaos ser vos mi criado."
Pues ¡vive Dios! que no basta
a quien de sus carnes gasta
y es ministro de un privado.
Esto es: uno piensa el bayo,

> *et cǽtera;* mas razón
> es, siendo el amo pelón,
> que sea calvo el lacayo.

The miserly glutton, Nineucio, did not, according to Tirso, believe in God nor in the immortality of the soul. When Lázaro urges charity on him, Nineucio's angry answer is (I, xiii):

> Saducea es mi opinión;
> la inmortalidad del alma
> niego; en muriéndose el hombre,
> todo para él acaba:
> ni espero premios del Cielo,
> ni el infierno me amenaza.

Elsewhere the miser tells his wife (II, v): "No hay Dios que me dé cuidado; / lo demás es desvarío." And he brings to an end this conversation with the blunt statement: "Nacer y morir: no hay más." Clemente, at the end of the play, brings the same charge against the *rico avariento* (III, xx): "la inmortalidad del alma negaba el torpe Nineucio."

That anyone ever labelled Olivares an atheist is not, insofar as I know, on record. In connection with the role of *alcahuete* that he supposedly played in his young King's love affairs, it was said that he was one of the "alumbrados" and that he induced Philip to accept their ideas about love to the end that the latter could sin in comfort. According to Dr. Marañón,[22] this was sheer gossip, fashioned by French travellers who were in Spain long after Olivares' death. What his fine biographer does not deny is that the Conde-Duque de Olivares was unduly superstitious (op.cit., pp. 186-87) and that he had the reputation of being a wizard. (His power supposedly resided in the cane [*muletilla*] with which he steadied himself!) In the *Cueva de Meliso* he is accused of dealing with black magic, an accusation that apparently finds its reflection in Tirso's play, *La fingida Arcadia*, as I pointed out some years ago.[23] But from such charges to that of atheism, the step is a fairly long one—even if we grant the credulity and love of gossip that must have abounded in that time, as it does today.

---

22 *El Conde-Duque de Olivares*, p. 37.

23 See my *Studies in Tirso, I: the Dramatist and his Competitors, 1620-26*, pp. 205-08. He was also labelled a "heretic" in 1632. See Marañón, op.cit., p. 179.

Tirso has stressed one note in Nineucio's characterization that is in diametric contrast to Marañón's portrait of the *privado*. Felicia would have liked to have had children from her union with Nineucio, but the latter refuses, saying (III, xiii):

> no apetezco herederos,
> ...........................
> yo he de heredarme a mí mismo.

Again, when Gulín points out to Nineucio that Felicia is ill, "por verte en su amor tan tibio," the husband replies brutally (III, xii):

> Muérase porque me ahorre
> de los gastos excesivos
> con que todas las mujeres
> empobrecen sus maridos.
> Todo lo que en mí no empleo
> me llega al alma.

Public gossip, in *Tanto es lo de más*, attributed their childless state to Nineucio's impotence. Flora says of Nineucio (II, ii):

> Todo hombre barriga
> es inútil para amante,

and Nisiro adds:

> Dios de impotentes es Baco,
> y por eso es barrigón;
> dios de la generación
> es Pan, y le pintan flaco.

Now Olivares and his wife, Inés de Zúñiga, had but a single child, "la rosa blanca." And when on July 30, 1626 she died in childbirth, a son to succeed him became a veritable obsession with Olivares. As Marañón[24] observes: "el sentimiento del linaje es parte esencial en la ambición de poderío del Valido." Even Novoa, bitter enemy to the Conde-Duque, grants the preoccupation of the *privado* over a son to inherit him ("la importantísima sucesión") and suggests (p. 279) that Olivares was so busy with public matters "que no podía acudir bien al fin y la sucesión del matrimonio." Tirso has other explanations, as we have seen above, for Nineucio's lack of issue.

---

[24] *El Conde-Duque*, p. 276.

It is time to sum up our findings. Comparison of the dramatic portrait of Tirso's play, when set alongside the one that history or tradition affords, shows that they agree on many things: in physical appearance, agreement is almost total, though Olivares undoubetly had black hair, not golden; but in matters of character and attitude, if there is agreement in some directions, there are broad contradictions in others. Olivares was, according to history, hyperactive, not the inert log that led Felicia to sum up his daily existence in just 13 words: "Desde la cama a la mesa y desde la mesa a la cama." To be sure, this very superactivity when in the public eye may have left him so tired "que no podía acudir bien a la sucesión del matrimonio," as Novoa suggests. But the suggestion hardly seems logical in a matter that was so intimately linked with his love of power and rule.

Nor was Olivares an atheist who denied a hereafter. "Saducea es mi opinión," Nineucio declares. Just possibly Tirso may, with this, have been alluding to the Jewish blood which undoubtedly flowed in Olivares' veins and to the Jewish concern with matters of *this* world rather than with those in the *next*. But again there is no real reason to assume that Olivares was an atheist, even though he was superstitious, as were many others of his time, and was accused in his day of believing in black magic.

In a play which developed from an *auto*[25] into a comedia around 1621-23, one that undoubtedly suffered yet further changes around 1626-27, let us point to four lines which are important in any attempt to identify Nineucio with the Conde-Duque de Olivares. When boasting of his riches in the opening scene of this play, Nineucio says:

> De suerte el Planeta real
> con diamantes me enriquece
> y esmeraldas, que parece
> que traigo el sol al jornal...

---

[25] I have in a recent study dealt with J. López Navío's belief that *Tanto es lo de más* is the auto, *Saber guardar su hacienda*, which Tirso had given into the hands of an *autor*, Juan Acacio, in September, 1612. I believe López Navío is correct in this assumption. However, I must reject his belief that the auto was developed into a long *comedia* around 1612. That *desarrollo* came, in my opinion, after Tirso went to Madrid, in 1621-23. It was later altered again, as Eugenio Asensio has shown in his *Itinerario del entremés*, pp. 128-29.

This is the only passage in which Tirso has indicated that Nineucio stands in any official relationship to his sovereign. It is all the more interesting because Philip IV was called "The Planet King"[26] by the poets and was often referred to as "The Sun."

Now I have no specific proof that the Planet King at any time ever "enriched" Olivares with diamonds and emeralds, but I can show that *the chances of his having done so are very good indeed.* In the first place, it is on record that "las joyas y alhajas de casa," which had belonged to Rodrigo Calderón,[27] valued at 184,000 ducats, all passed into the possession of Philip IV even before that unfortunate *privado* of Lerma and Philip III lost his head on the block. It is also recorded[28] that when Queen Isabel had to undergo a bloodletting, some time before October 14, 1621—one week before Calderón's death on the scaffold—Philip IV sent his wife, together with 100 *doblones*, "un mazo de tres mil perlas retas [sic: ¿netas?] ... todo de la almoneda de D. Rodrigo Calderón." Yet again, the anonymous *Noticias de Madrid*[29] states that Archduke Charles of Austria, shortly before his death in Madrid on December 26, 1624, left Philip IV such jewels of his collection as his majesty might desire: "Las joyas mandó que se llevasen al Rey, para que escogiese las que le gustasen." Philip IV, then, was known to be fond of precious jewels and presumably had plenty at his disposal, at least in late 1621 and again in late 1624.

That his collection of precious stones would have included emeralds is almost inevitable. It the first place, as the *Columbia Encyclopedia* tells us: "Good emeralds are the most highly valued of gem stones." According to this same *Columbia Encyclopedia*, the finest emeralds are found in South American Columbia where "they have

---

[26] As to the year in which the poets gave him this name, I have no documentary information, but almost certainly is was in late 1625 or early 1626 when Spanish forces were victorious from Bredá to South America. These verses concerning *"El Rey Planeta,"* which were in print in 1627 when this play was published in Tirso's *Primera parte* (Sevilla, 1627), point also to 1625-26.

[27] See Andrés Almansa y Mendoza, *Cartas*, p. 102.

[28] Idem, p. 79.

[29] See the anonymous *Noticias de Madrid* (p. 110), published by A. González Palencia in Madrid, 1942.

been mined continuously for over 400 years." Finally, "the trea-
sures taken to Spain by the Conquerors included emeralds." In
seems highly likely then that the Planet King's collection of gems
included some emeralds.

I have no statement to the effect that Philip IV had any diamonds in his collection, but *in general* princes of Tirso's time did not
disdain them for Royal gifts. Marañón (op.cit., p. 57, n. 10) has
described the content of a manuscript which he possessed, one
that at one time had belonged to the library of Cogullada's monastery. This mansucript states (p. 57, n. 10) that the Prince of Wales,
on leaving for England in September, 1623, gave to Olivares "un
diamante con una perla pendiente que vale 16000 ducados; a su
mujer, Doña Inés, una cruz de diamantes que vale 6000 ducados; y
a Doña María de Guzmán, la hija, dos sortijas de diamantes que
valen 3000 ducados." It is hardly possible then, that the collections
of don Rodrigo Calderón, of the Archduke Charles of Austria, and
of Philip IV himself should not have included both emeralds and
diamonds!

That Olivares would have been the recipient of some of the
jewels owned by Philip IV seems almost inevitable, given the
extraordinarily close relations that existed between the youthful
monarch and his favorite. It was all the more probable because, at
least after Rodrigo Calderón's death, Olivares realized that he was
on the defensive and that he was being criticized for receiving gifts
from the King that came out of the Royal Treasury. A gift in the
form of jewels could be made in private without attracting the
unfavorable criticisms that gifts from the Treasury would normally have brought. Soon after the execution of Lerma's favorite
(i.e., Rodrigo Calderón) on October 21, 1621, Olivares, recognizing
the shift of public sentiment, wrote Philip IV a letter, one dated
November 21, 1621, in which he first acknowledges, "véome a mí
más obligado al real servicio de V.M. que ningún otro vasallo,"
then goes ahead to beg his young sovereign to restrain himself "en
las mercedes *que hubieren de salir de su real erario*" (my emphasis). What
is more, according to Marañón (op.cit., p. 116), the Conde de la
Roca, official biographer of Olivares, tells us this: "Deseaba [Oli-
vares] engrandecerla [i.e., su casa] sin que el Patrimonio de la Real
Hacienda se defraudase, y así resolvió recibir todos sus medros de
mano del Rey, pero no del Patrimonio Real..." The almost inevita-

ble solution for Philip IV's generous instincts would have been gifts of valuable jewels taken from his personal possessions. He could in that way reward his friends without occasioning further public disapproval.

UNIVERSITY OF ARIZONA

# TABULA GRATULATORIA

Ramón Aguirre
John J. Allen
Nicolás E. Álvarez
David Lauri Anderson
Frederick A. de Armas
Samuel G. Armistead
M. S. Arrington, Jr.
Teresa R. Arrington
Auburn University,
  Ralph Brown Draughon Library
Juan Bautista Avalle-Arce
Mac E. Barrick
Theodore S. Beardsley, Jr.
Patrick Myner Blanchard
Donald W. Bleznick
R. S. Boggs
Louis Milton Bourne
Brigham Young University,
  Harold B. Lee Library
Paul W. Brosman, Jr.
Frieda S. Brown
Dolores Brown
Shasta M. Bryant
Barbara Foley Buedel
James F. Burke
Robert I. Burns, S.J.
Israel Burshatin
David G. Burton

303

Jose L. Cagigao
California State College,
  Bakersfield, Library
D. Lincoln Canfield
Anthony J. Cárdenas
Dwayne E. Carpenter
M. Jean Sconza Carpenter
James A. Castañeda
Pedro M. Cátedra García
Centre College of Kentucky,
  The Grace Doherty Library
Raquel Chang-Rodríguez
James R. Chatham
Ignacio Chicoy-Dabán
Anna McG. Chisman
Manuela M. Cirre
Dorothy Clotelle Clarke
Calvin Andre Claudel
Carl W. Cobb
Jane K. Cobb
Mitchell A. Codding
María Castellanos Collins
Judith S. Conde
Cornell University Libraries
Mechthild Cranston
Philip E. Cranston
Dalhousie University Library
Bruno M. Damiani
Elizabeth R. Daniel
George B. Daniel, Jr.
Frank Dauster
James H. Davis, Jr.
Mary E. Davis
William R. Davis
Nelle Smith Delgado
Bruce F. Denbo
Alan Deyermond
Ralph DiFranco
Marta Ana Diz

John Dowling
G. Francis Drake
Lee Dubs
Marilyn Lamond Eddington
Daniel Eisenberg
Glen Emmons
Marilyn Emmons
Alfred Engstrom
Mary Claire Engstrom
Jean Schneider Escribano
Robert O. Evans
Frances Exum
Charles B. Faulhaber
Martin Favata
Gastón J. Fernández
Robert L. Fiore
John H. Fisher
C. Bruce Fitch
Augusta E. Foley
Fordham University Library
Manuel da Costa Fontes
John F. Fox
Marion F. Freeman
Herschel Frey
Werner P. Friederich
Joseph G. Fucilla
Barbara E. Gaddy
John Steven Geary
Philip O. Gericke
E. Michael Gerli
Stephen Gilman
Nydia Rivera Gloeckner
Harriet Goldberg
Joaquín González-Muela
Arthur Graham
Lanin A. Gyurko
J. Richard Haefer
Robert W. Haney
Harvard College Library

Francis C. Hayes
Everett W. Hesse
Enrique Hoyos
Indiana University Library
Víctor Infantes de Miguel
Dolores W. Jácome
Charles Javens
Joseph R. Jones
Margaret Jones
James H. Johnson
William W. Johnson
Lloyd Kasten
L. Clark Keating
Ruth Lee Kennedy
Patricia Kenworthy
William W. Kibler
Richard P. Kinkade
Marjorie T. Kirby
Robert Kirsner
Kathleen Kish
Myron L. Kocher
Judith Irene Knorst
Kathleen Kulp-Hill
Walter G. Langlois
John H. LaPrade
Constance E. Lathrop
Thomas A. Lathrop
Luis Leal
Patrick J. Lecertua
William Ransom Ledford
Isaac J. Lévy
Lewis and Clark Colege Library
Libreria Gregoriana Editrice, Padua
John Lihani
Mrs. Robert White Linker
Pilar Liria
Anthony G. Lo Ré
Leon F. Lyday
Raymond R. MacCurdy

Robert A. MacDonald
McGill University Library
Norris MacKinnon
José A. Madrigal
Edward M. Malinak
Hester P. Matthews
Walter Mettmann
Robert B. Modee
Luis Monguió
Connie S. Mora
Moorehead State University Library
Frances W. Morgan
Ciriaco Morón Arroyo
Joann McFerran Mount
Richard Terry Mount
Dorothy M. Mulberry
Edward W. Najam
Eric W. Naylor
Lucy Ann Neblett
Colbert I. Nepaulsingh
New York University,
   Bobst Library
Georgia Pappanastos
Aristóbulo Pardo
Jack H. Parker
James A. Parr
Anthony M. Pasquariello
Mamie Salvá Patterson
James S. Patty
J. Hunter Peak
T. Anthony Perry
Mrs. Edwin B. Place
Alberto Porqueras-Mayo
Princeton University Library
Enrique Pupo-Walker
Purdue University Library
Daniel Rangel-Guerrero
W. F. Reagan
Katarina Real-Cate

Margaret G. Redd
Daniel R. Reedy
Agapito Rey
José Rey-Barreau
Gabriel de los Reyes
Joseph V. Ricapito
Donnie Richards
Ripon College, Lane Library
Romance Monographs, Inc.
Hector R. Romero
Fred de Rosset
Irving P. Rothberg
St. Mary's College (Minn.),
    Fitzgerald Library
Hortensia Sánchez-Boudy
José Sánchez-Boudy
Judith H. Schomber
Hugh N. Seay, Jr.
Karl-Ludwig Selig
Alberta Wilson Server
Lawrence A. Sharpe
Harvey L. Sharrer
Barton Sholod
Tanya Shook
Isidore Silver
Joseph H. Silverman
Merle E. Simmons
Carolyn F. Smith
R. Roger Smith
Josep M. Solá-Solé
Vicente Soler Gimeno
Jackson G. Sparks
Geoffrey Stagg
Edward F. Stanton
State University of New York,
    Buffalo, Lockwood Library
State University of New York,
    Fredonia, Reed Library
Charlotte Stern

Robert R. Stinson
H. Reynolds Stone
H. T. Sturcken
Harlan Sturm
Sara Sturm-Maddox
M. Laurentino Suárez
C. William Swinford
Frances Keller Swinford
Isamu Taniguchi
Robert ter Horst
Edward D. Terry
Earl W. Thomas
Roger D. Tinnell
Pedro N. Trakas
Trent University,
    Thomas J. Bata Library
Richard W. Tyler
Justo C. Ulloa
Leonor A. Ulloa
University of British Columbia Library
University of California,
    Berkeley, Library
University of California,
    Irvine, Department of Spanish
    & Portuguese
University of California,
    Irvine, Library
University of Delaware,
    Library
University of Georgia Libraries
University of Kentucky Libraries
University of Minnesota,
    Minneapolis, Libraries
University of North Carolina,
    Chapel Hill, Wilson Library
University of Pennsylvania Libraries
University of Santa Clara,
    Library

University of Victoria,
  McPherson Library
University of Wisconsin,
  Madison, Library
University of Wisconsin,
  Milwaukee, Library
Eduardo Urbina
Juan O. Valencia
Antony van Beysterveldt
David J. Viera
Frederick Vogler
Mary Frances Vogler
Gerald E. Wade
John K. Walsh
Bruce W. Wardropper
Billy R. Weaver
Weber State College Library
Edwin J. Webber
Ruth H. Webber
West Georgia College,
  Irvine Sullivan Ingram Library
Shirley B. Whitaker
Whitman College,
  Penrose Memorial  Library
Joseph W. Whitted
W. L. Wiley
Constance L. Wilkins
Heanon M. Wilkins
Raymond S. Willis
Winthrop College,
  Dacus Library
Hensley C. Woodbridge
Louis J. Zahn
Joseph W. Zdenek

ADDENDUM

Manuel Ramírez
María Jesús Lacarra